# BASIC CHRISTIAN DOCTRINE

◆ *Other books by John H. Leith*

From Generation to Generation: The Renewal of the Church According to Its Own Theology and Practice

Introduction to the Reformed Tradition: A Way of Being the Christian Community

The Church: A Believing Fellowship (Revised)

The Reformed Imperative: What the Church Has to Say That No One Else Can Say

John Calvin's Doctrine of the Christian Life


◆ *Books edited by John H. Leith*

Creeds of the Churches: A Reader in Christian Doctrine from the Bible to the Present

Guides to the Reformed Tradition:
    Worship
    The Church

Reformed Reader: A Sourcebook in Christian Theology,
Volume I: Classical Beginnings, 1519–1799
(with William Stacy Johnson)

JOHN H. LEITH

---------------- ❖ ----------------

# BASIC
# CHRISTIAN
# DOCTRINE

---------------- ❖ ----------------

Westminster/John Knox Press
Louisville, Kentucky

Scripture quotations from the Revised Standard Version of the Bible are copyrighted 1946, 1952, © 1971, 1973 by the Division of Christian Education of the National Council of the Churches of Christ in the U.S.A. and are used by permission.

Scripture quotations from the New Revised Standard Version of the Bible are copyright © 1989 by the Division of Christian Education of the National Council of the Churches of Christ in the U.S.A. and are used by permission.

For Acknowledgments, see page xviii.

*Book design by The HK Scriptorium, Inc.*

*First edition*

Published by Westminster/John Knox Press
Louisville, Kentucky

This book is printed on acid-free paper that meets the American National Standards Institute Z39.48 standard. ∞

PRINTED IN THE UNITED STATES OF AMERICA
9   8   7   6   5

Library of Congress Cataloging-in-Publication Data

Leith, John H.
  Basic Christian doctrine / John H. Leith. — 1st ed.
      p.    cm.
  Includes bibliographical references.
  ISBN 0-664-25192-7 (pbk. : alk. paper)

  1. Theology, Doctrinal.   I. Title.
BT75.2.L47   1992
230'.42—dc20                           92-9062

❖

For Henry and Caroline,
children of the divine covenant and of the family covenant,
who in diverse ways are the recipients and means of divine grace,

and

For the Presbyterian elders, deacons, and ministers
who have sought to renew the Church
by the serious study of theology
through their support
of the Colloquium on Calvin Studies (Davidson)
and the Fund for the Explication
and Application of Reformed Theology:

Annabelle Lundy Fetterman, Lewis Fetterman, Thomas Cousins,
Ann Draughon Cousins, James W. White, Julia T. White,
John Newton Thomas, Nancy White Thomas, F. Sidney Anderson,
Alec Cheyne, Vernon Broyles, W. Frank Harrington,
William F. Keesecker, E. Douglas Vaughan, Martha Vaughan,
Thomas Jefferson, Jr., William T. Stuart, Janet W. Stuart,
Arthur S. Link, Margaret D. Link, Charles Myers, Mrs. Thornton Brooks,
Richardson Preyer, Edward Lee Spencer, Jr., Mrs. Ellis Whitehead,
Neil O. Davis, Fowler Dugger, Elizabeth Young Davis, Jean McFall White,
Ann White Leith, Charles Cooke, Taylor Reveley,
Wallace Alston, Jerold Shetler, Charles Raynal,
Merwyn S. Johnson, Hughes Old, William Carl,
John Debevoise, William P. Wood, John B. Rogers,
Joseph Welker, Robert Bluford, Jr., James W. White, Jr.,
Vernon Hunter, Benjamin W. Farley, Kenneth B. Orr, Robert Bardin,
John Kuykendall, William Cockrill, and many others.

❖

# CONTENTS

Preface                                                                    *xi*

Acknowledgments                                                          *xviii*

1.  Christian Theology in Reformed Perspective                              1
    *A Christian Theology*                                                  *1*
    *Augustinian and Reformed*                                             *5*
    *Classical Statements of Reformed Theology*                            *9*

2.  Faith and Doctrine                                                     13
    *The Importance of Doctrine*                                          *14*
    *Theology Grows Out of the Worshiping Community*                      *18*
    *Forms of Doctrine*                                                   *19*

3.  The Human Situation, Mystery, and Revelation                          *21*

4.  The Doctrine of God                                                    40
    *Six Basic Affirmations*                                              *41*
    *God Is Defined by Jesus Christ*                                      *45*
    *The Triune God*                                                      *46*
    *The Attributes of God*                                               *50*
    *God Who Elects*                                                      *54*
    *God Who Covenants*                                                   *55*
    *God Who Is Transcendent and Immanent*                                *55*
    *How Do We Know God?*                                                 *58*

5.  Creation                                                               66
    *Creation as an Article of Faith*                                     *67*
    *Affirmations of the Doctrine of Creation*                            *71*

6.  Providence                                                    81

7.  The Human Creature                                            97
    *The Human Being as Creature*                                 98
    *The Uniqueness of the Human Creature*                        99
    *The Human Creature as Sinner*                               105
    *Specific Questions*                                         111

8.  Jesus Christ                                                 124
    *The History of Jesus Christ*                                125
    *Of the Same Substance (Being) as the Father*                131
    *The Person of Jesus Christ*                                 136
    *The Resurrection of Jesus Christ*                           140
    *The Ascension*                                              143
    *The Birth of Jesus*                                         144

9.  The Work of Christ                                           150
    *Jesus as Example*                                           151
    *Jesus as Teacher*                                           153
    *Jesus as Our Ransom*                                        154
    *Victor Over Sin, Death, and the Devil*                      155
    *Deification*                                                155
    *Forgiveness of Sins*                                        156
    *The Outreaching Love of God*                                158
    *Prophet, Priest, and King*                                  158

10. The Holy Spirit                                              160
    *Who Is the Holy Spirit?*                                    162
    *What Does the Holy Spirit Do?*                              163
    *How Does the Holy Spirit Work?*                             165

11. The Beginnings of the Christian Life                         166

12. Faith                                                        171
    *A Personal Act*                                             172
    *Faith as Knowledge*                                         173
    *Faith as Trust*                                             174
    *Faith as an Act of the Will*                                174
    *The Object of Faith*                                        175
    *Faith and Love*                                             175

*Faith and Hope*                                                     176
*Faith Is Not a Work*                                                177

13. Justification by Faith                                           178
*Faith Righteousness versus Work Righteousness*                      179
*An Imputed Righteousness*                                           182
*Received by Faith*                                                  183
*A Completed Act of God*                                             184
*Consequences of Justification*                                      184
*The Doctrine by Which the Church Stands or Falls*                   185

14. Sanctification                                                   186
*The Relation Between Forgiveness and Sanctification*                187
*The Doctrine of Sanctification*                                     190
*The Content of Sanctification*                                      193
*Good Works*                                                         198
*The Vision of the Holy Commonwealth*                                199

15. Christian Freedom                                                204
*God Alone Is Lord of the Conscience*                                205
*Freedom from the Rigor of the Law*                                  206
*Willing Obedience*                                                  206
*Things Indifferent*                                                 207

16. The Law and Moral Decisions                                      210
*Natural Law*                                                        211
*The Ten Commandments*                                               212
*The Law of Christ*                                                  214
*The Bible and the Example of Jesus*                                 215
*Gospel and Law*                                                     216
*Moral Inquiry*                                                      216

17. The Prevenience of Grace                                         220
*Grace as God's Favor*                                               221
*Grace in Creation*                                                  223
*Predestination*                                                     225
*Perseverance of the Saints*                                         229
*Assurance of Salvation*                                             230
*Reprobation and Damnation*                                          231
*Grace and Freedom*                                                  232

18. The Church and the Means of Grace                234
    *Creation of God*                                235
    *The Church Lives by Hearing the Word of God*    236
    *Congregation, the People of God*                238
    *One, Holy, Catholic, Apostolic*                 240
    *Visible, Invisible*                             244
    *Militant, Triumphant*                           245
    *The Church as Israel*                           246
    *Organization or Institution*                    249
    *The Means of Grace*                             251
    *Sacraments*                                     251
    *Preaching*                                      260
    *Mutual Conversation and Consolation*            261

19. Prayer                                           262

20. The Bible                                        270
    *The Word of God Written*                        270
    *The Authority of Scripture*                     271
    *The Testimony of the Holy Spirit*               272
    *The Canon of Scripture*                         273
    *Inspiration*                                    274
    *The Bible and Tradition*                        276
    *The Interpretation of Scripture*                276
    *The Bible and General Revelation*               277

21. Christian Faith and Living Religions             278
    *The Universality of Religion*                   279
    *The Uniqueness of Jesus Christ*                 281
    *Inclusive and Exclusive*                        282
    *Confessional*                                   284

22. The Christian Hope                               286
    *What Can We Hope for in History?*               288
    *Eternal Life*                                   292
    *The End of History*                             298
    *A New Heaven and a New Earth*                   301

Epilogue                                             304

Notes                                                307

---- ❖ ----

# PREFACE

This book has been written with three purposes in mind. The first is to provide a brief but comprehensive statement of Christian faith. The second is to interpret the Christian witness and tradition in language that is intelligible to contemporary people. The third purpose is to make available a brief but comprehensive statement of Christian faith for the Christian laity as well as for theological students and ministers. I hope that my two years as a student supply pastor, my fourteen years as a pastor, as well as thirty-one years as a seminary professor will be reflected in the book.

These purposes commit the writer to a statement of the Christian faith in its catholicity, in its fullness. This is the purpose of every truly Christian theology. Yet the recognition of one's own finiteness and the limitations of a sinful creature mean that catholicity must be an intention but never claimed as a fact. Hence the purpose of this volume is modest. The best that can be hoped for is the faith of the one, holy, catholic, and apostolic church, as it has been understood in particular by Reformed Christians.

The emphases of this particular tradition are clear. This statement of faith intends quite specifically to affirm the faith of the ancient creeds: the Apostles' Creed, the Nicene Creed, the Chalcedonian Definition, and the Athanasian Creed. It is also drawn deliberately from the theologians of the ancient church, in particular Athanasius, Augustine, and Gregory of Nyssa. The debt to Luther's great writings of 1520 will also be obvious. The more specific context is the Reformed theology that began with Zwingli and Bullinger in Zurich and Calvin in Geneva and was developed by the English Puritans.

The contemporary theologians who have been most influential in shaping the theology of the writer are Karl Barth, Emil Brunner, Reinhold Niebuhr, H. Richard Niebuhr, and William Temple. The writer is also greatly indebted to those who have taught him theology: G. G. Parkinson at Erskine College, W. C. Robinson at Columbia Theological Seminary, E. T. Ramsdell and Roy Battenhouse at Vanderbilt, and Albert C. Outler, Roland Bainton, and Robert L. Calhoun at Yale.

This book has also been written in the light of convictions that have evolved in recent years about the contemporary plight of churches and about the state of theology in relation to the churches. Theologies were once the sign of vitality in the churches. Augustine's theology was a significant factor in the Christian community's survival during the breakup of Roman civilization. It mightily shaped the emerging European community. The great revival of faith in the sixteenth century cannot be imagined apart from Calvin's *Institutes* and similar theologies. The theologies of Jonathan Edwards (1703–1758) and John Wesley (1703–1791) informed the revival of faith in the eighteenth century. But no new theology in the past two hundred years has led to a revival in the church, with the possible exception of the theology of Karl Barth.[1]

Contemporary theology has been impaired by desire for novelty and for relevance. The primary purpose of theology is always first to explicate in understandable language the deposit of faith that has been the tradition in the church. The language of the church grows out of scripture and out of the reflections of the worshiping, believing community of people now for two thousand years. Any departure from the language of the Bible and of Christian experience has always to be justified. Moreover, relevance to the contemporary situation is generally found through the faithful interpretation of the tradition combined with clarity of expression and simplicity of language. Theologies since 1955 have exhibited an inordinate desire for new vocabularies that do not grow out of worshiping communities as well as modifications of traditional faith more accommodative of a secular humanist culture than illuminative for worshiping congregations.

This book has been written in the conviction that we are now living in a period of religious revival.[2] It is also a time when church people who have emphasized the life of the mind have a great opportunity to witness to the people who have gone to college in greater numbers than ever before in history. It is becoming increasingly popular to speak about theology being marginal to educated people.[3] But usually the reference is made by persons in academic positions who seem to limit the educated to their particular departments and their professional disciplines. The simple fact, confirmed by personal observation and by statistical data, is that the brightest and most effective people in almost every community in America are eager to hear the gospel preached.

This study has also been written in the conviction that Christian faith is persuasive when it is proclaimed as the gospel of God, a gospel that heals the bruised consciences and wounded spirits of human beings. It is persuasive when it is explicated in a manner that reveals its own intelligibility and the intelligibility of the various dimensions of human life and society in the light of the faith.[4]

Theology is not first of all an academic exercise. It is a work of the community of faith. To theologize was once used in the same sense as to evangelize today. The Fourth Lateran Council of 1215 defined the theologian as "one who is to teach priests and others about the Sacred Page and above all to inform them of those things that are known to pertain to the cure of souls."[5] The seminal theologians of the Reformed tradition were all preachers and pastors: Zwingli, Bucer, Bullinger, Calvin.

The increasingly current definition of theology in academic terms defined in a secular university context is something new in the history of the church, as is the drawing of seminary faculties from secular graduate schools rather than from the life of the church. Yet there is no evidence in church history that theologies that do not begin with revelation—Jesus Christ as the word made flesh—and that do not grow out of worshiping communities, can gather and sustain congregations. Christian theology is primarily answerable as to its integrity to the faith of the believing community, and to human beings as human beings, not to the orthodoxies of secular universities. Theology calls forth faith when it is spoken in faith and received in faith as God's gracious word to the human creature. The commonsense wisdom of the Christian community over a period of time, or—to put it more theologically—the testimony of the Holy Spirit in the life of the church, is still the best arbiter of Christian doctrine, more reliable than either the papal authority or the academic graduate school.

Preaching and theology that show scant concern for modernity elicit quantifiable signs of life. The data on church attendance and church growth, as well as the presence of conservative churches in affluent and educated neighborhoods, indicate the persuasiveness of the gospel and the openness of modern people to the gospel. Yet critical and intellectually concerned people ought not to be forced to choose between preaching that ignores modern culture and preaching that so accommodates this culture as to deny or attenuate the Christian faith.

Intelligent people can and do find the Christian gospel improbable or false. Equally intelligent people find it to be the truth. Faith may contradict faith. The decision of faith is not the conclusion of an argument, but a human commitment involving the whole self, comparable to a decision to love or to choose a life vocation. Faith is no more the conclusion of a school argument than is any other major decision in life. Faith is the judgment and commitment of the whole person in which a persuasive statement of the faith may play a significant role.

The Protestant Reformers all insisted on translating the Bible into the language of the people. They were convinced that ordinary people can read the Bible, understand it and apply it to their lives. They also contended that theology should be in the language of the people.[6] Hence they rejected the specialized language of school (scholastic) theology and wrote theology in the language and idiom of the worshiping, believing congregation. This has also been an intention in the writing of this volume.

The special task of theology is first to certify the authenticity of the message for Christians. This means that all theology and preaching must be in accord with the revelation of God in Jesus Christ, attested in the scriptures.[7] While no theology can claim adequately to grasp the truth of revelation, the theological intention is to be transparent to the reality it discloses. The words of theology should be in some sense comparable to the elements of the sacraments, the occasion of the presence of God through the power of the Holy Spirit.

Theology also has the task of indicating how the revelation of God does justice to the facts of the world and of human life, illuminating human experience and making sense out of human life and society. In theology the false starts, the dead ends, the corruptions of human life should be uncovered and the grace of God proclaimed in such a way that human life is renewed. As Reinhold Niebuhr once put it, the first task of apologetic theology is to uncover the inadequacies of secular concepts in the understanding of human life and society. On the other hand, Christian faith is validated when theological reflection illuminates the crises, the decisions, the problems of human life and society as does no other faith.[8]

James Turner has documented how an overzealous effort to accommodate the culture outside the circle of faith actually contributed in the United States to the rise of unbelief.[9] The first concern of the Christian theologian must be the revelation of God in Jesus Christ, as attested in scripture, and its explication in the language of ordinary discourse.

All theology, Christian or otherwise, must have intellectual integrity. The critical point is that theology must be done from within the Christian community. The faith must be explicated on its own ground and not in the light of or in the context of the various faiths of a secular society or in particular in the context of social movements which, while denying basic Christian affirmations, are happy enough to make use of Christian resources to fulfill their own agenda.

Every theologian of any perspective and commitment is equally obligated
to acknowledge the authority of hard facts and to be subject to the rules
that govern responsible discourse. All theological statements must have warrants. Every Christian theology seeks to speak the truth and in speaking
the truth to utilize all the powers of the human mind in the service of God.
Yet it is critically important that the question of "faith" not be confused
with the question of "facts." Every fact is apprehended in some frame of
reference, and "questions of fact" are never comprehended apart from previously decided "questions of faith." Christian faith confesses certain crucial
events in history, such as the life of Jesus, his teachings, the witness to his
resurrection, and the remarkable inauguration of the church with signs
and wonders. In this respect theology resembles natural sciences. A fundamental task of theology is not unlike the natural sciences, namely, to
reflect on the interpretive framework through which faith views the world
of "facts." The adequacy of any theology, like that of any science, is based
on its internal integrity and on its ability to make sense of the "facts" as
we encounter them in the world and to illuminate human life and society.[10]

My own theological position intends to be catholic, protestant, and
reformed in an American context. In more contemporary terms the intention is to be critically orthodox. By orthodox I mean the reaffirmation
of the classical Christian faith, based on scripture and expounded in the
tradition, particularly the creeds of the ancient church and the writings
of the Protestant Reformers. By critical I mean that the faith has to be
expounded on this side of the Enlightenment and the nineteenth century.[11]

I have written this book while a resident member of the Center of
Theological Inquiry in Princeton, New Jersey, of which Daniel Hardy is
Director. I shall ever be grateful to a goodly number of friends who gave
me strength not only for the theological task but for human life itself.
Among these were Thomas and Barbara Gillespie, Arthur and Margaret
Link, Samuel and Eileen Moffett, Bruce and Isabel Metzger, Wallace and
Alice Alston, Christiaan Beker, Edward A. Dowey, William and Sally Sword,
James and Nancye Fitzpatrick, Cynthia Jarvis, David and Sally Willis-
Watkins, Diogenes and Jane Allen, James Charlesworth, Roland and Jean
Frye, William Harris, and many others. I am also indebted to Thomas F.
Torrance, whose commitment to Christian theology and the church is as
impressive as his learning, and who serves on the Advisory Council of
the Center. I also owe much to colleagues at Union Theological Seminary
and to former students, especially Stacy Johnson, now teaching on the
faculty of Austin Presbyterian Theological Seminary, for innumerable conversations about theology generally and about the particular issues of this
text. He also read the manuscript.

I am likewise indebted to Craig Dykstra and the Lilly Endowment for their confidence in granting funds that provided for secretarial and research assistance, without which the manuscript could not have been completed, at least not on schedule.

Martha Aycock Sugg, Associate Librarian, Union Theological Seminary in Virginia, has always supported my studies and writing far beyond her official responsibilities. I came to realize how much support this meant with her retirement in the past year. I am likewise indebted to William Harris, archivist of the Speer Library, Princeton Theological Seminary, who is also my friend, and who has likewise gone far beyond the call of duty and even friendship in searching out articles for me.

Kate Le Van of the Center of Theological Inquiry was most helpful to me during my residence there. Norma Kuhn, Helena Thomas, and Lois Bedell of the Union Theological Seminary staff have continued being helpful to an emeritus professor. Angela Basmajian typed the manuscript with competence and a cordial disposition. Daniel Griswold, a former student, was very helpful in running down references and in helping to put the manuscript in final shape. Peter Vanderbrake and Michael Bush, along with Kyle Fedler of Columbia Theological Seminary, assisted with the notes. William T. Stuart, M.D., Presbyterian elder and my friend, and Ann. W. Leith, my wife, read the galley proofs. Carl Helmich was the diligent editor for Westminster/John Knox Press. Sally Telford of the Press has always supported my publications.

The book has been given its final editing and form while I have been a visiting minister on the staffs of two great Presbyterian congregations, composed of people who by any standard of "modernity" are very bright, alive, and effective in contemporary society.

W. Frank Harrington, pastor of Peachtree Presbyterian Church, Atlanta, has stimulated my work on this book by the effectiveness of his ministry and most of all by his friendship. Peachtree Presbyterian Church, with ten thousand members, is a very remarkable community. It has given me confidence in writing a statement of Christian faith in our time.

While in Atlanta, I lived on the campus of Columbia Theological Seminary, whose president, Douglas Oldenburg, was in my first classes at Union Theological Seminary, and was a cordial host on the seminary campus. I have also profited from the friendship and theological conversations with George Stroup of Columbia Theological Seminary, and Brian Armstrong of Georgia State University. F. Sidney Anderson went beyond duty and even friendship to encourage me in my theological work.

I also served on the staff of the First Presbyterian Church of Charlotte, North Carolina, located in the heart of the business community, a leading financial center of the nation. The effectiveness of its witness as a community of Christian faith in that setting is impressive. William P. Wood, the pastor, was a student in my seminary classes and is my friend. Conversation with very "modern" people in highly successful business, professional, and social activities in Atlanta and Charlotte confirmed my understanding of the importance of what I have attempted in this book.

Richard Ray, formerly editor of John Knox Press and now pastor of First Presbyterian Church, Bristol, Tennessee, encouraged me in 1977 to sign the contract to write this book. It is a better book for the delay, but it may not have been written without his encouragement.

My personal gratitude must be expressed to medical doctors who have enabled me to continue working with chronic illnesses, especially Duncan Owen of the Medical College of Virginia, and Benjamin F. Thomas, Jr., of Auburn, Alabama. Wyndham H. Blanton, M.D., was chairman of the Union Theological Seminary Board when I was called there, and his office, especially the laboratory staff, and his sons, Wyndham Blanton, Jr., and Frank Blanton, have graciously attended my needs. I also profited from the presence of medical doctors and lawyers who attended my classes on the theology of John Calvin, including W. T. Thompson, W. M. Thompson, George Warthen, William T. Stuart, and Charles Cook.

Theology is written out of books that have been read and studied, but it is also and more profoundly written out of personal existence in a community of faith. This book is the Christian faith as I have come to know it in life and church, and it is the faith I have wanted and intended to believe and confess.

# ACKNOWLEDGMENTS

Grateful acknowledgment is made to the following for permission to reproduce copyrighted material.

Augsburg Fortress, from Martin Luther, "The Freedom of a Christian," reprinted from *Selected Writings of Martin Luther,* edited by T. G. Tappert, copyright © 1967 Fortress Press. Used by permission of Augsburg Fortress.

T. & T. Clark Ltd., from Karl Barth, *Church Dogmatics,* translated by G. T. Thomson, T. F. Torrance, G. W. Bromiley, et al. Published by T. & T. Clark, 1936–1969.

Macmillan Publishing Company, for material reprinted from *The Nature and Destiny of Man,* copyright 1941, 1943 Charles Scribner's Sons. Copyright © 1964 Charles Scribner's Sons. Copyrights renewed © 1969, 1971 Reinhold Niebuhr.

Oxford University Press, from Christopher Fry, *The Dark Is Light Enough,* copyright Oxford University Press 1954.

SCM Press Ltd., from Karl Barth, *Dogmatics in Outline,* published by SCM Press, 1949; copyright © 1959 by Harper & Row, Publishers, Inc. Used by permission of SCM Press and HarperCollins Publishers.

Westminster/John Knox Press, from *Calvin: Institutes of the Christian Religion,* edited by John T. McNeill, translated by Ford Lewis Battles, published by The Westminster Press and SCM Press. Copyright © MCMLX W. L. Jenkins; and from Emil Brunner, *Revelation and Reason,* copyright, MCMXLVI, by W. L. Jenkins.

World Council of Churches, for material from *Christ, the Hope of the World* (New York: Harper & Brothers, 1954).

CHAPTER 1

❖

# CHRISTIAN THEOLOGY
# IN REFORMED PERSPECTIVE

Theology in its broadest sense is critical reflection about the meaning of human existence and about the nature of the universe. As critical reflection it is distinguished both from religious enthusiasm and from prayer, though some have attempted to write theology as a prayer.[1] *Christian* theology is critical reflection about God, about human existence, about the nature of the universe, and about faith itself: (a) in the light of the revelation of God embodied in Jesus Christ and attested in the scriptures; (b) in dialogue with the way the church has understood the revelation in the past; (c) in conversation with human experience today, especially human experience within the church; and (d) in dialogue with and witness to culture, social life, and living religions. For the Christian community, Jesus Christ is the final revelation — the definitive revelation that is the criterion of all other revelation.

## A Christian Theology

Every Christian theology intends to be a *Christian* theology or a catholic theology. Yet no theology is *the* Christian theology or a truly catholic theology. Every theologian is a finite creature, limited by space and time, born and reared in a particular tradition and without either the experience or the intelligence to write a truly catholic or Christian theology. In addition, every theologian is a sinner saved by grace. Theologians — as do all people — hold the truth in unrighteousness (Romans 1:18, KJV).

The purposes of a Christian or catholic theology can best be served by accepting the perspective out of which the theology is written and by acknowledging the limitations of the theologian. This particular theology is written out of four perspectives and as such claims to be a Christian

1

theology but also confesses that it falls short of the breadth and depth of a truly catholic theology.

1. The foundation of the Christian community, and therefore the decisive authority for Christian theology, is Jesus Christ, the Word made flesh. The Bible is the original and authentic witness to this revelation of God. In a historical sense the Bible is a book of the church, the witness to Jesus Christ that the church certifies to be authentic and original or apostolic. In another historical and theological sense the Bible is prior to the church in that the original witness, to which scripture attests, is the foundation of the church's existence. The canon of scripture, the collection of authoritative writings, is not authoritative as a canon but as a collection of authoritative books, which the church acknowledged.[2] The church has also insisted that the Bible is not simply an original and authentic *witness* to the revelation of God but that it is also the means of God's revelation today. Hence, any Christian theology must be biblical. The revelation of God must not be construed, however, in terms of disparate texts. Theologies must be broadly based and be developed under the authority of a comprehensive understanding of the scriptures.

2. Christian theology must also be catholic, that is, reaffirming in every new time and place the theological achievements of the ancient catholic church. This ancient catholic church includes the Apostles' and comparable creeds from Eastern churches, the Nicene Creed (A.D. 325, 381), the Chalcedonian Definition (451), the doctrine of the Trinity, and the theology of Augustine (354–430), and Athanasius (c. 296–373). The theological foundation in the broad base of the biblical witness and the somewhat narrower but still broad base of catholic Christianity are the indispensable ground and source for Christian theologizing in all later periods. The ancient catholic church was compelled by its own reflections on the faith and by the pressure of an alien culture to give answers to the basic questions of Christian theology: Who is Jesus Christ? How shall we think of God? What does it mean to be a human being in a sinful world?

In the providence of God the church had able theologians to formulate the theological answers to these questions: It had the Cappadocians: Gregory of Nyssa (330–395), Gregory of Nazianzus (329–389), and Basil of Caesarea (330–379). It had schools of theology at Antioch and Alexandria; it had Athanasius and Augustine. Furthermore, it concentrated its energies on the theological questions with an intensity and a catholicity that have never been duplicated.

3. This particular theology intends also to be Protestant, that is, influenced and guided in particular by the writings of Martin Luther

(1483–1546) in 1520: *The Freedom of a Christian, The Babylonian Captivity of the Church,* the *Address to the Christian Nobility of the German Nation,* and the *Treatise on Good Works.* It includes theses, confessions, and early writings of the Swiss theologians, Zwingli's *An Exposition of the Faith,* Heinrich Bullinger's *Decades,* and Calvin's *Institutes of the Christian Religion,* as well as the homilies of the early English Reformation.[3] These early writings insisted on the supreme authority of the Holy Spirit speaking through scripture, justification by grace through faith (the forgiveness of sins), the priesthood of all believers, the sanctity of the common life, and a strong belief in personal decision and responsibility.

4. Within Protestantism this particular theology intends to be Reformed and therefore distinguishable from Lutheran theologies and Anglican theologies.[4] No one doctrine identifies a Reformed theology, but a number of nuances and perspectives are marks of theology in the Reformed way.

These perspectives or nuances are the following:

a. A strong perception of God's energy, activity, intentionality, and moral purpose. God is personal and inherently communicative.

b. An insistence on the purposive activity of God in human history as well as in nature and a conception of the Christian life as embodying the purposes of God in public as well as in private life.

c. A distinctive way of putting together God's grace as mercy which forgives our sins and God's grace as power that transforms us: forgiveness and sanctification. The early Reformed theologians were insistent that forgiveness of sins can neither be separated from nor be confused with the transformation of human life into the image of Christ. The purpose of the Christian life is not to be forgiven but to become a mature person in the image of Jesus Christ. Forgiveness is the presupposition, not the end, of the Christian life.

d. Reformed theology is also defined by a distinctive way of perceiving the transcendence and immanence of God. Reformed theologians have always emphasized the freedom of God the creator from his creation but at the same time have insisted on the immanence of God in terms of moral purpose and intentionality. Following the ancient school at Antioch the Reformed were very suspicious of any theology that minimized the moral, historical character of human life and the finiteness of every created object. This insistence on the transcendence of God and the immanence of God conceived of in personal terms gives a peculiar character to Reformed doctrines of the person of Christ, of the presence of Christ in the sacrament, and of the church as a divine and human institution. Neither in the doctrine of Christ nor the presence of Christ in the sacrament nor in the doctrine of the church does Reformed theology allow any intimation of a confusion of the divine and the human or the absorption of the human into the divine. The emphasis in the Christian life is on the integrity of moral decision and historical action.

e. Reformed theology is further distinguished by a particular way of relating general revelation and special revelation, church and society, creation and redemption. The revelation in Christ and redemption are related to the created order neither by denials nor by simple fulfillment but generally in terms of conversion. The peculiar way of relating general and special revelation, church and society, creation and redemption will be pointed out in the discussion of particular doctrines.

f. Reformed theology has always been characterized by an emphasis on the practical rather than the theoretical, on edification rather than vision. The end of the Christian life is not so much the vision of God as the kingdom of God, life and society transformed into the image of Christ.

These four classical statements of Christian theology (the scriptures, the theology of the ancient catholic church, Protestant theology, and Reformed theology) are the foundation of this particular statement of faith. No claim is made that they represent the fullness of the Christian tradition. Theological developments of the medieval period are minimally involved in this theological statement as well as the great theological achievements of Eastern Orthodox churches.

Any contemporary theological statement has to give attention to additional concerns.

First, the greatest divide in the modern history of Western culture was the Enlightenment and the nineteenth century. Any contemporary theological statement has to be made against this background. On the one hand, the significance of the Enlightenment ought not to be exaggerated. Few if any contemporary statements of Christian faith are more persuasive to the contemporary reader than some of the writings of Calvin or Luther or Thomas Aquinas or Augustine. However, the Enlightenment and the nineteenth century taught us truths about the world and about the nature of critical thinking that theology can forget only at its own peril.[5] A distinction has to be made between the dogmas of the Enlightenment and the spirit of the Enlightenment. The dogmas of the Enlightenment were in many instances denials of Christian faith, as, for example, the notion that scientific knowledge exhausted truth. Hence the dogmas must be subjected to criticism. Yet the spirit of the Enlightenment contributes strength to any theological inquiry. The insistence on freedom of inquiry in the long run is essential to good theology as well as to the integrity of the human mind. Because of the Enlightenment we know better than we did before that we cannot believe something that we know is not true, that any religion that requires a sacrifice of the integrity of the human mind is bad religion. Theology after the Enlightenment must come to terms with freedom of inquiry, with respect for facts, with insistence on the integrity of the human mind in theological work, and with the relevance of Christian faith for concrete human experience. For this critique of the Enlightenment, theology must be grateful.

Theology must also be written in the context of a particular locality and place. For the present writing, the context is the United States of America at the end of the twentieth century. Christian theology in America must seek to make intelligible the peculiar experiences of American people.[6]

In the writing of theology, attention must be given to a language adequate to express theological truths. There is good reason for seeking to write Christian theology in the language of ordinary human discourse. This follows the example of the early Protestant Reformers. It also builds upon the great achievement of those who shaped the English language in the sixteenth and seventeenth centuries and who were in large measure concerned with the language that would be adequate for speaking about God and God's work for our salvation. The influence of the King James Version of the Bible as well as much of Puritan literature on the English language has continued to this day. Every theologian has to give attention to the adequacy of language to express theological content and in particular to a language that is adequate and useful and understandable in ordinary human discourse. From the beginning Reformed theologians with few exceptions have written theology in the language of ordinary experience and in the language of the Christian community.

## Augustinian and Reformed

This particular theology in its method intends to be Augustinian and Reformed.[7] John Calvin, in agreement with other Reformed theologians, deliberately adopted the Augustinian way of theological reflection.[8] For Augustine and for Calvin, Christian theology begins with the revelation of God in Jesus Christ. Augustine knew that the decisive difference between classical culture and Christian faith was found in the Christian affirmation that the Word became flesh.[9] The Theses of Berne (1528), the first major public declaration of Reformed faith, began with the assertion that the church lives by hearing the word of God. The foundation for Christian theology is not some universal truth but the particular historical revelation of God in Jesus Christ.

This Augustinian way of doing theology, which was adopted by Calvin, can be summarized in five statements.

1. All human understanding is based on what is perceived to be "revelation" and on a faith commitment. As Augustine put it, "We believe in order to understand."[10] Faith and revelation are not the second story, as it were, to human knowledge and understanding. They are the means by which all people understand. The disparate facts of experience are always put together in the light of some faith.

All people, according to the Augustinians, live by faith. To be a human being is to live by faith. There is no other alternative. Insofar as a human being is truly human, personal faith is an inescapable dimension of human life. The events of life compel us to faith commitments whether explicit or implicit, conscious or unconscious. Each day before we have been up three hours we have made decisions in the light of some faith commitment about the nature of the universe, about the nature of the human being, about the significance of a human being, about the meaning of human life.

Human life is lived within brackets or parentheses, encompassed by mystery.[11] Within the brackets or parentheses we can have some limited understanding, but the words within a parenthesis do not really make sense unless we know the words of the encompassing sentence. Our human predicament is that we cannot escape from the brackets. We do not know from whence we came or whither we go. We do not know by our reasoning the origin of the universe or its final destiny. Neither do we know by the data we gain from the study of human beings whether human life has any abiding value or meaning.

Revelation provides the clue, the wisdom, the insight that enables us to understand. It is in the light of what we perceive to be the revelation of reality and in the light of the faith in that revelation that we evaluate the facts, organize the facts, and put them together in some coherent whole. The Communist and the Christian, for example, have access to the same facts about human life, the same biological, social, historical, and physical facts; but the Communist and Christian come to radically different answers to the question, Who is a human being? The difference is not in the facts but in the faith in the light of which the facts are understood.

A confusion about faith and facts exists in much popular understanding. The real issues in life are not between faith and facts but between faith and faiths. Every fact is understood in some frame of reference, of meaning, of faith. As shall be indicated later, the popular controversy about the origin of the world often misstates the question as though it were a controversy about facts. The real issue is not between creation and evolution. The real issue is between the faith that the origin of the world is chance or impersonal power and the faith that the origin of the world is found in purpose and, indeed as Christians contend, in the grace and love of God. The scientist as well as the Christian believer lives by faith. Hence, it is critically important for theology to uncover the faith by which people actually live and to explicate the Christian faith over against other faith possibilities. There is no escape for human beings from this dilemma. Every understanding of the world, of human life, and of the meaning and destiny of human existence is based on some faith commitment, whether it is conscious or unconscious. As Calvin liked to insist, the only options in life are between faith in God and faith in idols.[12]

All theology according to the Augustinian, Reformed way of thinking is confessional. We confess our faith on the basis of what we perceive to be the revelation of God. On this basis, all people are invited to stand with Christian believers, to receive the grace of God for the living of life, and to see the world as they do. The Christian claim is that Christian faith does more justice to the facts, makes more sense out of life, illuminates life, opens life more to the grace of God that forgives and heals wounded consciences and bruised spirits than does any other faith.

2. Reason as well as revelation has its place in theology. Augustine, as well as Calvin, knew that without the capacity for reason faith would not be possible. Faith requires comprehension and commitment. Also, reason serves as the means of critically examining faith. Augustine emphasized the distinction between credulity and faith.[13] Faith is not believing something that you know is not true, nor is it a denial of facts. Hence, reason serves the critical function of examining faith as to its consistency and as to its integrity in faithfully explicating what it declares to be a revelation of God. Reason also serves to distinguish faith from fantasy or delusion. We cannot believe something that we know on good rational grounds is not true. Finally, reason serves the useful function of explicating the meaning of faith, so as to illuminate human life.

3. Christian theology takes place in the worshiping community of believing people. As Augustine put it, "In order to know the truth we must first love the truth."[14] The Augustinians and the Reformed have always emphasized the affections and the will. Augustine knew that desire is an important factor in knowing.[15] This is true not only in matters of faith but also in life generally. Chemistry, for example, can be learned more easily by those who desire to learn chemistry than it can by those who have no desire. The more truth affects our lives personally, the more important it is to

love the truth in order to know it. Repentance, for Augustine and for Calvin, was an important factor in knowing the truth of God, as Reinhold Niebuhr has emphasized in our time.

William Temple, lecturing on an American college tour in the 1930s, was asked by an American college student if there was any evidence for the existence of God. Temple replied, "Do you want to believe in God?" Temple's point was that if one wants to believe in God there is a great amount of convincing evidence, but if one does not want to believe in God, no evidence will be convincing.[16]

4. Anselm, the great twelfth-century theologian, carried forward the Augustinian way of doing theology by declaring that faith seeks understanding, or intelligibility.[17] Faith is not simply declared but is understood. The task of Christian theology is to understand the act of faith itself and to bring the various truths apprehended by faith and repentance into some kind of coherent, consistent whole. The faith is not simply to be affirmed; it is also to be understood.

Faith also seeks the intelligibility of human existence and in particular of human existence in the universe and in all of human history in the light of the faith itself. Reinhold Niebuhr insisted that Christian theology must be apologetic and that the apologetic task was twofold. First, Christian apologetics exposes the alien faiths by which people live and makes explicit what is often implicit in the lives of people. Theology seeks to uncover the fact that all people live by faith which has consequences not only in their personal lives but in political, economic, and social life as well. The task of Christian theology, however, goes beyond the exposure of alien faiths to the positive task of showing how Christian faith makes sense of human life and experience. Niebuhr liked to insist that Christian categories, even such categories as original sin, enabled modern people to understand political and economic life better than the secular categories. In this way faith validates itself.[18]

The truth about the validation of faith can be illustrated in many realms of life. No one, for example, can prove that another person loves him or her. The conviction that one is loved by another person is always an act of faith. The self that stands over against one is never fully known but always has a depth of mystery. No one can ever demonstrate that a lover truly loves or that a friend is truly trustworthy. Any evidence presented is always subject to another interpretation. However, the faith that a person does love and that a friend is trustworthy is validated, as that faith makes sense out of one's experience with one's lover or with one's friends. Such a faith can encounter incidental facts that do not seem to support it; but if the experience generally supports the faith, it survives to be strengthened or weakened by further experiences. Love and trust grow stronger as the faith that one is loved or that one's friend is trustworthy illuminates and makes sense out of human experience. So it is with faith in God. The believer, who is always an unbeliever, overcomes unbelief in part by understanding.

5. Theology seeks to explicate the faith not in order to prove its truth but in order to persuade those who hear. The effort to demonstrate the faith has a long and indeed an honorable history in philosophy, as, for example, in the arguments for the existence of God. It has had practitioners within the Christian community. In contemporary theology many theologians are busily engaged in seeking some universal foundation for the faith. No such effort has ever succeeded, and there is very little reason to believe that it shall succeed today. As is true with almost every important decision in life, the question of faith is settled by persuasion, not by demonstration. For Calvin and for Augustine the "proof" of Christian faith was primarily rhetorical. The task of the theologian, like the task of the preacher, is to write theology in such a way as to persuade modern people.

## Classical Statements of Reformed Theology

The classical statements of Reformed theology can be found in the great systematic theologies and in the statements of faith that have through the years received approbation in the life of the Christian community, in particular the Reformed community.

### Reformed Theologians

Ulrich Zwingli (1484–1531), *The True and False Religion* (1525)
John Calvin (1509–1564), *Institutes of the Christian Religion* (1536, 1559)
Heinrich Bullinger (1504–1575), *Decades* (1549–1551)
Wolfgang Musculus (1497–1563), *Commonplaces of Sacred Theology* (1560)
Theodore Beza (1519–1605), *Confession of the Christian Faith* (1558)
Peter Martyr Vermigli (1500–1562), *Commonplaces* (edited by Robert Masson, 1576)
William Perkins (1558–1602), *A Golden Chain* (1591)
Amandus Polanus (1561–1610), *Syntagma Theologiae Christianae* (1609)
William Ames (1576–1633), *The Marrow of Divinity* (1623)
Johannes Wollebius (1586–1629), *Compendium of the Christian Faith* (1626)

Gisbert Voetius (1589–1676), *Selectae Disputationes Theologicae* (1648–1669)

Francis Turretin (1623–1687), *Institutio Theologiae Elencticae* (1679–1685)

Benedict Pictet (1655–1724), *Christian Theology* (1696)

Samuel Willard (1640–1707), *A Compleat Body of Divinity* (1726)

Jonathan Edwards (1703–1758), *A History of the Work of Redemption* (1744)

Heinrich L. Heppe (1820–1879), *Reformed Dogmatics* (1861) (Eng. trans. 1950)

Charles Hodge (1797–1878), *Systematic Theology* (1871)

Robert Louis Dabney (1820–1898), *Systematic and Polemic Theology* (1878)

Henry B. Smith (1815–1877), *System of Christian Theology* (1884)

Augustus Hopkins Strong (1836–1921), *Systematic Theology* (1886; 8th ed. 1907–1909)

William Shedd (1820–1894), *Dogmatic Theology* (1888)

Herman Bavinck (1854–1921), *Our Reasonable Faith* (1909)

Louis Berkhof (1873–1957), *Reformed Dogmatics* (1932)

Karl Barth (1886–1968), *Church Dogmatics* (1932–1957) (Eng. trans. 1936–1969)

Emil Brunner (1889–1966), *Dogmatics* (1946–1960)

Otto Weber (1902–1966), *Foundations of Dogmatics* (1955)

Hendrikus Berkhof (1914–), *Christian Faith* (1979; rev. ed. 1986)

Reformed dogmatics has also been enriched by the great number of theologians who have not written comprehensive systematic texts. These would include James Henley Thornwell (1812–1862), James Orr (1844–1915), Abraham Kuyper (1937–1920), Benjamin Breckinridge Warfield (1851–1921), Horace Bushnell (1802–1876), John McLeod Campbell (1800–1872), Nathaniel Taylor (1786–1858), James Denney (1856–1917), Hugh Ross Mackintosh (1870–1936), John Oman (1860–1939), John Baillie (1886–1960), Donald Baillie (1887–1954), P. T. Forsyth (1848–1921), Hendrik Kraemer (1888–1965), Reinhold Niebuhr (1892–1971), Thomas F. Torrance (1913–), and many others.

*Representative Reformed Confessions
of the Sixteenth and Seventeenth Centuries*

I. Early Theses
   Zwingli's Sixty-Seven Articles, 1523
   Theses of Berne, 1528

Theses of Rive, 1535
Theses of Lausanne, 1536

II. CONFESSIONS OF ZURICH AND BASEL
Confession to Charles V (Zwingli), 1530
Confession to Francis I (Zwingli), 1531
First Confession of Basel, 1534
First Helvetic Confession, 1536
Second Helvetic Confession, 1566

III. CONFESSIONS OF GENEVA, FRANCE, AND THE NETHERLANDS
Confession of Geneva, 1537
Consensus of Geneva, 1552
Gallican Confession of Faith, 1559
Belgic Confession, 1561

IV. THE ZURICH CONSENSUS (TIGURINUS), 1549
(*Joint statement on Lord's Supper of representatives
of viewpoints of Geneva and Zurich*)

V. THE RHINELAND
Tetrapolitan Confession, 1530
Heidelberg Catechism, 1563

VI. OTHER EUROPEAN CONFESSIONS
Confession of Czenger (Hungary), 1557 or 1558
Consensus of Sendomir, 1570
Confession of Sigismund, 1614

VII. ENGLISH LANGUAGE CONFESSIONS
Scots Confession of 1560
Thirty-Nine Articles, 1563 (Reformed in articles on predestina-
tion and the Lord's Supper)
Irish Articles of 1615

VIII. SEVENTEENTH-CENTURY CONFESSIONS
Canons of Dort, 1619
Declaration of Thorn, 1645
Westminster Confession, 1647
Helvetic Consensus Formula, 1675
London Confession, 1677, 1689

*Representative Catechisms*

Catechisms present systematic theology usually in a question and answer form and for elementary instruction in the Christian faith.

Geneva Catechism (John Calvin), 1542
Emden Catechism, 1555
Heidelberg Catechism (Zacharias Ursinus and Caspar Olevianus), 1563
Craig's Catechism, 1581
Zurich Catechism of 1609
Brief Method of Catechising (William Gouge), 8th ed. 1631
Short Catechism Containing the Principles of Religion (John Ball), 18th impression 1637
New Catechism, 1644
Endeavour of Making the Principles of Christian Religion, namely, the Creed, the Ten Commandments, the Lord's Prayer, and the Sacraments, Plaine and Easie (Herbert Palmer), 6th ed. 1645
The Shorter Catechism (Westminster Assembly), 1648
The Larger Catechism (Westminster Assembly), 1648
The Principle of Christian Religion with a Brief Method of the Doctrine Thereof (James Ussher), 1654
Draft Catechism of the Church of Scotland, 1954

❖

## CHAPTER 2

# FAITH AND DOCTRINE

Why is doctrine important? Faith is life, and many devout Christians have lived without reading a textbook in Christian theology or even a confession of faith. Why then write a summary of Christian faith?

Christian faith has been kept alive by the liturgy, by telling the story of Jesus, by the discipline of church practices, by the singing of hymns, by the prayers of people. The power of these practices has been demonstrated over and over again in Christian history. The law of prayer is the law of believing.[1] The church has existed effectively for many centuries in societies where few people could read or write, much less think abstractly.

Church history also includes those who have had every doctrine correct but who have not shown the signs of Christian faith. In protest against those who took theology seriously but who forgot about life, John Wesley emphasized the beliefs of the heart and committed himself "to promote, so far as I am able, vital, practical religion, and by God's grace to beget, pressure, and increase the life of God in the souls of men."[2]

Today many of the fastest-growing Christian communities in the world do not have academic theologians and quite obviously give worship, life, and work a priority over theology. The growth of these churches is closely related to preaching, to singing, to prayers, to human affections, and to community life. On the other hand, theologians, as has already been indicated, have not been distinguished in the last two centuries by the power of their theologies to gather churches and to build them up as the kingdom of God.

The New Testament places great emphasis on doing the will of God and promises that those who do the will of God shall know the doctrine (John 7:17). The will to believe is more basic than mental assent to doctrines. Yet this emphasis on doing, obeying, and willing makes sense only in a context where the faith is known and interpreted. The question still stands,

"But how are they to call on one in whom they have not believed? And how are they to believe in one of whom they have never heard? And how are they to hear without someone to proclaim him?" (Romans 10:14).

## The Importance of Doctrine

The reasons why Protestant and particularly Presbyterian churches must take seriously the writing and the study of theology are to be found first of all in the particular tradition and, second, in the nature of faith itself. The early church had no systematic theological texts for two centuries, yet the situations that led to the first comprehensive theological texts in the third century were present from the beginning. In every succeeding generation the life of the Christian community has been enriched by theological writing. Kenneth Scott Latourette in his seven-volume history of Christian missions found a positive correlation between theological vigor and the vitality of church life.[3]

1. Protestantism was born in a protest against the theological failures of medieval Catholicism. Martin Luther once declared with passion:

> Life is as bad among us as among the papists. Hence, we do not fight and damn them because of their bad lives. . . . I do not consider myself to be pious. But when it comes to whether one teaches correctly about the word of God, there I take my stand and fight. That is my calling. To contest doctrine has never happened until now. Others have fought over life; but to take on doctrine—that is to grab the goose by the neck! . . . When the word of God remains pure, even if the quality of life fails us, life is placed in a position to become what it ought. That is why everything hinges on the purity of the Word. I have succeeded only if I have taught correctly.[4]

Protestantism from the very beginning insisted that catechetical instruction, Bible reading, and the writing of theology were crucial for the church's existence. For this reason Protestants established schools adjacent to their churches to teach people to read the Bible and to read theology. Other forms of Christian faith can exist without literacy, without reading of the Bible, and without the study of theology. But the Protestant form of Christianity by its very nature is dependent on these practices. It is interesting to observe that the advent of Protestantism followed immediately the invention of the printing press. Without the printing press, Protestantism as we know it would not have been possible.

2. Presbyterian (Reformed) Christians have always been distinguished by their emphasis on the life of the mind in the service of God. The first Reformed theologians were greatly influenced by Christian humanism, and

they believed that ideas and books were influential in shaping society. John Calvin was always suspicious of feeling. Therefore he insisted on the importance of knowing what one believes and why one believes it. A person is as a person thinks. Augustine had emphasized that a person is as a person loves.[5] This theological tradition remains within the Reformed community, but it is significantly qualified by an emphasis on the service of God through the life of a mind.

The early Reformed sermons required that people think. They also, in a day of few schools, taught people how to think and how to express thought. This emphasis of the Reformed community on the life of the mind in the service of God is reflected in the large number of universities and colleges — including the most elite of secular universities — that had their origin in the Reformed community to train persons to serve God in the Christian ministry and in the commonwealth.[6]

Again, it is not necessary for a person to read a theological text to be a Christian. Yet it is necessary for Presbyterians to take theology seriously if they are to be Christian in the Presbyterian way.

Theology is rooted in the commands of Jesus himself. The warrant for theology is implicit in the admonition of Jesus to consider how the lilies grow (Matthew 6:28). It is explicit in the great commandment "You shall love the Lord your God . . . with all your mind" (Matthew 22:37). The apostle Paul insisted that the believer must take every thought captive to Christ (2 Corinthians 10:5). The author of 1 Peter declared, "Always be ready to make your defense to anyone who demands from you an accounting for the hope that is in you" (1 Peter 3:15).

Theology is also grounded in the nature of faith itself: "Faith is incipient theology."[7] Every faith commitment involves a spoken or an unspoken assertion about the final nature of things and about the meaning of human existence. In addition, faith always seeks understanding (intelligibility), in part because a person who believes has a mind as well as a heart and in part because faith, as well as the self, seeks to bring all things, all the diversities of life into some intelligible, coherent whole.

The significance of theology for faith, according to Karl Rahner, one of the most distinguished Roman Catholic theologians of the century, finds an apt analogy in the experience of human love.[8] A man may fall in love with a woman in such a way that his life is radically transformed. There is no question that this experience of love is real, that it is his and her own experience. It may be that in an intellectual and reflective way, the lover understands very little of what has happened to him. He may be able to speak of it only in a halting and stumbling manner or only in terms of his own feelings. The reflection of others on this experience and even the reflection of the man and woman themselves at a later time may disclose hidden depths in the experience of which they were both unaware intellectually. Reflection may open the way for future developments that they did not anticipate. The experience belongs to the person who is involved in it in such a way that it cannot belong to anyone who reflects on it from the outside or even to the person himself or herself reflecting on it later. Nevertheless, the later reflection is not unrelated to the experience itself. As a result of the reflection, similar experiences of others may be illuminated and the experience of the original lovers may be enlarged and deepened.

The disciples of Jesus experienced the presence of God in Jesus Christ in a way that has been decisive for Christians ever since. Yet it is possible that later Christians, as they have lived the life of faith in changing contexts and as they have reflected in study, have discovered meaning and significance that even the first disciples could never have perceived or articulated. No theology, just as no reflection on love, can ever be a substitute for the personal experience itself. Yet both human love and faith in God can be enhanced, deepened, and broadened by intellectual reflection.

Theology grows inevitably out of the experience of faith itself. It grows out of this experience because the person or the self who believes not only feels, not only wills, not only desires, but also thinks. No truly human activity can long survive unless it is supported by human thinking as well as human feeling and willing.

3. Theology is also required by the social context in which faith exists. Christians do not live unto themselves but in the larger world, which calls upon them not only to articulate their faith but to give a reason for it. This has always been true in Christian history, but it is especially true in contemporary culture. While Americans are possibly more religious today than they have ever been, the centers of information—in particular the mass media and the universities—are dominated by secular humanism. A fundamental dogma of the secular society is pluralism, that is, the convictions that there are many roads to God and that all religions not only have the right to exist equally in the community but also have equal validity. The Christian conviction that the Word, the mind and purpose of God, became incarnate in Jesus of Nazareth is anathema to a pluralistic and secular society. A basic dogma of such a society is the conviction that if there is a word to become incarnate, there cannot possibly be only one word. Hence in American society today it becomes crucially important for Christian people to know what they believe and why they believe it.

Furthermore, the teaching of Christian faith is no longer carried on by the structures of society but is done in the church alone.

4. Two developments in the early church that called for theology were false teachings and catechetical instruction.

Irenaeus's *Against Heresies,* sometimes called the first systematic theology, was written to give a clear statement of the Christian faith over against false teachings. The same concern was present in the writing of Origen, whose *De Principiis (On First Principles)* likewise shares the honor of being one of the first attempts at systematic theology.

Theological heresy is not a matter of such serious concern in contemporary society or even in the contemporary church. The reasons for this are found in history. The wars of religion finally caused revulsion. The fundamentalist-modernist controversies and the heresy trials of a few decades ago likewise resulted in a determination that the church would not again be torn asunder by such controversies. Yet tolerance of heresy easily became indifference to Christian truth. The secular presupposition of this indifference or tolerance was the notion that theology does not really matter. Many who advocated tolerance in theology were most intolerant in those areas of life that were significant to them, namely, political, economic, or ideological orthodoxies. Theological institutions today may be amazingly tolerant of all theological views, but contemporary theological as well as university campuses are unusually intolerant when political, social, and ideological orthodoxies are challenged.

Nevertheless, heresy—false teaching—is a fact that often endangers the very existence of the Christian community.[9] This is amply demonstrated in the quantifiable facts of church life. The Christian tradition is that which the church believes, confesses, and teaches as well as the practices that these actions entail and the fellowship they create. The boundaries of tradition are hard to define, but the central core is clear enough. There has been no enduring Christian community that has not believed that Jesus Christ is the Word made flesh and that by his life, death, and resurrection we are saved. There has been no enduring Christian community that has not treasured the Bible as the Word of God written. There has been no enduring Christian community without the fellowship and the ministry of compassion. The tradition, as Albert Outler has so well pointed out, is Jesus Christ; and the various human statements of the tradition in theologies and communities of faith are broken representations of it.[10]

Heresy exists in many forms.[11] It may be the truncation of faith as in Marcionism. It may be the dilution of faith as in Gnosticism. It may be the distortion of faith as in Montanism. It may be the denial of the fundamentals of the faith as in Arianism. In contemporary American society heresy grows out of biblical illiteracy, ignorance of the Christian tradition, and dilution of church life as well as theology by secular orthodoxies.

The first task of theology is always to maintain the integrity of the faith itself. The second task is to explicate the faith in an intelligible way so that believers may understand and unbelievers may be convinced. Theology always works for the intelligibility of faith itself and the intelligibility of human life and experience in the world in the light of that faith.

The second development in the ancient church that called for theology was baptism and catechetical instruction. Catechetical instruction has always been more than receiving doctrines and then learning them. Every doctrine raises questions that must be answered. Every doctrine must be understood with the mind as well as accepted by the heart, and this requires explication.

Even the most basic Christian instruction, even the singing of "Jesus loves me, this I know; for the Bible tells me so" is filled with theological assertions that the growing child needs to understand.

# Theology Grows
## Out of the Worshiping Community

Christian theology at its best always grows out of the worship, practice, and reflection of the Christian community. Christian theology can be studied outside the Christian community, even in a secular university whose dogmas disallow the basic Christian assertion that the Word became flesh. Yet it can originate and be developed only within the Christian community itself.

Christian theology at its best has always developed out of the life of the believing, worshiping, obeying community. The Apostles' Creed, for example, has no author. It simply grew out of the life of the church. Theologians in the ancient and medieval churches were monks and bishops. The creative theologians of the Protestant Reformation were preachers. Scholastic theology was written in schools that were closely related to the church. The practice of writing theology in secular, humanist universities and under the authority of academic guilds is new, and all the quantifiable data seem to indicate that such theologies have great difficulty in being persuasive either in calling Christian communities into being or in sustaining the life of existing communities. Theologians who write in secular universities may also participate deeply in the life of the Christian community, and therefore the writing of a Christian theology in a secular university is not an impossibility. Yet the impact of the dogmas of a secular humanist culture in the last four decades has continually eroded basic and distinctive Christian commitments.

## Forms of Doctrine

Christian theology exists in many forms. Dogmas are those Christian beliefs which are fundamental for the Christian community and which are necessary for salvation. Protestantism has no officially defined dogmas, but quite obviously in creeds and confessions there are certain convictions, such as the doctrine of the person of Christ, that are the foundation for every Christian community as well as for theology. Doctrine is a looser term than dogma and is applied to those Christian beliefs which the church regards as important and about which there is general agreement, but which do not have the definitive character as "dogmas." Christian thought is an even broader concept, which includes not only the doctrines that are held to be essential as well as the doctrines that have received church approval but also the thought of responsible theologians within the church.

Outside the range of dogmas, doctrines, and thought there exists a whole body of materials from the life of the Christian community that have great theological significance, namely, hymns, prayers, devotional writings, and worship practices. In writing theology for today the theologian has to take seriously not only the dogmas, doctrines, and Christian thought but also various data of the Christian community's life.

Christian theology is written under the conviction that Jesus Christ is the embodiment of the wisdom and the power of God, that Jesus Christ is in actual fact the Word made flesh. All theology must be *biblical*. The Bible is the original and authentic witness to the revelation of God in Christ. It is more than a witness; it is itself a means of revelation. As Jesus Christ is the Word made flesh, so the scriptures are the Word of God written. Theology that is truly Christian must be biblical.

Theology is also written in the light of the Christian community's reflection on the revelation of God in Jesus Christ. The *history of doctrine* is in a real sense the history of the way the church in various times and places has interpreted and understood scripture. This historical theology becomes part of the inherited wisdom of the theologian.

Christian theology must also take into account the experience of the Christian community and the concrete actuality of the faith as it is lived by Christian people in the world. Hence theology includes ethics, theological reflection on the moral life. It is also concerned with the practices of church life to the end that these practices may grow out of and enhance the faith.

Christian theology must also be written in dialogue with culture and with an awareness of living religions. It is apologetic in that it seeks to engage people where they are and to invite them to share in the life of the community of faith.

The decisive human test of the authenticity of a theology is the approbation of the people of God over a period of time. Theology must finally commend itself to the commonsense wisdom of the Christian community— or, more theologically, to the testimony of the Holy Spirit in the life of the church. Protestantism has no magisterial office that can define theology. Even if there were a magisterial office, orthodoxy cannot be imposed upon people, for faith and assent are actions of the self. Christian theology must be persuasive and capable of winning the consent of those who read it, especially in a free and pluralistic society.

Christian theology is no substitute for the living faith of believers and for the living faith of the worshiping, believing community. Yet it arises necessarily out of the nature of human beings who believe and out of the nature of the faith itself. Arising out of faith it can enhance faith, broadening it, deepening it, and illuminating life in the light of the faith.

## CHAPTER 3

❖

# THE HUMAN SITUATION, MYSTERY, AND REVELATION

A genuine faith resolves the mystery of life by the mystery of God. It recognizes that no aspect of life or existence explains itself, even after all known causes and consequences have been traced. All known existence points beyond itself. To realize that it points beyond itself to God is to assert that the mystery of life does not dissolve life into meaninglessness. Faith in God is faith in some ultimate unity of life, in some final comprehensive purpose which holds all the various, and frequently contradictory, realms of coherence and meaning together. A genuine faith does not mark this mysterious source and end of existence as merely an X, or as an unknown quantity. The Christian faith, at least, is a faith in revelation. It believes that God has made Himself known. It believes that He has spoken through the prophets and finally in His Son. It accepts the revelation in Christ as the ultimate clue to the mystery of God's nature and purpose in the world, particularly the mystery of the relation of His justice to His mercy. But these clues to the mystery do not eliminate the periphery of mystery. God remains *deus absconditus.*

> Reinhold Niebuhr, *The Essential Reinhold Niebuhr:*
> *Selected Essays and Addresses,* ed. with introduction
> by Robert McAfee Brown, 238–239

Long ago God spoke to our ancestors in many and various ways by the prophets, but in these last days he has spoken to us by a Son, whom he appointed heir of all things, through whom he also created the worlds. He is the reflection of God's glory and the exact imprint of God's very being, and he sustains all things by his powerful word.

> Hebrews 1:1–3

Theology is basic human wisdom. No other knowledge is so critical for human life. It determines alike our destinies on earth and in heaven. Theology is knowledge of God and knowledge of ourselves.[1] Knowledge of God and knowledge of human beings are bound together so that we cannot know the one without the other. We cannot know who a human being is apart from our knowledge of God, and we cannot truly know God apart from our knowledge of human beings. Knowledge of God and knowledge of human beings are so bound together that we cannot tell which precedes the other. This means that theology, even in the strict sense of knowledge of God, cannot be separated from the concrete realities of human experience in the world.

The necessity for theology grows out of the human situation. Theology always seeks to explicate human experience.[2] It is not a system of belief or even a process of critical reflection that is arbitrarily imposed on human beings from without. Yet the facts and realities of human experience do not in themselves force us to be theologians, however much they may raise theological questions. Animals, so far as we know, are not theologians. Human beings become theologians because of the powers of the human self to transcend itself, to ponder the origin and destiny of the self, to recognize signs of a transcendent intelligence and purpose in human experience and in the world. The human spirit has not only the capacity to objectify the self's existence and to reflect on it but also the power to go beyond every human achievement and knowledge or love toward an ever-receding horizon. Real knowledge of ourselves, like the pot of gold at the end of the rainbow, is always beyond us.

The human spirit reaches out beyond every human achievement, and for this reason all human achievements in the end fail to satisfy the deepest yearnings of the human self. Furthermore, the facts of human experience are never self-explanatory, and the human mind cannot escape asking the meaning and significance of these facts.[3] Theology in the broad sense of reflection on the meaning of human experience is a universal human enterprise, even if it is carried on sometimes in unconscious and incoherent ways. Thus, theology is not strange or alien to human experience. Some form of theology is made necessary by human experience itself and by the critical capacities of the human self.

## The Fact of the Human Mystery

The emergence of human beings in the history of the universe is as certain as any human knowledge can be. We know from immediate experience that we exist. We know that the world exists, for we can no more doubt the reality of the world than we can doubt our experience of it. Yet neither our existence nor the existence of the world is self-explanatory.

The emergence of the human self is a wonder and a puzzlement. Somehow in the history of the universe the human mind emerged with remarkable powers to read off the facts of the universe and even to think the universe itself. When scientists have checked their theoretical reflections by observation they have found the world to be in considerable measure as they thought it would be. In addition, the human will has the remarkable capacity to organize the energies and vitalities of life toward intangible goals and in contradiction to momentary desire. The human spirit has the incredible power to objectify the self's own existence, to reflect about it in praise or blame, to transcend every human achievement in the world itself, asking what is beyond as well as behind every fact and every human undertaking. The human capacity for loyalty, commitment, sacrifice, love, devotion as well as capacities for imagination, analysis, and language can only be, when reflected on, a cause for amazement. The fact that the human self appeared on this planet is a marvel and an enigma that calls for some explanation.

The universe is itself a wonder and a puzzlement. We know far more than previous generations have known about the history of the universe. We know that the universe came into existence about fifteen to twenty billion years ago with a terrific explosion that is beyond our comprehension. Radios and telescopes have picked up "a dying remnant of the fireball that filled the universe at the time of the explosion."[4] The fact that we can today detect the noise and fire of the explosion only adds to the mystery. Yet we cannot get beyond the fireball, which apparently destroyed everything that went before. So far as we now understand, we cannot know the forces that created the explosion or brought the universe into being.[5] The evolving history of the universe is becoming clearer to us at least in outline. The earth came into existence about four and a half billion years ago, and life emerged some three and a half million years ago. Human origins are very indistinct, most of the evidence having been destroyed in the passing of time. One anthropologist who has spent his life trying to recover evidence of human origins in the Olduvai Gorge in Africa writes, "The urge to know what happened is very great, an irresistible inbuilt curiosity about our origins. . . . If we are honest we have to face the fact that we shall never truly know."[6] Early human beings appeared some three to five million years ago.[7] Decisively human activities must be dated much later: fire, 25,000–50,000 years ago; the wheel, about 5,500 years ago; agriculture, 10,000–20,000 years ago; writing, 5,000–6,000 years ago. Much more difficult to date are the emergence of human language, the ability to communicate symbolically, and the emergence of self-consciousness and the power to objectify one's own existence and to reflect on it—that is to say, the emergence of a human being. The precise details of how human beings came to be and how they developed is probably forever closed to us, however interesting the hints of that development may be. Nevertheless, there is no doubting the facts. Human beings—so remarkable that if they did not exist there is no probability that they would exist—do, in fact, exist.[8]

The phenomena of the universe and the phenomena of the human we can in practical life neither doubt nor escape. Yet there are puzzlements. Human existence is bracketed.[9] Like words in a parenthesis, human existence in the universe itself depends on what is outside the parenthesis for its meaning. Within the parenthesis there are only intimations of meaning. The forces that brought the universe and human beings into existence appear to be beyond the reach of human inquiry. The knowledge that is within human grasp may tell us a great deal more about what is within the brackets, but knowledge of what is beyond the brackets is forever closed to us. This is to say, human life is enclosed in mystery.

The interesting fact is the continually receding horizon of human existence. The more we know, the more the horizon recedes. We never reach the boundary. A receding horizon is different from a missing link. Human knowledge may fill the gaps in our knowledge and in our power. Yet the more knowledge and the more power we have, the more the horizon recedes. At least this has been our experience thus far, and no evidence indicates that it will ever be different.

There does not seem to be any escape from the mystery that encompasses us.

## Mystery

Mystery is not a word that appeals to many contemporary persons.[10] Some of the death-of-God theologians in the 1960s envisioned life without mystery. Modern people, it was affirmed, can live without religion and without asking the questions that are rooted in the mystery of existence. They do not ask the meaning of life; they simply find the meaning of life in the living of life.[11] Yet the confidence that the puzzlement of existence could be resolved is refuted by the proclivity of modern people to practice astrology, divination, and even witchcraft. Furthermore, the vitality of religion in contemporary society defies the prediction of those in the nineteenth century who attempted to explain it away in terms of economic forces or psychological factors or even as a stage of history.

Mystery must be distinguished, as a number of modern theologians have insisted, from problems and puzzles.[12] Problems are due to ignorance or ineptness. The application of human resources, science, technology, and logical analysis can resolve problems. Some problems, such as the cure for cancer, are very complex and very resistant to human efforts to resolve them. The same is true of problems in the social and political spheres. In fact, many problems may be so complex that they will never be resolved. The point, however, is not whether they will be solved or not but that in principle they are solvable. They could be solved, if only sufficient knowledge and skill and commitment were brought to bear on them. For the past three centuries persons in the Western world have been amazingly successful in solving problems, from growing crops to curing diseases, from overcoming problems of travel and communication to the convenience of heating and air conditioning for physical comfort. This success has been the source of the temptation to believe not only that all problems can, in fact as well as in principle, be solved but also that life itself can be understood and handled as a problem.

Life can also be viewed as a puzzle.[13] A puzzle may at first glance have the appearance of mystery. We do not know nor can we immediately imagine how the parts fit together, yet once we discover the clue, the parts all fit together neatly and the puzzle becomes a rational pattern. Some puzzles may be very resistant to human efforts to solve them, and conceivably some puzzles may never be solved. The important fact, however, is that puzzles are solvable, if only we can discover the clue. They may be frustrating, but they do not in the end elicit awe or wonder.

Mystery is essentially different from a problem or puzzle. First of all, mystery is not in principle, much less in practice, solvable. It is outside the reach of scientific inquiry. Mystery impinges on us at the boundary of our existence. It elicits the powers of the human spirit to transcend itself, but it is never within our grasp.

Mystery may be construed as a presence that encounters us in the depths and at the boundaries of our existence. The mystery defies objectification and every effort to grasp it or to get a hold on it. For we are within the mystery, and we cannot view it as a spectator. "A mystery is something in which I am myself involved, and it can therefore only be thought of as a sphere where the distinction between what is in me and what is before me loses it meaning and its initial validity."[14]

Gabriel Marcel, whose analysis of existence has construed mystery in this way, has understood the contrast between mystery and problems. Problems can be objectified. They can be subjected to human scrutiny and review. Mystery defies "every technique." Mystery meets us a Subject, as Presence. It is "capable of recognition." By the same token, it can be ignored or denied.[15]

The responses to mystery and to problems differ. The proper response to problems is study, hard work, and the application of techniques and procedures. When problems are solved, any "mystery" dissipates. The proper response to mystery, however, is awe, wonder, and prayer. The more mystery is recognized, the more mysterious and wondrous it becomes.

There is still a further difference between problems and mystery. Problems when once solved can be repeatedly solved by those who have learned the formula. Solutions to problems, once they are known, do not call upon inner resources or involve one's personal existence. The recognition of mystery cannot be repeated at will. It involves being grasped by a presence. All the deeply personal factors that are involved in the recognition of another person are also involved in the recognition of mystery.

Mystery can also be approached from another angle. It is embodied in the ancient question, Why does something exist and not nothing? Marcel's analysis of mystery has been criticized by those who emphasize this particular perspective.

> Marcel, in discussing mystery, nowhere raises the question about the existence of the world. For him, the ontological mystery is not a cosmological mystery. Ontological mystery is always rooted in some person, whether human or divine. It has as its locus some center of value, affection, and concern. The world does not provoke mystery, since it is not a person.[16]

Milton Munitz formulates the question in opposition to Marcel as follows: "Is there a reason—for—the—existence—of—the—world?"[17] In sum, mystery is involved in the ancient question of Parmenides, Why is there something and not nothing?

Mystery may also be approached, as has been suggested, in terms of the transcendence of the human spirit.[18] The human spirit transcends and goes beyond every human achievement. All achievements and knowledge only raise further questions. All acts of love only open up further possibilities of love. The horizons of human existence always recede as we seek to approach them. The whither of the spirit goes beyond anything that it can grasp and make an object of its scrutiny. This orientation of the human self toward what is beyond the self and its world, this experience of the indeterminate openness of human life, is primordial, prior to conceptualization and to the objectification of the experience and reflection.

Attention may be turned away from it or distracted from it, but there is no escape from it.

Mystery likewise confronts us as a dimension of ordinary human experience.[19] Ordinary human experiences, when subjected to analysis, cannot account for themselves. There is, for example, the pervasive conviction that life is worth living. Whence comes this conviction? There are signals of transcendence in a mother's giving comfort to her child, such as in her assurance to the child that everything will be all right. In Peter Berger's well-known analysis, the mother either implicitly affirms the reality of God or misrepresents reality to a child.[20]

We experience meaning and love in life, but what are the foundations of meaning and of love? Are they fantasies of the human spirit, convenient ways we talk about human experience, or do they have roots in the very ground of existence itself?

This discussion of the impingement of mystery on human life must be said over against the denial of transcendence and mystery in modern life, even in theological circles.[21] The significance of the signals of transcendence that infuse human experience will have to be assessed. Yet it is worth mentioning that denials of transcendence seem in our culture to elicit practices that are a tribute to the dimension of transcendence. It is a significant fact that in the midst of the secularism of contemporary culture astrology, divination, and even witchcraft should have flourished.[22] It is also noteworthy that, against the predictions of an increasingly secular culture and the pronouncement by theologians that modern people could not believe in the supernatural, a revival of religion in conservative and supernatural forms thrives. In a culture that found difficulty with Christmas narratives, movies such as *Close Encounters of the Third Kind* and *Star Wars* were box office hits. In a society that dismissed angels, the conviction that intelligent beings exist on other planets is widespread.

How then can the human experience with mystery be evaluated? Karl Barth, whose theology begins with revelation, knew that the realities of human existence can be studied as phenomena, which as such are neutral and indifferent. The frontier situation that confronts us when the boundaries of existence impinge on us does not carry any guarantee of a counterpart. Yet Barth acknowledges that there is a questionableness about existence that cannot be denied.[23] Human existence and the world alike raise questions. The theologian of revelation may not methodologically correlate revelation and questions, but the fact is that revelation does address the concrete realities of the human situation.

The questionableness of existence is not in itself proof that human existence is anything more than questionable. In fact, the questionableness of human existence has been explained away in terms of economic experience or as a stage of historical development, or as a psychological phenomenon. Yet it is significant that the questions persist after the "explanations." The secularist may deny the validity of any revelation, but its potential relevance to the human situation cannot be denied.

# Revelation

The counterpart of mystery is revelation. As religion generally is a response to the mystery of human existence, so revelation also is a universal religious conception.[24] Whatever human beings may contrive for the future, the fact is that in the past, throughout human history until now, a human has been human by his or her being in one way or another transcendent-oriented.[25]

The roots of religion are more inclusive than mystery, and revelation is not an exhaustive concept. There are other religious objects and functions. Yet in all religion there is some perception of a disclosure of the nature of things. The disclosure may be so general and so readily available as to call into question the use of the word "revelation" rather than "discovery" and so vague as to challenge its cognitive content. Yet even in these cases there is always the making known of that which is beyond human grasp.

Revelation, as a general term, has been understood in different ways even in Christian history.[26] Believers experience what they perceive to be the presence of God in terms that make sense in their own cultures. Revelation has been understood as the powerful word of God that makes covenant with his people, as the image of God in Jesus Christ, as the illumination of the human soul, as law, as the disclosure of a body of doctrine about God and humanity, even as information, as God graciously and personally encountering human beings. The common element in all these perceptions of revelation is the *disclosure* of mystery, of the unknown upon which we depend.

Revelation in some form is universal. Human beings generally order the disparate facts of life in the light of some "revelatory moment," some experience or event that provides the clue for organizing the experiences of life in a meaningful way. The critical question is whether "revelation" is a disclosure from within the brackets[27] or from outside the brackets, that is, from the mystery that encompasses us. The Christian doctrine of

Jesus Christ expresses the conviction of Christians that in Jesus Christ, God, the creator of heaven and earth, has made himself known. As the letter to the Colossians puts it— "the knowledge of God's mystery, that is, Christ himself, in whom are hidden all the treasures of wisdom and knowledge" (Colossians 2:2–3); "For in him all the whole fullness of deity dwells bodily" (Colossians 2:9).

Hendrik Kraemer, a Reformed theologian and a specialist in the comparative study of religions, has sought to express the Reformed understanding of revelation in this way.

> Revelation as a formal concept is not at all an exclusive Christian idea or Biblical presupposition. It is a universal religious conception. All religions know about mysteries that have to be revealed and which cannot be known except through revelation. This is not made less true by the fact that the word revelation is so often used in a very loose and improper sense. When what is called revelation properly should go by the name of enlightenment, a sudden intuitive insight, a luminous idea, or knowledge about so-called occult facts. Revelation in a proper sense is by its nature inaccessible and remains so even when it is revealed. The necessary correlate to the concept of revelation is therefore faith. It lies in the very nature of the divine revelation that the only organ for apprehending it is faith; and for the same reason faith, in a strict religious sense, can only be appropriately defined as at the same time a divine gift and a human act.[28]

Theologians in every age have been tempted to identify revelation with the communication of information and to make faith assent to proposition. Revelation does have a cognitive element, as does the revelation of one self to another. Furthermore, reflection on revelation does issue in propositions that the believer is convinced are true. The relation of personal disclosure to informative statements cannot be disavowed, but neither is revelation to be identified with information.

The insistence on the cognitive dimension of faith has a long history among the church's best theologians. The Augustinian formula is: to believe is to think with assent.[29] Faith agrees that what is said is true.[30] Thomas followed Augustine. The mind is moved by the will to assent. The act of faith consists essentially in cognition, and there is its perfection.[31] The goal of faith is perfect knowledge, which will be given in eternal life. Augustine and Thomas knew that faith involves assent, and they rightly emphasized this dimension. Yet when faith is primarily understood as assent, revelation easily becomes the disclosure of information and faith becomes simply believing these propositions are true. Over against this notion of faith Luther insisted on the fiducial, personal quality of faith.[32]

A. A. Hodge (1823–1886), who was confronting the challenge of the critical historical study of scripture, also gave theological expression to the notion of revelation as the communication of factual knowledge. "As a matter of fact, an infallible record of the supernatural revelation has been given, which conveys, when interpreted with the illuminating assistance of the Holy Spirit, information, the knowledge of which is essential to salvation, which reason could by no means have anticipated."[33] In American fundamentalism revelation as a communication of information became a primary article of faith in the doctrine of verbal inerrancy.

Revelation came to be understood as communication of information of the same order as information that is available to the human mind through its own working but beyond its reach. Yet in no case was this identification of revelation with the communication of information and the understanding of faith as assent complete. There was always an awareness that the truths of revelation are not the same as the truths of human science and that faith was more than assent.

How shall we think of revelation today?

1. Revelation is the personal disclosure of God, not simply the communication of ideas that might have been attained in the way of scientific knowledge if our skills had been sufficiently acute. The content of revelation is God himself. By revelation Barth, Emil Brunner, and John Baillie, among Reformed theologians, and William Temple, an Anglican, have meant an event analogous to a person's revealing himself or herself to a friend. In such a disclosure the character, the attitude, and the disposition of one personal subject are made known to another. In addition, Christian revelation is more than a personal disclosure; it is also a divine action for the renewal of life. Revelation means grace.[34]

Contemporary Reformed understandings of revelation generally have two characteristics. First, revelation is not simply the disclosure of information that human beings, if they were wise enough and diligent enough, could have gotten in some other way. It is rather the disclosure of God himself mediated through some created object and understood according to the analogy of the way one person is personally perceived by another. Second, revelation is the moment of disclosure in history which illuminates the meaning of history—personal history and world history. Revelation, in the words of H. Richard Niebuhr, is the "intelligible event in the light of which other events become intelligible."[35] Revelation is a clue that enables one to put together the disparate experiences of life into a meaningful, coherent whole, to see a pattern and purpose in human history, to overcome the incongruities between what life is and what it ought to be. It is the experience that reconstructs our ideas about God and human life and that transforms our existence. Revelation is not so much information as it is insight, as it is illumination, disclosure, message, assurance, and healing. Revelation is the key to the human situation. It is the clue that enables us to understand and the grace which heals. Revelation is information, but never simply information.

2. The truths of revelation are apprehended by faith and repentance and issue in the transformation of life.[36] Revelation as a self-manifestation of God can only be perceived and received in the personal response of the believer, that is, faith. Revelation is an engagement between subjects, not between subjects and objects. It is analogous to the way in which a person makes himself or herself known to another and the other responds in trust and confidence.

Revelation is not an object that exists independently of being received. It is never a given, an object that we can grasp. In revelation there is not only the act of the revealer but also the illumination of the believer to perceive and receive it. Revelation as a personal act can be received only by the personal response of faith. Faith is first of all a description of a personal relationship of trust, confidence, and commitment. Only in a secondary sense can it be applied to an I-it relationship, that is, to assent to facts or propositions. Faith is also commitment—in relationship to God, unconditional commitment.

In the course of Christian history there has always been a temptation to substitute faith as assent for faith as trust. The reason for this is that faith as trust always involves knowledge of facts. A son believes in his father in part because he has witnessed his father's behavior and believes that his father is trustworthy. Yet faith as mental assent can never be a substitute for faith as trust, confidence, and commitment. Likewise, revelation can never be received in the same way in which we accept facts and master those facts. Revelation as a personal act calls forth a personal response; in the case of the Christian revelation it requires repentance as well as faith (Mark 1:15).

3. Revelation always comes as a gift. In revelation the initiative belongs to the revealer. Here again revelation is different from objective data, which can be grasped and mastered. In this case also there is an analogy in the way persons know each other. There is a body of objective knowledge that one person can obtain about another person without that person's consent, such as body weight or color of hair. This objective knowledge may extend to such intimate matters as composition of the blood, the electric waves of the brain, knowledge that in some instances may be of critical

importance. There is much that can be known about a person even without the person's consent. Yet no one can know another person as a person except as that person chooses to speak and to reveal the innermost commitments of personhood. A person does reveal himself or herself routinely in work, in appearance, in style; yet this general revelation of one's personhood is always ambiguous until it is confirmed in deliberately revealing acts.

The initiative in divine revelation is with the Revealer. Infinitely more than any created object that in some measure is in human grasp, God is beyond human knowing, except insofar as he chooses to make himself known. In the Bible, God makes himself known sometimes when he is least expected and even in opposition to the will of those to whom he is revealed (Acts 9:11–19).

The Christian community, like all human communities, has been tempted to try to control the revealing activity of God. Some have attempted to fasten the infinite and indeterminate God to that which is finite and determinate, as in the sacramental elements of bread and wine and water, or to the words of scripture. Still others have attempted to bind God to techniques, formulas, and rituals. The end is idolatry. Revelation is always the free act of the revealer.

4. Revelation is always mediated.[37] No one has ever seen God at any time is the ancient dictum (Deuteronomy 33:20; John 1:18). God cannot be known by sense perception. We cannot see, touch, or taste him. This means that if God is to be known he must be known through something other than God. The medium is occasional, the choice of the revealer. It may be a rock, or a burning bush, or a book, or the ideas and images in one's mind, or a person. Knowledge of God is also knowledge of something else at the same time. This something else is the medium of revelation, but the medium cannot be identified with the revelation. The medium points beyond itself to the divine realities that are disclosed in and through it.

The temptation that has always confronted the church is to confuse the media of revelation with revelation itself. Theologically this ends with idolatry, substituting the creature for God. Practically it ends in personal sterility, for the personal action that elicits trust is missing. Religion becomes magic or a new law.

The medium of revelation is never simply a material object nor an image nor a symbol.[38] For revelation always takes place in the historical context and is a historical occasion. The historical context is more decisive than the rock or the burning bush or the book. There is no revelation apart from the history that provides the context. Hence, it must be emphasized that the medium of revelation is always a historical occasion, even though it involves a rock or a book or a symbol.

The experience of revelation is direct but not immediate. Over against the mystic, who wishes to experience God immediately, Christian faith has always insisted on a medium. Over against the rationalist, who limits our awareness of God to an inference, Christian faith has insisted on the direct personal experience in and through the medium. John E. Smith finds an analogy to revelation in the knowledge we have of a self who is not known immediately but only through facial expressions, gestures, and words.[39] The self is known directly through these media, not as an inference from them. Yet the media are not the self that is known. The media of revelation must not obscure the act of revelation. In revelation the personal reality of God is manifested. The mystery of the divine reality encounters and engages the mystery of the human self. Revelation as personal encounter must not be confused with theological reflection, which may infer by logical arguments the reality of God from the media of revelation. Revelation is not an inference. It is an encounter or an engagement of a subject with a subject, a self with a self.

5. Revelation has increasingly been described in recent theology as an event.[40] The revealing God is a God who acts and who reveals himself in and through his actions. Revelation as an act of God or as an event stands in contrast to the conception of revelation as the communication of ideas. The difference is not as clear as it first appears. Historical events do not as such pass on information. Yet there is no event without interpretation. Revelation as an act of God is not complete without the illumination of the mind that receives it and interprets it. William Temple writes, "In effective revelation two factors must normally be present, the objective event and the mind qualified to interpret it; but behind each is the purposive action of the living God."[41] Furthermore, revelation as an event, interpreted by mind, is productive of theological symbols, ideas, and propositions.

The understanding of revelation as event is pervasive in theology today. Yet it does not fully embrace all that the church has traditionally included within the gamut of revelation. Austin Farrer has objected that the theory of revelation as event is no more satisfying than the theory of revelation as dictated information. We can all agree, he writes, that "the primary revelation is Jesus Christ himself." Yet he goes on to insist that "divine truth is supernaturally communicated to men in an act of inspired thinking which falls into the shape of certain images."[42] Revelation, as Söderblom argued, takes place in the soul of the prophet.

William Abraham, in a recent discussion of revelation, insists on the necessity of understanding revelation as "God speaking."

> Most, if not all, revelation has been confined to revelation in deed, without sufficient awareness of the potential emptiness of this doctrine when little is done to specify the deeds that reveal God, and without sufficient awareness of the importance of divine speaking in deciding what deeds God has done in history.[43]

He goes on to argue:

> Classically the recipients of the speech acts of God have been the prophets. They constitute paradigm cases of men who have been spoken to by God but divine speaking has by no means been limited to these; in the Biblical tradition it embraces figures as far apart as Abraham and Paul and extends outside that period into the lives of ordinary believers in the present. As regards revelation in deed, there is little doubt as to what constitutes a paradigm instance of this form of revelation. It is the incarnation of God in Jesus Christ. As the writer of Hebrews puts it: "In many and various ways God spoke of old to our fathers by the prophets; but in these last days he has spoken to us by his son, whom he appointed the heir of all things, through whom he also created the world." The contrast drawn here between the revelation through the prophets and revelation through Jesus has been central to Christianity. Jesus has been set apart as being unique in the tradition as a bearer of revelation, and classically this has involved an account of the work of Jesus that posits direct divine action of a unique kind. The term "incarnation" has been central to the account of divine activity which has captured the mind and imagination of Christendom. In any attempt to determine the significance of divine intervention in Christianity, it would surely be a major lacuna were this act of God to pass unnoticed.[44]

6. Revelation is general and also special or intensely focused.[45] Yet whether it is general or special it is always a self-revealing act of God and is made possible by the Holy Spirit in the divine illumination of the believer's heart and mind. Hence, the term "natural revelation," which has been frequently used in theology, is misleading. Whenever revelation occurs it is a divine act, not a neutral fact. Natural theology and natural revelation may more properly refer to the intellectual and logical inference of God from the facts of the world. God in this sense is a fact of the same order as other facts that may be grasped by the activity of the human mind. Even if it is granted that this inference of God is correct, the inferred proposition is far removed from revelation as personal encounter with God through the medium of the created order, which the Christian community has understood revelation to be. One may, however, properly argue that if God cannot

be rationally inferred from reflection on the created order, then the possibility of revelation would be questioned.

John Calvin was sure that nature, especially when seen through the spectacles of scripture, was a theater displaying the glory of God,[46] and the Belgic Confession (1561) declares that nature is "before our eyes as a most beautiful book in which all created things, whether great or small, are as letters showing invisible things of God to us."

No one has affirmed the universal revelation of God in all of his creation more vigorously than William Temple:

> Unless all existence is a medium of revelation, no particular revelation is possible. . . . Either all occurrences are in some degree revelation of God, or else there is no such revelation at all; for the conditions of the possibility of any revelation require that there should be nothing which is not revelation. Only if God is revealed in the rising of the sun in the sky can he be revealed in the rising of the son of man from the dead.[47]

Temple goes on to argue that an impersonal God would be revealed equally in all events and things. If God is personal he will reveal himself in some events more than others. This is analogous to the way in which human beings disclose who they are. We truly know who human beings are only as they respond personally to challenging situations. H. H. Farmer has written:

> If we speak of a general revelation of God in nature, the most we can mean . . . is that God may make any situation into which man may come at any time, the medium of his revealing word to the soul. . . . Our position is, then, that wheresoever and whensoever God declares himself to the individual soul in such ways that he is apprehended as holy will actively present within the immediate situation, asking obedience at all costs and guaranteeing in and through such asking the soul's ultimate succor, there is revelation. . . . It follows from this conception of revelation that not all situations are equally calculated to be a medium of it, though any situation may become such, owing to a peculiar relevancy to the individual's life history which it may at any moment assume.[48]

The significance of general revelation over against special revelation has been variously regarded in different times and situations. Theologians such as Karl Barth have insisted that the Christian's attention should be focused on the revelation of God in Jesus Christ. More apologetic theologians whose attention has been focused less on the church and more on those outside have given general revelation a larger place. Reinhold Niebuhr has summarized the mutual relationship of the general revelation with the public historical or special revelation in Jesus Christ. Without the special revelation the general revelation is confused, incoherent, and incomplete. Special revelation corrects, clarifies, and completes general revelation. On the other hand, special revelation without general revelation would lack credence, as William Temple also argued.[49]

7. While revelation dispels mystery, it also includes mystery. In a very real sense revelation is mystery. In revelation the mystery that encompasses us is changed into meaning, yet the mystery remains in the act of revealing. We still see through a glass darkly. Sergius Bulgakov of the Orthodox Church has put it this way:

> Mystery ceases to be mystery, if it is not disclosed, or, on the other hand, if it is resolved or exhausted by the process of revelation. It is equally characteristic for a mystery to disclose itself and remain hidden, for it always remains a mystery in the process of being disclosed. . . . Revelation, therefore, is of the very nature of Deity. God is a self-disclosing mystery.[50]

The analogy of the disclosure of a human self holds for the mystery of God. The fullest disclosure of a human person does not exhaust the reality of that person, who stills remains a mystery even to the closest of friends. In human relationships the relations of trust, devotion, and commitment are tied to the mystery. We do not trust or love that which we fully know. Even on the human level the more a great human self makes himself or herself known, the more the mystery of the self is enhanced.

The "provisional" character of revelation has been emphasized by Hendrikus Berkhof.[51] We know God only in indirect and hidden ways. We do not see God face to face. Much of human existence remains a puzzle to us and even an absurdity. Revelation makes sense of life and human experience but only partially. We walk by faith, but not by sight.[52]

The reasons for the hidden and "provisional" character of revelation are at least threefold. The first is our sin, which obscures our understanding of God. The second is our creaturely, human, historical character. We cannot get outside our creaturely position to see ourselves as we are. This is what it means to be a creature. No finite creature can ever know God fully. The third reason is the majesty of God, the unfathomable source and ground of our existence. A God whom we could fully know would not be God.[53]

The "provisional" character of revelation must not be allowed to obscure the authenticity of what is revealed. The fact that we do not know everything does not mean that what we do know is not true. Revelation is true even if it is incomplete. The revelation in Jesus Christ will be enlarged and confirmed in the consummation of all things.

8. The adequacy of the concept of revelation for Christian theology and also for contemporary experience has been called into question in recent years. Within the Christian community it has been argued that there is "no clear knowledge of God" and that therefore the use of the word "revelation" is unjustified.[54] Such an argument goes beyond the provisional or partial character of revelation as indicated above.

Others have argued that the concept of revelation is too intellectualistic. As Gustaf Aulén has put it,

> The word "revelation" is heavily burdened with intellectualism. Theology has often combined Reason and Revelation as two ways toward the knowledge of God. . . . Certainly Christian faith is conscious of having the true knowledge of God. But this knowledge does not mean only certain ideas or a certain doctrine about a being called God; it means the personal relation brought into existence through the action of God. And therefore, if we use the word revelation in our Christian language, revelation must always be connected with *the activity of God;* and it must signify the self-communication of God through his own activity. This self-communication of God is, in the language of faith, known as "revelation."[55]

The word "revelation" means more than information, and it must always be used in the context of the order of salvation and not as general knowledge. Nevertheless, the use of the word is necessary to any traditional understanding of Christian faith. Without the concept of revelation, the doctrine of salvation has questionable validity. Without the disclosure of God, how can we know God's salvation?

The concept of revelation has also been criticized by James Barr. "The use of revelation as central and normative concept may not only be harmful to general theology but may also form an obstructing and distorting influence to the more empirical analysis of Biblical evidence."[56] While Barr provides a useful critique of the use of the concept "revelation" in some contemporary theology, he does not provide an adequate alternative. "Communication," which he suggests as an improvement, is surely open to the same critique. Moreover, the real alternative to revelation in a secular society is the limitation of all human insight to human efforts alone, to the empirical study of human experience and the world.[57]

9. The validation of any revelatory experience is an increasingly critical problem as human society becomes more pluralistic and secular. The line of demarcation between faith and credulity, between faith and magic, is easily obscured by human emotions and by the pressure of the social context. The nature of revelation itself precludes proof. Any proof of revelation would be more ultimate than the revelation itself. Hence revelation

must be in and of itself an intelligible experience, authenticating itself. The recipient of revelation knows that it is true in the same manner that lovers know that love is true or friends know that friendship is authentic.

The criteria, by which the validity of what is perceived to be a revelatory experience can be checked, cannot be conclusive; but they are not unimportant. They serve to confirm experience and to call into question other claims to revelation. First of all there is the check of community. Other persons have been so apprehended and one's own experience can be compared to the experience of others. There is no absolute reason why revelation cannot come to one person, but a solitary revelation would lack the confirmation of others' experience. Furthermore, the solitariness of revelation would have to be conformable with the nature of the God who is revealed. Revelation is also validated by its coherence and internal intelligibility. Second, revelation must itself be intelligible. Third, revelation is validated by its power to make sense out of human experience generally and to do justice to the hard realities of life as we know them. Fourth, revelation is confirmed by its adequacy in dealing with the great issues of human life: guilt, meaninglessness, and death. Fifth, revelation is validated by fruitfulness in life. The consequences of revelation in human life and society are indications of its source. Sixth, the historical event by which revelation is mediated and apprehended is also subject to critical examination. None of these criteria can possibly be decisive, but they do serve as checks to expose credulity and fraud as well as wish fulfillment.

10. Any discussion of revelation must face what Christian theology knows as the christological question.[58] The question is not what is being revealed but who is doing the revealing. The Christian community in the fourth century when confronted by this question answered with the Nicene Creed and the doctrine of the person of Christ.

Every person lives by faith and in the light of some "revelation."

> Anyone who tries to understand human life and its relation to the world cannot avoid selecting among the data available; and for such a one particular events or a particular person in which it seems to him important facts or principles are brought into sharp focus, are sure to seem of special revelation value. . . . Whatever one's choice, the point is the same. One cannot avoid selecting, and special illumination will seem to him to be found in one place or in another.[59]

All people live in the light of experiences or events that happen to them and seem to unveil reality, to declare what is important and what is the meaning of life.

Many people are not critically aware of these "revelatory moments." They do not reflect on them. Yet few questions are as important for human beings as the identification and evaluation of those "occasions" that have revealed to them life's meaning. The consequence is that many live in the light of "revelatory moments" that are superficial and on the surface of life.

Christians by definition are people for whom reality has been revealed in Jesus Christ. The Christian community, having been apprehended by the presence of God in Jesus Christ, has reflected on the event of Jesus Christ with its best critical and intellectual resources and affirmed that in Jesus Christ God, creator of heaven and earth, was present, speaking through the words and deeds of Jesus Christ—his life, death, and resurrection. Critics may deny that Jesus Christ is the Word made flesh, but no one can deny that the Christian community has made its commitment not only with the heart but with the best theological resources it could muster, especially in the fourth and fifth centuries. Moreover, it has heard the critiques of an Enlightenment culture and of nineteenth-century historians and philosophers. No other religion has equaled Christianity in its analysis of what it believes to be the revelation of God or has listened as much to the critique of a secular culture.

11.  The very possibility of revelation has been questioned by an Enlightenment secular culture. In such a culture revelation that unveils the "mystery" encompassing human life is impossible or unnecessary. The only human possibilities are reflection on human life and the world and the imagination of the human mind. Post-Christian theologies are written as if there were no personal, saving revelation from God the creator. Theology is another human conversation, but no one knows if any reality corresponds to what theologians call God.[60]

The minimizing or denial of revelation leads to the collapse of the distinctly Christian doctrines. The life of the Christian community is based on the conviction that God has revealed himself. Every Christian theology and every Christian community stands or falls on the reality of the revelation of God in Jesus Christ.

❖

## CHAPTER 4

# THE DOCTRINE OF GOD

We confess and acknowledge one God alone, to whom alone we must cleave, whom alone we must serve, whom only we must worship, and in whom alone we put our trust.

Scots Confession of Faith (1560), Chapter 1

God's being as He who lives and loves is being in freedom. In this way, freely, He lives and loves. And in this way, and in the fact that He lives and loves in freedom, He is God, and distinguishes Himself from everything else that lives and loves. In this way, as the free person, He is distinguished from other persons. He is the one, original and authentic person through whose creative power and will alone all other persons are and are sustained. With the idea of freedom we simply affirm what we would be affirming if we were to characterise God as the Lord. But His lordship is in all circumstances the lordship of His living and loving.

Karl Barth, *Church Dogmatics* II/1, 301.

There is but one only living and true God. . . .

Westminster Confession of Faith, Chapter 2.1

What is God?

God is a Spirit, infinite, eternal, and unchangeable, in his being, wisdom, power, holiness, justice, goodness, and truth.

Westminster Shorter Catechism, Question 4

But Moses said to God, "If I come to the Israelites and say to them, 'The God of your ancestors has sent me to you,' and they ask me, 'What is his name?' what shall I say to them?" God said to Moses, "I AM WHO I AM." He said further, "Thus you shall say to the Israelites, 'I AM has sent me to you.'" God also said to Moses, "Thus you shall say to the Israelites, 'The LORD, the God of your ancestors, the God of Abraham, the God of Isaac,

and the God of Jacob, has sent me to you':
>   This is my name forever,
>   and this my title for all generations."

Exodus 3:13–15

Hear, O Israel: The LORD is our God, the LORD alone. You shall love the LORD your God with all your heart, and with all your soul, and with all your might.

Deuteronomy 6:4–5

No one has ever seen God. It is God the only Son, who is close to the Father's heart, who has made him known.

John 1:18

The reality of God, or at least the question of God, is inescapable for human beings.[1] It is written into the structure of human life at its center and at its boundary. Attempts to explain away the question of God have never succeeded.[2] The question of God inevitably is elicited by the puzzlement or the aporia of human existence. It is raised by the universal human experiences of love, loyalty, devotion, and meaning. It is inherent in reason and the rational processes. It is called forth not only by the wonder of human life but also by its fragility. The origin of life and in particular of the human person with the power of mind and will is so inexplicable that one observer rightly concludes it is highly improbable that human beings should exist at all.[3] The question of God is inescapable for human beings who ask about love, meaning, reason, and the worthwhileness of their own existence.

The question of God is universal, but the Christian doctrine of God rose out of what Christians perceive to be God's specific revelation; and it was formulated in the light of the experiences and the reflections of a particular people to whom, they believe, God had made himself known.

## Six Basic Affirmations

The explicit formulation of the Christian doctrine of God presupposes at least six basic affirmations about the reality of God.

1. Confessions of the church — in particular, Reformed confessions — emphasize "the one only living God" (Westminster Confession 2.1). In addition, the Bible speaks of God in terms of life. God is alive, in contrast to dead or inert powers. When the Bible speaks of the living God, it also includes the conviction that the living God is active and effective in the world. The living God acts upon and through his creation.

2. God is as God reveals himself. In scripture the living God encounters human beings, speaking to them, testing them, commanding them, and showing mercy to them. This conviction about God can be stated more abstractly in the rubric that God is always subject, never object, though Christians believe that God has accommodated himself to our sinful and finite existence and objectified himself in Jesus Christ. God makes himself known to his people but God is never an object for human beings to observe and study.[4]

The insistence that God is always subject means that God is never an object that we can control, manipulate, study, or analyze. We cannot by searching find our God. Indeed we cannot find God: the world is much too vast. Many have used the remarkable gifts of the human mind to fashion God according to human reason or to describe God in terms of their investigations of the world. Rationalistic concepts of God as well as empirical theologies have always enticed philosophers and thinkers, but neither the empirical nor the rational concept of God has created communities to worship God. Worshiping communities have been called into existence by God's self-revelation, in which God lays hold of human beings, declares that he is our God and that we are his people.

Blaise Pascal (d. 1661) affirmed the God of Abraham, Isaac, and Jacob, not the God of the philosophers.[5] This is not to depreciate the work of philosophers or even to oppose their work except when it becomes a substitute for the God of Abraham, Isaac, and Jacob. Christian theology rests on the conviction that God, who is beyond our grasp, has made himself known to us not only in his creation but particularly in his incarnation in Jesus Christ.

3. The one living God who encounters us as the subject who makes himself known to us is personal. The Bible and theology until quite recently took the personal character of God for granted. The scriptures continually speak of God in personal terms as the one who creates, who wills, who loves, who judges, who tests, and above all who shows mercy. The decisive revelation of God is Jesus Christ, a person. Everything in Christian theology presupposes that God is personal—that is, a proposing, knowing, willing, acting I who elects and who covenants. God is "the One who (in His own way) loves us, who (in His own way) seeks and creates fellowship between Himself and us, [who] also informs us what a person is. . . ."[6] Barth's definitive statement about the being of God as the one who loves in freedom emphasizes that God is more, not less, than a human person. For Barth, God is *the* person, and from his revelation we learn the meaning of the human person. We do not know God as personal

because we are persons. Rather we know what it is to be persons because God has made himself known to us in a personal way.

4. God is the name that refers to the Reality that encounters us. The Christian affirmation of God is not a human fantasy or speculation. It is not simply a manner of speaking or way of committing our lives or declaring that life is meaningful. The name God refers to the reality that encounters us in the depths of human existence.[7] Augustine long ago emphasized that if we penetrate deeply enough within our own being we come to an awareness of that reality that enables us to make any meaningful human statement, to the God who created the world with a structure, a rationality, a coherence that makes human thought possible.[8] God is also the name we give to the reality that we encounter at the boundaries of human existence, as that reality upon which we are utterly dependent or to which we are unconditionally obligated.

For Christians the name God refers in particular to the subject who encounters us in Jesus Christ. Hence the name God has a quite specific reference, a reference to facts of human experience and to the historical reality of Jesus Christ. It is true that the reality that encounters us in life and above all in Jesus Christ may be and is sometimes perceived by others as an impersonal force or, as in the case of Jesus Christ, simply another human being. The presence of God in creation and in history is apprehended only by faith and repentance. The point is that the word "God" has a referent that must be called either God or something else.

The purpose of this book is to explicate the Christian understanding of God who is the source of our existence, the Lord of our lives and the one who blesses us with his steadfast love and mercy. Those who do not apprehend these realities as God encountering us are obligated to give their own account of the mystery that encompasses human life.

5. God is the mystery that encounters us, but God is a mystery that we cannot grasp, a mystery who is beyond our knowing unless he makes himself known to us. God is not the greatest being in a series of beings.[9] God is not objectifiable, and therefore is not an object for our study, as are all other created things except the human self.

The mystery of God has an analogy in the mystery of the human self. The self cannot be objectified, to the great disgust of those who wish the self were a scientific object. The self can be known only as that self freely chooses to give expression to the self's intentions and purposes. We can speak of another self only as that self speaks to us and in analogy to our own experience of self.

We cannot speak of God directly but only by way of analogy. There is an analogy between the way God is and the way we are. When we say that God loves, we do not mean exactly what we mean when we say a human being loves, nor do we mean something totally different. We do mean that there is an analogy between the way God loves and the way we love. God loves in a way that is appropriate to his being as God, and we love in a way that is appropriate to our being as created human beings. All our language about God is analogical whether it is abstract or concretely human.

6. We say God is or God exists. Yet we do not mean that God exists as we dependent, finite beings exist. We mean that God exists in a manner appropriate for one for whom to be and to exist are identical. God has existence within himself. Existence for human beings is a gracious gift.

Helmut Gollwitzer has written that God enters the conditions in which particular being is expressed.[10]

> The fact is, that with the approach of God the fruitless effort to evade anthropomorphism by means of abstraction, or by keeping as consistently as possible to "non-objective" talk of God, has become superfluous — and not only so, but plain wrong: it is no longer a case of avoiding anthropomorphism as much as possible, but only (a) of examining what kind of anthropomorphic talk is appropriate, and (b) of leaving no doubt about the "improperness" of such talk. . . . That our talk of God is inevitably anthropomorphic, and that by his approach he has explicitly authorized us to speak anthropomorphically of him, does not mean that now there can be a free-for-all, that anything we say will *a priori* already correspond to him, that all words, concepts and ways of speaking have an equal chance of corresponding and are equally appropriate.[11]

Gollwitzer goes on to conclude that

> (a) particular and concrete ways of speaking have the preference over general and abstract ones, (b) personal ways of speaking have the preference over impersonal, neuter ones. "Preference" means: the non-preferable way of speaking is not absolutely ruled out, but must submit to the standard of the other, which has the precedence, and must receive its content from the latter.[12]

Gollwitzer concludes that theology has to say "God is," but with the awareness that this statement is not comparable to saying a tree is or a person is.

> "God is" is not a neutral statement in the indicative which asserts in the first instance an existence as such and still leaves it an open question what that existence means for us. It immediately changes our situation and can thus only really be said in the form of confessing to that change, acquiescing in

that change. The grammatical subject of this proposition is indeed from the start no empty subject, but contains the whole event of revelation. Thus if a man really recognizes what this proposition says and in recognizing it accepts it, then he not only accepts an existence of God in itself, but also assents to God's being what he encounters us as in his revelation. The proposition thus means: The Lord is, the Judge is, the living and life-giving One is; he is really what he discloses himself to be, and we are thus really what we are revealed to be by what he is—and we not only are that, but through him, through what he says to us, we have become people who joyfully and at the same time with fear and trembling assent to, and no longer resist, no longer assert our denial of, the fact that he is. To accept God's existence means, to be willing that God is and is no other and nothing else. Hence we have not here to do with one of the truths which we can ascertain without any change in our own being, but with the truth which must change us in order to be able to be accepted by us, which we are not free for without much more ado, which we have no desire for as we are, but for which we have to be made free by itself. In the proposition "God is," the enmity between God and man is done away.[13]

## God Is Defined by Jesus Christ

God, for Christians, is defined by Jesus Christ. God is revealed in all his works, but this revelation, as has been noted, is inchoate, confused, and incomplete. God's presence is focused in Jesus Christ who is the Word, God in his self-expression, embodied in a human life (John 1:1-14). The historical reality of Jesus Christ is the starting point for the Christian doctrine of God.

The deity of Jesus Christ, for this reason, has always been the crucial Christian affirmation. The only Son, as John's Gospel puts it, has made God known to us (John 1:18). Jesus Christ has lived in our midst and in the light of this revelation we know not only the Son but also God the Father and God the Holy Spirit. Hence the doctrine of the person of Jesus Christ is the crucial doctrine upon which all Christian theology rests.

Jesus acknowledged the God of Abraham, Isaac, and Jacob (Mark 12:26; Matthew 22:32; Luke 20:37). He also declared his faith in the words of Deuteronomy 6:4, "Hear, O Israel: the Lord our God, the Lord is one" (Mark 12:29). Yet he goes beyond the faith of Israel in the revelation of God to him and through him as Father in a very intimate sense. The Gospel traditions affirmed that Jesus addressed God as Father. In Israel God had been addressed as Father, but Jesus is unique in the consistency with which he addressed God as Father and by the intimacy of the address, speaking of "my" Father and using the personal and intimate word "Abba." In addition to his speech, the life of Jesus bears the same witness. Jesus lived confidently under the care of the Father.

The intimacy of Jesus' address does not nullify the power of the Creator of heaven and earth or the majesty of the Lord of history. Every word Jesus spoke and every deed presupposes the Creator and the Lord of history. But his words and life reveal that the Creator and the Lord of history is also "my Father" and "our Father." "No one knows the Son except the Father, and no one knows the Father except the Son and anyone to whom the Son chooses to reveal him" (Matthew 11:27).

In recent literature the word "Father" as the name for God has come under criticism. In response to the criticism it must be noted (1) that in scripture Father has no sexual meaning when applied to God; (2) that father does not mean domination or arbitrary power. The use of the word "father" comes out of ordinary experience and better than any other human word it conveys what Jesus understood God to be. Yet Barth is correct in insisting that the human definition of father must be modified by the revelation of the meaning of Father in God's action in Jesus Christ.

The naming of God as "my Father" or "our Father" cannot be excised from the life and teaching of Jesus Christ. No equivalent substitute has been found for it in theology as a name for God or in the designation of Father, Son, and Holy Spirit in Trinitarian theology. "The God and Father of our Lord Jesus Christ" is the most adequate name Christian theology has for God (Romans 15:6; 2 Corinthians 11:31). God and Father are defined in this name by the words and life of Jesus Christ.

# The Triune God

The unique statement of the Christian understanding of God even more than the cross is the doctrine of the Trinity. Karl Barth argued over against Schleiermacher that the doctrine of the Trinity belongs at the beginning of a statement of Christian faith.

The doctrine of the Trinity received its classic formulation in the fourth and fifth centuries, but it was present from the beginning in the acts of God in creation and redemption, in the language of Christian piety, and in the liturgy of the church, especially the baptismal formula.

The doctrine arises out of the experience of the Christian community. On the one hand, Christians declared that God is one. The first Christians had been nurtured in the faith of ancient Israel. "Hear, O Israel: The

LORD is our God, the LORD alone. You shall love the LORD your God with all your heart, and with all your soul, and with all your might" (Deuteronomy 6:4–5). Yet the Christian community was constituted by the presence of Jesus Christ in the midst of his disciples: a presence that compelled them to acknowledge him as their Lord and their God, to believe that God was uniquely present in Jesus Christ. Devout people who had always said "the Lord our God is one Lord" now spoke of Jesus Christ as God. In addition, the Holy Spirit descended on them and empowered them in new and remarkable ways. Yet they knew the Holy Spirit as the power of God in their midst, and they knew the Holy Spirit as the Spirit of Christ. Out of the revelation of God there arose the theological task of saying that God is one, and also acknowledging Jesus Christ as God and the Holy Spirit as God, present in the power of the divine personhood amidst his people.

In the formula of baptism and in the life of the church generally Christians spoke of God as the Father, the Son, and the Holy Spirit. Earlier attempts to deal with the theological problem took the form either of a spirit Christology in which Jesus Christ was filled with the spirit of God or of a Sabellianism which defined Father, Son, and Holy Spirit as successive modes of God's existence. Here the effort was to maintain the unity of God, the "monarchy," and at the same time to do justice to the facts of the Christian revelation and Christian experience. Dynamic monarchism, the doctrine that Jesus Christ was filled by the spirit, failed because it did not do justice to what Christians believed was the decisive presence of God in Christ and moreover did not do justice to the Christian experience of the Holy Spirit. Sabellianism maintained the unity of God but introduced a chronological succession whereby God is now Father, now Son, and now Holy Spirit, a trinity not of essence but of revelation.

The Nicene Creed, which rejected Arianism and which declared that Jesus Christ was truly God, became the occasion for more serious discussion of the doctrine of the Trinity. In the East the Trinitarian doctrine received its classical form in the work of the great Cappadocian theologians Gregory of Nyssa, Gregory of Nazianzus, and Basil of Caesarea and its creedal formulation in the Niceno-Constantinopolitan Creed of 381. Here the doctrine was stated in the language of Christian piety rather than in the language of technical theology: "And in the Holy Spirit, the Lord and life-giver, Who precedes from the Father, who is worshipped and glorified together with the Father and the Son, who spoke through the prophets. . . ." The Niceno-Constantinopolitan Creed is a clear affirmation that God is one and that the Father, the Son, and the Holy Spirit are truly God. In the West the doctrine of the Trinity received its classic expression in Augustine's great work *On the Trinity*.[14]

The development of the doctrine of the Trinity necessitated a precise vocabulary. As early as the beginning of the third century, Tertullian had provided the technical formula which the church in the West used: God is one substance in three persons. By substance Tertullian meant that God is one being. By person he did not mean, as we do in contemporary language, an individual. His own definition of a person is imprecise, but he was attempting to say that in the being of God there is a threefold distinction of existence.

In the East the formula that became definitive for the Trinity was one *ousia* in three *hypostases*. The precise working out of a formula was difficult because *ousia* and *hypostasis* could be and were used interchangeably. In addition, there was the problem of relating the Greek vocabulary to the Latin vocabulary of the West. In the end the formula of one substance in three persons became normative in Western theology and one *ousia* in three hypostases became normative for Eastern theology.

The Greek word *ousia* and the Latin word *substantia* can best be translated into contemporary English as "being."

> The faith and the confession of one being, (*ousia*), three persons does not rest on any preconception or definition of the Divine Being, but on the very being of God as he has named himself "I am who I am—I shall be who I shall be" (Exodus 3:14), the ever-living and self-revealing God who truly and really is, beside whom there is no other. This revelation of God as "He who is who he is" is mediated to us in the gospel through the one act of God the Father, through the Son and in the Holy Spirit. Thus in the doctrine of the Holy Trinity the "one being" of God does not refer to some abstract essence, but to the "I am" of God, the eternal living being which God is of himself.[15]

The three persons in the traditional Trinitarian formula are more difficult to define in contemporary language. Traditional theology on the one hand has refused to think of "the persons" as functions, and on the other hand it has refused to think of them as individuals. When the doctrine was being formulated, the word "persons" did not have all the connotations it does today but was used to "describe the permanent and objective form or persons in which the godhead is presented alike to human vision and to the divine self-consciousness."[16] In Greek theology *hypostasis* came to designate the Trinitarian person, and it meant "a positive concrete and distinct existence."[17] In recent theology, Karl Barth and Protestant theologians defined "persons" in terms of "mode of being" or ways of existing as God,[18] and the Roman Catholic Karl Rahner as "way of existing" or "modes of presence."[19] God is one personal subject, and within the personhood of God there are three personal existences. The unity of God is personal, not mathematical.

Theologians have sought analogies to the Trinity, but none of the analogies is fully adequate. Tertullian spoke of the sun, the rays proceeding from the sun, and the sunbeam as reflected by some object on earth, and also of the spring, the river, and the lake.[20] These analogies, as is immediately clear, are all spatial, but the Trinity is spirit or personal. Augustine tried to find analogies within the depths of human life. He distinguished memory, intelligence, and will. By these he meant the contents of the mind, the act of thinking and the will. All three are involved in the act of self-reflection.[21]

A faint analogy may be found in human existence. A person is not a mathematical unity but a personal unity. In one human person, through the power of self-transcendence, different "selves," roles, or ways of being a unified person may be present. A person can include in one personal unity, for example, the father, the teacher, and the coach. The problem with this analogy is that it seems to treat the persons in the Trinity as functions. Perhaps in the unity of the human person they are not so much functions as three ways of being a person, three existences united in one person, three ways that are mutually engaged in one person. These ways of being a person may sometimes involve anguish in the human person or at other times mutual support.[22] For example, the person as father and the person as coach may be in conflict. This analogy, like all others, is very inadequate. As Karl Barth once put it, God is not three "I's" but one I three times over.[23]

(The doctrine of the Trinity does not mean that there are three Gods,) nor does it mean the mathematical absurdity that three and one are the same. In the doctrine of the Trinity, the early church was giving expression to the fact that the one God had apprehended them as Father, Son, and Holy Spirit. God was God in three ways. God was God as the unfathomable ground of existence and the source of all things, as the one who has acted for us and as the one who is creative of all things and who became incarnate in Jesus Christ for our redemption, and as the God who is present with us in the power of the Holy Spirit. God is transcendent, creative, and immanent.[24]

The doctrine of the Trinity is more profound than saying God is God in three ways. The doctrine is Christian reflection on the way God has revealed himself and the Christian community's apprehension of this revelation. Christians knew God as the unfathomable source of all things; they knew God's presence in Jesus Christ and particularly in his death and resurrection; they knew God in Christian experience. The doctrine of the Trinity affirms that God is in *his own* being as God has revealed himself. The sending forth of the Son is the way God is eternally. The Son is derived from the Father but nonetheless God. The Father loves his Son and the Son glorifies the Father. In the death of Christ the Son experiences forsakenness without being any less God, and the Father experiences the loss of the Son without being less God. The Holy Spirit proceeds from the Father through the Son but likewise is nonetheless God. God is one, not a mathematical unity, but as in a remote analogy the unity of the human self is personal and not mathematical.

The doctrine of the Trinity is the "attempt to clarify the nature of God who reveals himself in Jesus Christ."[25] The going forth of God in revelation and redemption is not an accidental happening. This is who God is, the way God is in his own being. Thus the doctrine of the Trinity even more than the cross is the unique Christian doctrine, clarifying how the transcendent God is present in his creation and more particularly how God is present in the death and resurrection of Jesus Christ as well as in Christian experience without being any the less God.

The theologians of the fourth and fifth centuries also developed the doctrine of coinherence or, as Augustine put it, "the works of the Trinity are outwardly indivisible."[26] This means that no person of the Trinity can be isolated from the whole being of God. In every act all three persons participate. In the act of redemption the Son becomes incarnate but the Father sends the Son and the Holy Spirit makes the Son known. Hence no sharp division isolating Father, Son, and Holy Spirit from each other is permissible, though with this understanding, theologians "appropriately" assigned particular works to each person.

# The Attributes of God

The character of God, as well as the doctrine of the Trinity, is very difficult for human beings to define. God is beyond our highest thoughts. Yet even theologians such as Calvin, who minimize any discussion of the characteristics or attributes of God, still find it necessary to speak of particular aspects of God's character.[27] The difficulty in speaking about the character of God is sometimes defined as the problem of the attributes. Any discussion of the character or the attributes of God may become abstract and boring; it may simply *attribute* certain characteristics to God; and it may destroy the unity of God. Hence it is important to remember that the attributes of God are the characteristics of God or simply the divine nature in relationship to the world and to the human creature.

Theologians have organized the attributes or characteristics of God in different ways.[28] There are the incommunicable attributes such as God's self-existence, eternity, immensity, and simplicity; and there are the communicable attributes such as love and mercy, which human beings in some measure share. Others have defined the attributes in terms of the negative and the positive, the negative attributes saying what God is not and the positive saying what he is. Karl Barth has organized the attributes under the perfections of the divine loving: grace—holiness, mercy—righteousness, patience—wisdom; and the perfections of divine freedom: unity—omnipresence, constancy—omnipotence, eternity—glory.[29]

In this discussion the traditional attributes of God will be defined without regard to any particular order.

The *holiness* of God is God's self-differentiation, the willed energy by which God asserts and maintains the fact that he is wholly other against all else.[30] Gustaf Aulén has written that holiness meets us as an unconditional majesty. Every attempt to transform Christianity into a religion of satisfaction and enjoyment is doomed to failure. Egocentricity masquerading in the robes of religion is excluded.[31]

Rudolf Otto emphasized that *holiness* is the basic religious emotion. It is the creaturely feeling, the sense of awfulness, the sense of majesty in the presence of the wholly other. Yet as Otto said, the God who is holy also fascinates and attracts those who acknowledge their unworthiness to be in his presence.[32]

God is *love*. Love is not a quality or an attribute. Love is the very nature of God. Yet love is not God. God is also truth.

Karl Barth has insisted on four qualities of the love of God. (1) God's loving is concerned with seeking and creating a fellowship for its own sake. In loving us God does not give us something. He gives us himself. (2) God's loving is concerned with the seeking and the creation of fellowship without any reference to existing attitudes or worthiness on the part of the loved. God's love is free. (3) God loves because he loves; because this act is his being, his essence, his nature. (4) God's loving is necessary, for it is the being, the essence, and the nature of God. For this reason it is also free from every necessity in respect to its object. God does not owe us our being or in our being his love. God's love is freely given.[33]

*Almightiness* or omnipotence is usually attributed to God, but in

Christian theology what does it mean to say that God is almighty? Any definition of the divine attributes must begin by insisting that God is as God has revealed himself. Almightiness is not defined in general terms; it is the almightiness of the God and Father of our Lord Jesus Christ. Hence the almightiness of God is not sheer power and certainly not neutral power. Almightiness is defined in these abstract and general terms in questions such as Can God make a stone so large he cannot carry it, or can God make a prostitute a virgin? Can God make a selfish person happy?[34] Hence it is important to define almightiness in terms of God's revelation of himself. As Karl Barth has put it, God's power is the power both to do the sum of what is possible for him and therefore genuinely possible and also not to do what is impossible for him and therefore completely impossible.[35]

Christian theology has also insisted that God has limited his almightiness in the creation of an independent world and in the creation of human beings for freedom.[36] God limits his power in that he comes to us in Jesus Christ as one who wants our willing consent.

Emil Brunner has stated with clarity the meaning of almightiness in the light of God's revelation in Jesus Christ.

> There is a Divine Omnipotence which is exercised in compulsion—His work in the realm of Nature, and in that which man experiences absolutely as Destiny. But there is also a Divine Omnipotence where man decides in freedom, and this is His "Omnipotence" proper, that which most clearly expresses His sublime divine Nature: His Nature as the Holy Lord, and as the Loving Father, God so wills to be "almighty" over us, that He wins our hearts through His condescension in His Son, in the Cross of the Son. No other Almighty Power of God could thus conquer and win our hearts. The heart is the one sphere which cannot be forced. No love can be forced— God the Creator makes us so free that even His coercion could not force us to love Him. But He has indeed created us so free because He wills to reveal Himself to us as love, because our free love is the highest that He desires. If we would describe the Omnipotence of God, we would have to do it in the way in which Rembrandt depicts the Passion. Everything which might otherwise be described as "Omnipotence" would have to be left wholly or half dark, and all the light would be concentrated on this One point: the love of the Crucified—which, as the only power that can do so—subdues our pride, conquers our fears, and thus wins our hearts. The turning of the rebellious despairing heart of man to God as the result of His turning to man, man being dethroned from his position of likeness to God by the stooping down of God from His Throne—that is the supreme proof of the divine Omnipotence, because it is His most difficult work. At its highest the Omnipotence of God is one with His Holiness and His Love.[37]

God is also *omnipresent.* This means that God is not limited by space.[38]

In older theologies this doctrine was expressed in terms of the immensity of God. Most simply put, it means there is no place in creation where God is not. Gustaf Aulén, a Lutheran theologian, has insisted that God's omnipresence must be understood from the viewpoint of the sovereignty of divine love.[39] Omnipresence implies the ability of divine love to maintain itself everywhere unhindered by limitations of time and space. God can reach us wherever we are, and it is useless to flee God's presence. Paul Tillich speaks of God's presence as his participation in the spatial existence of his creatures. In the certainty of the omnipresence of God we are always in the sanctuary.[40] Whenever omnipresence is experienced it breaks down the distinction between sacred and profane.

The Christian doctrine of the omnipresence of God is not only extensive but also intensive, not only quantitative but also qualitative. We speak of God as far away or near, just as a person sitting in the same room may be far away or near to us. God's presence is focused for us in certain experiences, in certain places and in particular in Jesus Christ. Yet God's presence is always an act of God's freedom. We cannot command God's presence; he makes himself present to us in qualitative ways when and where he chooses.

Christian theology also speaks of the *omniscience* of God. This is to say that God knows everything there is to be known. Our knowledge is bound by time and space and limited by our intellectual capacities, but God's knowledge is unlimited. He knows everything there is to be known and in a way appropriate to its being known. For example, God knows that which takes place in freedom in a way that is appropriate to its taking place in freedom. Finally God's omniscience is also qualitative as well as quantitative. God's knowledge is an interested knowledge.[41]

The *eternity* of God means that God is not limited by time, just as he is not limited by space. As Aulén puts it, eternity is the sovereignty of divine love in relation to time.[42] Eternity also means God's sovereignty over time. God is able to anticipate the future and also to re-create the past. As has been indicated, time is the creation of God, and it has significance not only for human beings but also for the eternal God.[43]

Eternity is not timelessness. Neither is it endless time. Eternity embraces time anticipating any possible future and not being bound by the past in that God in creating the future can re-create the past.

Christian theology has also spoken of the *impassibility* of God. God is free from suffering. In contemporary theology there has been a major reaction against any such doctrine.[44] An abstract doctrine of the impassibility of God cannot be related to the revelation of God in Jesus Christ and to the doctrine of divine love. Yet in the ancient church the doctrine of impassibility had theological significance. It underscored the tran-scendence of God.[45] The sufferings and sins of human beings cannot impair the blessedness of God. A God who can be forced to suffer is incompatible with the belief that God is independent of the world. Furthermore, if God suffers, it can be argued that God is at the mercy of human beings. This is illustrated over and over again in human affairs when the ability to cause one to suffer becomes a technique for getting control over other people.

The impassibility of God as it was defined in the early church implies moral freedom.

> It safeguards the truth that the impulse alike in providential order and in redemption and sanctification comes from the will of God and is not depen-dent on a created universe. In so far as the doctrine of the suffering of God is affirmed it presupposes the freedom of God whereby God suffers because God freely associates himself with the world's suffering.[46]

The characteristics of God also include *immutability*—unchangingness and constancy. The doctrine of immutability appears abstract, and when abstractly considered it does violence to the God about whom we read in scripture. The doctrine of the immutability of God attempts to say that God is not deficient, that God is not in the process of becoming something God was not in the past. It must be conceived of more like the steadfastness of a good person than the unalterable properties of a triangle. Hence Karl Barth prefers "constancy" to "immutability."[47] The constancy of God is the consistency of his character.

God is also *patient*. This attribute was especially meaningful to Karl Barth. For him the patience of God meant that God provides space and time for those who have forfeited their existence in his sight and are unable to justify themselves. God is patient, unafraid of running out of time, and therefore God can give time to Cain, who has forfeited the right to time.[48]

## God Who Elects

God is the one who elects. The Bible from the beginning to the end emphasizes God's election. God chooses nations and peoples. God chose Israel rather than Israel's choosing God. The whole story of Israel's history is told in terms of God's choosing and calling forth his people. Before God liberated the Israelites from the pharaoh, he chose them to be his people. The same theme runs through the New Testament: "You did not choose me but I chose you" (John 15:16). The letter to the Ephesians puts the whole Christian life in the context of God's election: ". . . he chose us in

Christ before the foundation of the world to be holy and blameless before him in love. He destined us for adoption as his children through Jesus Christ, according to the good pleasure of his will, to the praise of his glorious grace that he freely bestowed on us in the Beloved" (Ephesians 1:4–6). The doctrine of election establishes a community that is not constituted by race, nationality, ethnic origin, gender, or even history. Election takes precedence over every other activity. God chose Israel before he liberated Israel.

## God Who Covenants

God is also understood as the one who covenants and, by making covenant, creates his people. Covenants play a major role in the religion of Israel—the covenants with Noah, Abraham, and David—covenants that Christians believe were fulfilled in the covenant in Jesus Christ. As Jeremiah put it, "I will be your God, and you shall be my people" (Jeremiah 7:23; 31:33). The concept of covenant also plays a significant role in the New Testament: "This cup is the new covenant in my blood" (1 Corinthians 11:25). The new covenant fulfills Jeremiah 31 and defines the character of the Christian community (Hebrews 8:6; 9:15; 12:24; 2 Corinthians 3:7–14; Ephesians 2:12).

Covenant is rooted in election, but it includes the human response. Covenant thus became the characteristic of the church and of human communities under God.[49]

## ⁓God Who Is Transcendent and Immanent

God is also transcendent and immanent. By transcendence theology means God's separation or independence from the world. "Immanence" is God's involvement in the world. The scriptures everywhere assume that God is both independent of the world and yet actively involved in the world.

The conceptualization of transcendence and immanence has been made more difficult by the psychological impact of modern science. How can God's transcendence of the world as well as his immanence in the world be understood, especially in a world whose structure and processes can be described in scientific textbooks?

Christian theology has always insisted that God is both transcendent and immanent, separate from the world yet involved in the world. God is transcendent in his being. For God, existence and being are one.[50] For all created things existence is dependent on a source outside themselves.

Yet God's transcendence is not simply ontological; it is also a transcendence in knowledge, in goodness, in holiness, in personhood. No attribute of God is the character and attribute of a creature raised to its highest form. This emphasis on the transcendence of God is seen in the theological protest against every idolatry that seeks to fasten the infinite and indeterminate God to some finite and determinate object.

Christian theology also declares that God is immanent in the creation. The scriptures on the one hand affirm God's transcendence ("I, I am the LORD, and besides me there is no savior" [Isaiah 43:11]) and on the other hand continually speak of God's personal activity in the world. According to the scriptural metaphors and images, this activity is direct and immediate and continual.

How can we conceive of God's transcendence and immanence with our modern scientific awareness of how the world works? The problem has been accentuated by modern science, which emphasizes the universe operating according to its own nature, procedures, and processes. The issue of God's transcendence and immanence became crucial with the science of Isaac Newton at the end of the seventeenth century. Newton understood the world in terms of mathematics and mechanics.

The scientist theologians who worked with Newton and under his influence came to think of God's transcendence and immanence according to the analogy of a clockmaker.[51] The clockmaker gave the clock its structure and provided it with the power to operate for long periods of time. Then the clockmaker withdrew. The clockmaker could, of course, return to fix a mechanism that had gotten out of order and also on occasion to rewind the clock. Here, God's transcendence and immanence are understood in spatial terms. God has his space; the created order has its space. The created order operates on its own until something goes wrong or until its energy dies down; then God moves from his space and does what is necessary to maintain the created order. This particular view of God's immanence became known as deism. God gives the world its existence and its structures and for the most part is absent from its operation.

The deistic understanding of transcendence and immanence stands over against pantheism, in which God is identified with forces in the world and has no transcendence over the world. Panentheism, or "dipolar" theism, holds that God's inclusion of the world does not exhaust the reality of God and emphasizes the divine-creaturely interaction in its critique of what it perceives as traditional theism.

God's activity in the world can also be conceived of in terms of God's speaking or addressing human beings. In the very influential book *Jesus Christ and Mythology,* Rudolf Bultmann declared that God's action in the world is God's address.[52] The world, according to this theology, has its own structures, which operate according to their natures, but in some way God speaks to human beings and addresses them. Nature and history alike are minimized in this particular theological perspective, and the Christian life becomes a dialogue between God and the believer.

The scriptures relate God's activities to the world in personal categories. God is one who listens, who hears, who judges, who tests, who moves the hearts of human beings, who visits his anger upon people and who also shows mercy. In the Old Testament God's activity in the world is very immediate and very personal. The independence of the world as a created order with its own procedures receives little emphasis.

Until the rise of modern science, theology continued this tradition of relating God's transcendence and immanence to the created order in personal categories. The uncritical character of this understanding means that it cannot be simply repeated in contemporary culture; yet the comprehension of God's transcendence in personal categories is the most productive way in which the transcendence and immanence of God are understood in our particular culture.

William Temple, in his remarkable book *Nature, Man and God,* defines the transcendence of God in this way:

A person is properly described as transcendent of his acts. He is expressed in these, but he has an existence apart from them. His circumstances on any occasion may be strictly accidental; that is to say, the causes conditioning them may be wholly other than his own will or any causes conditioning this, so that it is possible to conceive him, while himself unaltered, being at that time in other circumstances instead. His acts in the two sets of circumstances would be quite different. Indeed he would express that special identity which he is by the difference in his acts in different circumstances. His self is not only distinguishable but separable from the acts in which it is revealed. What is important in the assertion of transcendence is the affirmation, not of unexhausted resources, though this may be true, but of capacity for that infinite delicacy of adjustment to varying conditions in which purposive as distinct from mechanical or chemical action consists. An unusual or unexpected act may appear to exhibit a special volume of energy, but that is because our minds are obsessed by the mechanical categories, and we suppose that additional energy is needed to counteract a supposed natural tendency to do always the same thing—a moral inertia. But what is required for heroic sacrifice as compared with selfish acquisitiveness is not more volitional force; it is a different volitional direction. *What a true doctrine of divine transcendence will assert is not a reservoir of normally unutilised energy, but a volitional as contrasted with a mechanical direction of the energy utilised.[53]*

God is transcendent and immanent in the world in a way that is analogous to a person's transcendence over and in his or her own work. God is not spatially transcendent, but personally transcendent. One analogy to the transcendence and immanence of God is the relationship of the self to the body. Ian Barbour, in *Issues in Science and Religion,* suggests that this analogy may be too intimate in not giving sufficient independence to the created order, but at the same time it is very suggestive.[54] The human body operates according to its own energy systems and procedures and yet the human self can direct or influence these procedures without interrupting them. Even the heartbeat or blood pressure can in some measure be determined by the human self. If a person raises his or her arm, the physicist and biochemist can explain that act in biochemical and physical terms. Yet the person knows that the real reason that the arm was raised was the decision of the human self.[55]

The conception of the transcendence and the immanence of God in personal terms means that the integrity of the world as the created order is maintained and yet at the same time holds that this created order is open to the personal intentions and purposes of the creator. This conception of the transcendence and immanence of God in personal categories also modifies all religious activities. On the one hand, God is not at our control, and we cannot "lose ourselves in God" as the mystics claim. On the other hand, God is present in all creation and especially to human creatures. Our relationship to God is analogous to our relationship to other human beings and to the way in which human beings are transcendent and immanent in their own relationships or in groups. God's transcendence and immanence must be understood in personal analogies. The doctrines of the person of Jesus Christ, of the presence of Christ in the sacraments, and of the church are all shaped by this understanding of transcendence-immanence.

## How Do We Know God?

We know God as God reveals himself. Every proposition in this statement of faith is intended to be based on God's self-revelation in the history of Israel culminating in Jesus Christ and the giving of the Holy Spirit. Furthermore, God is not within our grasp; we cannot objectify God. We can know God only in ways comparable to the knowing of another human self. We can objectify another person and acquire significant knowledge. We know the composition of the blood, the general appearance of the body. In certain situations this knowledge is very important. We can know a great deal about a human self through the activities of that self. Yet we cannot truly know another self unless the self freely chooses to reveal himself or herself to us, unless the self tells us who he or she is. We cannot know God unless God chooses to reveal himself.

Yet the further question arises, Does God reveal himself only in the history of Israel and in the revelation in Jesus Christ? The scriptures as well as Christian theology always insisted that God has revealed himself in all of his creation. Even Karl Barth, whose theology is narrowly focused on the revelation of God in Jesus Christ, knows that God reveals himself through his entire creation.[56] We know God not only as Christians who have been encountered by God in the history of Israel and in Jesus Christ, but as human beings apart from this history. Christian theology has generally affirmed that God is known at least in an elementary way through the created order. Karl Barth himself declares that, having known God in Jesus Christ, we can engage those outside the Christian faith in conversation, based on this general revelation.[57] Having known God in Jesus Christ, we see God's action more clearly in all his creation.

1. We know God in the immediacy of human experience. This was the emphasis of Augustine and also of Calvin.

> Augustine finds reason for recognizing God as the *arché* or *principium* of his being, thought, and purpose; and belief in God assumes the character of *intima scientia,* a kind of "inner knowledge" akin to belief in the self; it is presumed or presupposed in the consciousness of his own existence and activity. This belief neither requires nor admits of "external" verification; scientifically speaking, it is both undemonstrated and undemonstrable. Nevertheless, it yields a knowledge of the Divine Being, the *intellectualis visio Dei,* sufficiently clear and precise to make it possible for him to say that, "Next to myself, I know God."[58]

John Calvin also believed that we know God with the same immediacy with which we are aware of ourselves and the world.[59] He spoke of the *sensus divinitatis,* the awareness of God that arises out of our experience as human beings. He also spoke of the immediate knowledge that arises out of conscience or in an awareness of the disparity between what we are and what we ought to be, an awareness that we are obligated and responsible. For Calvin this immediate knowledge of God is always distorted by human sin and leads to idolatry. Yet for Calvin the awareness of God is so immediate that the only possibilities for human beings are faith in the living God or faith in idols.[60]

Christian theologians who have emphasized knowledge of God that arises out of the depths of human existence have also been moved by the ontological argument for God's existence. The ontological argument developed in the tradition that found God by reflecting on the depths of personal existence and on the life of the mind itself, on what is involved in thinking. This argument received its classical form from Anselm.

> For no one who understands what God is can think that God does not exist, even though he says these words in his heart—perhaps without any meaning, perhaps with some quite extraneous meaning. For God is that than which a greater cannot be thought, and whoever understands this rightly must understand that he exists in such a way that he cannot be nonexistent even in thought. He, therefore, who understands that God thus exists cannot think of him as nonexistent.[61]

The crux of Anselm's argument is the power to think of a being than which no greater can be conceived. If one cannot conceive of such a being, the argument falls apart.

Anselm's argument received vigorous criticism especially by Immanuel Kant (1724–1804), who contended that the argument was flawed in that it regarded existence as a predicate. Descartes used the illustration of a triangle. The essential property of a triangle is that its angles add up to a constant sum. All triangles have this property. Properties do not entail existence. Anselm himself had faced this argument from Gaunilon in a writing entitled *On Behalf of the Fool*. One can conceive, Gaunilon contended, of the most blessed and perfect island that can possibly be conceived, but this does not mean that it exists. We can conceive of the most perfect form of many objects, but this conception does not entail their existence. In all ordinary cases Kant's and Gaunilon's objections hold true.

Anselm's argument, however, does not apply to ordinary objects, nor to the "chief member of a class, but the supreme Ground of the being of all classes." Existence of that being than which no greater can be conceived cannot be compared to the existence of particular things. "It is rather being which is presupposed by the existence of particular things, but which is presupposed no less by the ability to define any character whatsoever."[62] Unless there is an undergirding order of being, more fundamental than being possible or actual, no meaning can be given to logical predicates.

The ontological argument has always had its critics, but it persists. If one can really conceive of a being than which no greater can be conceived, then many find it impossible to doubt that this being exists.[63]

2. God can be known, a long tradition in theology and philosophy has contended, by reflecting on his works. In the Christian tradition this perspective found its classic expression in the theological work of Thomas Aquinas, who rejected the ontological argument but was convinced that by reflecting upon the work of creation human beings could arrive at the knowledge that God is, and by analogy come to other conclusions such as God is one. Sense perception provides the data upon which the reason can operate. The existence of God can be demonstrated on the basis of the knowledge that we have of the natural world. Hence arguments for God's existence begin with the sensible facts of the realm of nature.[64]

Thomas formulated his proofs for God in five arguments.[65] The first is from motion. We are aware of motion. The mover either must be the ultimate source of motion or dependent on a previous mover. Thomas was aware that one can conceive of an infinite regress of movers, but he also contended that an endless regress made no sense. "In a world where everything is merely relative, then nothing is even relative, nothing exists at all, nothing is definable. Only if we have a frame of reference to which those relative states which develop in a process of change can be referred are we able to define a process of change even as change."[66]

The second argument is from efficient cause. As in the case of motion, efficient cause makes sense only if there is an uncaused cause.

The third argument is from contingent, dependent being to necessary being. Again, in order to affirm contingent being one must affirm being that is noncontingent in order to make sense.

The fourth argument has to do with the existence of degrees of greatness and of goodness. We continually make distinctions between better and worse, greater and less. Thomas contended that this gradation of being implied an order. For there to be grades of goodness or distinction between good and evil there must be a supreme instance of goodness.

Thomas's fifth argument was from design (teleological argument). This is one of the most ancient and impressive of the arguments for God's existence. The evidences of intelligence, of order, and of meaning in the universe point to an orderer. Those who have advocated this argument are well aware of the data that do not seem to agree, but the evidences of design have been impressive both in ancient times and even today.[67]

Thomas Aquinas expressed the arguments from sense data for God's existence in abstract language. These arguments can be put in more concrete language. William Temple impressively argues for the reality of God on the grounds of the appearance of the human mind and the human person in the history of the universe. The appearance of the human mind is a most remarkable fact. The mind has the capacity for language, for concepts. It can read off the facts of the universe; it can even think the universe. Moreover, the universe itself corresponds to the human mind. It is impossible to conceive of the mind in a universe that is utterly irrational and whose processes do not correspond to the processes of the mind. A very remarkable fact about the human mind is not simply its ability to read the facts of the universe but its capacity to think the universe. How else can one explain a universe accessible to a mind and a mind that appears in the history of the universe unless there is behind them both mind spelled with a capital M?[68]

Temple also argues from the fact of the human person. Human beings not only think; they are also selves with the capacity to be conscious of the world and to be self-conscious, that is, with the power to objectify the human self and reflect on it. This power of self-objectification provides freedom so that human beings are not simply the consequence of instinct and impulse as is the life of animals, but are shaped in part by the power of the human self to reflect on the self and to organize all the vitalities and energies of the self in the pursuit of a freely chosen goal. How is it that the human person with the power to organize the energies of life, with a capacity of love and to give oneself in devotion and sacrifice, how is it that such a person emerged in the world unless there is behind the world a Person?[69]

The traditional arguments for God's existence are not widely used today, as they are not thought to be persuasive. Yet eminent scientists are moved to see evidence of design or a transcendent intelligence in the world they study. Owen Gingerich, Senior Astronomer at the Smithsonian Astrophysical Observatory, Harvard University, in a moving address declares that he finds evidence of a transcendent intelligence at work in the world. He concludes: "For me, it makes sense to suppose that the superintelligence, the transcendence, the ground of being in Paul Tillich's formulation, has revealed itself through prophets in all ages, and supremely in the life of Jesus Christ."[70]

3. Others have argued for the existence of God on the grounds of goodness, beauty.

The argument on the grounds of goodness is based on the almost universal awareness of moral obligation, a sense of being obligated. Also there is an almost universal awareness of the disparity between what human beings are and what they ought to be. The content of what is perceived to be good and evil varies. The distinction between good and evil, right and wrong, is virtually universal.

The human experience of "oughtness," the conviction that I must do certain things not because they will help me or society but simply because they are right, reveals something about the universe.

> The good man who thinks out to the end the implications of his loyalty to the moral good . . . will find that he is pledged to something more than simple recognition of an ideal of conduct as entitled to his unqualified respect. He is committed . . . to a belief in the final coincidence of the "ought" and the "is," in virtue of their common source in a transcendent living and personal Good — one, complete, eternal — the only belief which rightfully deserves to be called belief in God.[71]

Human beings have almost universally had an awareness of beauty. They have been deeply moved or filled with ecstasy by the sheer wonder of a sunset or the majesty of a mountain, or by the pleasantness of some object that deeply moved them with its symmetry of shapes and colors. Those who argue from beauty ask how it is that one can come to say that a particular scene or act is beautiful. Beauty cannot be reduced to pure subjectivity. It is not a whim of the observer. Those who are deeply moved by beauty affirm that there is a reality that stands over against them and that has intrinsic value in and of itself. The question arises: Is the beauty of a sunset simply an accidental collocation of atoms? The affirmation of beauty seems to involve a creator and a purpose behind it.

The experience of beauty at least for many implies an artist. The beautiful is the expression of purpose, of meaning. A. J. Balfour in *Theism and Humanism* has written:

> The feeling for natural beauty cannot, any more than scientific curiosity, rest satisfied with the world of sensuous appearance. But the reasons for its discontent are different. Scientific curiosity hungers for a knowledge of causes; causes which are physical, and, if possible, measurable. Our admiration for natural beauty has no such needs. It cares not to understand either the physical theories which explain what it admires, or the psychological theories which explain its admiration. It does not deny the truth of the first, nor (within due limits) the sufficiency of the second. But it requires more. It feels itself belittled unless conscious purpose can be found somewhere in

its pedigree. Physics and psycho-physics, by themselves, suffice not. It longs to regard beauty as a revelation—a revelation from spirit to spirit, not from one kind of atomic agitation to the "psychic" accompaniment of another. On this condition only can its highest values be maintained.[72]

In addition to the arguments from goodness and beauty, others have been impressed by the fairly universal presence of belief in God. Religious experience is another testimony to the reality of God. In the nineteenth century the Marxists explained religion in terms of economics. Freud and others explained it in terms of psychology and wish fulfillment. Historians explained it away as a stage of human development. Yet religion did not disappear. It persists in spite of political oppression and intellectual assaults.[73] The testimony of religious experience comes from rich and poor, learned and ignorant, the comfortable and the oppressed, in all times and places. Those who deny the reality of God are called upon to account for religious experience, especially its persistence, more effectively than they have thus far. For those who believe, it strengthens faith.

How then shall we evaluate these arguments for the existence of God? They have received very vigorous criticisms especially from Immanuel Kant. The weaknesses of the arguments are clear enough. (1) The evidence is ambiguous in such arguments as those from design. Many aspects of human life appear to be absurd and to contradict the belief in a rational creator. (2) The arguments go beyond our experience. As Kant insisted, our knowledge is limited to our experience.[74] In all the arguments we make a jump from the range of our experience to that which is beyond our experience. (3) They do not point to the God whom Christians worship but to a First Cause or a Designer.

The arguments for the existence of God in the final analysis are as futile as arguments for why a person should love another person are in eliciting love. Faith in God is a personal act, of which reason is only one factor. In every area of life, no argument is conclusive to any person who does not wish to believe it.

The arguments for the existence of God, however, have real value. First of all they clarify belief. They indicate quite clearly what it is to say there is no God. This is no inconsiderable service. Apart from the arguments for the existence of God, it becomes very easy for one to deny the reality of God without taking responsibility for what one is actually saying. To declare that there is no God is to declare, for example, that there is no purpose behind the universe or at least that human beings cannot know it. A secular humanist culture will have to explicate the meaning and significance of purpose, truth, and love, of birth and death, or face a collapse similar to that of communism, which was unable to account convincingly for these experiences.

The arguments for the existence of God also confirm faith. They may not compel faith. They may not be the primary reason we come to faith, but they do demonstrate the rationality of faith. This leads to a third service. The arguments for the existence of God complete faith by showing how faith makes sense of the world we experience, how faith enables us to understand the world better than it can be understood on any other basis.

4. We also come to know God by participating in the fellowship of those who affirm the reality of God and who worship his name.[75] It is doubtful if any faith conviction can be maintained apart from a supporting community, and this is especially true in the instance of faith in God. Christian life as well as theology is based on the conviction that we come to know God by the power of the Holy Spirit, especially as the Holy Spirit speaks through the words of scripture in the fellowship of the church. Persons come to know God in a great variety of ways. God's spirit is free. It is possible that the Spirit of God will deeply move one who is playing golf on Sunday morning, but it is more likely that the Spirit of God will deeply move our hearts and renew our minds in the conviction that God is and, more than that, that God knows us and that God loves us through participation in the worshiping, believing community of Christian people.

Faith in God grows out of the deep experiences of life. We do not come to know God by reading a book on the arguments for the existence of God or taking a course in the university. We come to know God in the deep experiences of life, in particular in experiences in the company of those who already believe in God, and by the power of the Holy Spirit through the means of grace.

# CHAPTER 5

❖

# CREATION

What do you believe when you say: "I believe in God the Father Almighty, Maker of heaven and earth"?

That the eternal Father of our Lord Jesus Christ, who out of nothing created heaven and earth with all that is in them, who also upholds and governs them by his eternal counsel and providence, is for the sake of Christ his Son my God and my Father. I trust in him so completely that I have no doubt that he will provide me with all things necessary for body and soul. Moreover, whatever evil he sends upon me in this troubled life he will turn to my good, for he is able to do it, being almighty God, and is determined to do it, being a faithful Father.

Heidelberg Catechism, Question 26

In the beginning when God created the heavens and the earth, the earth was a formless void and darkness covered the face of the deep, while a wind from God swept over the face of the waters. . . . Then . . . God saw everything that he had made, and indeed, it was very good.

Genesis 1:1–3, 31

Have you not known? Have you not heard?
The LORD is the everlasting God,
 the Creator of the ends of the earth.

Isaiah 40:28

In the beginning was the Word. . . . All things came into being through him, and without him not one thing came into being.

John 1:1, 3

He is the image of the invisible God, the firstborn of all creation; for in him all things in heaven and on earth were created, things visible and invisible, whether thrones or dominions or rulers or powers—all things have been created through him and for him. He himself is before all things, and in him all things hold together.

Colossians 1:15–17

The works of God that are emphasized in scripture are creation, redemption, and sanctification.[1] These works are bound together by being the work of the one Triune God and cannot be separated. Redemption, for example, cannot be isolated from creation any more than it can be separated from sanctification and the consummation of all things. Ideally we should speak of creation, redemption, and sanctification together, but as created human beings we have to speak about one thing at a time.

## Creation as an Article of Faith

The confession "I believe in God the Father Almighty, creator of heaven and earth" is the first article of the Apostles' Creed. It is an article of faith. The obvious reality of the world (that is, obvious to ordinary human beings) suggests that the doctrine of creation, unlike some other Christian doctrines, is within our own experience and reflection. We are tempted to conclude that we know the creator and creation, as we know other facts about our world.

The misconception of the doctrine of creation as a historical or scientific statement sets the stage for the debate between the so-called creationists and the so-called evolutionists. Creation, as a theological conviction, and evolution, as a scientific description, are not comparable terms. The radical issue of faith can better be expressed in the contrast between the conviction that the universe is a chance happening, or the product of forces with no prevision of their end, and the conviction that the universe is the expression of purpose—or, more particularly in the Christian understanding, of grace. The real controversy is not between two sciences but between conflicting faiths, even when faith masquerades as science. The scientist has no more facts about why the universe is than does the theologian. The theologian and the scientist alike live by faith.

The doctrine of creation is a conviction of faith, not a scientific conclusion. Christians have sometimes been misled into confusing theology with science by the first two chapters of Genesis, which seem to make scientific as well as historical statements about the creation of the universe. The literary power of Genesis 1–2 is very impressive and even overwhelming. The simplicity of the style, the clarity of thought, and the remarkable correspondence of the Genesis account with what we know from science tempts readers to think of these chapters as science or history. The creation accounts were the attempt to describe within the language of human experience what is clearly beyond human experience.

Karl Barth has insisted that the first chapters of Genesis should be understood as saga.[2] He rejects the word "myth" because in popular understanding it means falsehood or fantasy. Saga distinguishes Genesis 1–2 from history and also from myth and scientific description. Saga is necessary because no human being was a spectator to creation. Modern science has found ways of recovering a remarkable knowledge of the first developments of the universe, but these are all accounts from within the universe. Neither the scientist nor the theologian was a spectator to creation.

In a book entitled *God and Personality,* C. J. Webb described Plato's use of myth in a manner that illuminates Genesis 1–2.

The myth . . . takes the place of History, where a historical question is asked, but the materials for a historical answer are lacking.

How did the world come into being? How did society begin? What will happen to our souls after death? It is to such questions as these that Plato offers replies in the form of myths. Philosophy cannot answer such questions, any more than it can tell me where I dined this day last year or where I shall dine this day next year. For an answer to the former of these two inquiries I should consult my personal memory or my journal; and if I wished for information about something that happened before I was born, I should seek for it in the history books. But if what I want to know must have happened at a time whereof there is no record extant, what can I do? The best I can do, says Plato, is to frame a myth, a story which, if not the truth, will at any rate be like the truth. But this cannot merely mean that it is to be like what actually occurred, for *ex hypothesi* I do not know what did occur, and hence cannot tell what would be like it and what not.

What it means for Plato, however, is not doubtful. It means that the myth is to be in accord with those conclusions as to the general nature of things which *I derive not from History but from Philosophy.* Just as you could not tell me where and on what I dined this day last year, but could confidently assert that it was not in fairyland and not on nectar and ambrosia, so too we are sure that whatever took place in the unrecorded past must have been consistent with what we know to be the eternal nature of Reality; whatever we have reason to think is incompatible with the eternal nature of Reality we have reason to think did not occur in the past and will not occur in the future.[3]

Saga is the use of historical or mythical language to say what actually happened, but it does so through the imaginative use of historical materials to describe what is beyond human experience. The critical test of saga is not history or science but the theological integrity of the account. The crucial question for the Christian is how the creation account in Genesis is related to the revelation of God in Jesus Christ.

The Bible also affirms the created reality of the world in simple propositional terms, as in the words of the prophet Isaiah:

> I made the earth,
>     and created humankind upon it;
> it was my hands that stretched out the heavens,
>     and I commanded all their host.
>
>                                                     Isaiah 45:12

The doctrine of creation is not science; neither is it history. It is the attempt to say with the materials and images available to Christians from history and human experience what they believe is the origin of the world. It is the attempt to speak the truth about the world. The world is not all there is. An intelligence and a will transcend the world. Tokens of this transcendence in the created order are apprehended by Christians through the eyes of faith. This transcendent intelligence and will, Christians believe, spoke through the prophets and was embodied in Jesus Christ.

No scientific or historical account of creation is possible for the scientist and the historian. They, no more than the theologian, have ever been outside the universe or have been spectators at creation. When a scientist declares that the world is all there is, all there has ever been and all there ever will be, the question must be asked, How does the scientist know? The scientist and the historian and the theologian alike speak by faith, if they speak at all concerning the origin of the universe.

The recognition that the doctrine of creation is an article of faith means also that it is not the conclusion of an argument or the result of reflection on the universe. Karl Barth has emphasized this particular point.

> The doctrine of the creation no less than the whole remaining content of Christian confession is an article of faith, i.e., the rendering of a knowledge which no man has procured for himself or ever will; which is neither native to him nor accessible by way of observation and logical thinking; for which he has no organ and no ability; which he can in fact achieve only in faith. . . .
> As the Christian philosopher does what other philosophers and inventors of myths have always been able to do and have in fact done, i.e., as he constructs a view of things by way of observation and reflection, he comes to the conclusion that the assumption of a principle which is superior to the world is unavoidable, and decides to accept the reality of this unavoidable principle and to call it God.[4]

Barth's point is that a first cause that can be known by philosophical reflection is not what Christian theology means by the creator.

The doctrine of creation is neither history nor science nor the conclusion of an argument. As an article of faith it is a doctrine of revelation. The location of the doctrine of creation as the opening chapters of the Bible is logical, but theologically misleading. The affirmations of creation in Genesis, in Psalm 104, in Isaiah, or in the New Testament are alike rooted in the history of Israel and the Christian church as a believing community and are based on the experience of God as redeemer and sanctifier. Isaiah knew God as creator because God had encountered him as the lord of history. In the New Testament it is the presence of Jesus Christ that is the ground and basis of the doctrine of creation. The prologue of the Fourth Gospel declares that the Word that was in the beginning with God and through whom all things came to be is the Word that was made flesh in Jesus Christ (John 1:1–14). Paul quotes an early confession: "Yet for us there is one God, the Father, from whom are all things and for whom we exist, and one Lord, Jesus Christ, through whom are all things and through whom we exist" (1 Corinthians 8:6).

A powerful statement of the significance of Jesus Christ for the doctrine of creation is found in the letter to the Colossians in the verses quoted at the opening of this chapter (1:15–17). The letter to the Hebrews likewise declares, "Long ago God spoke to our ancestors in many and various ways by the prophets, but in these last days he has spoken to us by a Son, whom he appointed heir of all things, through whom he also created the worlds" (Hebrews 1:1–2).

The really critical point in the Christian doctrine of creation is not that the world is created or that there is a first cause, but the character of the creator. The creator is the God who is present in Jesus Christ and known in human experience by the power of the Holy Spirit. Karl Barth has insisted "that the reality of creation is and can only be known with clarity and certainty in the person of Jesus Christ. . . . Jesus Christ is the Word by which the knowledge of creation is mediated to us because He is the Word by which God has fulfilled creation and continually maintains and rules it."[5] To know the creator in Jesus Christ is to know that the creator is personal and gracious, as well as powerful and intelligent.

The Christian doctrine of creation is determined by the experience of the creator in Jesus Christ. Yet the revelation of the creator in Jesus Christ would not be possible if there were not signs of the creator in the creation. The scriptures affirm that the heavens declare the glory of God (Psalm 19). No theologian has emphasized the signs of God's presence in human experience and in the wonders of the created order more than John Calvin.[6] In our own time those who study science sometimes are compelled by the sheer wonder of the creation to acknowledge a transcendent intelligence. Fred Hoyle, one of the most distinguished of contemporary scientists, was overwhelmed by the discovery of the remarkable nuclear arrangement that made carbon possible, an element that is necessary for human existence. The discovery shook his atheism:

> Would you not say to yourself, "some supercalculating intellect must have designed the properties of the carbon atom, otherwise the chance of my finding such an atom through the blind forces of nature would be utterly minuscule"? Of course you would. . . . A common sense interpretation of the facts suggests that a super intellect has monkeyed with physics, as well as with chemistry and biology and that there are no blind forces worth speaking about in nature. The numbers one calculates from the facts seem to me so overwhelming so as to put this conclusion almost beyond question.[7]

The importance of the revelation of God in Jesus Christ for the Christian doctrine of creation cannot be minimized, but it ought not to obscure the signs of the creator that are to be found everywhere in creation. Belief in creation is not "purely an extrapolation from the belief in redemption."[8] Creation is a doctrine revealed by God, but it must not be isolated from human experience in the world.

## Affirmations of the Doctrine of Creation

The doctrine of creation does not make scientific or historical statements about the world. It does make affirmations about the nature and the purpose of the universe. On the basis of faith in Jesus Christ, it does believe that these statements are true, accurate descriptions of the way the world is.

1. The doctrine of creation means that the world and human life cannot be understood by scientific analysis or by observation. Knowledge of how the world works does not give us knowledge of why the world should work or for what purpose. The world is not self-explanatory, though this is the implicit assumption of a secular culture. "If the fundamental truth about this universe be that it owes its existence to His will, then in our efforts to understand it, the last word will be in terms of His intention and purpose."[9] We know the true meaning of things and beings, animal as well as human, in the light of the purposes of God and only in a secondary sense in the light of scientific knowledge and analysis.

2. The doctrine of creation means that the universe is the expression of the purpose and grace of God. In human experience the greatest human

works are those that express purpose and love. The doctrine of creation means that the universe is more, not less, than the highest human work. No one has put this more emphatically than Karl Barth: "Creation . . . is already the work of the free, fatherly grace and mercy of God. . . . Creation follows the covenant of grace since it is its indispensable basis and presupposition."[10] Barth's theology insists that the origin of the world is not simply the expression of thought or even of purpose but above all of grace and favor. In this way Barth argues more clearly than any previous theologian that the world and human life are gifts of God and that the Creator is much more than "a first cause." The doctrine of creation means that the world and human life are gifts, that there is a giver, and that the giver can be trusted.

Creation means that the universe and human beings are not thrown into existence by some mechanical or energetic or rational necessity. Human life and the world do not have to be. They were created by God in his freedom. God does not have to have the world or human beings. He freely chose to create the world and human beings. The freedom expressed in the creation of the world is more fully embodied in Jesus Christ.[11]

3. Creation means that the world is dependent and finite. The mystery and immensity of the world together with its energies and vitalities have always tempted human beings either to deify forces of nature or to fear them. The doctrine of creation desacralizes the world. Ancient Israel had a continual struggle with neighboring peoples who deified the forces of nature in the worship of Baal, and thus Israel insisted that the creator, not the creation, should be worshiped. Early Christians so clearly denied any divine quality to nature or to religious and political structures that they were accused by their contemporaries of atheism.[12]

The finite and dependent character of creation came to expression in the doctrine of creation *ex nihilo*. This doctrine, which is implicit in scripture, was developed by early Christian theologians.[13] It means that the world is neither an emanation from God and therefore divine, nor a self-existent reality over against God and therefore an outside limitation on the power of God. This doctrine was an attempt to say that the universe is because God wills it. It expresses the sheer wonder of creation and answers the ancient question of why there is something and not nothing.

Athanasius (c. 296–373) declared: "For God creates, and to create is also ascribed to men; and God has being, and men are said to be, having received from God this gift also. Yet does God create as men do? Or is his being as man's being? Perish the thought. . . . For God creates, in that he calls what is not into being, needing nothing there unto."[14]

The practical consequence of the doctrine of creation is that human beings should not expect to find in creation or in the energies and vitalities of nature the fulfillment of life. The doctrine of creation also means that the forces and even the immensities of the created universe are not to be inordinately feared. The universe can do no more and no less than a creation that is totally dependent on the God whom we know in Jesus Christ. Human life can only be fulfilled in God, the creator. Augustine declared: "Thou hast made us for thyself and restless is our heart until it comes to rest in thee."[15]

4. The doctrine of creation means that the world has a reality of its own with a relative independence, though dependent and finite. It has structures, processes, and energy systems of its own. God's governance of the world is primarily through the processes he has created. God need not be conceived of as ordering directly and immediately each event. The natural world operates according to its structures. Within the order of human freedom and history God can be loved, hated, blasphemed, rejected. In this world there are irrationalities, accidents, even absurdities, as when beautiful plants or animals develop in nature only to be destroyed by nature. The Christian doctrine rejects pantheism, which places God's action immediately in every event in history and nature. It also rejects any ultimate dualism that gives the world an existence apart from God.

5. The doctrine of creation means that the highest form of created existence is personal. Creation is a personal act of the Triune God. That which is most real is personal. "It is in personal relationships we experience the highest form of reality known to us."[16] The subpersonal, the material, exists as material for fashioning the personal.[17]

6. The doctrine of creation affirms that the created order is good. The goodness of the world is not self-evident. The conviction that the world is evil is one of the most persistent in the history of the human race. For some the world of flesh and blood that we can see, taste, touch, and handle is a prison house of the soul, and salvation is escape from this material world. Others have concluded that the world is the creation of an evil god. The first great heretic in the history of the church was Marcion (c. 85–160), who came to believe that the creator, the God of the Old Testament, was a lesser god than Christians know in Jesus Christ. Marcion did not like many features of the world (snakes, alligators, and the way babies come into the world, for example), and he believed any good god would not have created such a world. In modern times "parasitic ingestion" has been used in a similar fashion to illustrate the carnage and bloodshed of an evil world.[18] The church of the second century responded to Marcion and

the Gnostics with vigor, affirming with clarity that the God of the Old Testament is the God whom we know in Jesus Christ and that the creator is the Word who became flesh in Jesus Christ.

The goodness of creation cannot be defined abstractly or arbitrarily. Creation is good if it both expresses and serves the purposes of the creator. It becomes clear in the doctrine of providence that many difficulties arise when one assumes that the purpose of creation is to provide a safe and comfortable life for human beings. Many difficulties disappear if God's purpose was at least in part to provide a suitable environment to bring human beings to maturity. The goodness of creation is defined by its appropriateness for the purposes of God as revealed in Jesus Christ.

The goodness of creation means that the universe is intelligible, consistent, ordered, and expressive of purpose and redemptive love. Human life has meaning and purpose. The goodness of creation means that human beings enjoy the universe and use it under God for the enhancement of human life. The goodness of creation means that the world is appropriate for God's purposes for the world and especially for human beings.

Augustine of Hippo (354–430) so strongly insisted that the world is good that he defined evil as a privation of the good, a falling away from the good.[19] Insofar as anything truly is, it is good. Evil is that which God does not will and therefore has no real existence.

The affirmation that the world is good has not only religious but cultural significance. The conflict between Christian faith and science has frequently been emphasized, but it ought to be noted that science developed in a culture informed by the Judeo-Christian tradition, which emphasized that God created the universe and saw that everything he had made was good. Modern science could never have developed in a culture that minimized the goodness of creation and the significance of history, as for example in Hindu culture. Today a secular culture has appropriated the Judeo-Christian conviction that the universe is good; but there are signs that apart from belief in the creator who is good, one cannot for long believe that creation is good.[20] Creation cannot provide more for human life than is appropriate for the created order. When human beings worship the creation rather than the creator, the creation itself becomes in the end meaningless.

The goodness of creation, however, does not mean that the creation is perfect. Karl Barth has spoken of the shadow side of creation,[21] and other theologians have spoken of the provisional character of the created order. In human experience we encounter a creation that is filled with wonders and evidences of purpose and meaning, but we also encounter a creation that appears at times irrational, absurd, purposeless, and wasteful.

How shall we interpret this aspect of the created order? First, we can recognize that we do not fully comprehend either the creation or the purposes of the creator. A second answer is to admit with Hendrikus Berkhof that we cannot explain it. "Why has God (provisionally) wanted something which nevertheless (ultimately) he does not want? The only answer we can give is no answer; apparently it was never God's purpose to call into existence a ready-made and complete world. He evidently wants his creation to go through a history of resistance and struggle, of suffering and dying."[22]

Augustine, who unqualifiedly affirmed the goodness of creation, dealt with this problem in terms of the plenitude of beings or the symmetry of a tapestry. Some "heretics" are not able to acknowledge the good creation,

> because there are, forsooth, many things, such as fire, frost, wild beasts, and so forth, which do not suit but injure this thin-blooded and frail mortality of our flesh, which is at present under just punishment. They do not consider how admirable these things are in their own places, how excellent in their own natures, how beautifully adjusted to the rest of creation, and how much grace they contribute to the universe by their contributions as to a commonwealth; and how serviceable they are even to ourselves, if we use them with the knowledge of their fit adaptations? So that even poisons, which are destructive when used injudiciously, become wholesome and medicinal when used in conformity with their qualities and design; just as on the other hand, those things which give us pleasure, such as food, drink, and the light of the sun, are bound to be hurtful when immoderately or unseasonably used.[23]

Augustine goes on to declare: "For as the beauty of a picture is increased by well-managed shadows, so, to the eye that has skill to discern it, the universe is beautified even by sinners, though, considered by themselves their deformity is a sad blemish."[24]

7. For Augustine, the doctrine of creation declares that space and time are the creation of God and do not exist apart from the creation. This is an article of faith, for none of us has been present at the beginning of time or at the edge of space. We cannot imagine time or space having either a beginning or an end. All of our thinking must be done within the context of space and time, which we do not fully comprehend.

For Augustine and the ancient theologians such as Gregory of Nyssa (330–395) and Athanasius, the Christian doctrine of time was set over against the notion that time continually repeated itself. When time is understood to have no beginning and no end, achievement in history becomes impossible. As Marcus Aurelius said, "How many a Chrysippus, how many a Socrates, how many an Epictetus has time already swallowed up? And let the same thought occur to thee with reference to every man and thing."[25]

For Augustine time had a beginning and a goal. It was filled with unique unrepeatable events that would be embodied in history. Moreover, all history moves toward God's consummation of history and creation in the new heaven and the new earth. Time was more than chronology. It was a dimension of the human self and of human history.

> It is manifest and clear that there is neither times future nor times past. Thus it is not properly said that there are three times, past, present, and future. Perhaps it might be said rightly that there are three times: a time present of things past; a time present of things present; and a time present of things future. For these three do coexist somehow in the soul, for otherwise I could not see them. The time present of things past is memory; the time present of things present is direct experience; the time present of things future is expectation.[26]

Karl Barth has spoken eloquently of space and time as God's gifts.

> Creation as history fashions the world as a sphere for man who is to be a participant in this grace. And it fashions man as a being who precisely in this sphere is to become grateful to God for this grace and to correspond to it. As creation is itself history, the Lord of the subsequent history of the covenant will not really enter a strange land which does not belong to Him from the very outset, but in the words of John 1:11 will come to His own possession, so that even if His own people will not receive Him, they will have no excuse on the score that they were not His from the very outset.[27]

Barth very suggestively defines the patience of God in terms of God's provision of space and time for sinful human beings, space and time that they do not deserve.

> We define God's patience as His will, deep-rooted in His essence and constituting His divine being and action, to allow to another—for the sake of his own grace and mercy and in the affirmation of His holiness and justice— space and time for the development of its own existence, thus conceding to this existence a reality side by side with His own, and fulfilling His will toward this other in such a way that He does not suspend and destroy it as this other but accompanies and sustains it and allows it to develop in freedom.[28]

8. Creation means that unity and diversity are alike the will of God. In human history monistic philosophies have frequently sought to reduce all things to one. The spiritual practices of Eastern religions and of many mystics likewise move toward the absorption of the individual into the unity

of all things. At other times the diversity of creation has been exalted at the expense of unity. The Christian doctrine of creation teaches that all creatures and things are the one creation of God and that each particular thing or being has its place guaranteed by the creator. Creation is the one work of God; yet within creation individuality, diversity, and plurality are likewise established by God's decree.

9. The Christian doctrine of creation ascribes a special place to human beings in the created order. The Bible is a very anthropocentric book (see, e.g., Genesis 1–2, Psalm 8, Matthew 6:25–34), and theologians from the beginning down to Karl Barth have affirmed the special place of human beings in the created order: "He (in His humanity) is the centre of all creation, of the whole reality of which the creed says that God created it, that it has duration and existence through God alone."[29]

Some theological and philosophical writers have recently argued that the centrality of human beings is no longer tenable in so vast and mysterious a universe.[30] No one, it is said, can be aware of black holes and still affirm Psalm 8.[31] On the other hand, some scientists who deal with the immensities of space are also overwhelmed by the utter improbability that human beings could ever have come into existence or that they would come into existence if they were not already a reality.[32] The confidence that intelligible beings exist elsewhere, a very widespread conviction a few decades ago, is now much more modest. The place of human beings in the presence of God is independent of what may or may not be true for the existence of intelligible beings elsewhere. Christian theology has always affirmed God's particular concern for each human being, and for his people.

> But now thus says the LORD,
>     he who created you, O Jacob,
>     he who formed you, O Israel:
> Do not fear, for I have redeemed you;
>     I have called you by name, you are mine.
>
>                                        Isaiah 43:1

Psalm 8 in the Old Testament and Matthew 6:25-34 in the New Testament are integral to Christian faith, to the Christian doctrine of creation as it has been traditionally formulated. This doctrine affirms that God called human beings into existence, that he knows them by name, that he redeems them by his love. The significance of human life is not the mystery of the human being and cannot be attributed to the wonder of our biochemical existence or the achievement of culture, but to the conviction that the Creator addresses each human being by name and that human life is fulfilled by no earthly achievement. No finding of the physical or social sciences establishes the value of a human being.

The dominion over nature that is ascribed to human beings in scripture (Genesis 1:28; 2:15, 19–20; 9:1–7) and was generally affirmed in theology until the last few decades is an aspect of this central position given by Christian theology to human beings in the created order. Critics of this doctrine have asserted that it has led to the exploitation of nature in the Western world. It is also demonstrably true that this capacity to exercise dominion over nature has contributed much to the maintenance of the natural order and enhanced human life on this planet. In the Western world generally, floods, earthquakes, and tornadoes create far less havoc than they do in areas of the world where the capacity of human beings to exercise dominion over nature has not been recognized or developed. In any case dominion over nature must be understood in the light of accountability to God, the creator. Dominion must be consonant with the faith and cannot be arbitrary and exploitive.

10. Christian theology has also spoken of "orders of creation" and of "natural law." Orders of creation refer to those structures that God has embodied in the being of nature itself that determine human life. Examples of the orders of creation are the unique, indissoluble relationship between one man, one woman, and one child, or the order between children and parents, or the necessity and structures of the civil order. Natural law refers to the will of God as embodied in creation and as accessible to human reason. The natural law tradition was taken over by Christian theologians from the Stoics in the second century and remained a part of Christian theology until modern times.

The orders of creation and natural law have been called into question in contemporary theology. Throughout the history of these traditions, the clarity of the will of God in the orders of creation and in natural law has been obscured, especially by human sin. Furthermore, human beings have used the orders of creation and natural law to justify practices that are disruptive of other affirmations of Christian faith. The breakup of Christendom, in which society itself recognized the origin of the created order in the will of God, has contributed to a loss of influence for orders of creation and natural law.

The Bible (Romans 1:18–32; Acts 14:15–18; 17:22–23) and Reformed theology[33] admonish believers to pay attention to what nature teaches. Paul Ramsey, a contemporary ethicist, has warned that the more human action deviates from the order of nature, the more seriously the moral ramifications of that action should be observed.[34]

11. The created world includes all intelligible beings. Angels, evil spirits, and the devil appear throughout the Bible, and theologians down to Barth have given them serious attention. The basic teaching has always been that all intelligible beings are created and are therefore finite and dependent. Second, any evil spirit or devil is a "fallen" angel. All intelligible creatures were created good and subject to God.

In a secular society angels have a problematic place. They are scorned by the same persons who are caught up in the excitement of intelligible beings on distant planets, an expectation that is much more sober today. In addition, Andrew Greeley, a sociologist, has noted that those who banish angels frequently fill their place with the fantasies of science fiction.[35]

Barth is rightly insistent that the question of angels must not be answered on the assumptions of a secular culture or an alien philosophy. It must be answered by listening to scripture and in the light of the faith. Some who have listened to scripture have often been sure of the presence of angels. Moreover, those who have lived in the midst of monstrous evil have been convinced of the reality of the devil.[36]

Any Christian doctrine will insist that angels are created and that they do the will of God. The devil is not the opposite of God but a creature subject to God's rule. The implausibility of angels in a secular culture is itself a reason Christians should be open to the possibility of angels and to the accounts of scripture.

12. The doctrine of creation calls forth a piety that includes wonder, humility, and thanksgiving in the presence of the created order.

The world is a wonder, a mystery, an expression of purpose and of love. Hence the world cannot be, for those who believe in the creator, a dead, inert thing with no purpose or meaning. The only proper response is a sense of wonderment and awe in the presence of so great a mystery.

The world is also a mystery beyond our comprehension. Only those who are convinced that the universe is simply a chance happening, an accident or the product of forces with no prevision of their end can overlook the mystery, the sheer miracle of the world and especially of human life.

The psalmist has expressed in a very apt manner the response of those who experience the world as a wonder of God's creation.

Bless the LORD, O my soul. . . .

You set the earth on its foundations,
  so that it shall never be shaken.
You cover it with the deep as with a garment;
  the waters stood above the mountains.

At your rebuke they flee;
  at the sound of your thunder they take to flight.
They rose up to the mountains, ran down to the valleys
  to the place that you appointed for them.
You set a boundary that they may not pass,
  so that they might not again cover the earth.

You make springs gush forth in the valleys;
  they flow between the hills,
giving drink to every wild animal;
  the wild asses quench their thirst.
By the streams the birds of the air have their habitation;
  they sing among the branches.
From your lofty abode you water the mountains;
  the earth is satisfied with the fruit of your work.

You cause the grass to grow for the cattle,
  and plants for people to use,
to bring forth food from the earth,
  and wine to gladden the human heart,
oil to make the face shine,
  and bread to strengthen the human heart.

O Lord, how manifold are your works!
  In wisdom you have made them all;
  the earth is full of your creatures.

Psalm 104:1, 5–15, 24

John Calvin wrote that the knowledge of the creator means first of all that one will not "pass over in ungrateful thoughtlessness or forgetfulness those conspicuous powers which God shows forth in his creatures."[37] This means the believer will reflect "upon the greatness of the Artificer."[38] It also means "to recognize that God has destined all things for our good and salvation but at the same time to feel his power and grace in ourselves and in the great benefits he has conferred upon us, and so bestir ourselves to trust, invoke, praise, and love him. Indeed, . . . God himself has shown by the order of Creation that he created all things for man's sake."[39] To acknowledge the creator and to know the world and human life as God's creation is to live with humility, gratitude, and thanksgiving.

John Calvin insisted that our use of the world should be guided by four principles. Proper use of the world is determined (1) by thankfulness, (2) by a sense of wonder, (3) by stewardship under God that uses the world for the purposes God created it, and (4) by vocation, an awareness of being called by God to live responsibly in his world.[40]

## CHAPTER 6

# PROVIDENCE

We confess and acknowledge one God alone, to whom alone we must cleave, whom alone we must serve, whom only we must worship, and in whom alone we put our trust. . . . By whom we confess and believe all things in heaven and earth, visible and invisible, to have been created, to be retained in their being, and to be ruled and guided by his inscrutable providence, for such end as his eternal wisdom, goodness, and justice have appointed, and to the manifestation of his own glory.

Scots Confession of Faith (1560), Chapter 1

And now do not be distressed, or angry with yourselves, because you sold me here; for God sent me before you to preserve life.

Genesis 45:5

But if God so clothes the grass of the field, which is alive today and tomorrow is thrown into the oven, will he not much more clothe you—you of little faith?

Matthew 6:30

We know that in everything God works for good with those who love him, who are called according to his purpose.

Romans 8:28 (RSV)

Hallelujah!
For the Lord our God
  the Almighty reigns.
Let us rejoice and exult
  and give him the glory. . . .

Revelation 19:6–7

The doctrine of providence is the conviction that God is personal and that God is personally active in all his creation, in nature and in history, preserving, sustaining, and governing the created order.[1] The heart of the doctrine is the conviction that the God whom we know in Jesus Christ is also the God who is personally active in nature and in history and in governing not only the affairs of the world but also the affairs of human life.

Emil Brunner defined providence thus:

> The idea of Divine Providence is also the absolute denial of the idea that the universe has no meaning, that things only happen by "accident." All that is, and all that happens, takes place within the knowledge and the will of God. Thus there is nothing "casual" about life, nothing that happens "anyhow." Everything that happens has its final ground in God. All that happens is connected with the divine purpose; all is ordered in accordance with, and in subordination to, the divine plan and the final purpose.[2]

Providence, according to Albert Outler, is God's provision of the energy systems, structures, and processes of the universe and of their openness to reason, love, and grace.

> When, . . . then, we speak of divine providence and purpose in Christian terms, we are trying to point to God's provision for the processes and prospects of the human enterprise. We are confessing our belief in God's resourcefulness in his dealings with any and all his human creatures, his unfaltering love in sustaining them in their wayward histories and his pardoning mercy in salvaging their corrupted aims and hopes. Providence does not mean the divine predetermination of historical events. It means rather the provision that such events may be affected by reason, grace, and hope. It means the provision of a community of faith and grace in which men may cultivate their consciousness of God's presence and imperative love, in Word and Sacrament, in faithful witness and sacrificial service.[3]

Providence, with its emphasis on the purposive action of God in the created order, stands over against doctrines that define human life in terms of chance, fate, fortune, astrology, or natural law. The conviction that human life as well as the universe is under the governance of a personal God whose grace has been made known in Jesus Christ came as great good news to the ancient world. Charles Cochrane argues that the Christians' doctrines of providence and predestination came as good news to those who felt oppressed by fate and fortune.[4] The providence of the Triune God was personal and established human personhood. It denied that nature is a "closed system of 'necessary' physical laws. 'The stars . . . are not the fate of Christ but Christ is the fate of the stars.' . . . Our souls, therefore, are by nature subject to no part of physical creation, even to that of the heavens."[5] Human personhood and freedom are established by the person-hood and freedom of the Triune God, whose providence governs all things. As a modern historian has observed, "Either you trace everything back in the long run to blind chance, or you trace everything to God."[6] Human life is lived within the personal providence of God or in the context of impersonal powers, so vividly set forth by Bertolt Brecht:

> Praise ye from your hearts the unmindfulness of heaven! . . .
> No one knoweth if you are still there.[7]

## Providence as an Article of Faith

Providence, like creation, is an article of faith. Karl Barth writes: "The Christian belief in providence is faith in the strict sense of the term, and this means first that it is a hearing and receiving of the Word of God."[8] Belief in providence "is simply and directly faith in God Himself, in God as the Lord of His creation watching, willing and working above and in world-occurrence."[9] Providence is not the consequence of contemplation or observation, nor is it a conclusion from an argument. Providence is given its peculiar form by the fact that it is the lordship of the God and Father of our Lord Jesus Christ. A believer comes to affirm providence not from observing the world but from participation in the worship of God and in reflection on the world in the light of that faith.

Providence is closely related to the doctrine of creation, and some theologians have tended to regard providence as an aspect of creation. Other theologians, such as Augustine, Calvin, and Barth, have maintained that providence must be treated separately. Only in this way can the independent reality of creation be maintained. The emphasis on creation as the activity of God that subsumes providence ends in a denial of the independent reality of creation. It does not clearly affirm the relative independence of that order.[10]

Providence is also closely related to the doctrine of predestination. Generally speaking, providence refers to God's total activity in observing, sustaining, and governing the created order. Predestination has to do with God's election of human beings. Calvin at first discussed predestination and providence together, but in the final edition of the *Institutes,* he discussed predestination at the conclusion of the Christian life. This location seems to suggest his conviction that predestination is best understood as one looks back over one's experience and reflects that God's grace preceded every human action.[11] More recently, Karl Barth has given predestination a place in his dogmatics prior to providence. The primary fact is God's election of his people, and providence is the means to that end. Barth writes:

> Predestination is more than a special example of the general divine government of the world. . . . Predestination is rather the presupposition, and its fulfilment in history the constitutive centre, of God's overruling, and the basis and goal of its realisation. In predestination we certainly have to do with the creature under God's lordship, but with the creature, i.e., man, as the object of the original, central and personal intention of God, with man as the partner in the covenant of grace made by God in and with creation. In providence, on the contrary, we have to do with the creature as such and in general; with God's active relation to the reality created by and therefore distinct from Himself.[12]

Barth's distinction between providence and predestination enables him to discuss providence in the context of an emphasis on the reality of the world. God has given the world an order, energy, and processes that work according to their created natures. Activity in the world is not simply God's activity but also the activity of God's creation. On the other hand, predestination is the more personal activity of God calling a particular individual or community to the fulfillment of the purpose for which the individual was created. Of greater significance is Barth's insistence that the grace of election is prior to creation and providence.

Karl Barth has emphasized the distinctively Christian character of a Reformed doctrine of providence with a clarity that is missing in Calvin as well as in later Reformed theologians.

> The Christian belief in providence is given its content and form, and therefore its distinction from other views apparently similar, by the fact that the lordship of God over the world which is its object is not just any lordship, but the fatherly lordship of God. And this "fatherly" does not mean only "kind" and "friendly" and "loving." It means all this, yet not abstractly, but on a specific basis. Similar attributes of the supreme ruler or principle of the world are to be found elsewhere, but only in a way which is non-obligatory, contingent and problematical. In the language of the Christian belief in providence, "fatherly" means first of all, quite apart from any such predicates and as their solid foundation, that the God who sits in government is "the eternal Father of our Lord Jesus Christ."[13]

The Reformed doctrine of providence was given classic expression by Zwingli and Bullinger in Zurich and Calvin in Geneva. For each of these theologians the doctrine of providence was of crucial importance as a statement of the doctrine of the all-governing God and also for Christian experience. Zwingli had "the strong sense of providence and God as the cause of all things."[14] Yet "providence for Zwingli is never simply a matter of the mind, seeking to understand the mystery of the world or the mystery of God's being. It evokes in the godly a response of wonder, gratitude and surrender to God."[15]

The most influential formulation of the Reformed doctrine of providence was provided by John Calvin, especially in the *Institutes of the Christian Religion*. As was true for Zwingli's theology, Calvin's doctrine of God emphasized power, energy, activity, and intentionality. Calvin likewise insisted that the Christian life is intensely focused on God's providence, asking what God is saying to us in the events of our lives. Calvin's doctrine was also characterized by its biblical character. In scripture we see God's providence at work and learn to understand it in our own lives. In the preface to his commentary on Psalms, Calvin outlines how he understands his own life in the light of the Psalms.[16]

The most striking characteristic of Calvin's doctrine of providence is his emphasis on the immediacy of God's personal activity in the created order. The falling of a leaf or a drop of rain occurs at the command of God.[17] This immediacy cannot be translated perfectly into the vocabulary of an age informed by modern science, though it is possible for true piety to affirm that what happens simply through the structures of the created order is still God's will.

Calvin himself acknowledged second causes, the structures and processes which God has established in the created order. He insisted that Christians should be diligent in making use of second causes. Calvin did not theoretically deny second causes, but in practical piety he believed that life should be lived with an awareness that every event, whether a routine operation or God's more direct and personal act, is God's act. Calvin, while greatly influenced by Augustine, minimized Augustine's emphasis on natures and structures as well as the concept of God's permitting evil.[18]

In his tracts Calvin discusses providence under three heads: the general governance of the world, the governance of human beings, and the governance of the church. He builds on the distinction that Augustine makes between nature and history. R. A. Markus has summarized Augustine's doctrine as follows:

> Augustine came to think of the creation of rational beings as introducing a forking of ways in the universe. Up to this point the processes established in the world could all be described as "natural." God was at work in a great garden, "giving growth even to the trees and to the grass." But at this point the divine gardener grafted reason into the universe "as on a great tree of things," and thereby inserted an element of novelty which could no longer be subsumed among "natural" processes. The activities of rational beings, though still present to God's providence were present to it in another way.

Providence henceforth operates through two channels: through the order of nature, and through the acts of wills and the events in which these issue. Augustine calls the providence behind the first *providentia naturalis,* that behind the second *providentia voluntaria.* Dependent on the two streams of providence, there are two kinds of order to be found in the world: the order of nature and the order expressed in human choices and enacted in human actions and its result. This duality of order in the world underlay all Augustine's later reflection on society.[19]

Calvin likewise insisted that God's providence was appropriate to the creation, to that over which it was exercised. God does not deal with human beings as though they were stones or pieces of wood but as persons with minds, affections, and wills.[20] Providence does not "intervene" or destroy the integrity of the creation.

Calvin understood God's providence as the means by which God accomplishes his purposes in the world and in particular his purposes in human communities. For this reason Calvin interrupts his doctrine of providence to include an entire chapter on the teaching and nurturing function of providence.

> Therefore the Christian heart, since it has been thoroughly persuaded that all things happen by God's plan, and that nothing takes place by chance, will ever look to him as the principal cause of things, yet will give attention to the secondary causes in their proper place. Then the heart will not doubt that God's singular providence keeps watch to preserve it, and will not suffer anything to happen but what may turn out to its good and salvation. But since God's dealings are first with man, then with the remaining creatures, the heart will have assurance that God's providence rules over both. As far as men are concerned, whether they are good or evil, the heart of the Christian will know that their plans, wills, efforts, and abilities are under God's hand; that it is within his choice to bend them whither he pleases and to constrain them whenever he pleases. . . .
>
> Gratitude of mind for the favorable outcome of things, patience in adversity, and also incredible freedom from worry about the future all necessarily follow upon this knowledge. Therefore whatever shall happen prosperously and according to the desire of his heart, God's servant will attribute wholly to God, whether he feels God's beneficence through the ministry of men, or has been helped by inanimate creatures. For thus he will reason in his mind: surely it is the Lord who has inclined their hearts to me, who has so bound them to me that they should become the instruments of his kindness toward me. In abundance of fruits he will think: "It is the Lord who 'hears' the heaven, that the heaven may 'hear' the earth, that the earth also may 'hear' its offspring" [cf. Hosea 2:21–22, Vulgate; 2:22–23, Eng.]. In other things he will not doubt that it is the Lord's blessing alone by which all things prosper. Admonished by so many evidences, he will not continue to be ungrateful.[21]

Later Reformed theologians would discuss God's governance of the world in terms of the three general categories of preservation, concursus or sustaining activity, and the governance of the world. Generally these theologies were more precise and exact than those of Augustine or Calvin, but they lack the awareness of mystery and a sense of the openness of the world to the freedom of God.[22]

Karl Barth has followed this same pattern but with greater imagination. He speaks of the Divine Preserving, the Divine Accompanying, and the Divine Ruling.[23] Providence, as is the case with the doctrine of creation, is an article of faith. It is derived from the revelation of God in the history recorded in scripture and in particular in Jesus Christ. Karl Barth's doctrine of providence has its focus in God, who as the king of Israel ordered and coordinated creatures and events into a community. In Israel and in the church one finds the revealed God with a revealed purpose.[24]

In this community there are four signs of the presence of God. The first is the Bible, by which Barth means not so much the text as its origin and transmission, its exegesis, and its influence in the course of history generally. "If we accept the witness of Holy Scripture, then implicitly we accept the fact that, quite irrespective of the way in which they were humanly and historically conditioned, its authors were objectively true, reliable and trustworthy witnesses."[25] Likewise, evidences of God's providential care are in the completion and transmission of the canon of the Old and New Testaments as well as in the place that exegesis and exposition had in human affairs. In a similar manner Barth emphasizes the history of the church and the history of the Jewish people as evidences of God's providential ruling in history.[26]

The fourth evidence is the limitation of human life. "All life has to be lived as limited life."[27] All people have to live within a definite limit, and this is one of the "traces which it is always and necessarily rewarding to contemplate as traces of the divine Lord of the world."

> It is still the case that I myself am a sign and testimony of the divine world-governance, and I myself am always present to myself: I myself, who am somewhere on the way between the beginning and the end, and conditioned by both; I myself, who once was not, and one day will be no longer; I myself, with my own individual life characterised by its individual limitation; I myself as the object of this disposing.[28]

The contemplation of the fact that human life has a beginning and an end, neither of which we choose or govern, leads to serious reflection that points in the direction of providence.

It is I who live, but both in my birth and in my death it is made clear that to live is something which I myself cannot take, or give, or maintain; something which is ordained and given to me. It is I who live, but in so doing I do not belong to myself; I am indebted to the power which ordained that I should live within the limits laid down not by myself but by that power. It does not make any difference whether we call the ordination permission or command; as permission it is command, and as command permission. And it certainly does not make the slightest difference whether we find it acceptable or otherwise. Obviously it is not for us to interpret it in either the one way or the other. Either way it is an ordination, an act of lordship, which encloses our whole life and to which we owe its spontaneity.[29]

The Christian doctrine of providence comes to its climax in eschatology, the consummation of all things by the power of God. The universe and human history do not end in chaos and debris but in the fulfillment of the divine purposes. This conviction was expressed with great drama in the concluding chapters of Isaiah (60–66) and also in the final book of the Bible, Revelation. Providence means that, now and in the end, God reigns.

## Providence in Contemporary Experience

The theological task now is to formulate the Christian doctrine of providence in a way that, on the one hand, is true to scripture and to the tradition and, on the other hand, illuminates contemporary experience, especially experience in the church. Any such effort will include at least five theological statements.

1. First, Christians all acknowledge that everything that happens is the will of God. No one has ever been more insistent on this than John Calvin.

There can be no doubt that the will of God is the chief and principal cause of all things. . . . God holds within Himself the hidden causes of whatever is made, and these are not made resident in created things. He gives effect to them not by the operation of providence by which he upholds the nature of things in being but as he administers them as he wills, so he created them as he wills.[30]

Hence Calvin rejects the unqualified distinction between God's permitting and God's willing. "It is easy to conclude how foolish and frail is the support of divine justice afforded by the suggestions that evils come to be not by His will, but by His permission."[31] Calvin quotes Augustine with approval:

So that in a wonderful and ineffable manner nothing is done without God's will, not even that which is against his will. For it would not be done if he did not permit it; yet he does not unwillingly permit it, but willingly; nor would he, being good, allow evil to be done, unless being also almighty he could make good even out of evil.[32]

Calvin was insistent that God's will is simple and one. Yet this will of God appears to us to be manifold because of our mental incapacity to grasp how in diverse ways God wills and does not will something to take place. Here again, Calvin builds on the teaching of Augustine. In contemplating providence it is necessary to acknowledge on the one hand that everything happens because God wills it, but then it is important to ask in what sense does God will it. Calvin, like Augustine, contended that some things happen according to God's will which are at the same time against his will. It is not enough, therefore, to affirm that the world and everything that happens are the will of God. We must also ask in what sense and in what way a particular event is God's will. Above all, the will of God must be understood not as fate and an impersonal power but as the personal activity of the Triune God.

The providence of God is expressed first of all in the rational and intelligible character of the created order, in its reliability and its consistency. These qualities of the created order can be described in textbooks in chemistry and physics and biology. They are also the basis for human life, for we plan our days on the basis of the consistency of this order. Things always fall down rather than up in this particular corner of the universe. Fire is always hot; ice is cold. Sunshine, rain and snow, seedtime and harvest come in patterns that we can anticipate and in large measure describe. The same consistent patterns of the universe which ensure that automobiles can be driven safely also are the occasion of terrible accidents. In human affairs the consistency of the universe has both its benign and also its terrifying qualities.

We have the responsibility of living our lives in the context of this world which we only partly understand. We can relate to it as a cold, impersonal fact, or we can relate to it in the words of the Sermon on the Mount: "But if God so clothes the grass of the field, which is alive today and tomorrow is thrown into the oven, will he not much more clothe you—you of little faith? For . . . your heavenly Father knows that you need all these things" (Matthew 6:30, 32). We can accept the reliability and consistency of the created order as God's gracious gift.

2. The doctrine of providence also affirms that it is God's will that

human beings should live in this consistent, intelligible world with the powers of *human freedom* and *self-transcendence.* Human beings can objectify themselves, set goals and organize the energies of life to achieve those goals. They can also violate the patterns, the consistencies, the intelligibilities of the world. Human freedom means that a human being can organize the energies of life for works of compassion, love, and mercy and live for the glory of God. On the other hand, this same freedom means that human beings can organize all of life's energies in the pursuit of selfish purposes and the denial of the rights of other people. God chose to create human beings with power and freedom, so that they can grow to be mature persons. God could have made human beings creatures of instinct and impulse who live as the animals do, so far as we know; but God chose to endow human beings with freedom so that they can break the chain of instinct and impulse and organize the energies and vitalities of human existence pursuing a goal that arises out of personal decision.

3. God's will for a consistent universe and God's will for human beings to be free give qualities to the natural world and to human history that are important for the life of faith. The first is the impartiality of the universe in its relationship to human beings. The universe does not play favorites. Human life is placed in the context of law-abiding, consistent structures. There is no neat and simple correlation between goodness and one's fate in this world. Infectious germs, defective genes, the implacability of a consistent natural order provide an impartial and in one sense impersonal context for the living of life. As the Gospel of Matthew puts it, the Father in heaven "makes his sun rise on the evil and on the good, and sends rain on the righteous and on the unrighteous" (5:45).

The question must be asked, Why did God make the world impartial to all people, to good and evil alike? The reason must be that God designed the world not for human comfort but as a school for character, as a vale of soul making. The Puritans liked to insist that the purpose of the human journey in the context of the world of nature and through human history was growth into the image of God and preparation for the fruition of life in the celestial city. Human life came to be described as a pilgrimage.

A mature person by definition cannot be created. Maturity comes only through personal decisions. God could have created perfect animals, but God could not without contradicting himself create perfect human beings. The perfection of human life involves the decision of the human heart and comes through growth of character and personhood, as will be indicated in a later chapter.

When Rome fell to the barbarians, Augustine was asked why it was that Christians were so badly treated. He first answered that, on the contrary, many of the Christians found safety in the refuge of the church, for the gospel has been preached even in an Arian form to the barbarians. But this was not Augustine's real answer. Augustine said that the difference between people is not in what happens to them but in how they respond to what happens to them.[33] The world deals with Christians and non-Christians alike with amazing impartiality. Christians differ from other people not in what happens to them so much as in the fact that they respond to what happens to them with faith, hope, and love. The world therefore must be understood not as a place designed for human comfort, so much as the provision of a context in which human beings can grow into the fullness of Christ.[34] Admittedly the understanding of the world as a school for character or a vale of soul making does not solve all problems. The questions can be still asked, Is the suffering not excessive? Could not the purposes of God have been achieved in a world less brutal and at times less capricious to human beings?

The consistency of the natural order and human freedom mean that the world is precarious as well as impartial. Neither a good person nor an evil person, neither strong nor weak, can make human life secure. An astronaut can orbit the earth only to trip over a rug or fall in the bathtub. No human effort can take the risk out of life or guarantee its future. Accidents happen in this world to good and evil alike. If we ask why God made the world precarious and liable to human accidents, the reason must be to teach us to trust in him. As no human achievement fulfills life, so no scientific, political, economic, or social achievement can give life security in nature or in history. The security of the human creature is only in God.

As Jesus put it, we cannot by taking thought add inches to our height or years to our life (Matthew 6:25–33). Although we have learned how to add a few inches to height and a few years to life, human life remains fragile and limited. Our political, economic, and social achievements likewise remain fragile and finite. Hence Matthew 6:25–33, the heart of the Sermon on the Mount, remains the heart of human piety as well as the embodiment of the doctrine of providence in human life.

4. Providence not only means that God made the world with consistency and intelligibility and decreed that human beings should be free; it also means that God made the world so that it is open to reason, love, and grace. This is true on the human level. Human reason can mitigate the damages of floods and tornadoes and earthquakes. Agricultural studies

can develop plants that grow in areas with little water. In many ways the world is open to human reason. It is also open to love, as when human beings aid one another and thus modify the ravages of nature as well as the violence of human history. On the human level history is open to grace, particularly in relationship to other human beings, whereby the gracious favor of one person transforms the life of another. Grace in the human heart may also open up possibilities in nature that would not be available apart from this graceful response.

Providence means that the universe is open to the grace and the love of God the creator. God did not create the world and then abandon it to run itself, nor does God simply supply the energies and the processes for the universe and human life. Christian theology has always insisted that God works personally in the created order. The discussion here presupposes what was said about transcendence and immanence under the doctrine of God. God's relationship to the world can best be conceptualized in terms of personal analogies. The ways in which God is transcendent and immanent in the world are analogous to the way a human being is transcendent and immanent in his or her work. The personal activity of God in the created order does not mean that God arbitrarily interrupts or intervenes in the created order, but that the divine will moves the created order in ways analogous to the way the human self moves the human body without disrupting the natural processes by which the body lives. The universe is not a closed system. It is constantly open to God.

The openness of the created order to God's grace and the conviction that God is personal are the base for the conviction that some events are "acts of God," or miracles. On a fundamental level everything is an act of God. Apart from God's willing nothing would exist. For this reason Schleiermacher said, "Miracle is simply the religious name for an event."[35] In this sense everything is an "act of God." Miracle, in the New Testament meaning of a sign or wonder, is an event perceived by faith to be the focused personal act of God in distinction from world occurrences that are the will of God for the structures, processes, and energy systems of the created order.

Nathaniel Micklem suggests that a human blush is the best analogy to the way God works in the world, which is finally beyond our power to conceive. The origin of the blush is very much in the life of self, the embarrassment of the self. It expresses itself in the flushing of the face yet without disrupting the biochemical processes in the human face.[36] Miracle, as God's personal act, does not "intervene" in or disrupt nature, for nature is responsive to his will. When a person raises his or her arm, that action can be explained totally in scientific terms without uncovering the real reason the arm was raised, namely, the decision of the self to raise the arm. In an analogous way God may work in the world or in human acts that are intensely personal. Events in nature and history can be perceived only by the eyes of faith to be acts of God or miracles. A miracle is not an event that we do not understand, for no event is really understood until we see the hand of God in it.[37] A miracle is an event in which God's personal activity is focused and is perceived by faith.

"Acts of God" or miracles may not differ from other events when scientifically or historically analyzed. They are not interventions in the sense of disrupting the structures and processes of the natural order. They can be perceived only by faith and repentance.

In scripture and Christian piety some events are called "acts of God" or miracles, because in them God's presence is focused and in them the believer perceives God's purposive action. In these events God makes himself known as he is not known in the routine events of life. An analogy is seen in human life. A person may perform many routine functions without revealing who he really is. The decisive revelations of the self are found in critical events, in response to a crisis, when a person's presence is focused. God, who is personal, will reveal himself more in some actions than in others.

5. The Christian doctrine of providence becomes clear in the Christian conviction that God is personal and that God personally sustains and governs the created order.

The Christian doctrine of providence includes God's governing the world as well as God's preserving the world and concurring in all of its activities. God's ruling the world means that all events, natural and historical, occur under God's lordship and that the history of the universe as well as human history moves to the conclusion that God has ordained. The doctrine of providence presupposes that God is the creator and that God is personal. In providence as in creation the crucial question is not so much the reality of God as it is the character of God. The Christian doctrine of providence presupposes that the God who provides is the God and Father of our Lord Jesus Christ.

God's governance of the world cannot be demonstrated from a study of the world; evidences of it can be found in the signs of design and intentionality in the natural order. God's providence can be seen also in the self-destructive character of evil. Human evil is overruled by the natural order: rivers, mountains, seas, space, and time. Daniel Day Williams has written that the redemptive activity of God becomes real to us in the destruction which God visits upon intolerable evil.

Wrath means that life has within it certain ineluctable structural principles which can be defied only at the risk of losing the good of life itself. When these are defied there is set in motion whether in individual life or in the social order, a chain of consequences which may take the form of vast destruction and misery; or which may work silently in an individual soul in the loss of meaning of life, the fading of the glory.[38]

Evidences of God's ruling and overruling can also be seen in history, when it is viewed from the light of the Christian faith; however, this evidence is likewise always ambiguous. The doctrine of providence is based first of all on God's revelation of himself in scripture and above all in Jesus Christ.

## Providence as the Universal Lordship of God the Father

The Christian doctrine of providence means that the Christian lives under the universal lordship of God the Father.[39] What does it mean for the Christian to live under the providential care of God?

The Christian doctrine of providence involves the recovery of an awareness that the world is God's creation, in which we know God's presence. This awareness goes beyond the emotional and the aesthetic. It includes rational reflection on how God works in his creation and on the various forces that play their roles in the events in which we participate and which happen to us. Any such reflection must relate human life first of all to what seems to be the stable order of the universe. To live under the providential care of God is to *accept* God's ordering of the universe, his provision of the structures, the natures, and the processes and energy systems of the world as God's gracious gift.

The world has structures, processes, and natures as well as energy systems which can be analyzed in the laboratory and described with some precision in scientific textbooks. Scientific study has enabled us to harness these powers for human good. We can fly an airplane overcoming the problems of space, and we can devise medicines to protect us from many diseases. The scientific description of the universe is very impressive, not simply in what it has contributed to our comfort and convenience but also in the completeness of the explanation. Modern people have confidence that the secrets of the universe will be open to investigation and disclosure. In actual fact, the universe is not as open to our investigations as it first appears. On further examination, the secrets of how the universe operates seem very resistant to our mastery of them by human intelligence. Yet our knowledge of how the world works is sufficiently impressive that it has obscured the more fundamental question of why there is a world anyway and why it works at all.

The doctrine of providence begins with the cultivation of the awareness that the universe is God's creation, operates by his power, and is subject to his rule. G. K. Chesterton once declared that the sun rose every morning because God said, "Get up!"[40] George Buttrick argued that the regularity of nature is but the faithfulness of God.[41] These statements contradict the seemingly independent structures and processes of nature. Can we sing and mean that God has brought us safely through another day or week? Can we praise God every morning for the rising of the sun, seeing in it evidence of a providence operative not only in its creation but also in its continuing care and ever-present activity? For twenty centuries a piety that affirms God's personal activity has been at the heart of the church's life. To live under the providential care of God is to be aware that the universe is open to God's personal acts. To live under the providence of God is to pray knowing that God hears our prayers and responds to our petition. It is this faith in God's providential care that makes prayer more than meditation and an exercise in self-development.

Christians must live their lives in a universe that operates according to the structures and processes and energy systems that have been given to it in God's created order. This universe, as has been indicated, is very impartial. Yet life within this universe need not be conceived of as fate but as God's gracious gift in which we may learn to live with the awareness that the God who cares for the lilies of the field also cares for his people. Living in the providential care of God's world means a life of faith, obedience, and prayer. In the context of the impartial structures of nature, Christians trust God, seek to do his will, and pray for manifestations of his love and spirit that cannot be anticipated simply on the basis of nature itself.

Living under the providential care of God finally means living with the awareness that the grace of God is universal. In every event in the world and in particular in every event in human life, there is always God's grace. The tragedy, the frustration, or the evil in the human situation is never the last word. The last word is the grace of God, which enables those who love God to bring good out of every event.

Calvin encouraged Christians to find in the doctrine of providence a means of deepening and enlarging their own Christian life. This means the acceptance of the world as the expression of God's personal will, not as a fate or as a fortune that is imposed upon us.

The Christian heart, since it has been thoroughly persuaded that all things happen by God's plan, and that nothing takes place by chance, will ever look to him as the principal cause of things, yet will give attention to the secondary causes in their proper place. Then the heart will not doubt that God's singular providence keeps watch to preserve it, and will not suffer anything to happen but what may turn out to its good and salvation. But since God's dealings are first with man, then with the remaining creatures, the heart will have assurance that God's providence rules over both. As far as men are concerned, whether they are good or evil, the heart of the Christian will know that their plans, wills, efforts, and abilities are under God's hand; that it is within his choice to bend them whither he pleases and to constrain them whenever he pleases.[42]

This conviction gave a certain serenity to Christians living in a precarious and uncertain world.

Calvin in addition believed that providence was a means by which God teaches an individual person the meaning of his or her own life. Each person must ask the significance of events, challenges, and crises for growth as a Christian believer and as a member of the Christian community. In prosperity and in adversity alike, the Christian asks, What is God teaching through these particular events? What does it mean to be a person living in this particular time and in this particular place? The Christian doctrine of providence therefore confronts us not with the unraveling of the mysteries of the universe but with the focusing of our own lives so that they embody the divine purposes.

The Heidelberg Catechism answered the question of the meaning of providence in this way: ". . . that we are to be patient in adversity, grateful in the midst of blessing, and to trust our faithful God and Father for the future, assured that no creature shall separate us from his love, since all creatures are so completely in his hand that without his will they cannot even move" (Question 28).

## CHAPTER 7

❖

# THE HUMAN CREATURE

The being of man . . . rests upon the election of God; and . . . it consists in the hearing of the Word of God.

Karl Barth, *Church Dogmatics* III/2, 142

O LORD, our Lord,
   how majestic is thy name in all the earth! . . .

When I look at thy heavens, the work of thy fingers,
   the moon and the stars which thou hast established;
what is man that thou art mindful of him,
   and the son of man that thou dost care for him?

Yet thou hast made him little less than God,
   and dost crown him with glory and honor.
Thou hast given him dominion over the works of thy hands;
   thou hast put all things under his feet,
all sheep and oxen,
   and also the beasts of the field,
the birds of the air, and the fish of the sea,
   whatever passes along the paths of the sea.

O LORD, our Lord,
   how majestic is thy name in all the earth!

Psalm 8:1, 3–9 (RSV)

The Christian doctrine of the human creature can be summarized under four heads: (1) the human creature as created by God, (2) the human creature created uniquely in the image of God, (3) the human creature broken by sin, and (4) the human creature redeemed in Jesus Christ. The first three topics will be considered in this chapter, and the last in a series of chapters on Jesus Christ and the redemption that God wrought in him.[1]

## The Human Being as Creature

The Bible is clear in declaring that human beings are creatures. "The LORD God formed man from the dust of the ground, and breathed into his nostrils the breath of life; and the man became a living being" (Genesis 2:7).

> All people are grass,
>     their constancy is like the flower of the field.
> The grass withers, the flower fades,
>     when the breath of the LORD blows upon it;
>     surely the people are grass.
>
> Isaiah 40:6–7

What does creaturehood mean for human life?

1. It means that human beings are defined by the purpose of God the creator. A human being is a child of God. God thought of each human being before that human being was, and God has called each human being into existence and given to each one an individuality, an identity, a name. From beginning to end the Bible clearly affirms that God knows each human being by name.

2. Creatureliness means that human life is not self-explanatory. It cannot be defined by scientific analysis, by biochemical, physical, psychological, or social studies. The meaning of human life is determined by the creator. Why did God create human creatures and for what purpose?

3. The good God created human beings, and therefore human existence is good. Each life is a gift from the graciousness of God and must therefore be received with gratitude and thankfulness. What each person claims for himself or herself must also be attributed to every human creature.

To exist as a human being is good, and human creatures rightly rejoice in their existence as well as in the time and in the place in which, in the providence of God, they do exist.

4. To be a creature is to be limited and dependent. Each person is dependent on powers and forces outside himself or herself. Modern science has enabled us in remarkable ways to make use of the created world, but there is no evidence that human beings will ever be able to exempt themselves from dependence on the powers and energies and processes of the created order. To be created is to be dependent, dependent not simply on the powers that we experience in everyday life but dependent on the creator whose will brought the creation into existence.

To be a creature is to be limited by time and space. A creature can be in only one particular space—here and not there. A creature knows not only the shortness of his or her time but also its irreversibility. To be a creature is to be young only once. Just as we cannot occupy all space, the human creature has to accept the limitation of time and learn to "number our days" (Psalm 90:12, RSV).

As creatures, human beings are limited not only by space and time but also by energy and intelligence. Each of us has been given just so much energy, and when it is used up human life ceases on this planet and in history. We have also been given just so much intelligence. Even the most intelligent cannot comprehend all that human beings desire to know. Moreover, we know everything only as it can be known from our particular situation and perspective.

5. The limitations of creaturely existence come to focus in death, which is universal. It limits all human achievements, personal and public. The New Testament describes death as the last enemy to be destroyed (1 Corinthians 15:26). Death, as part of God's creation, is not in and of itself evil; but it becomes the occasion of great evil when it is faced without trust in God, who is the creator and the redeemer. Thus death is not only the symbol of our creatureliness; it is the final test of faith.[2]

## The Uniqueness of the Human Creature

Christian theology affirms that human beings are creatures, but unique creatures. This uniqueness is recognized apart from faith and has been defined in many ways. Within the Christian community the "image of God" has been the symbol of human uniqueness (Genesis 1:26–28). The task here is to summarize in a brief and comprehensive way what is generally accepted by all Christian people. The classic text is Genesis 1:27–28.

> So God created humankind in his image,
>   in the image of God he created them;
>   male and female he created them.
> God blessed them, and God said to them, "Be fruitful and multiply, and
> fill the earth and subdue it; and have dominion over the fish of the sea. . . ."

What does it mean to be made in the image of God? Claus Westermann, an Old Testament scholar, has summarized the meaning of the text in this way:

> The creator created a creature that corresponds to him, to whom he can speak
> and who listens to him. The strength of this explanation is only seen when
> the question is put in another form. It is not one of many possible answers

to the question "What is the image and likeness of God or in what does it consist?" But an answer to the question: "What is the meaning of this further determination in the account of the creation of human beings?" It consists in determining further the nature of the act of creation which enables an event to take place between God and humans; it is not a question of equality in human beings. . . . This means that the creation of human beings in the image of God is not saying that something has been added to the created person but is explaining what a person is. There is no essential difference between the creation of humans in Genesis 1:26 and Genesis 2; the person is also created by God as his counterpart in Genesis 2 so that something can happen between the creator and the creature. The difference is that Genesis 2 expresses it in story form and not in conceptual terms. . . . God has created all people "to correspond to him," that is so something can happen between creator and creature. This holds despite all differences among people; it goes beyond all differences of religion, beyond belief and unbelief. Every human being of every religion and in every place, even where religions are no longer recognized has been created in the image of God. . . . Seen from another point of view, the sentence means that the uniqueness of human beings consists in their being God's counterparts. The relationship to God is not something which is added to human existence; human beings are created in such a way that their very existence is intended to be their relationship to God.[3]

To be created in the image of God means that human beings have the uniqueness as well as the essential meaning of their existence defined by their relationship to God. To be created in the image of God is to be answerable, responsible to the creator.

Christian theology has spent much effort defining the image of God in terms of those structures and capacities of human existence that make possible the personal response to God. The uniqueness of human beings has been variously defined in terms of cranial capacity, in terms of tool making, and in particular in terms of the powers of the human mind. The human mind is a most remarkable capacity. It has the ability for language, for conceptual thought, and for analysis. It can read off the facts of the world. To some limited extent it can even think the world without observation. It enables human beings to understand the world that the creator has made. William Temple declared "that next to a life of love the human mind in the service of God is the most wonderful thing in all the world."[4]

The uniqueness of human existence can also be described in terms of language which is more than sign making. As will be discussed later, language is a means of human self-transcendence as well as the means by which human beings can engage in deeply mutual relationships.

Language enables human communities to be organized beyond the association that is established by instinct and impulse and geography.

The uniqueness of human beings can be also defined as the power of memory. Augustine was always deeply moved by the wonder of human memory, which enables human beings in some measure to transcend time. Augustine said that if no one asked him, he knew what time was; but if someone asked him he had difficulty saying. He concluded that time was best understood as a dimension of the human soul. There are three times, he concluded: time past, which is memory, time present, which is experience, and time future, which is anticipation. In every human experience time past and time future concur in the present event.[5]

A cultural memory enables human beings to build on the achievements of the past. Animals, so far as we can tell, build on their own contemporary achievements. They cannot build on the achievements of previous generations of animals. Human beings have a cultural memory, and therefore they do not have to begin life anew with each human birth. The achievements of the past are conserved in individual memories and in cultural memories. Each generation, for example, does not have to rediscover fire, or invent the wheel or the airplane. Each generation builds on what previous generations have achieved.

Yet Augustine found the real uniqueness of human existence not in the mind, not in language, not in memory, but in the power of the human self to objectify itself and to transcend itself. Human beings have the remarkable capacity to regard as an object their own existence. They are not only conscious; they are also self-conscious. They can stand outside themselves and reflect on their past, their present, and their future. This capacity of the human self to transcend itself gives it a remarkable freedom.[6]

This capacity provides the freedom to transcend instinct and impulse. Animals, so far as we know, are creatures of instinct and impulse. Therefore for animals eating and sex are not moral problems; they are determined by instinctual needs. Moreover neither eating nor sex is complicated by the power of the human mind and imagination. For human beings eating and sex are never simply natural acts. They are always complicated by the human spirit. Yet this capacity to transcend instinct and impulse gives to human beings a certain measure of freedom. When food is placed in the presence of a hungry dog, the dog eats. When food is placed in the presence of a hungry human being, the human being may or may not eat. The human creature has the capacity to deny himself or herself food in order to feed hungry people a thousand miles away who are not visible to the eye. Or a human creature may simply want to lose weight. This power of the human self to transcend itself, to objectify itself, to reason about its own behavior, to imagine what cannot be seen, gives every human being in some measure a power and a freedom over the demands of instinct and impulse.

The power to objectify human existence also gives human beings the capacity to transcend their culture. Every human being knows that he or she was born in a certain situation and by reflection can comprehend the various ways history and culture have shaped human life. Moreover, each human being has the capacity to imagine himself or herself being born in a radically different culture and in a very different geographical location. This capacity of the human self to transcend the self gives us a certain knowledge of how culture determines our lives and also a certain freedom from that determination.

This power to objectify the self and to transcend the self gives the human creature a power over his or her past and a capacity to exercise some freedom in shaping the future. By the power of self-objectification, a human creature knows that he or she did or said or failed to do or say certain things yesterday. The power of transcendence gives one the capacity to stand in judgment on one's past, to praise oneself or to blame oneself. It is this capacity, which enables us to take the past and to use it in the achievement of a future, that at least in some measure is freely chosen. The transcendent self has the unique capacity to organize all of the energies and vitalities of human existence, or at least an amazing number of them, in the pursuit of a goal that has been formulated through this power to objectify one's own existence and to transcend one's self.

The power of self-transcendence also enables every human being to transcend every human achievement. For this reason, no human achievement ever exhausts the possibilities of life. Every human creature knows there is always something more. No act of love ever exhausts the possibilities of love. Each act of love opens up new possibilities. The power of self-transcendence means that human beings can be satisfied finally with no earthly achievement. No matter how great the achievements may be, the human self knows there is something more. Augustine took the power of human transcendence to mean that the human self reaches out toward God by its very nature as the creature made in the image of God. As Augustine himself put it, "Thou hast prompted him, that he should delight to please thee, for thou hast made us for thyself and restless is our heart until it comes to rest in thee."[7]

To be made in the image of God means that every human being is created to respond to God and that the fulfillment and meaning of life are in hearing the word of God.

To be a man in responsibility before God is to know God. Man knows God because God declares to him His Word, and therefore first knows him. For this reason it takes place as a spontaneous act of gratitude, in which the history inaugurated by God becomes man's own subjective history, that, following on that divine knowledge by the Word as thunder follows lightning, man knows God. Thanksgiving is a readiness to acknowledge. It is a matter of knowing the God who tells man in his Word that He is gracious to him, and therefore of knowing this benefit. But the Benefactor Himself, His own saving and keeping initiative on behalf of mankind, is this benefit, just as His Word in the creaturely mode of existence is again Himself, God the Creator. To know grace as His work is thus to know God Himself as the gracious God. As this takes place, as man does this, he fulfils his responsibility before God and therefore fulfils his own being.[8]

The image of God is not simply a formal capacity. It also has a content embodied in human life. Christian theology finds the content of the image described in the New Testament. First, the content is Jesus Christ, who is "the image of the invisible God" (Colossians 1:15), who is the "reflection of God's glory and the exact imprint of God's very being" (Hebrews 1:3). The manner of the life of Jesus—his words, his deeds, his friendship with persons such as Mary, Martha, Lazarus, and Mary Magdalene, his eating with sinners and thereby bringing them into God's presence, his death on the cross—this is what it means to live in the image of God. Second, the content of the image is embodied in the forgiven and sanctified person. Sanctification is the process of transforming human life into God's image so that human life is responsive to God's grace. Thus, the New Testament passages that have to do with how Christians live in the world and how human life is transformed by the grace of God also describe the content of the image of God.

Traditional Reformed theologies spoke of man's original state as one of "original righteousness." In the light of what we know about human origins it is now difficult to conceptualize a historical period of human existence as one of original righteousness, except as a period comparable to the innocence of childhood. Yet the persistence of some golden age in human imagination is also grounds for continuing to take the doctrine of original righteousness seriously. Original righteousness is the "memory" we have of our original creation, or, as Reinhold Niebuhr writes, our consciousness of "original righteousness" is in the moments when the self transcends itself and history and remembers its origin and true destiny.[9]

In defining the content of original righteousness, Niebuhr distinguishes

between the essential nature of man and the virtue and perfection which would represent the normal expression of that nature. The essential nature of man contains two elements; and there are correspondingly two elements in the original perfection of man. To the essential nature of man belong, on the one hand, all his natural endowments, and determinations, his physical and social impulses, his sexual and racial differentiations, in short his character as a creature imbedded in the natural order. On the other hand, his essential nature also includes the freedom of his spirit, his transcendence over natural process and finally his self-transcendence.[10]

The virtues that correspond to the first element of human nature are the laws of nature. Even though everything a person does is influenced by the human spirit, the requirements of a human being as a creature of nature remain.

The virtues that correspond to the freedom of the spirit are faith, hope, and love. The content of this "original righteousness," which even a sinful person has—not as a possession but in the sense of something lacking—must be further explicated.

It contains three terms: (a) The perfect relation of the soul to God in which obedience is transcended by love, trust and confidence ("Thou shalt love the Lord thy God"); (b) the perfect internal harmony of the soul with itself in all of its desires and impulses: "With all thy heart and all thy soul and all thy mind"; and (c) the perfect harmony of life with life: "Thou shalt love thy neighbour as thyself."[11]

The Genesis account of creation speaks of the dominion of the human creature over animals and of the command to subdue the earth. In recent years some have contended that this scripture has led to the exploitation of animals and of the earth by Christian people.[12] Yet in this context "subduing" and "dominion" must be understood in terms of the conviction (1) that God is the creator of the earth and of all living things, (2) that God sees his creation as good, and (3) that human beings are made in the image of God and are therefore answerable to God. The human being's relationship to the rest of creation is that of a person who is responsible to the creator.

In Genesis the fruit trees and plants are food for human beings and animals alike. In Genesis 9:3 divine permission is given for human beings to use animals for food. Dominion over the earth does not mean that the human creature can do anything he or she chooses. It does mean that human beings, who are also creatures, must exercise dominion as persons accountable to the God and Father of our Lord Jesus Christ.

# The Human Creature as Sinner

The third Christian affirmation declares that human beings have been broken by sin. The goodness of creation is a basic rubric of Christian theology. How then did sin enter into human history?

## The Origin of Sin

The most pervasive and influential answer at least in Western theology and literature is based on the story of Adam and Eve in Genesis 3 and as expounded in the theology of Augustine and given imaginative literary expression in Milton's *Paradise Lost*.

Adam and Eve appear created as mature human beings. (For Luther and for Milton they resemble college graduates.[13]) Their lives were in perfect harmony until they ate the forbidden fruit. In this act they understood one part of the created order (the fruit) in the light of another part of the created order (the serpent) without any reference to God.[14] Sin in its basic form is living life in terms of the creation with no reference to God, or—as Augustinian theologians have put it—it is aversion to God and conversion to the created order.[15] This sin had disastrous consequences for Adam and Eve and for their posterity. Their eyes were opened; they knew good and evil; they were ashamed of their nakedness. They were cast out of the garden, and childbearing, toil, and tilling the earth were complicated by this sin. The sin of Adam and Eve did not affect themselves only; it became the heritage of the human race.

How shall we understand this account of the origin of human sin in the light of our knowledge of how human beings appeared on this planet. It is not likely that we shall ever know precisely how human beings emerged in the history of the universe, but all that we do know contradicts the story of the Garden of Eden, if understood as history. The writer used the language of history to convey what is the truth about human origins, but origins to which we have no witness.

Augustine understood more clearly than any theologian before him that once sin happened, human history was forever changed. No child is any longer born into a situation of innocence. The sins of the society and the sins of the parents precede the child and corrupt the child.

How the sins of the parents affect the child and how sin is passed on from generation to generation are in part mystery. Thus Augustine, who was aware of the mystery, was perhaps too preoccupied with sex and especially with sexual intercourse as a means of transmitting sin and guilt.[16] Augustine knew that every act of sexual intercourse is complicated by the human spirit and therefore complicated by human sin, by such sins as envy, greed, selfishness, and irresponsibility in bringing children into the world without the acceptance of responsibility for their nurture.

Original sin became embodied in the structures of society in the moral failures of the family. The simple fact is that no child, however fortunate, is born into a situation of innocence, but into a situation in which sin is already present, in which sin limits the possibilities of his or her life and, more than that, corrupts human life.

Original sin is passed on in the mysterious ways one human life penetrates another human life, especially in the intimate relationships of life. There is good evidence that a child's personal life begins before birth.[17] There is also good evidence that a child's experiences at birth and immediately after birth make it easier or more difficult to trust God later.[18] The relation of genetics and biochemistry to original sin is difficult to comprehend. Certainly original sin is not some biochemical component that is passed on, as it were, in the blood. Sin centers in the self, not in one's physical nature (animals cannot sin). Yet the increasing evidence of the influence of one's physical nature on human conduct is reason for caution in discussing the transmission of original sin, as well as the actual freedom a person has over genetic inheritance, over instincts and impulses, over the consequences of glandular and biochemical factors for human conduct and for faith itself.[19]

The older theologians—for example, John Calvin and the writers of the Westminster Confession of Faith—insisted that original sin was a source not only of corruption but also of guilt. Some recent Reformed theologians have insisted only on corruption. Yet in human life secularists who are amused by the doctrine of original sin somehow conclude that children to the second and third generation are accountable for their parents' and grandparents' "sins." In recent years there has been a proclivity among social activists to speak of the sins of groups and of the accountability of new generations for the sins of older generations. The history of the doctrine of original sin should provide some warnings about glibness in talking about the transmission of sin from generation to generation and about the guilt of groups.[20] At the same time, the fact that in the secular order guilt is believed to be transmitted from generation to generation and that groups are guilty suggests that theologians should give more attention to these factors. Original sin, someone once said, is the only Christian doctrine that is empirically verifiable.[21]

The doctrine of total depravity is closely related to the doctrine of original sin. This doctrine, as Calvin formulated it, does not mean that a person is totally evil. It does mean (1) that all people are sinners, (2) that every dimension of the human self is corrupted by sin, and (3) that the bondage of the will is total at the crucial point of human existence, so that a sinful person cannot turn from self and the world to God through his or her own efforts. The problem to which the so-called doctrine of total depravity points is the inability of a self-centered person to become unself-centered by his or her own efforts. Certainly self-centeredness can be overcome within limits, but self-centeredness remains. The self-centered individual becomes unself-centered in his or her family, or church, or race, or nation. The final dilemma of life is that sinful pride can be cast out only by more sinful pride, as T. S. Eliot put it.[22]

Calvin and Reformed theologians after him emphasized the *bondage* of the will. By bondage they meant that the will cannot escape from itself unless some outside power elicits a willing response. A selfish will is free to be a selfish will, but it does not have the ability to be what it is not. The human will is free, Calvin insisted, in that it is not coerced or constrained by some external power. The will is not free to choose what it is not. The will is under the necessity of being what it is. A person's will is enslaved to itself. The powers of self-transcendence by which the self objectifies itself and reflects on itself does provide some freedom of choice. Yet the self in its self-transcendence is still the sinful self. The highest human freedom is the power of the human spirit to recognize its own bondage. The final human predicament, the bondage of the will, is that the self-centered self cannot become God-centered by trying hard. This is the human situation to which predestination is addressed. God's grace encounters the human will and elicits a willing response. This ultimate human predicament has many human analogies. An ungrateful person cannot become grateful; a proud person cannot become humble; and an unloving person cannot become loving by trying hard. Grace alone—divine grace or, on the human level, human grace—can save the self from the bondage of an evil selfhood.

The origin of sin is a deep mystery for which no rational explanation has been possible. Indeed, no rational explanation is possible, for then sin would not be sin. It would be justified by some cause or condition. Christian theology has always insisted that human sin does not have a cause apart from the freedom of the human self.[23] Yet Christian theology has never affirmed that human beings invented sin. In the Genesis narrative it is the serpent who entices and corrupts Eve, so the origin of sin is pushed back from human beings to the devil. With greater imagination human sin has been explained in terms of the fall of the angels, who in turn corrupted human life. Kierkegaard said that sin always posits itself.[24] We would not sin if sin were not already present.

The simple fact is that there is no rational reason why human beings created in the image of God should turn against God. In this sense, as Emil Brunner insisted, human sin is utterly irrational and beyond explanation. If we could explain it, it would not be sin.[25]

Augustine, in the most influential conceptualization of human origins and the first human sin, conceived of Adam and Eve as mature individuals. Other theologians have conceived of the first human beings more as infants or as children who are learning how to live in God's world and who learn what it is to be truly human somewhat by trial and error.[26] In this sense, the tempter is the fascination of the created world, which turns human beings away from God. The first sin, therefore, would be comparable to the fall a child suffers as the child learns to skate. In order to learn to skate one must try, and in these initial efforts there will be many falls; but through the falls one comes to the maturity of a competent skater. Irenaeus conceptualized human origins very much in this way. Augustine's way of conceptualizing the human origins had the advantage of affirming the goodness of creation and also of making the first sin all the more inexplicable. The Irenaean way has the advantage of greater intelligibility in the light of what we know of human origins, but it also minimizes other basic Christian doctrines such as the goodness of creation as well as the mystery of human freedom and the mystery of human sin that cannot be rationalized.

## The Nature of Sin

Sin is personal. It is the condition, disposition, and direction of the person. Hence we speak of people as sinners. Yet sin is also expressed in acts that are called sins. Fundamentally sin is aversion to God, the living of life without regard to God.

Sin is *unbelief* or unfaithfulness. Augustine, John Calvin, and Reinhold Niebuhr always insisted that this is the fundamental sin out of which all other sins flow.[27] Unbelief in this sense must not be understood as the denial of propositional truth. Unbelief is an emptiness or a rejection of a trustful confidence in God the creator and the redeemer. Unbelief is an aversion to God, and out of this fundamental sin all other sins flow.

Sin is *pride*—that is, self-centeredness—determining everything by its relation to the self. Augustine and Calvin and the mainstream of Western theology have always regarded pride as the most pervasive form of sin.[28] Reinhold Niebuhr in a remarkable analysis has pointed to the ways that pride leads to brutality, to injustice, and to dishonesty.[29]

Sin can also be understood as *rebellion*. Rebellion emphasizes the dynamic quality of sin and underscores the fact that sin is a rejection of God, the forsaking of God, the leaving of God.

Sin has also been understood as *disobedience* to the law of God. Here the law of God is understood as God's personal presence and gracious will for humankind. This understanding of sin is very helpful. Yet when law becomes simply a matter of prescriptions and regulations it does not adequately express God's will. Sin when conceived as disobedience sometimes leads to an imagery of God as an army sergeant barking out orders and a soldier obeying.

Sin is *idolatry*. The prophets of the Old Testament spoke vigorously against idols. From the very beginning of Reformed theology, idolatry has been a major definition of sin.[30] Idolatry is the worship of the creature rather than the creator. On the religious level idolatry is the attempt to have a manageable God, to identify God the creator with some object that is within our control, whether it be the bread and wine in the sacraments or the techniques of an evangelist or a political or social reality such as the state. On the practical level idolatry is making some created good the center of life and "the revelation" in the light of which life is understood. Thus money, sex, fame, for example, may become the focus that orients life and the object to which many give their highest devotion.

Sin is *apathy* or *sloth*.[31] This sin, known as acedia, frequently appeared fourth on medieval lists of the seven deadly sins. It can be translated as sloth, apathy, indifference; yet it is something more than this. Apathy is a loss of enthusiasm for life, a "don't care" attitude, a giving up on the meaningfulness not only of personal existence but of human history and the world in which we live.

Karl Barth has a very remarkable passage on sloth.

> In its form as man's tardiness and failure, sloth expresses more clearly than pride the positive and aggressive ingratitude which repays good with evil. It consists in the fact, not only that man does not trust God, but beyond this that he does not love Him, i.e., that he will not know and have Him, that he will not have dealings with Him, as the one who first loved him, from all eternity. In relation to God there is no middle term between love and hate. . . . It may be that this action [sloth] often assumes the disguise

of a tolerant indifference in relation to God. But in fact it is the action of the hate which wants to be free of God, which would prefer that there were no God, or that God were not the One He is—at least for him, the slothful man. This hatred of God is the culminating point of human pride too.[32]

Sin has also been understood as the *privation of the good* or *nothingness*. It is the falling away from creation, and it therefore has no real existence. Sin is what God does not will, and therefore, finally, it is nothingness.[33] Augustine, who insisted on the goodness of creation, thought of sin as a falling away from creation. Insofar as something truly is, it is good.[34]

Sin as the privation of good is closely related to the character of sin as parasitic. A truly sinful society could not exist. There has to be honor even among thieves for a community of thieves to maintain order. Sin cannot exist on its own.[35] It always has to live parasitically on the good.[36] Hence the notion of sin as privation or falling away from real existence contains some very important insights into the nature of sin itself. Sin, because it is not willed by God, always in the end self-destructs.

Sin is also understood as *sensuality* and is preeminently regarded as sensuality in popular thought. Sensuality creates havoc in human relationships and anarchy in society; generally in the end, it becomes repulsive. Hence, it is understandable that for many persons sin is equated with sensuality.

The understanding of sin as sensuality must be formulated in such a way as not to deny the goodness of the impulses, vitalities, and instincts of life. God's gift of food and the joy of eating together must not be obscured by the sin of gluttony. The significance of sex in the propagation of the human race and in the mutuality of human love must not be denied by the perversions of sex. The created order, the world of nature, of food, of sex, of drink, is good. God created human beings to be sensual; sensuality as sin is a perversion of human creation.

Sins of sensuality are self-limiting. While they are obviously very destructive, the extent of their destruction is limited by the nature of the sin itself. For example, a glutton can eat only so much. Sins of sensuality soon reach satiety. In addition, sins of sensuality always in the end become repulsive and self-defeating. Sins of sensuality therefore are in contrast to sins of pride and greed, which are unlimited. No one ever has as much fame or money or power as he or she desires. Hence sins of the spirit, such as pride and greed, are far more devastating in human history than sins of sensuality, which occupy so much of our time and attention.

Sins of sensuality may be an expression of pride, preoccupation with oneself and with one's own happiness and joy.[37] Sins of sensuality may be idolatry when the object of one's love is made the center of one's life.

Sins of sensuality may also be closely related to apathy, as an attempt to escape from life. Unable to face the crises, challenges, and decisions of life, a person loses himself or herself in the stream of nature—in alcohol, in drugs, in sex, or in gluttony. In this sense sensuality is a sin of escape.

Søren Kierkegaard, the great Danish theologian and psychologist, distinguished sins of strength from sins of weakness.[38] Sin is on the one hand a person's attempt to be more than a human being. This sin of pride issues in injustice and dishonesty as human pretensions have to be supported by power and wealth and falsehoods. There are also sins of weakness, in which human beings seek to escape the responsibilities of human life.

Sin finally and most decisively must be understood by Christian people in the light of the revelation of God in Jesus Christ.[39] We do not really know what sin is apart from this revelation. Jesus Christ not only reveals God's intention for human beings and creation but, in revealing God's intention, also makes known what God does not intend, namely, sin. The various ways in which the Christian tradition has understood sin must always be reexamined in the light of the reading of the Gospels and our knowledge of what Jesus Christ said and did. In our knowledge of what Jesus Christ said and did sin takes the form of unbelief, of failing to trust the Father in heaven, who cares for the lilies of the field and the birds of the air. Sin is the action of the prodigal who leaves his father's home. Sin is self-righteousness, the conviction that one is already good and does not need salvation (Matthew 9:9–13). Sin is the refusal to receive mercy. The only people whom Jesus could not help were not the rich or the outcasts or those whom society regarded as sinners, but those who did not know they needed the physician, those who did not want to be helped. In the light of what Jesus said and did one has to conclude that self-righteousness and the arrogance of those who think they are already good and do not need help is a fundamental form of human sinfulness. No neat summary of sins can be formulated in the light of the revelation of God in Jesus Christ. We have in the life of Jesus a portrait—a statement not in propositions but in human life and personhood—of our true human destiny, in the light of which we know our failures.

Sin is a defiance of God. It is also the corruption of the good. We sin in our best deeds as well as the worst.

## Specific Questions

The doctrine of the human creature raises many questions that have not been covered under the discussion of the human creature as created in the image of God and as the sinner. These will now be discussed briefly.

## Soul and Body

The Bible does not contain a neat and finished anthropology, but throughout the scriptures there is the assumption that human beings are soul and body. The word "soul" has a strange sound in a secular culture, and it is well to begin by noting that the closest synonyms to "soul" in common speech are "self," "I," or "person." Charles Hodge defined the soul as that reality of which one is immediately self-conscious and which expresses itself through the body. The soul "is that which thinks and feels, which may be saved or lost, which survives the body and is immortal. The soul is the man himself, that in which his identity and personality reside."[40] Karl Barth defined the soul as the person or the self in all of its powers and reasoning, of willing, of self-transcendence.[41] The soul is the self that contemplates the self and organizes all the energies and vitalities of life for freely chosen goals.[42] The soul is the human being in his or her knowledge of God and in the awareness that human life is not simply animal existence of instinct and impulse. The soul hears the word of God.

Traditional theology has spoken of the soul as immortal. The New Testament also speaks of immortality. Yet in Christian theology any use of the concept immortal must be qualified by two emphases: (1) The soul is created and must be sustained by the creator. It is not divine or self-sustaining. (2) The soul cannot be isolated from the body through which it expresses itself and its own historical existence and identity.

The Bible always emphasizes the unity of soul and body, and nowhere does it depreciate the human body.[43] The soul has a body as a creation of God. It is on the one hand a sign of the goodness of God, and it is on the other hand a sign of the creatureliness of a human being. The body means that we can be only in one place, that we are subject to many physical limitations, and that finally we die. Yet the Bible never depreciates the body. The body is united to the soul. It is the means through which the soul expresses itself. The body enables human beings to make their calling as hearers of the word of God concrete and actual in history.

The relation of the self and the body is very complex. There is no generally agreed scientific or philosophical understanding of the relationship. "The link between brain structures and processes on the one hand and mental dispositions and events on the other is an exceedingly difficult one."[44] It may well be that the true understanding of the self and the body, especially the brain, will never be resolved. Materialists of one kind or another think of the self or the mind as a function of the brain. Yet there is good reason to insist that the self uses the brain as its instrument.

Wilder Penfield, in an autobiographical essay, states that he began his work believing that the mind was a function of the brain, but after years of practicing neurosurgery he came to the opposite conclusion. He observed that he had through manipulation of the cerebral cortex compelled people to recall memories that they had forgotten, to see things more vividly than they had ever seen them before, to utter words and to make bodily movements. However, he had never been able to elicit a truly personal response in which the person said I do this or I choose this. The person always declared, You made me do this. Thus Penfield concluded that no one could elicit a truly personal response by manipulating the brain.[45]

The mind is not an instrument of the brain, but the mind uses the brain as a computer or as its own instrument.[46] John Eccles, a neurologist and Nobel Prize winner, concluded:

> The self-conscious mind is not a powerful operator upon the brain, it is an interpreter, attempting to get meaning out of it and gradually to modify it, as we know when we are actively searching for meaning, or searching for words, or causing actions. It is not power that distinguishes the brain action, but the fact that we can operate it voluntarily by taking thoughts. I think the point I want to make is that even though there is a brain machine behind the whole interpretation, yet the interpretation itself in a meaningful manner is . . . an integrated achievement of my self-conscious mind.[47]

The mind is, for Eccles, best understood as a special creation of God.

Contemporary people sometimes imagine the possibility of building a machine that can think as does a human being.[48] No one has yet done it, and it may be more improbable than many optimistic modern people think. In any case, the likelihood that human beings can ever create a machine with the capacities of the human self to transcend itself, to organize its energies by the power of the human will in the pursuit of a freely chosen goal, to devote life to a great cause, to live with love, sympathy, and devotion defies imagination or even science fiction.

Christian theology has never committed itself to any particular doctrine of the origin of the human soul. It has always affirmed without equivocation that the origin of human beings and of each human being in particular is the will and purpose of God. The way in which God's will is accomplished in the history of the universe and in the emergence of each human person is a mystery. John Eccles was so impressed with the wonder of human existence that he came to reassert the old doctrine of ensoulment, that at a particular point God creates a soul in each human being.[49] Some theologians in the early church tradition understood the origin of the human soul in terms of traducianism. This doctrine insisted that all souls were in Adam and were passed on to his posterity. On the other hand, other theologians insisted on creationism, that each human soul is a particular creation of God.[50]

The critical Christian doctrine is that each human soul or person is God's creation and that God knows the person by name. The soul or the person has a body through which the soul expresses itself and makes concrete its personal decisions in human history.

## The Human Creature as Worker

According to the creation narratives in Genesis, "human existence includes occupation or work. . . . Work is regarded here as an essential part of human existence. Life without work would not be worthy of human beings."[51] The work that God mandates "is part of human existence because the living space which the creator has assigned to his people demands work."[52] While sin has made work less pleasant, work as such belongs to those activities that are distinctive of human existence.

No theologian has ever understood that more clearly than John Calvin.

> We know that God does not expect us to be lazy, living in this world. . . .
> Even before sin came into this world and we were thus condemned by God
> to painful hard work, it was already necessary for men to exert themselves
> to some work. And why? Because it is against our nature to be like a useless
> tree trunk. Thus it is quite certain that we need to apply ourselves to some
> type of labor our whole life long.[53]

Again Calvin writes, "Nothing is more unseemly than a person who is idle and good for nothing, who profits neither himself nor others and seems born only to eat and drink."[54]

To be human is to work or at least to desire to work. In the New Testament Paul admonishes Christians to bear their own loads as well as to bear their neighbor's burdens (Galatians 6:2–5), and he commanded the Thessalonians, "If anyone will not work, let him not eat" (2 Thessalonians 3:10, RSV).

## Male and Female

Barth has insisted that the creation as male and female is closely related to what it means to be made in the image of God.[55] Yet the significance of male and female can be exaggerated in that this does not distinguish human beings from other creatures. Animals are male and female. Identity as male and female indicates what it is to be God's creatures. The words of Genesis, that God created human beings male and female, that it is not good for man to be alone, that God created woman as a "helper fit for him" do not necessarily or primarily refer to the sexual relationship between men and women, but constitute a paradigm of the human community.[56] The truly human is neither male nor female but man and woman in community. Barth has argued there is no such thing as a self-contained and self-sufficient male life or female life.[57] "In the Lord woman is not independent of man or man independent of woman" (1 Corinthians 11:11).

God did not make human beings to live alone, and the fullest development of human life is always life in community. Individuals who live in large measure alone are still human beings and may achieve elemental community, but their aloneness impoverishes life. Certainly marriage is not necessary for truly human existence, but it is a paradigm and the most intense form of the relationship between human beings that is essential for our humanity. God made us not simply as individuals with our own identity but also to live in community with and for each other. Claus Westermann writes,

> A human being must be seen as one whose destiny it is to live in community; people have been created to live with each other. This is what human existence means and what human institutions and structures show. Every theoretical and institutional separation of man and woman, every deliberate detachment of male from female, can endanger the very existence of humanity as determined by creation.[58]

Marriage as the paradigm of human community must not be conceived of only as sexual attraction.

> The Bible nowhere bases marriage simply on the basis of sex but includes it in marriage. Family, social and economic elements as well as the part parents have played in the arrangement of the marriage of their children have a very significant role in both monogamous and polygamous marriages in the Old Testament.[59]

God created human beings as individuals whom he knows by name, and he also created human beings to live in community with one another. No one can be a true human being in isolation from other human beings, and no one can be a truly human being in community without first being an individual. God created both individuality and community. Even in community, as one flesh, we remain male and female.

Individuality and community, human differences and unity, are alike the creation of God. The differentiation of male and female is given to us in creation. Christians have often depreciated their creation as embodied human beings, but the reality is: we are embodied human beings. Male and female are not interchangeable, as the birth of every baby makes clear. This is the goodness of creation in which Christians rejoice. Differences of culture, nationality, language, and even race are less structural and embodied, but they too are none the less real.

Human beings, however, are not only embodied human beings. They are also mind, will, and spirit that give to every human being the power to transcend human differences. The deepest human difference, greater than male or female, culture, nationality, or race, is faith. Faith distinguishes people on the deepest level of human existence. Within the context of Christian faith Paul declared, "As many of you as were baptized into Christ have clothed yourselves with Christ. There is no longer Jew or Greek, there is no longer slave or free, there is no longer male and female; for all of you are one in Christ Jesus" (Galatians 3:27–28). There is a unity that transcends the differences, yet within the unity the differences remain and enrich human life as part of God's good creation.

## Sexuality

Sexuality is a powerful energy in human life and community. It is also part of God's creation. In an increasingly secular society how are we to understand sexuality?

1. Christian theology declares human sexuality to be a created good. This means that human sexuality has all the limitations of created existence. It is dependent on the creator; its powers are finite. Finally, as part of the created order, it cannot fulfill the meaning of human life, however much it may enhance it.

2. Human sexuality also reminds human creatures of their limitations. Augustine, the great theologian of the fifth century, was himself personally and theologically distraught by the power of sexual energy to overrule the human will. Human sexuality reminds us of the created existence we share with animals and also of the limited power we have as human beings. Augustine knew that sex was a part of the created order, a part of paradise, but in paradise it is subject to the human will.[60]

3. Human sexuality is a created good. Yet the power of human sexuality to overrule the human person, to lay bare the interior life of the person, and to create anarchy in the human community has led many people to think of sex as dirty, as shameful, and as destructive of human life.[61] Over against the notion of sex as dirty and shameful, Christians in our society have joined with a secular culture in celebrating sex. Sex ought to be

celebrated, as is true of all the energies and vitalities of life; but in order for it to be truly celebrated, it must be celebrated in the context of a faith that human existence is more than sex and the vitalities of nature. Sex must be affirmed as part of the goodness of God's creation and therefore, when celebrated in an ordered life, a means of good for human beings and human community alike.

4. Christian theology not only declares that sex is a created good, but it also declares that sex is never a purely natural act, as it may be for animals. When the Kinsey report emphasized sex as a natural act, Reinhold Niebuhr was vigorous in his reply that no human act is ever simply a natural act.[62] Every human act is complicated for good or for evil by the human spirit, by the human will, and by the human imagination. For human beings sex serves many purposes that range far beyond animal desire. Every sexual act for human beings is intensified by the powers of the human imagination and by the capacity of the human self to set goals and purposes for human existence. This means for human beings that sexuality can on the one hand be far more destructive than it is for animals, and on the other hand it can be creative of far greater good than is possible in mere animal existence. The critical point that Christian theology makes is that human sexuality is never purely a natural act but is always an activity of a human person made in the image of God.

5. Christian theology affirms that human sexuality is the means by which God has willed that the human race should be replenished in all the earth. One of the first commands in Genesis is to replenish the earth (Genesis 1:28). Human sexuality is the means for procreation. No human act surpasses the dignity and the responsibility of bringing a new human life into existence. No human acts are more fraught with possibilities for good and evil than the bringing of a child into the world. God has established as an order of creation that a relationship exists between this man and this woman and this child which is unique, unrepeatable, irreversible, and unbreakable.

Because procreation for human beings is not simply a natural act, there is a fundamental difference between the breeding of rabbits and two human beings covenanting together to bring a new human being into existence. The silence of the church and the silence of our society on the great personal significance and responsibility of the decision to have a child is one of the tragedies of our time. No sin is fraught with graver consequences for individual human beings and for society than the procreation of children by human beings acting on the level of animal existence, that is, without responsible decision and without accepting the responsibilities of this act.

The social witness of the church begins with an emphasis on human responsibility in bringing children into the world.

6. The human body is the medium through which the soul or the self expresses itself in words, action, and also in sexuality. Human sexuality, as is the case with the human voice and with the human hand, is a means by which human beings express themselves to other people. It confirms and enhances the words that humans speak and thus becomes a means of community. Its form ranges from a handshake, to a facial expression, to a touch, to a hug, to sexual intercourse, which is in a qualitative, personal way as well as in a physical way the most intense unity human beings experience.

Human sexuality as a means of human expression and communication can either enhance or damage human life and community, as is true of all human communication. From speech to sex, integrity and mutuality are crucially important, and the more serious the words or intense the act, the greater the need for integrity and love. The level of truth and love must be appropriate to the words or to the act. This is what it means to be human, and this is what distinguishes human sexuality from animal sexuality. Love and truth are the tests of all human relations. Sexual intercourse without the commitment appropriate to it is demonic.

Human sexuality can enhance human life in community, or it can become prurience and pornography. The *Wall Street Journal* (February 9, 1973) in a film review declared the movie *Last Tango in Paris* to be pornography, primarily "because it conceives man totally in terms of his erotic being, because it separates his sexual identity from his total identity, and makes everything that it presents relative to the exotic sequences at its core." When separated from love and when separated from the whole of responsible personal existence, the exercise of human sexuality always is prurience and pornography. Animals are never guilty of prurience or pornography, but human beings have the self-determination and self-transcendence to corrupt God's gracious gift of sexuality.

7. The New Testament's relative silence about human sexuality must be taken with great seriousness by the church in a secular society that exults in the "celebration" of sex. Neither does the New Testament have a developed doctrine of marriage or of what we today call the Christian family. For Jesus and for Paul the family is subordinate to the kingdom. A person must be willing to forsake wife or husband for the sake of the kingdom (Matthew 10:34–39). One who is married should be able to rejoice in living with one's spouse, but also in the freedom to live without a spouse (1 Corinthians 7:29–31). Marriage in the New Testament is

understood as a response to the command to replenish the earth; as the means of ordering the vitalities of life; and, with less emphasis than in Genesis, as a means for human community and for the fulfillment of the human self. Later Calvinists, especially the Puritans, came to understand marriage as the fulfillment of the purposes of God in society and history.[63]

The early Christian community took over the traditional mores concerning marriage and family. Yet in so doing they transformed marriage, for they insisted that these standards are now to be observed "in the Lord." Children are to obey their parents "in the Lord" (Ephesians 6:1). Fathers are not to provoke their children but bring them up in the instruction of the Lord (Ephesians 6:4). Wives are to be subject to their husbands, which was the custom of society, but Paul added "as to the Lord." The husband is head of the wife as Christ is head of the church. Yet Paul begins this instruction by saying that, in the ordering of family and society, husbands and wives are to be "subject to one another out of reverence for Christ" (Ephesians 5:21).

The relationship between father, mother, and child is the structure of physical, biological, psychological, and covenantal reality, and for it there is no equivalent alternative. Yet there is no final doctrine of family or home in the New Testament. The traditional Protestant family has embodied Christian faith and has been enormously beneficial to the church and to society, but it is not the only form of Christian life. The family in one form or another is universal, and Christian faith modifies those forms by insisting that they must be "in the Lord" and according to his teaching. Christians are not free to invent any form of the family or any life-style they wish. The nuclear family has been established in creation and confirmed by Jesus Christ.

There is little in the New Testament about marriage as the embodiment of God's purposes or about the relationship between a man and a woman in marriage either enhancing human personality or building up community life. The New Testament speaks very little about the positive role of human sexuality or marriage and the family.[64] This silence should be understood in terms of the historical situation. Celibacy was thought to be an aid to Christian vocation. It freed persons to do what otherwise they could not accomplish. This has been the most responsible justification of celibacy in the Christian church—that is, celibacy as a means to Christian vocation, not as a higher form of Christian life.

The sublimation and minimizing of human sexuality seemed necessary to the worship of God and the cultivation of a new way of life in a pagan, erotic society. The early Christians were in protest against the magnification of sexuality in a pagan society. They believed the time was short, and so they advised believers to forgo marriage if they were able. Widows were advised to remain widows unless marriage was necessary for the ordering of human vitalities and energies (1 Timothy 5:3–16).

The New Testament's relative silence concerning sexuality must be understood also in the light of the protest of the prophets against Canaanite religion. The religion of Baal exulted in the vitalities and energies of life; sexual energies disclosed the meaning of life, and temple prostitutes became part of worship. The New Testament stands clearly over against a paganism that found life's meaning in the enhancing of human vitalities. It looked askance at ecstasy produced by human sexuality. The New Testament's emphasis is on the personal, moral, historical character of human existence and on sex as a created but limited good.

The Christian doctrine of human sexuality may be developed as a part of the doctrine of creation that the New Testament everywhere affirms. The God and Father of our Lord Jesus Christ is also creator of the world. This means that the world is good and that it is part of Christian piety to rejoice in the world, and in the gift of sexuality. Christian doctrine of human sexuality is also enhanced by those passages in the Old Testament, and in particular the Song of Solomon, which exult in the wonders of sexual love.

## Homosexuality

Homosexuality, which has become a focus of discussion in the church, is the occasion for questions, not only about sexuality but also about human existence. As homosexuality arouses passionate opinion, any consideration must have as its first intent neither to approve it nor to defame it but to understand it. Understanding is not simple, as studies thus far do not seem to be conclusive. Homosexuality appears to be both a constitutionally disposed and a learned behavior.

The scriptures (e.g., Leviticus 20:13 and Romans 1:27) consistently condemn homosexual practices.[65] The Christian community has likewise consistently rejected homosexual practices up until recent years, when some exceptions have been made. Homosexuality is not an order of nature or a created determination of the two sexes as are the relationships between male and female. As a personal and historical activity, it cannot perpetuate itself and is dependent for its existence on the sexual union of male and female.

Christian theology has no basis for idealizing homosexuality, much less for accepting it as an alternative to heterosexual relationships or as God's

will for human life. Even as a constitutional "given," it cannot be ideal-
ized any more than other constitutional dispositions, such as excessive
aggressiveness.

Christian theology cannot legitimize homosexuality, yet it must take
seriously the "given" character of homosexuality, the constitutional determination of life, just as it must respect other constitutional "givens" in
life. Homosexuality may always be abnormal, but it is not always perverse.
The Christian community must on theological grounds insist on charity
and pastoral care and support. This emphasis is in accord with the example
of Jesus, who was always more lenient with those who were guilty of sins
of the flesh than with those who were guilty of sins of the spirit, especially the sin of self-righteousness.

## The Beginning of Life and Death

The beginning of the life of the human creature and the end of historical
existence in death are lively concerns today because of public controversies
about abortion and medical care for the old and the dying. In the light
of these controversies it is imperative to affirm that life is good; and, more
than that, it is God's gracious gift. Christians have a strong bias to life
in all moral decisions. God wills life. This is true of the life of a tree, of
a dog, but above all of a human being. Yet God's will for life is not God's
only will. In scripture and in theology there are warrants for taking the
life of a tree, of a dog, and even of a human being.

Human beings have been created as persons made in the image of God
with gifts of reason, will, and self-transcendence. They are created to live
not by instinct and impulse or social pressure but in accord with faith and
by moral decisions. This personal responsibility comes to focus in the bringing of a human being into existence and in attitudes toward those whose
historical existence is ending in death.

Just as sex is never simply a natural act for human beings, the bringing
of a child into existence ought to be a very personal and responsible act
between a man and a woman. This emphasis on responsibility before God
in "replenishing the earth" must be emphasized in theology because it is
not emphasized in a secular society and even in the contemporary witness
of the church.

Christian theology is emphatic that each human soul or person is the
creation of God and is known by him by name. Yet the Bible does not
teach and Christian theology has no doctrinal consensus about when a
human being comes into existence.[66] Some theologians have argued that

a human being comes into existence at the moment of conception,[67] and at the other extreme it is argued that individual human life exists only at birth.[68] Theologians as distinguished as Augustine did not know when a human being comes to be.[69] Gratian's *Decretum* (1140), a summary of ecclesiastical legislation, distinguished between the "formed" and the "unformed" fetus. Scientific knowledge of the growth of the fetus can point to significant developments and dates, but none of this data is conclusive.[70] In any case, from the beginning the fetus is life destined to be a human being, life that is potentially human, perhaps a form of human life.[71]

Any decision about abortion must include deep and profound respect for all life and especially human life as a gift of God. It must include an assessment of the consequences for other people of a human being's coming into existence — above all, the consequences for the potential human being. The decision must be based on reflection about when a human being comes into existence. Christians differ concerning this decision, but all Christians must make it conservatively in respect to the preciousness of life. John Eccles states concerning the doctrine of ensoulment: "We may never be able to describe when or how ensoulment takes place as this is an act of God and an act which is worked out through the natural processes that scientists can describe. The essential point is the remembrance that all life is God's gift and that personal existence is God's special creation."[72]

Death, the end of historical existence, is the moment when Christians should be most aware of the preciousness of human life. Yet in contemporary society many factors conspire to undermine this awareness. Modern medicines and medical skills have enabled people to live much longer and for illness to be greatly prolonged. Hence the question has arisen in its most crude form: Has the state the right to declare that "certain sick people are unfit to live and therefore to resolve and execute their annihilation? We have in view the incurably infirm, the insane, imbeciles, the deformed, persons who by nature or accident or war are completely immobilised and crippled and therefore 'useless.' "[73] Barth wrote these sentences against the background of Nazi Germany.

The Christian community can never afford to take for granted respect for life. What has happened in various places in the world in the twentieth century can also happen to Christian communities. Hence an emphasis on the preciousness of human life must always be the witness of the church. The preciousness of a human being is not calculated in terms of that person's productivity or usefulness to society, but in the fact that a human being exists by the will and the purpose of God and that God knows this human being by name.

A man who is not, or is no longer, capable of work, of earning, of enjoyment, and even perhaps of communication, is not for this reason unfit to live, least of all because he cannot render to the existence of the state any notable or active contribution, but can only directly or indirectly become a burden to it. The value of this kind of life is God's secret."[74]

Neither can the preciousness of a person be determined by the value of that person to family or to friends. The preciousness of human life is grounded in the will of God.

Care for the dying is enhanced as well as complicated by modern medicine. On the one hand the pain of illness can be relieved, and hygienic care can be more effective. On the other hand bodily functions can be maintained when the person is dead, and the process of dying is thus violated. At least three dispositions toward the dying grow out of theological concerns. First, there is no substitute for human love and for respect for the preciousness of a person. Second, there is no substitute for Christian wisdom and judgment, which grows out of human experience and life in the church. In many cases there are no right answers to questions of medical care. Paul Ramsey has argued for a "medical indications policy" that will take *impending* death decisively into account.[75] Yet this does not solve the problem because of the ambiguity in medical indications and the influence of secularization in the practice of medicine. Even for "medical indications" wisdom and Christian commitment are crucial, as well as medical competence. Hence the third disposition toward the dying is a conservatism in identifying death that is rooted in the Christian awareness that human life is God's gift. Human beings who have entered the process of dying must be allowed to die with the support of human love and with dignity. Yet no Christian theology can support a choice of death or the precipitation of the process of dying.

It is crucially important to take seriously warnings that much of the rhetoric and practice connected with the coming of a human being into the world and with dying are slippery slopes. Words and deeds that at first seem reasonable may in the end undermine the preciousness of human life, which is based on Christian doctrine. Hence the doctrine of the human creature as the child of God must be the basis of every decision about bringing a child into the world, about abortion, and about dying.

## CHAPTER 8

❖

# JESUS CHRIST

Christology . . . is the touchstone of all knowledge of God in the Christian sense, the touchstone of all theology. "Tell me how it stands with your Christology, and I shall tell you who you are." This is the point at which ways diverge, and the point at which is fixed the relation between theology and philosophy, and the relation between knowledge of God and knowledge of men, the relation between revelation and reason, the relation between Gospel and Law, the relation between God's truth and man's truth, the relation between outer and inner, the relation between theology and politics. At this point everything becomes clear or unclear, bright or dark. For we are standing at the centre. And however high and mysterious and difficult everything we want to know might seem to us, yet we may also say that this is just where everything becomes quite simple, quite straightforward, quite childlike.

Karl Barth, *Dogmatics in Outline,* 66

And [we believe] in one Lord Jesus Christ, the only-begotten Son of God, begotten from the Father before all time, Light from Light, true God from true God, begotten not created, of the same essence [reality or being] as the Father, through Whom all things came into being, Who for us men and because of our salvation came down from heaven, and was incarnate by the Holy Spirit and the Virgin Mary and became human.

Niceno-Constantinopolitan Creed (A.D. 381)

He said to them, "But who do you say that I am?" Simon Peter answered, "You are the Messiah, the Son of the living God."

Matthew 16:15–16

In the beginning was the Word, and the Word was with God, and the Word was God. He was in the beginning with God. All things came into being through him, and without him not one thing came into being. . . . And the

124

Word became flesh and lived among us, and we have seen his glory, the glory
as of a father's only son, full of grace and truth.

John 1:1–3, 14

Every Christian doctrine is determined by the life, death, and resurrection of Jesus Christ. Christian faith cannot be adequately expressed or communicated apart from telling "the old, old story of Jesus and his love."
When theology forgets the history of Jesus it becomes dull and unpersuasive.
When the Christian life is severed from the history of what Jesus said and
did it loses its unique and distinctive character as well as its vitality.[1]

Emil Brunner has cogently observed that the Christian community is
constituted by two historical facts.[2] The first is the life, death, and resurrection of Jesus Christ. The second is the apostolic witness to this life,
death, and resurrection. Without these two historical facts there is no Christian community. Christian faith remains Christian only if it is committed
to Jesus Christ, not as some illustration of a general principle but as a
unique, concrete, irreplaceable disclosure of God. The Christian message
has as its purpose the telling of what God has done for our salvation in
Jesus Christ.

# The History of Jesus Christ

The communication of Christian faith involves the telling of the story,
the recounting of the history of Jesus Christ as he was and is remembered
in the Christian community. This foundation of Christian faith is the source
of two problems that need to be noted and faced. The first is the reliability of this history, and the second is the transition from the history of
a particular man to the belief that God acted in this particular person.
These issues were stated with clarity by Gotthold Ephraim Lessing
(1729–1781):

> To this I answer: who will deny (not I) that the reports of these miracles
> and prophecies are as reliable as historical truths can be? But if they are only
> as reliable as this, why are they treated as if they were infinitely more reliable?
>
> And in what way? In this way, that something quite different and much
> greater is founded upon them than is legitimate to found upon truths
> historically proved.
>
> If no historical truth can be demonstrated, then nothing can be demon-
> strated by historical truth.
>
> That is: accidental truths of history can never become the proof of
> necessary truths of reason.
>
> If on historical grounds I have no objection to the statement that Christ

raised to life a dead man; must I therefore accept it as true that God has a Son who is of the same essence as himself? To jump with that historical truth to a quite different class of truths and to demand of me that I should form all my metaphysical and moral ideas accordingly . . . "if that is not a transformation to another kind" then I do not know what Aristotle meant by this phrase . . . that is, then, the ugly broad ditch which I cannot get across, however often and however earnestly I have tried to make the leap. If anyone can help me over, let him do it, I beg him, I adjure him. He will deserve a divine reward from me.[3]

This quotation quite clearly lays out the two basic problems. The first is the problematic character of all historical knowledge. We cannot be fully certain about the facts of history; there is always a provisional character to historical knowledge. Yet faith is sure and certain. How can faith in the living God be tied to the uncertain facts of history? Are the Gospel narratives reliable accounts of the earthly life of Jesus Christ?

The second problem is the transition from the facts of history to the truths of faith, from the historical facts that Jesus of Nazareth lived in a particular time and place to the truth of faith that God was in Christ. Even if we should overcome the provisional character of all historical knowledge, we would still face the question of the leap or the jump from historical knowledge to affirmations of faith about ultimate reality, the leap from the fact of Jesus to the witness of faith that God was in Christ reconciling the world unto himself. Theology, which is critical reflection on Christian faith, must give attention to the reliability of the knowledge of Jesus Christ.

All historical knowledge, as has been indicated, has a provisional quality. We cannot provide absolute proof of any historical event. We take a great deal of historical knowledge for granted; yet we are as certain of its reliability as we are of anything else in human experience. We cannot demonstrate that our knowledge is true. Hence there is always the temptation in Christian theology, since the advent of critical historical studies, to minimize historical knowledge. This was especially true of such modern theologians as Rudolf Bultmann and even of Barth and Brunner. There is hesitancy to put Christian faith at the risk of historical knowledge and theology under the control of a historian.

The other extreme response to the problem of the historical reliability of our knowledge of Jesus Christ is a doctrine of the inerrancy of scripture. Theology is then based on the belief that the scriptures are historically inerrant. This puts the historical data of scripture beyond the critical study of the historian.

Christian theology is based not simply on the historical reliability of the account of Jesus' life but also on the historical fact of the apostolic witness to Jesus Christ. The witness of faith that God was uniquely present in Jesus Christ, that in Jesus Christ God wrought our salvation, and that God raised Jesus Christ from the dead is the heart of Christian faith. Yet the substitution of the witness of faith for the concrete data of what Jesus said and did impoverishes theology. The witness of faith to the theological significance of Jesus Christ should lead to an even greater emphasis on the deeds and the teachings of Jesus. The meaning of the witness of faith is intelligible in the light of the life that Jesus lived. Theology has no doubt been greatly influenced by the fact that the Pauline epistles say very little about the life of Jesus but put his death and resurrection into a cosmic setting. Yet it is very difficult to believe that Paul preached in his missionary journeys without telling people what Jesus said and did or without knowing that some of the people to whom he spoke had heard the story of what Jesus said and did.

This cleavage between the Jesus who actually lived in history and the witness of faith is no new problem. In the ancient catholic church the christological debates were raised with great fury between the theological schools of Antioch and Alexandria.[4] The school at Antioch began with the man Jesus of Nazareth. The school at Alexandria began with the dogma or the witness of faith that the Word became flesh. It may be that we have two ways to come to Christian faith. One is to begin with Jesus of Nazareth, with the disciples as they knew him as just another human being, and then to come gradually to confess him as Lord and as God. The other way of becoming a Christian is to begin with the witness of faith: Jesus is the Christ or the Word become flesh. In the latter case, if the witness of faith is to have great significance, we need to know what Jesus said and did.

Is Christian faith therefore at the mercy of the historians? Do we have to choose between radical skepticism and a fundamentalist doctrine of the inerrancy of scripture? Can we with integrity of mind affirm the reliability of the Gospel portrait of who Jesus Christ was?

The first response to these questions must be the willingness of the church to submit its documents to critical study. Christians and theologians have to come to terms with historical study. They cannot in practice, in piety any more than in theory, exempt the life of Jesus, the records of what he said and did, from critical review. The integrity of the human mind demands that Christians, as well as theologians, ask if the record is reliable. Little is gained, however, if we simply replace an idolatry of the Bible with an idolatry of the study of history or with the idolatry of historians. The believing community can neither exempt its scriptures from critical study, nor can it surrender its scriptures to historical critics or elevate the historian to papal authority.

History is not an exact science. "The laws that govern all tradition and the rubrics that are used to determine reliable accounts from false accounts are always tenuous and there is no historical-critical method but a great variety of methods."[5] Moreover, these methods are significantly influenced by the experiences and the ideological commitments of the historian. The historian finds records reliable or unreliable in part because he or she wants to find them reliable or unreliable. The judgment concerning the reliability of historical documents depends not simply on technical qualifications but on the judgment and the wisdom of the historian. Reinhold Niebuhr stated that the "root error of modern culture" rested on the failure "to recognize the intimate relation between reason and interest and passion in all historical judgments."[6] In assessing the reliability of a document it may be better in many instances to trust the wisdom of a person who has experienced life over a long period of time in broad and deep ways without being a historian over against the judgment of a young Ph.D. in history who has not experienced life in its depth and in its breadth.

Paul Althaus has dealt specifically with this problem. He insists that the believing community is not dependent on the historians for their knowledge of Jesus Christ.[7] Human beings in general, he argues, have a direct intuitive encounter with their past. Even the scientific historian requires an intuition and an imaginative encounter with the data of history in order to gain understanding.

Our knowledge of another human being is not tied to the empirical, inductive method. On the first encounter with another human being, we make certain basic judgments about that person. The immediacy of our knowledge of the past is analogous. This personal, intuitive encounter with historical materials is no substitute for historical scholarship. It gives certainty to our judgment only on large issues, not on points of detail. It does not undermine the necessity for careful historical work, but it does indicate that our knowledge of the validity of historical accounts is not wholly, not even primarily, dependent on scientific methods of analysis.

John Knox argues in somewhat the same way as Althaus.[8] The believer, writes Knox, is not dependent finally on historical studies. It is impossible for the Christian to entertain any real doubt as to the existence of this person Jesus Christ, for the memory of him is an essential element of the Christian life itself. The man Jesus can be known only as he is remembered. We have no prior, independent, or objective knowledge of him. It is Jesus, as he was remembered and interpreted, who alone is important for the Christian community. It is this Jesus with whom both faith and history are concerned. The perception of the event of Jesus Christ invests the whole New Testament picture with a kind of immediate and unquestionable historical value—the event of Jesus Christ with precisely that totality of fact and meaning (a fact responded to, remembered, and interpreted) which is indubitably set forth in the New Testament and is thus itself indubitable.

Knox goes on to give an illustration. Suppose a historian approaches you with a proposal to write a biography of a deceased friend whom you knew intimately and loved for many years. You have complete confidence in the historian and you give him your approval and your help in writing the story. He goes his way and then, after months of study and writing, he returns with the historical account. The historian may discover many things about your friend which you did not know. He may discover that you are mistaken about certain facts. He may even demonstrate that since your friend died, your own assessment of him has changed. All of this the historian may do, and all of this may be very helpful and enlightening to you. But on the matter of the historicity of your friend you do not need the historian's help. You are already sure that you remember your friend. It is in some such way that the church bears in its heart the memory of Jesus and would find it inconceivable that historical methods should ever discredit that memory.

Herbert Butterfield, a modern historian, also illuminates this problem. Butterfield was the son of a Methodist minister. He wanted to be a minister himself but did not feel he had the qualifications; however, he became one of the preeminent British historians of his generation.

In his Gifford Lectures entitled *The Origins of History*, he relates the problem of our historical knowledge of Jesus Christ to that of our knowledge of Winston Churchill.

I am always reminded of the stories which are told about Winston Churchill and the hundreds of sayings of his which have come into the general currency during the last quarter of a century. We may read these things in newspapers and books, but I wonder if we realize how often they appear to depend ultimately on a verbal report given by a single man. I am not sure of the truth of any of the Churchillian anecdotes that has come to us by this particular route. I notice that even academic historians that are utterly reliable in their field of study find it hard to recall a story at dinner-time without adding something to round it off or to make it more piquant. So, it would not be easy to establish in a water tight manner the truth of a great many

of the single stories about Winston Churchill. Yet I have a hunch that many
of them are true (though I cannot do the distinguishing), and that in any
case the whole corpus of them shows us Churchill the man in quite an effective
manner. Even a Churchillian story that ultimately proved to be apocryphal
might well be more true in a sense, more typical of the man, than another
which could be established as absolutely correct. The person who invents
such a story or rounds it off in order to give it the Churchillian ring is just
the one who struggles to produce what contemporaries will accept as typical.
It might even be true that anecdotes in the mass can bring us nearer to the
man than an historical work which absolutely restricted itself to the things
that can be documentarily demonstrated. At the first level of analysis the
historian is in a somewhat analogous position in respect to the man Jesus.
It is more possible for us to form a general picture of him than to distinguish
which of the detailed anecdotes are authentic.[9]

Butterfield comes to the record of what Jesus said and did with considerable confidence. He is aware of the principles that New Testament
scholars use, such as the rubric that the stories and sayings that neither
support the early church nor agree with Judaism, stories and sayings that
do not obviously serve a polemical purpose, are more likely to be valid.
But he finds this argument oversubtle. The fact is that human history is
not so neat and rational. In many instances, the things more inherently
improbable actually happened. Butterfield is willing to grant only a very
limited usefulness to such rubrics. He is much more impressed with the
tenacity with which men of ancient times maintained their positions and
with the spirit of honesty and humility with which the Christian tradition was recorded.[10]

These citations from Althaus, Knox, and Butterfield do not resolve the
problem. They do, however, indicate that the believing community must
be aware that "all historical work is influenced by the presuppositions of
historians, and they themselves are children of their own time."[11] They also
give us confidence about much of the material in the Gospels, and especially
about the general picture of Jesus as given to us in the Gospels.

Good grounds exist for confidence that Jesus as he was remembered
by the community is not in contradiction to the Jesus who lived.[12] The
remembrance of Jesus in the light of the experience of Easter, and in the
light of the faith that God was in him reconciling the world, is not in conflict with the Jesus whom the disciples knew and who was seen by other
persons to be just another human being.

The historical record of the life and death of Jesus Christ has been subjected to greater critical scrutiny than is the case in any other ancient
historical document. Yet the data that meet the criteria of very severe
historical studies remain considerable, more in the case of Jesus than of

almost any ancient figure. There can be little doubt that Jesus was a Galilean prophet and that he had been a disciple of John the Baptist. There can be little doubt that he went about teaching about the kingdom of God and exerting a remarkable influence on those who heard his words and who fellowshiped with him; that in his presence remarkable events occurred; that he ate with sinners, making them aware of God's presence; that he gathered a community and chose disciples. He was executed by the Roman governor. In addition there can be little historical doubt that his disciples encountered him, the crucified Christ risen from the dead, and that using the words of ordinary historical experience they declared that they heard him, saw him, and were commissioned to be his disciples.[13] There is no need for Christians to be alarmed by destructive skepticism or be swept away by unbridled fantasy. The confidence that the portrait we have of Jesus, what he said and did, the manner in which he related to his disciples, is based on solid and reasonable historical grounds.

The theological work of an Augustine or a Calvin generally began with the witness of faith to Jesus Christ, that is, with the epistle to the Romans. Theologians today can begin with the witness to faith in Paul's theology, but only if they support the witness of faith with the record of what Jesus said and did in the Gospels of Matthew, Mark, and Luke. A knowledge of the Synoptic Gospels is foundational not only for theology but also for life in the church. The dogma that the Word became flesh or the theology that puts the crucified and resurrected Christ in a cosmic context does not mean very much, unless it affirms what Jesus actually said and did. Christian theology as well as the Christian life depends on the historical account or, to use the current word, the story of Jesus Christ.

The Gospels are not simply post-Easter confessionals; they are post-Easter confessionals full of and shaped by pre-Easter remembrance. The risen Christ was the Christ they had known. James Charlesworth goes on to argue that "the claim that 'the early Christian sources show no interest' in 'the life and personality of Jesus' is simply inaccurate. One of the interests of the earliest Christians was in Jesus' life and self-understanding; otherwise the production of the gospels is unthinkable."[14] Theologies that emphasize the Word made flesh have theological as well as historical reasons to emphasize the record of what Jesus said and did.

## Of the Same Substance (Being) as the Father

The Christian witness of faith to the fact of Jesus Christ received its classic theological formulation in the Nicene Creed (A.D. 325, 381). This is the most universal Christian confession, having authority in Eastern

Orthodox churches, Roman Catholic churches, and Protestant churches. It rejected the most important Christian heresy (Arianism), and it affirmed the most distinctive Christian doctrine. It declared that God was present in Jesus Christ without any diminution of his deity. Hence for all those who confess the Nicene Creed, God, the creator of heaven and earth, is defined by his presence in Jesus Christ.

The formulation of the Nicene Creed was precipitated by an Alexandrian presbyter named Arius, who raised very clearly the theological issue involved in the church's belief in Jesus Christ. The basic teaching of Arius was the transcendence and the uniqueness of God. In a letter to Bishop Alexander of Alexandria Arius declared the faith which he had learned from his forefathers and even from Alexander himself: "We acknowledge one God, alone ingenerate, alone everlasting, alone without beginning, alone true, alone having immortality, alone good, alone sovereign; Judge, Governor, and Provider of all, unalterable and unchangeable, just and good, God of the law and prophets and the New Testaments."[15] God is unique and transcendent, and no other being can share his nature with him. Hence any other being must be less than God. Arius understood the radical distinction between creator and creature. With this background Arius went to the heart of the question of who is the Son, the Word, the Logos who was present in Jesus Christ. Does the Son or the Logos have the nature of the creator, or does the Son or the Logos have the nature of a creature?

The Christian community had always spoken of Jesus Christ as if he were God. They had spoken of Jesus Christ as the Lord, the Savior, the Word of God, the Son of God, the Son of Man, prophet and priest. All of these titles referred to the activities of Jesus Christ in relationship to his disciples and to his value or meaning for them. For a long time and in many situations this language of faith and piety was sufficient. The disciples knew the reality of God through Jesus Christ.

Arius changed the question. He did not ask, How is Jesus Christ related to us or what does he mean for us? He asked a prior question: Who is Jesus Christ? Is Jesus Christ really God, or is he a creature? Arius's own answer to this question was as clear as his question. The Son or the Word is a creature. He is the noblest of all creation, the most perfect of all creatures, the firstborn of all creation, but he is still a creature. He was made (created); he came into existence by the will of the Father. There was a time when he was not.[16]

The question that Arius raised had to be answered; and all later Christians should be grateful for the clarity with which he put the question, even if they do not agree with his answer. The New Testament describes what Jesus Christ is to us and for us, but sooner or later the question had to be raised who Jesus Christ is himself. In what sense is he God? The Christians as well as the Old Testament prophets spoke of the one God, the creator of heaven and earth. What is the relationship of Jesus Christ to the creator? Such questions as these inevitably arose as the Christian community reflected on the faith and were also raised by observers from outside. Hence there was no escape from the question that Arius formulated. We should be grateful that he stated the question so clearly and that he answered it so specifically and so vigorously that he forced the church to devote its energies to clarifying its own understanding of the nature of the Son of God or the Word of God as incarnate in Jesus Christ.

Arius's theology immediately aroused controversy in the church. Alexander, Arius's bishop at Alexandria, vigorously opposed him and suspended him from office. Arius was an attractive spokesman for his theology, and his theology was rational and appealing. He safeguarded one truth that the church was determined to maintain, namely, the monarchy, or the sole rule, of God. The church had a basic abhorrence of polytheism, but by making the Son or the Word a demigod, Arius opened the way to the polytheism he sought to avoid. The controversy became so intense that it aroused the concern of Constantine, the emperor, who had only recently acknowledged the Christian faith, which he hoped would unite, not divide, the empire.

In June of 325 an ecumenical council under the sponsorship of Constantine as well as the bishops met at Nicaea. Three theological positions were clearly represented at the council. One group, under the leadership of persons such as Eusebius of Nicomedia, strongly espoused the Arian position. The middle party, headed by Eusebius of Caesarea, a friend and advocate of the emperor, sought a middle ground. The third position was advocated by Alexander, and it vigorously opposed Arius's theology. The council after debate took a creed of an Eastern church and added to it four phrases that Arius could not say without giving up his own understanding of Jesus Christ. The council then added a paragraph of anathemas condemning some of Arius's specific teachings. The creed that was adopted at Nicaea was as follows, with the four critical phrases in italics:

### The Creed of Nicaea

We believe in one God, the Father All Governing, creator of all things visible and invisible;

And in one Lord Jesus Christ, the Son of God, begotten of the Father as only begotten, that is, *from the essence* [substance, being, reality] *of the*

*Father,* God from God, Light from Light, *true God from true God, begotten not created, of the same essence* [being or reality] *as the Father,* through whom all things came into being, both in heaven and in earth; who for us men and for our salvation came down and was incarnate, becoming human. He suffered and the third day he rose, and ascended into the heavens. And he will come to judge both the living and the dead.

And [we believe] in the Holy Spirit.

But, those who say, Once he was not, or he was not before his generation, or he came to be out of nothing, or who assert that he, the Son of God, is of a different *hypostasis* or *ousia,* or that he is a creature, or changeable, or mutable, the Catholic and Apostolic Church anathematizes them.

The crucial phrase is "of the same essence [substance, being, reality], as the Father." The council wanted to make unmistakably clear that the Son or the Word was truly God. Later Athanasius, Alexander's great successor and the great theologian of Nicene theology, would come to see that this meant that the being of the Son is identical to the being of the Father.[17]

Many in the church did not like the phrase "of the same substance [essence] as the Father." It was not biblical language, and it had been associated with heresy. It had material connotations. For fifty years the Nicene theology was vigorously debated, and the church tried many substitutes for the phrase "of same substance [essence] as the Father." Some of these phrases were "like the Father," "like the Father in all things," "exact image of the Godhead," "of like substance with the Father," "like the Father according to the scriptures," "unlike the Father." All substitutes proved inadequate, and the church came to a consensus on the phrase "of the same substance as the Father" at the First Council of Constantinople in 381.[18] The creed that we use today in the liturgy of the church and that we popularly call the Nicene Creed represents the theological work of this council. It subsequently became the universal creed in that it is used by the Orthodox churches as well as by Roman Catholics and Protestants.

Athanasius saw very clearly the implications of Arian theology for Christian faith, and he underscored the theological significance of the Nicene Creed.

[Arius] has dared to say that "the Word is not the very God"; "though He is called God, yet he is not very God," but "by participation of grace, he, as others, is God only in name." And, whereas all beings are foreign and different from God in essence, so too is "the Word alien and unlike in all things to the Father's essence and propriety," but belongs to things originated and created and is one of these. Afterwards as though he had succeeded to the devil's recklessness, he has stated in his *thalia* "that even to the Son the

Father is invisible," and "the Word cannot perfectly and exactly either see or know his own Father;" but even what he knows and what he sees he knows and sees "in proportion to his own measure," as we also know according to our own power.[19]

Athanasius understood that if the Word or Son is a creature, then his knowledge of God is of the same order as our knowledge of God. As the firstborn of all creatures he may know more about God than any other creatures, but his knowledge is still that of a creature. Furthermore, if the Son is a creature then he cannot have the value of God for us, nor can he unite us with God.

The great leap of Christian faith is the assertion that in Jesus Christ we are encountered by God himself. In Jesus Christ the divine presence is focused for us, and in the light of this revelation all other revelations of God are identified and understood. Christians are people for whom God is defined by Jesus Christ.

In popular piety we sometimes say that Jesus is like God, but this kind of piety always leads to Arianism. To say that Jesus is like God assumes that we already know who God is and therefore can judge whether Jesus is like God. We also have the further problem of determining how much Jesus Christ is like God. If Jesus is like God, someone may come along who is more like God, and Jesus Christ becomes only one of many mediators of the divine presence. The Christian claim is that this Jesus whom we know from his life among us is the embodiment of God himself, the focused presence of the living God.[20] This is the faith that must be validated in our experience, as it enables us to deal with the facts of experience, as it puts the facts together in some coherent whole, and as it illumines and makes sense out of our common human experience. Paul Tillich has summarized the significance of the Nicene faith in this way:

> The most serious Christian heresy was overcome. Christ is not one of the many half-gods; he is not a hero. He is God himself appearing in divine essence within the historical person. It meant a definite negation of paganism. In Arius paganism again raised its head after it had been defeated in the antignostic struggle. The victory of Arianism would have made Christianity only one of many possible religions. . . .
>
> The negative character of the decision is especially evident in the condemnations. The creatureliness of Christ is negated. He has no other *ousia* than the Father; but what the *homoousios* [of the same substance] is was not explained. It was not decided whether the three *prosopa* are really differences in God, and if so whether they are eternal or historical. And no doctrine of the Spirit was given. Only one thing was determined: Jesus Christ is not

an incarnated half-god; he is not a creature above all others; he is God. And
God is creator and unconditioned. This negative decision is the truth and
the greatness of the Council of Nicaea.[21]

The first Christian doctrine that the church settled in an ecumenical
council and that has subsequently received approval in the life of the church
through the centuries had to do with the deity of Jesus Christ. The church
made clear at Nicaea what it was convinced had always been the faith of
Christian people. In Jesus Christ human beings are confronted by God.

# The Person of Jesus Christ

The councils of Nicaea (325) and Constantinople (381) affirmed the
most decisive Christian doctrine, but they did not end the theological task.
In fact the Nicene faith made two additional tasks the immediate concern
of the church. The doctrine of the Trinity, which was worked out in its
classical form at this time, attempted to state how Christians can believe
that God is one and that Jesus Christ is also truly God. The church also
had to explain its doctrine of the person of Jesus Christ.

At Nicaea the church had said unmistakably that in Jesus Christ we are
confronted by God himself. Yet the church had always said that Jesus Christ
was also man. The controversies of the next few centuries would demonstrate that the church found it as difficult to say that Jesus Christ is fully
human without any diminution of his humanity, as it had found it difficult
to affirm his deity. At the Council of Chalcedon (451) the church would
reaffirm the Nicene faith and also declare the true humanity of Jesus Christ,
with the human and the divine concurring in one Lord Jesus Christ.

The doctrine of the person of Christ was worked out in the four
ecumenical councils from First Constantinople (381) to Third Constantinople (681). An unusually able group of theologians concentrated their
attention on the doctrine of Christ with a catholicity of spirit that has
never been duplicated. The consequence is that the doctrine which they
worked out was confirmed by the consensus of the church and provides
the framework or the boundaries in which any contemporary doctrine of
Jesus Christ must be articulated.[22]

Apollinarius, a brilliant Nicene theologian, was the first to direct his
attention to problems that Nicaea raised, such as the question How can
Jesus Christ also be human? Apollinarius, very vigorous in affirming the
Nicene faith, concluded that the divine Logos replaced the psychological
center of the human self. The consequence was that Jesus was a divine

person expressed in and through a human body. Apollinarius's solution to the problem has always found support among the devout who find it easier to affirm the physical humanity of Jesus Christ than to declare his psychological humanity. The church rejected Apollinarius's doctrine at the First Council of Constantinople (381), because it did not do justice to the true humanity of Jesus Christ.

Nestorius, bishop of Constantinople (d. 451), attempted to solve the problem by conceptualizing the union between the divine and human as a conjunction or an indwelling. Nestorius had been scandalized by those who spoke of Mary as the mother of God. He had been trained in the school of Antioch and insisted on the radical distinction between creator and creature and also on the integrity of the human life of Jesus Christ. The church rejected Nestorianism at the Ecumenical Council in 431, because it did not do justice to the real personal unity of the divine and the human in one acting subject. Nestorius would later insist that he himself was not a Nestorian. In any case Nestorius's theology did not seem to many to place adequate emphasis on the unity of the divine and the human.

The Alexandrian school of theology emphasized the unity of the divine and the human. Cyril and the Alexandrians generally began with the dogma that the Word became flesh, and then they had the problem of how to do justice to the humanity of Christ.[23] They liked to speak of "from two natures into one nature."[24] Some like Eutyches carried this emphasis to an extreme and even spoke of a divinized flesh.[25] If Antioch had a problem of asserting the unity between the divine and the human, Alexandria had the problem of doing justice to the humanity.

Theologians divided between those who advocated the word-flesh Christology and those who advocated a word-person theology. For the Alexandrians the tendency was to say that the Word took on human flesh. Others, especially in Antioch and Rome, emphasized that the Word united with the human in one acting subject.

The controversies of this period received their resolution and their classic statement at Chalcedon in 451.

### The Definition of Chalcedon

Following, then, the holy fathers, we unite in teaching all men to confess the one and only Son, our Lord Jesus Christ. This selfsame one is perfect [*teleion*] both in deity [*theotēti*] and also in human-ness [*anthrōpotēti*]; this selfsame one is also actually [*alēthos*] God and actually man, with a rational soul [*psychēs logikēs*] and a body. He is of the same reality as God [*homoousion tō patri*] as far as his deity is concerned and of the same reality as we are ourselves [*homoousion hēmin*] as far as his human-ness is concerned;

thus like us in all respects, sin only excepted. Before time began [*pro aiōnon*] he was begotten of the Father, in respect of his deity, and now in these "last days," for us and on behalf of our salvation, this selfsame one was born of Mary the virgin, who is God-bearer [*theotokos*] in respect of his humanness [*anthrōpotēta*].

[We also teach] that we apprehend [*gnōrizomenon*] this one and only Christ—Son, Lord, only-begotten—in two natures [*dyo physesin*]; [and we do this] without confusing the two natures [*asynchytōs*], without transmuting one nature into the other [*atreptōs*], without dividing them into two separate categories [*adiairetōs*], without contrasting them according to area or function [*achōristōs*]. The distinctiveness of each nature is not nullified by the union. Instead, the "properties" [*idiotētos*] of each nature are conserved and both natures concur [*syntrechousēs*] in one "person" [*prosōpon*] and in one *hypostasis*. They are not divided or cut into two *prosōpa,* but are together the one and only and only-begotten Logos of God, the Lord Jesus Christ. Thus have the prophets of old testified; thus the Lord Jesus Christ himself taught us; thus the Symbol of the Fathers [N] has handed down [*paradedōke*] to us.[26]

The first paragraph of the definition emphasizes the confession of "the one and only Son, our Lord Jesus Christ." Yet it immediately balances the divine and the human. This one and only Son is perfect in deity, actually God, of the same reality as God. The one Lord Jesus Christ is also perfect in humanness, actually a man with a rational soul and body, of the same reality as we are as to his humanness.

In respect to his deity, "the one and only Son, our Lord Jesus Christ" was begotten of God before time but in respect of his humanity in these last days and for our salvation he was born of Mary, the Virgin. Mary can properly be called God-bearer in respect to his humanness. This first paragraph of the definition makes clear that any statement about Jesus Christ must declare on the one hand that he is truly God and on the other hand that he is truly human.

The second paragraph specifies how the divine and human are united. Over against those who wanted to say *from* two natures into one, the Chalcedonian definition declares that we apprehend this one and only Christ *in* two natures. The two natures are not to be confused or changed into the other or be divided into separate categories or be contrasted with regard to function. Each nature, the divine and the human, maintains its integrity. Yet the two natures concur in one acting subject, in one person.

A common criticism has been that Chalcedon used the substance categories of Greek philosophy. The theologians of the fifth century did use the terminology that was familiar to them, but when they spoke of substance they did not mean things or objects. The two natures of Jesus Christ refer to the mystery of the divine self and the mystery of the human self and the conviction that in Jesus Christ the mystery of the divine self concurred with the mystery of the human self in one acting subject.[27] Chalcedon did not mean that two different things became one thing. Furthermore, we find some distant analogy to this doctrine whenever we witness the power of one human person to enter into the life of another human person so that this person reflects not only his or her self but also the self that influences his or her behavior. At Nicaea and Chalcedon the church was saying that in Jesus Christ, who is truly, authentically human, the very reality of God is expressed and the very reality of God encounters us in one acting subject, one person.

The Definition of Chalcedon did not fully satisfy the church of the fifth century or the church since then. The Second Council of Constantinople in 553 interpreted Chalcedon in a monophysite (one nature) direction with the emphasis on the unity of the divine and the human, affirming the right to speak of Mary as mother of God and emphasizing that the Lord Jesus Christ who was crucified in the flesh was true God.

The Third Council of Constantinople in 681 moved in the Antiochene direction with an emphasis on the integrity of the two natures. "We also proclaim two natural willings or wills in him, two natural operations, without separation, without change, without partition, without confusion."[28] These interpretations of Chalcedon indicate the difficulty of holding together its chief concerns: on the one hand maintaining the integrity of the mystery of the human self and the integrity of the mystery of the divine self, and on the other hand insisting on the *hypostatic* or genuine personal union of the human and the divine in one acting subject. The Chalcedonian Definition is not a final statement, but it is the place in history where the church devoted its theological gifts to the problem of the person of Jesus Christ with the singleness of interests that is hard to duplicate and with a catholicity that helped to keep the discussion in balance. Chalcedon is the place "in the history of Christian thought where the New Testament compound was explicated in exact balance so as to discourage the four favorite ways by which the divine and the human 'energies' of the Christ event are commonly misconstrued."[29]

Chalcedon did not put an end to thought about Jesus Christ, but there is good reason for believing that it set the boundaries within which all thought about Christ must be done if it is to do justice to the New Testament witness. Any statement must declare that Jesus Christ is truly man, truly God, in one person. Within these boundaries theologians may use contemporary knowledge to throw light on the mystery. But there is no evidence that a Christology which abandons the true deity, the true humanity, and the union in one person can maintain itself in the church.

## The Resurrection of Jesus Christ

The epistle to the Romans declares that Jesus Christ "was descended from David according to the flesh and was declared to be Son of God with power according to the spirit of holiness by resurrection from the dead" (Romans 1:3–4). The Jesus whom wicked people sought to destroy, God raised from the dead (Acts 2:24). On the occasion of the crucifixion of Jesus the disciples went back to their old tasks with heavy hearts, having lost not only a friend but also a great hope. The pivotal event in human history is God's raising Jesus Christ from the dead, vindicating the life and ministry and declaring him to be Lord.

The resurrection of Jesus Christ is not simply a historical event, but the New Testament never understands it to be less than that. The New Testament consistently speaks of the resurrection as something that happened in time and space, that is concrete and objective. But it always speaks of the resurrection as something overpowering, something of a puzzlement, something of a mystery. The New Testament never envisaged Jesus Christ entering history again. The first Christians believed that God by a mighty act had raised Jesus Christ from the dead, empowering him to represent the kingdom of God in history. The disciples were witnesses to that elevation because God had made Jesus Christ visible to them. The power and the unanimity of the New Testament witnesses are impressive. Every sentence in the New Testament presupposes the resurrection of Jesus Christ, and so does every Christian theology.

Karl Barth, while recognizing the unique character of the resurrection, has emphasized the reality of the resurrection as an event that happened in time and space.

> If Jesus Christ is not risen—bodily, visibly, audibly, perceptibly, in the same concrete sense in which He died, as the text themselves have it—if He is not also risen, then our preaching and our faith are vain and futile; we are still in our sins. And the apostles are found "false witnesses," because they have "testified of God that he raised up Christ, whom he raised not up" (I Corinthians 15:14f.). If they were true witnesses of His resurrection, they were witnesses of an event which was like that of the cross in its concrete objectivity. . . . The apostles witnessed that Jesus Christ risen from the dead had encountered them, not in the way in which we might say this (metaphorically)

of a supposed or an actual immanence of the existence, presence and action of the transcendent God, not in an abstract but in a concrete otherness, in the mystery and glory of the Son of God in the flesh. . . . We can therefore say quite calmly—for this is the truth of the matter—that they attested the fact that He made known to them this side of His (and their) death only in the light of the other side, and therefore that he made known to them the other side, His (and their) life beyond, wholly in terms of this side, even as spoken in His resurrection from the dead, as the Yes of God to Him (and therefore to them and to all men) concealed first under the No of His (and their) death.[30]

Barth likewise emphasizes the role of the empty tomb as a guide to understanding the resurrection.

It is, in fact, an indispensable accompaniment of the attestation. It safeguards its content from misunderstanding in terms of a being of the Resurrected which is purely beyond or inward. It distinguishes the confession that Jesus Christ lives from a mere manner of speaking on the part of believers. It is the negative presupposition of the concrete objectivity of His being. Let those who would reject it be careful—as in the case of the Virgin Birth—that they do not fall into Docetism.[31]

The New Testament is simple and chaste in what it declares. There is very little of the baroque and sensational that characterizes the apocryphal accounts. No one witnessed the resurrection. The New Testament simply declares, "This Jesus God raised up, and of that all of us are witnesses" (Acts 2:32). The New Testament writers assumed that Jesus was raised in a way congruent with the empty tomb. While they do not expect Jesus to enter again in their history, they do not doubt that he was raised up, that he is alive, that he was seen by them, and that he spoke to them. Any interpretation of the resurrection as a vision, a hallucination, or an event in the human heart contradicts the New Testament witness. Moreover, it leaves one at the mercy of the impersonal powers that seem relentless in governing this world, leading not only to our deaths as individuals but to the extinction of life on this planet. The resurrection means that the ultimate power is not the impersonal forces but the purposive, loving action of God. The possibility of the resurrection rests upon the power of God to act personally in the created order. The question of the resurrection is finally a question about God and God's action in the world.

We cannot reconstruct what happened in the resurrection of Jesus Christ and in his appearance to his disciples. Karl Barth emphasized that the resurrection was not historical, in the sense that it could be observed independently of the standpoint of the onlooker.[32] It is not historical in the sense that it is analogous to other events in history or that it was the consequence of powers in nature or history. The death of Jesus can be described simply as an event in history, but not the resurrection. The New Testament did not speak of the resurrection as the resuscitation of a corpse or as a return to earthly life. The resurrection is the transformation of the body of Jesus into a reality unknown to us. Paul spoke of the change from the physical, perishable, and mortal body to a spiritual body (1 Corinthians 15). We may speculate that the energy of the physical body was translated into the energy of the resurrected body in such a manner that his disciples recognized him. It was Jesus of Nazareth who was raised from the dead, and the disciples who had known him in the flesh recognized him as the crucified Christ. As such the resurrection is the mighty act of God, not the consequence of physical and historical causes. It is historical in that the disciples were witnesses. Using the language of ordinary experience to describe what was beyond their comprehension, they declared that they saw, heard, and recognized the crucified Christ, who commissioned them to be his witnesses in all the world. The validity of their witness was confirmed by their lives.

The resurrection is a mighty act of God that overturned what evil people had done, conquered death, vindicated the life of Jesus, made the risen Jesus present to his disciples, and empowered him to represent the kingdom of God in history. Yet the resurrection is more than this. In Jesus' appearance to his disciples, the disciples were established in their discipleship and were commissioned and sent forth into all the world to baptize, to teach, and to make disciples of all people. The resurrection of Jesus Christ is gospel because it is an event that happened in time and space, because the risen Christ was seen and heard and known by his disciples. The importance of this clear affirmation of the New Testament is made vivid in Rodion Shchedrin's oratorio *Lenin in the People's Heart,* where the red guardsmen sang at Lenin's deathbed, "No, no, no, no, that cannot be. Lenin lives, Lenin lives."[33] Lenin lives in the cause, in memory, in the heart. This means there will come a time when the cause, the memory, and the heart also die. Paul put the issue very clearly. If Christ has not been raised, our preaching is in vain, and your faith is in vain, and we are of all people most pitiable (1 Corinthians 15:12–19). But in fact Christ has been raised from the dead.

The resurrection is a confirmation of the life of Jesus, of his words and deeds. It is the verdict of the Father, as Barth puts it. It declares that what Jesus said and did is undergirded by the power of him who created the world and in whose power the world exists. Indeed, Paul speaks of God as one who calls that which was not into being and raises the dead (Romans 4:17).

The resurrection is an answer to the problem of historical evil. On Good Friday a good man named Jesus was put to death by a Roman governor named Pilate, by Caiaphas the priest, and by howling, senseless demonstrators in the streets. On Good Friday evening it appeared as though the Pilates, the Caiaphases, and the demonstrators in the streets represented reality. On Good Friday one could only wish that the world had such a structure that it supported the life of a good person such as Jesus. And therefore the disciples were in despair. They went back to "the real world," to their fishing boats. But God raised Jesus Christ from the dead on Easter morning, undoing what wicked and evil persons had done on Good Friday. The "real world" is the resurrection of Jesus Christ.

The resurrection is also an answer to the problem of physical evil. Paul Tillich has said that the *Crucifixion* by Matthias Grünewald (c. 1470–1528) is the greatest portrayal of the incarnation in the visual arts.[34] The basis for this judgment is the sheer horror of the dead body on the cross. It puts in visual form the theological question of the incarnation: Can this man be the Son of God? Physical evil is devastating in dramatic forms such as tornadoes and earthquakes and in forms that more frequently affect us individually such as cancer. On Good Friday physical evil had devastated a beautiful, wonderful life. Is this the way it ends? But God raised Jesus Christ from the dead, demonstrating in human history that there are resources of divine mercy and power that can take the broken, wounded pieces of life and put them together again.

The risen Christ lives and sends forth his Spirit. The Spirit of Christ is the presence of the risen Christ in the world and the power of the risen Christ to work out his purposes in individual lives and in human communities. The power and the presence of the Spirit of the risen Christ in the life of the church have confirmed the witness of the resurrection.

# The Ascension

The ascension marks the end of the revelation of Jesus Christ and the beginning of the work of the Holy Spirit, making his presence alive in all the world. Easter and the ascension have very much the same content, but there are good theological reasons for separating them, as does the New Testament. The ascension is difficult to conceptualize. Hence the New Testament uses the language of space and time, of history, to say what is true but beyond our power to describe. Jesus is pictured in the New Testament and in Christian art as rising spatially into the heavens. Karl Barth likewise referred to the ascension as the homecoming of the Son, who had wandered into a far country.[35] Yet neither Luther nor Calvin nor Barth believed that the ascension was a spatial movement.

The ascension means that the earthly ministry of Jesus has ended. A new epoch in human history has begun. The resurrection and the ascension are two episodes in the same event. "Yet there is a clear distinction between them in theological meaning. It is one thing to assert that Jesus had been raised from the dead: it was another to assert that he now shared in the sovereignty of God over heaven and earth."[36] In the story account in Acts 1:6–11 the ascension brings to an end the Easter appearances and promises that "you will receive power when the Holy Spirit has come upon you; and you will be my witnesses . . ." (Acts 1:8).

The ascension means that the incarnate life of Jesus Christ is taken into the very being of God; that the ministry of Jesus Christ, formerly limited by space and time, is now universal by the power of the Spirit of God; that Jesus Christ is at the right hand of God ("right hand" was a symbol for a position of power); that he makes continual intercession for us and has opened for us the way to the presence of God (Romans 8:34; Hebrews 7:5; 9:24); and that he has been given all authority in heaven and earth. The risen and ascended Christ reigns over all things and intercedes for his people.

The doctrine of the ascension intends in the words of ordinary experience and of space to describe that which is beyond ordinary experience and is not contained in the space we know. Hence, when taken literally, the description of the ascension baffles us. Yet how better can we say (1) that the Easter appearances have ended, (2) that the human life of Jesus Christ has been taken into the very being of God, (3) that the risen Christ reigns, (4) that the risen Christ intercedes for us, and (5) that a new epoch in human history has begun with the sending of the Spirit and the mission of the church.[37]

# The Birth of Jesus

The birth of Jesus has acquired considerable significance in the life of the Christian community in recent years, in part because the fundamentalist-modernist controversy made the virgin birth the test of orthodoxy and in part because Christmas is the most important festival in American society. The birth narratives in Matthew and Luke very impressively express the faith that in the birth of Jesus God became human and acted for our salvation. In the transmission of the faith through sixteen centuries, Christmas carols, the birth narratives, and the celebration of Christmas have been very meaningful and powerful statements of the faith.

The birth narratives in the New Testament are only one of the ways the Christian community attempted to say what happened in Jesus Christ. The Gospel of Mark, which does not mention the birth narratives, declares the significance of Jesus in the record of his baptism, "You are my Son, the Beloved; with you I am well pleased" (Mark 1:11). The Gospel of John likewise has no mention of the birth of Jesus but accounts for the significance of his life by declaring "the Word became flesh and lived among us" (John 1:14). Paul does not discuss the birth of Jesus but in the epistle to the Romans declares that Jesus Christ "was declared to be Son of God with power according to the spirit of holiness by resurrection from the dead" (Romans 1:4). The birth narratives are not the only way of telling what happened in the coming of Jesus Christ. Yet they do so with a beauty and a compelling power.

The attention of the early church was focused on the death and the resurrection of Jesus Christ. The resurrection was celebrated from the very beginning as Christians gathered on the first day of the week to worship God, because on this day God raised Jesus Christ from the dead.[38] The celebration of Easter in the middle of the second century was sufficiently developed for a controversy to arise concerning the different dates for celebrating Easter in Asia Minor and elsewhere in the Mediterranean world, particularly, Rome.[39] By the third century the celebrations of the passion and the resurrection had become very elaborate and were the occasion when catechumens were admitted to membership in the church.[40]

The celebration of the birth of Jesus came much later. At the beginning of the fourth century the birth of Jesus was celebrated on January 5–6. This occasion also celebrated Jesus' baptism and the changing of the water into wine at the wedding feast of Cana, in addition to the coming of the wise men from the East and the star that led them to the child of promise. Christmas thus had its origin during the Epiphany feast of January 6, in which it was celebrated along with other events.[41]

The date January 6 had no relationship to the actual date of the birth of Jesus. It was the date on which the non-Christian world celebrated the lengthening of days and also

in the night before January 6 the waters of the Nile were said to possess special miraculous power. This fact explains why the disciples of Basilides chose this date for the festival of Christ's baptism: it was in order to proclaim a distinction from the heathen, that the true divine being who had appeared

upon earth was Christ, who entered the world in the Jordan at the moment
when the voice uttered the words: "Thou art my beloved son."[42]

The birth of Christ came to be celebrated in Rome on December 25
sometime between 325 and 354. Again, the determining factor in the choice
of the date was a pagan festival. The non-Christian world observed
December 25 as an important festival in honor of the sun. In the festival
of Epiphany on January 5–6 and Christmas on December 25, the Christian community deliberately set the Christian celebrations over against the
pagan celebrations of the powers of nature. For Christian communities
Jesus Christ was the son of righteousness. Augustine declared that we
celebrate not the sun but him who created the sun. The choice of a birth-
date for the celebration of the coming of Jesus Christ was done not on
historical grounds but on theological grounds.

It is also significant that Christmas developed after the promulgation
of the Nicene Creed. In the case of the Epiphany and Christmas festivals,
the Christian community on theological grounds was saying that the
ultimate fact in life is not the forces of nature—neither the mysterious powers
of the Nile nor the light of the sun—but God, who is incarnate in Jesus
Christ.[43]

The celebration of Christmas in the northern hemisphere came at the
time of the winter solstice. The Christmas festival was the theological
answer that Christians gave to the encroaching darkness, a darkness that
must have been overpowering before the days of electric lights or even good
gas lanterns. From the beginning the significance of Jesus was expressed
in terms of light. As the Nicene Creed declares, he is "light from light."

Christmas was the Christian community's answer to a paganism that
sought to find the meaning of life in the enhancement of the vitalities and
energies of life. Yet the ironic fact is that the Christian community has
always been subject to the temptation to turn Christmas back into a nature
festival. For this reason the Protestant Reformers, especially Calvin and
the Puritans, opposed the observance of Christmas.[44] Christmas had
become the occasion for gluttony and for excessive drinking as well as
idleness. Instead of being the Christian community's answer to paganism
that found the meaning of life in the exultation of the vitalities and energies
of life, Christmas became itself the time when those vitalities and energies
were exploited.

Christmas is appropriately a time for great joy—and, in particular, joy
in the created world. The God who became incarnate in Jesus Christ is
also the God who created the world. Hence, no good theological purpose

is served by denying that Christmas is a time for joy, for love, for the sharing of gifts and greetings, and for family festivals.

The birth narratives have also been the occasion for theological controversy. An Enlightenment and secular society has difficulty in comprehending the birth narratives. They presuppose a lively faith in a personal God who acts in history. Matthew and Luke used narratives such as the story of the shepherds and the wise men to tell what actually happened in Jesus Christ. The historical data are difficult or impossible to specify, yet they tell the truth about what actually happened with amazing power.[45] In fact, no other way of telling what happened in Jesus Christ has been as powerful, especially among ordinary people as have the Christmas stories and the Christmas carols.

The theological controversy concerning the birth of Jesus centers on the virgin birth.[46] In the fundamentalist-modernist controversies in the first half of the twentieth century, the affirmation of the historical, biological virgin birth of Jesus became the test of orthodoxy. This controversy gave to the birth of Jesus a centrality that it does not have in the New Testament, where it is mentioned only in the narratives of Matthew and Luke. So far as we know, the writer of the Fourth Gospel either did not know the narratives of the birth of Jesus or was not sufficiently interested in them theologically to record them. The same was true of the writings of the apostle Paul.[47]

It should be noted first of all that the theological doctrine of the virgin birth is not simply the affirmation of a biological and historical virgin birth. There could be a million virgin births without an incarnation. The truth is that the Word became flesh. The virgin birth is a way of confessing that this has actually happened; moreover, there is a beauty in the congruence of the Christian doctrine that the Word became flesh and the remarkable narratives of the virgin birth. Yet the crucial question is not, Was Jesus born of a virgin? but rather, Did the Lord God, creator of heaven and earth, become incarnate in this particular person? It is clear both in the New Testament and in subsequent church history that one can affirm the deity of Jesus Christ without necessarily affirming the virgin birth.

The reasons why one affirms or does not affirm the virgin birth are more important than the actual affirmation or refusal to affirm. A refusal to affirm the virgin birth on the grounds that God does not work in the created order, that the virgin birth is not a possibility, creates very serious theological problems. On the other hand, one may believe that God does work in the created order, that God has become incarnate in Jesus Christ, and yet become convinced that the historical evidence for the virgin birth is not sufficient to support an affirmation. Historical judgments, however, are significantly determined by faith commitments. For those who want to see in the narratives historical evidence for the virgin birth of Christ, there are more persuasive grounds for so affirming than for those who do not want to find the evidence. Yet for those who wish to affirm, the historical evidence is not conclusive.

The most exhaustive study of the birth narratives has been done by Raymond E. Brown. His conclusion about the virgin birth is as follows:

> In my book on the virginal conception, written before I did this commentary, I came to the conclusion that the scientifically controllable Biblical evidence leaves the question of the historicity of the virginal conception unresolved. The resurvey of the evidence necessitated by the commentary leaves me even more convinced of that. To believers who have never studied the problem critically before, this conclusion may seem radical. To many scholars who have long since dismissed the virginal conception as theological dramatization, this conclusion may seem retrogressively conservative. (And I would shock them more by affirming that I find it is easier to explain the NT evidence by positing historical bases than by positing pure theological creation.) I hope only that I have presented the evidence accurately enough to have induced the readers to further study and to their own conclusions about the evidence.[48]

Emil Brunner rejects the virgin birth on both theological and historical grounds. "The doctrine of the virgin birth does not belong to the kerygma of the church of the New Testament."[49] He does not find that the virgin birth protects the central doctrine of the New Testament, the doctrine of the incarnation. In fact, for Brunner there is tension between the virgin birth and the doctrine of the incarnation of the Son of God, though he admits that the doctrine and the birth narrative can be brought into harmony. Moreover, "the historical credibility of this narrative . . . is not such that of itself theological misgivings would be silenced. Although we cannot say absolutely that the narrative of both Synoptists is evidently non-historical, yet we must admit that the historical basis is uncertain."[50]

Karl Barth, on the contrary, is much more positive in his assessment of both the historical possibility and the theological significance of the virgin birth.

> In the Creeds the assertion of the Virgin Birth is plainly enough characterised as a first statement about the One who was and is and will be the Son of God. It is not a statement about how He became this, a statement concerning the basis and condition of His divine Sonship. It is a description of the way in which the Son of God became man. . . . The Holy Spirit has

never been regarded or described by any serious theologian as the divine Father even of the man Jesus. In the exposition of this dogma—and thoroughly in the sense of its New Testament presuppositions—it has been frequently and energetically explained that it might have pleased God to let His Son become man in some quite different way than in the event of the miracle attested as the Virgin Birth. It did in fact please Him to let Him become man in this way, but this event is not the basis of the fact that the One who there became man was the Son of God. It is the sign which accompanies and indicates the mystery of the incarnation of the Son, marking it off as a mystery from all the beginnings of other human existences. It consists in a creative act of divine omnipotence, in which the will and work of man in the form of a human father is completely excluded from the basis and beginning of the human existence of the Son of God, being replaced by divine act which is supremely unlike any human action which might arise in that connexion, and in that way characterised as an inconceivable act of grace. "Conceived by the Holy Ghost" does not, therefore, mean "begotten by the Holy Ghost." It means that God Himself—acting directly in His own and not in human fashion—stands at the beginning of this human existence and is its direct author. It is He who gives to man in the person of Mary the capacity which man does not have of himself, which she does not have and which no man could give her. It is He who sanctifies and ordains her the human mother of His Son. It is He who makes His Son hers, and in that way shares with humanity in her person nothing less than His own existence. He gives to her what she could not procure for herself and no other creature could procure for her. This is the miracle of the Virgin Birth as it indicates the mystery of the incarnation, the first attestation of the divine Sonship of the man Jesus of Nazareth, comparable with the miracle of the empty tomb at His exodus from temporal existence.[51]

In the birth of Jesus God acts again as the Creator, "but now not as the Creator out of nothing; rather, God enters the field and creates within creation a new beginning, a new beginning in history and moreover in the history of Israel."

❖

## CHAPTER 9

# THE WORK OF CHRIST

The doctrine of the Incarnation, properly understood, gives us the Christian apprehension of God, with all its saving power; leads us, in short, to the Trinitarian conception, which is the true basis for sound Christian living. But this is not a sufficient answer. If the central tradition of Christian theology through the centuries has been right, the full answer cannot be given without a consideration of the whole problem of sin and forgiveness, atonement and reconciliation. There can be no doubt that this is what the Christian witness has said from the beginning. "Faithful is the saying, and worthy of all acceptation, that Christ Jesus came into the world to save sinners." "Verily the Son of Man came . . . to give his life a ransom for many." God "sent his Son to be the propitiation for our sins." It is true that some of the Greek Fathers seem to give less emphasis than was given by the New Testament and by Latin Christianity to the thought of salvation from sin through the death of Christ, and that they sometimes think of God as assuming human nature in order to transform it by illumination and so make it immortal. But the thought of Christ having come into the world to die for our sins was never very far away. Thus Christology was continually passing into Soteriology, and throughout the whole Christian tradition the supreme human exigency to which the doctrine of the Incarnation had to be related and made relevant has been the need of salvation from sin, the forgiveness of sins.

Donald Baillie, *God Was in Christ,* 159–160

So if anyone is in Christ, there is a new creation: everything old has passed away; see, everything has become new! All this is from God, who reconciled us to himself through Christ, and has given us the ministry of reconciliation; that is, in Christ God was reconciling the world to himself, not counting their trespasses against them, and entrusting the message of reconciliation to us.

2 Corinthians 5:17–19

For to this you have been called, because Christ also suffered for you, leaving
you an example, so that you should follow in his steps.
> "He committed no sin,
>       and no deceit was found in his mouth."
When he was abused, he did not return abuse; when he suffered, he did not
threaten; but he entrusted himself to the one who judges justly. He himself
bore our sins in his body on the cross, so that, free from sins, we might live
for righteousness; by his wounds you have been healed.

1 Peter 2:21–24

What does Jesus Christ do for us? How does his life change, transform,
and heal our lives? The question Who is Jesus Christ? and the question
What does Jesus Christ do for us? are interrelated. We know who Jesus
Christ is because of what he has done for us. We also know what he has
done for us, because we know who he is. The two questions belong together,
and whenever they have been severed the answer to each question has been
impoverished. The two questions are the heart of Christian faith, and they
have been the focus not only of Christian proclamation but also of
theological reflection through the centuries.[1]

The church has answered the question of who Jesus Christ is more
precisely than it has answered the question of what Jesus Christ does for
us. There is no theological statement on the work of Christ that carries
comparable authority to the Nicene Creed or the Chalcedonian Definition.

The church has been satisfied with a variety of answers to the question,
What does Jesus Christ do for us, and how does he transform our lives?
The variety of answers defies summary in any one doctrine and provides
a depth and a breadth to the saving work of Christ that might otherwise
be lost. The variety in the ways the church has understood what Jesus Christ
actually does for us has its foundation in the New Testament.

## Jesus as Example

Jesus Christ is our example. An influential theological tradition has
insisted that we come to know who Jesus is through his benefits, through
what he does for us.[2] The same tradition has insisted that we come to
say that Jesus is my Lord and my God only if we have first known him
as a person who could be mistaken by his friends as just another human
being. This was true of the theological school of Antioch, and it was also
true for Augustine, as these statements from his sermons make clear:

> The Lord gives baptism, having been baptized by a servant, showing the way
> of humility and leading to the Lord's baptism, that is, his own baptism, by

offering an example of humility, because he himself did not reject the servant's baptism. And in the baptism of the servant a way was prepared for the Lord; and the Lord, having been baptized, made himself the way for those coming. Let us hear him: "I am the way, and the truth, and the life." If you seek the truth, hold fast the way; for the way is the same as the truth.[3]

(2) This is where you are going; this same is the way by which you are going. You do not go through one thing to something else; you do not come through something else to Christ. You come through Christ to Christ. How through Christ to Christ? Through Christ the man to Christ the God, through the Word made flesh to the Word which in the beginning was God with God, from that which man ate to that which everyday the angels eat. For so it was written, "He gave them the bread of heaven; man ate the bread of the angels." Who is the bread of angels? "In the beginning was the Word, and the Word was with God, and the Word was God." How did man eat the bread of angels? "And the Word was made flesh and dwelt among us."[4]

For Augustine, Jesus Christ is the way, the truth, and the life.

John Calvin, when he turns to the discussion of the Christian life in book 3 of the *Institutes,* refers not to the exposition of the Ten Commandments but to the example of Christ:

It [the Scripture] not only enjoins us to refer our life to God, its author, to whom it is bound; but after it has taught that we have degenerated from the true origin and condition of our creation, it also adds that Christ, through whom we return into favor with God, has been set before us as an example, whose pattern we ought to express in our life.[5]

The work of Christ as an example has its basis in New Testament teaching itself. After washing his disciples' feet, Jesus said, "For I have set you an example, that you also should do as I have done to you" (John 13:15). The apostle Paul writes, "Let the same mind be in you that was in Christ Jesus" (Philippians 2:5).

Jesus becomes our example not simply through the words that he spoke but also through the life that he lived. Proclaiming the gospel involves the telling of the story of Jesus of Nazareth as this story is given to us in the portraits of the four Gospels.

I love to tell the story
  Of unseen things above,
Of Jesus and his glory,
  Of Jesus and his love.

This hymn is more than warmhearted evangelical piety. Telling the story in both theology and preaching establishes our identity as Christians, for Jesus is the kingdom. Telling the story is the beginning of our salvation.

The story of Jesus is concretely the story of his life, as attested in the

Gospels. Otherwise, Jesus becomes a symbol for various ideological concerns. The Christian confession "Jesus is Lord," for example, has no content until informed by his story. The lordship of Jesus, apart from the story, can be filled with alien ideas and made the instrument of human causes contrary to his purpose.[6]

The story of Jesus is twofold. It is, first, his life of trust in God, of openness to other human beings, and of keenness in the ability to perceive and to acknowledge reality. He was among the people as a servant and in that way made known the Father. He was honest and at the same time humble in his dependence on God. His deeds and words were remarkably consistent.

The story of Jesus is also what he did. (1) He preached, announcing the nearness of the kingdom of God, calling people to faith and repentance. (2) He taught the will of God. (3) He healed the sick in body and person. (4) He graciously, at meals or in homes or in the presence of human needs, brought people into the presence of God's grace and mercy. (5) He gathered a community of disciples and sent them forth to preach, to teach, and to baptize. The disciples first knew Jesus as a very remarkable human being. They followed and listened to his words. In fear and trembling they accompanied him as he journeyed to Jerusalem and to his death. As witnesses to his resurrection they came to exclaim, "My Lord and my God!" In a similar manner people through the centuries have come to Christian faith, as they have heard the story of Jesus as told in the Gospels.

This story is an example for us. Some have tried to imitate the life of Jesus. The imitation of Christ will always be an important theme in Christian living.[7] Yet the vocation of Jesus Christ is not the vocation of every person in different times and places. He did not assume many responsibilities in society, such as maintaining civic order. As the Christ, his vocation is not the work of any other person. Hence there is a rigidity and at times an irrelevance to the imitation of Christ. The example of Jesus is more the pattern in the light of which we make the concrete decisions of daily life. Christian vocation is to be like Jesus amid the challenges and demands of our particular time and place. Jesus Christ saves us by giving us an example of trust in God, of openness to the neighbor, and of responsibility for the gift of life itself.

## Jesus as Teacher

Jesus Christ is our teacher. Much of Jesus' own ministry was involved in teaching the people. The parables of Jesus as well as his sayings constitute a major portion of the Gospels.

Jesus teaches us who God is. This teaching is not only in his words and parables but supremely in his life, as the disciples came to see that in Jesus, God the creator of heaven and earth was acting for their salvation. And the disciples came to affirm that the creator is the God and Father of our Lord Jesus Christ or, more particularly, that the creator is the Word that became flesh and lived among us (John 1:1–4; Colossians 1:15–16). Jesus in his death on the cross made known the love of God, for the disciples came to understand his cross as God's taking upon himself the sins of human beings.[8] Jesus teaches us by his word and by his life who God is.

Jesus also teaches us who we are. We cannot define the image of God or what it is to be an authentic human being by studying human nature itself. Human nature has been fractured and distorted by sin. Jesus in his life demonstrates what God made all human beings to be. Thus Jesus teaches us who we are. He is the answer to the question, Who is a true human being?

The role of Jesus as a teacher can only in part be summarized in sentences and propositions. He taught us by speaking to us and by telling parables. Yet the teaching of Jesus is more than propositions. Through familiarity with the life and teaching of Jesus we gain an insight, an illumination that enables us to know our own lives and the meaning of the world in which we live. The Christian assimilates in his or her own consciousness the record of the life of Jesus, the Lord and master, and through this assimilation shapes his or her own life. In this sense Jesus Christ saves us by being our teacher or our illuminator. In every age of the church this has been a consistent theme.

## Jesus as Our Ransom

Jesus Christ redeems us, ransoms us.[9] Here the symbolism is that Jesus Christ paid the price for our freedom and for our deliverance. When the church used the New Testament metaphor of redemption, of buying back, it was emphasizing something quite fundamental in general human experience. Whenever there is deliverance from evil, a price has to be paid to the evil in the situation. Each spring people die in the James River because they venture out too far into the swirling waters. Some drown; others are rescued. Yet whenever there is a rescue from potential drowning, a price has to be paid to the evil in the situation. The price may be no more than the gasoline for a helicopter, but it may involve the risk of human life on the part of those who venture out to the rocks to deliver persons from potential death. Whenever there is deliverance from serious evil, even in general human experience, a price has to be paid, a ransom given to the evil in the situation. The theologians of the early church were convinced that, though God is omnipotent, it would be inappropriate for God to save human beings in an arbitrary way. Even the devil has to be treated fairly. Deliverance from evil has to be an appropriate authentic deliverance, not a violent and arbitrary rescue.

## Victory Over Sin, Death, and the Devil

A fourth way in which Jesus Christ brings us salvation is through his triumph over sin, death, and the devil.[10] Here Christ is the victor. The early Christian imagination was very vivid in elaborating the ways in which Jesus Christ won the victory over the principalities and powers of this world. This elaboration makes more vivid the fact that once there lived in history a human being who was not overcome by evil but who overcame evil by good. In the life of Jesus, evil could not turn love into hate. Even from the cross, Jesus prayed, "Father, forgive them; for they know not what they do." Furthermore, Jesus Christ is the instance in human history of a human being who could not be destroyed by death. God raised him from the dead.

This triumph over sin, death, and the devil was not only a foretoken of God's final salvation; it was also a victory with which believers could identify and in which they could participate. Irenaeus spoke of the work of Christ as recapitulation. Jesus recapitulated in himself the long history of human evolution, undoing what human beings had done to themselves and fulfilling God's intentions for them.[11] We appropriate and participate in this recapitulation.

Our participation in the victory of Christ is illustrated in many events in our common life. In university communities persons who have neither the physical abilities nor the inclination to play in college sports yet identify with their team in a way that enables them to participate in its victories and losses. They do not even say the college won or lost; they say "we" won or lost. Hence the early church spoke of our participation in the victorious life of one who could not be destroyed by evil or death or the principalities in this world.

## Deification

Early Christians spoke of the work of Jesus as deification. Jesus Christ became man that we might become God.[12] As Second Peter expresses it, the work of Jesus Christ enables us to participate in the very being of God (2 Peter 1:3). For Eastern Christians especially this has always been an important theme. The fundamental human predicament has been our corruption and our mortality, our separation from God. Jesus Christ unites us with the life-giving energies of God and opens to us mystical experience, enabling us to become all that we are capable of being.

## Forgiveness of Sins

From the time of the New Testament on, Christians have spoken of Jesus as the victim or the sacrifice. The letter to the Hebrews compares Christ to the faultless victim who through his vicarious death assures forgiveness and communion with God (Hebrews 10:10ff.). Paul tells us that Christ became a curse for us (Galatians 3:13) or that Jesus was "raised for our justification" (Romans 4:25). In Colossians 2:14 we read that God erased "the record that stood against us with its legal demands. He set this aside, nailing it to the cross."

In the history of doctrine, this particular understanding of the work of Christ found its classic expression in Anselm's *Cur Deus Homo*.[13] Living in the twelfth century, Anselm used the imagery of a feudal society. Sinners have dishonored God, and satisfaction has to be made or punishment is necessary. Since the injury has been done to God, only God can provide an adequate satisfaction. Since human beings have done the injury, only human beings can make the satisfaction. Therefore satisfaction can only be rendered by the God-Man, who in his life rendered perfect obedience to God and who in his death bore our sins. Satisfaction has been made; forgiveness is possible without violence to the moral order.

Anselm's understanding of the work of Jesus Christ has always been subject to caricature and can appear remote from human experience. Yet in actual fact he was saying something that was very significant, and his understanding of the work of Christ is the most profound in the Christian tradition.

> Anselm makes it possible for God to forgive without loss of perfect righteousness. The law has been fulfilled now. The penalty has been paid, not in the form of punishment, but in the form of satisfaction, according to the principle either punishment or satisfaction. Either will suffice.[14]

Anselm knew that forgiveness is not simple. Forgiveness does not say that what one did or did not do does not matter. Forgiveness declares that the guilt has been borne and the possibilities of life are now altered.

Something like this always happens in human relationships when one person forgives another. Whenever there is true forgiveness, there is always, as H. R. Mackintosh put it, the suffering of atonement on the part of the forgiver, who accepts the wrongdoing and bears the guilt, and the suffering of repentance on the part of those who receive forgiveness.[15] There can be no forgiveness even in human relations without taking the guilt or atonement, on the one hand, and without repentance, a true sorrow for the wrongdoing, on the other. The death of Jesus Christ, therefore, belongs to the very being of God.

From the beginning, the Christian community always insisted that God's salvation has to be appropriate to the world that God has made. God cannot simply by fiat declare human beings saved; he cannot forgive out of a general disposition. Salvation has to come in ways that are appropriate in the light of the nature of God, the moral structure of the universe, and the nature of human existence itself. Anselm's way of understanding God's forgiveness is the most profound in the history of the Christian community, because it attempts to say that salvation is appropriate. It is an answer to the question of whether history, both public and individual, is simply a series of judgments or whether there are resources of divine mercy which can overcome sin and evil without sacrificing the divine intention for human life.

For Anselm and for Calvin, the heart of salvation is to be found in the death of Jesus Christ. The good news is paradoxically the death of Christ, a death that bought our salvation. The death of Christ could have been seen as the fate of a good life in a world dominated by evil persons. It could have been seen as an example of the way in which we are to respond to evil, that is, as an example of martyrdom. The early Christian communities never understood it either as a terrible fate or as a godly example, but as the redemptive act of God. The death of Christ is the actualization in human history of what happens in the very being of God. God takes our sins upon himself and forgives us.[16] The atonement is the answer to George Bernard Shaw's contention that forgiveness is a beggar's refuge, we must pay our debts (*Major Barbara*, 1905). The debt or the penalty or the satisfaction has been paid. This understanding of our salvation is the most profound of all.

From the beginning Christians have recognized that the death of Christ belonged to the very being of God. When they spoke of God as impassible (without suffering) they meant, as G. L. Prestige has argued, that God was not swayed from without, in the way that human beings are at the mercy of those they love, but that God's activity in providence, redemption, and sanctification comes from the will of God.[17] His love is not wrung from him by pity. This means that God is the same yesterday, today, and forever. In this sense the death of Christ belongs to the very being of God. In the incarnation of the Son of God, God on his own initiative took death into his own being.

## The Outreaching Love of God

The Christian community has never allowed Anselm's theology to stand alone. Very quickly, within a century, Abailard (1079–1142) caricatured what Anselm had been saying by contending that it would be cruel and wicked to demand the blood of an innocent person as the price for anything, or that God should consider the death of his son so agreeable that by it he should be reconciled to the whole world.[18] For Abailard, the work of Christ was not the bearing of our sins so much as it was a manifestation of the outgoing love of God, which lays hold of us and frees us from slavery to sin and wins for us the true liberty of children of God, so that we do all things out of love rather than fear.

Anselm is surely more profound, and without Anselm's understanding of the cost of forgiveness no doctrine of atonement is satisfactory. It can also be said that without Abailard's emphasis on the whole work of Christ as the outreaching love of God, no other understanding is complete. God's great work for our redemption in Jesus Christ cannot be adequately stated or summarized in neatly written sentences or propositions. Salvation is God's confronting us in a person. On the purely human level no personal engagement can be exhaustively described in words. Yet various facets of what God did to redeem us are clear enough. Our salvation is the work of God in Christ, who did for us what we could not do for ourselves. God in Christ suffered vicariously for us, made satisfaction for our sins, and in the person of Jesus not only condemned sin but overcame sin and death. Yet God's salvation is also the outreaching love of God and the demonstration of God's will for human beings in Jesus Christ, which elicits and evokes love and discipleship among us. This is the truth in the old evangelical way of describing salvation as coming to know Jesus.

## The Descent to Hell

This controversial phrase in the Apostles' Creed made its first credal appearance in the Fourth Formula of Sirmiun, 359. The New Testament basis for the descent to hell is primarily 1 Peter 3:19 and 4:6. It is suggested in Romans 10:7 and Colossians 1:18 and perhaps also Acts

2:27–31. It can be found as a part of the early Christian teaching in the writings of Ignatius, Polycarp, Irenaeus, and Tertullian. This phrase came to have theological significance as a way of presenting Jesus Christ to the Old Testament saints and also to those outside of the Hebrew tradition who had not known Jesus in the flesh. Another interpretation placed the emphasis upon the "harrowing" of hell. Christ invaded the very citadel of the devil and conquered him. The phrase gave expression to the triumph of Christ over sin and death and the devil, as well as offer salvation to all people.

John Calvin was aware of these earlier interpretations of the phrase. He too affirmed that it represented the triumph of Jesus Christ over sin and death and the devil, but he goes beyond this to perhaps the profoundest interpretation in his analysis of the Creed in the *Institutes of Christian Religion*: "The point is that the Creed sets forth what Christ suffered in the sight of men, and then appositely speaks of that invisible and incomprehensible judgment that he underwent in the sight of God in order that we might know not only that Christ's body was given as the price of our redemption but that he paid a greater and more excellent price in suffering in his soul the terrible torments of a condemned and forsaken man" (2.16.10). The descent into hell is the personal and psychological counterpart to the physical sufferings on the cross. In the incarnation, God suffered in human life the utmost depths of human anguish.

## Prophet, Priest, and King

John Calvin's doctrine of the work of Christ stands in the tradition of the school of Antioch with its emphasis on the humanity of Jesus Christ and on his life and example. It also stands in the tradition of Anselm, replacing Anselm's emphasis on satisfaction with penal substitution. Calvin summarized the work of Christ under the offices of prophet, priest, and king. Jesus Christ is our prophet who declares God's will to us and teaches us how to live and die. He is our priest who bears our sins, makes amends for the evil we do, and offers continual intercession for us. He is our king who rules over us and defends us from all our enemies. The Westminster Shorter Catechism popularized this understanding of the work of Christ among English-speaking Protestants.

Jesus came preaching the kingdom of God and calling people to repentance. More than that, he was in his own life the embodiment of that kingdom in history. As the risen Lord, he is the Lord of the church in which we prepare for the coming of the kingdom in glory.

CHAPTER 10

❖

# THE HOLY SPIRIT

The Holy Spirit, for whose work the community, and in and with the community the believing Christian, is thankful, is not the spirit of the world, nor is He the spirit of the community, nor is He the spirit of any individual Christian, but He is the spirit of God, God Himself, as He eternally proceeds from the Father and the Son, as He unites the Father and Son in eternal love, as He must be worshipped and glorified together with the Father and the Son, because He is of one substance with them. He is not man's own spirit and He never will be. He is God, attesting Himself to the spirit of man as his God, as the God who acts for him and to him. He is God, coming to man, and coming to him in such a way that He is revealed to him as the God who reconciles the world and man to Himself, in such a way therefore that what He is and does for him as such becomes the Word which man can hear and actually does hear, in such a way, therefore, that man allows himself to be reconciled with Him (2 Corinthians 5:20). God's self-attestation makes what He does the Word which is spoken to this man and received and accepted by him. The Holy Spirit is God in His self-attestation—God in the power which quickens man to this profitable and living knowledge of His action. He is God intervening and acting for man, addressing Himself to him, in such a way that He says Yes to Himself and this makes possible and necessary man's human Yes to Him. . . .

It is strange but true that fundamentally and in general practice we cannot say more of the Holy Spirit and His work than that He is the power in which Jesus Christ attests Himself, attests Himself effectively, creating in man response and obedience. We describe Him as His awakening power.

Karl Barth, *Church Dogmatics* IV/1, 646, 648

Jesus said to them again, "Peace be with you. As the Father has sent me, so I send you." When he had said this, he breathed on them and said to them, "Receive the Holy Spirit."

John 20:21–22

160

"This," he [Jesus] said, "is what you have heard from me; for John baptized with water, but you will be baptized with the Holy Spirit not many days from now."

Acts 1:4–5

The Holy Spirit is God's personal and powerful presence in the world, who calls forth faith and unites human beings with what God has done for them in Jesus Christ. In the words of Reformed orthodoxy, the Holy Spirit applies to us the redemption wrought by Christ.[1] As Calvin put it, "As long as Christ remains outside us, and we are separated from him, all that he has suffered and done for the salvation of the human race remains useless and of no value for us."[2] It is by the power of the Holy Spirit that salvation becomes a reality in human life and in human society. Hence the New Testament advised those who wanted the promised salvation to wait for the Holy Spirit (John 20:22; Acts 1:1–8).

This emphasis on waiting for the Holy Spirit stands in judgment on any notion that salvation and the church are human works. When salvation becomes a human achievement, we save ourselves, build the church, and bring in the kingdom. In the New Testament human salvation, the church, and the rule of God are first of all the works of God. The Holy Spirit is the chief agent in the life of the church. Every religious activity is empowered by the Holy Spirit. Christians pray in the Spirit, and the Holy Spirit prays in them and for them (Romans 8:27–28).

Christians recognize the presence of God in Jesus Christ by the power of the Holy Spirit (1 Corinthians 2). The Holy Spirit, poured into their hearts, enables them to confess that Christ died for them and that God commends his love in Christ's death (Romans 5:1–11). Christians are bound together in community by the power of the Holy Spirit (1 Corinthians 12; Ephesians 4:1–7). The Holy Spirit gives the gifts of the spirit, including the ability to speak in tongues and to prophesy. The Holy Spirit opens the meaning of scripture (1 Peter 1:10–13). The Holy Spirit gives the first installment or guarantee of our redemption (2 Corinthians 1:22; 5:5; Ephesians 1:14; 1 Peter 1:1–12). In the New Testament the Holy Spirit is the presence and the power of God that awakens the human heart and makes Christian believers alive to the presence of God. Moreover, the Holy Spirit empowers the believer to be transformed into the image of Christ and to bear witness to Jesus Christ.

# Who Is the Holy Spirit?

The Holy Spirit, according to John V. Taylor in a remarkable book, *The Go-Between God,* is the power of the divine personhood.[3] The human spirit is the power by which a person makes himself or herself present and known, so the Holy Spirit is that power by which God makes himself present and known to human beings. The Holy Spirit is God active in the world in the power of the divine personhood.

The word "spirit" is confusing in ordinary speech, for it sometimes stands in contrast to the material. The spiritual is popularly thought to be the ethereal over against flesh and blood, which are material. In the New Testament the opposite of spirit is not the material but the impersonal. The spiritual is the personal, and the spirit is the person. Some difficulties in theology are resolved if we remember that the spirit is closely related to what we call the person, and spirituality is closely related to the personal. Each stands in contrast to the impersonal, not primarily in contrast to the material.

The word "spirit" encounters a second difficulty in common speech: it has no content. There are many spirits loose in the world, and some of them are quite evil. Hence it is crucially important for the Holy Spirit to be defined. For Christians the Holy Spirit is defined by Jesus Christ. Jesus Christ is the concrete revelation of God in human history, and it is through Jesus Christ that we know the Father and that we know the Holy Spirit. Barth has well said that "we cannot say more of the Holy Spirit and His work than that He is the power in which Jesus Christ attests Himself, attests Himself effectively, creating in man response and obedience."[4]

The definition of the Holy Spirit by the life and death and resurrection of Jesus Christ is embodied in the controversial phrase of the Nicene Creed, *filioque* (who proceeds from the Father *and the Son*).[5] This phrase does not appear in the Nicene Creed as it was adopted by the First Council of Constantinople in 381. It came into use among Augustinian theologians in western Europe and gradually was added to the creed. Charlemagne attempted to have popes make this the official version of the creed in the West, but they refused. However, in 1012 the German emperor persuaded a German-born pope to add this clause to the creed used in the Roman church. Today the use of this phrase in the West is the source of contention with Eastern Orthodox churches. The controversy may be resolved by the use of the phrase that was common among Eastern theologians that the Holy Spirit proceeds from the Father through the Son. The important point is the definition of the Holy Spirit by Jesus Christ.

The importance of the *filioque* clause is clarified by a homely illustration. A slide projector may send only clear light with no content through a clear slide; but if the slide has color, content, a picture on it, then this becomes the substance of what is projected on the screen. In some such way the church was attempting to say in the *filioque* clause that Jesus Christ is the content of the Holy Spirit. The identity of the Holy Spirit is what we have seen and heard in the life, death, and resurrection of Jesus Christ. The Holy Spirit is Christ's spirit at work in the world sent forth by the Father through the Son.

The Holy Spirit is also bound to the Word of God, according to a traditional emphasis of Reformed theology.

> For by a kind of mutual bond the Lord has joined together the certainty of his Word and of his Spirit so that the perfect religion of the Word may abide in our minds when the Spirit, who causes us to contemplate God's face, shines; and that we in turn may embrace the Spirit with no fear of being deceived when we recognize him in his own image, namely in the Word.[6]

In this way classical Reformed theology was emphatic that the Holy Spirit cannot be separated either from the revelation of God in Jesus Christ or from the Holy Scripture, which is the word of God written.

## What Does the Holy Spirit Do?

The Spirit first of all unites us with Jesus Christ. Christ becomes ours, and he dwells within us. We are ingrafted into him (Romans 11:17) and we put on Christ (Galatians 3:27). Christ, Calvin insisted, means nothing to us until we grow into one body with him. This union is obtained by faith through the power of the Holy Spirit. It is important to note that our union with Christ is personal, comparable to the way in which we are united with other persons whose personalities penetrate our very existence and with whom we feel as one. Union with Christ is not substantive but personal. This is a characteristic of all of Calvin's theology. Grace is the personal act of God, and therefore Calvin resists every attempt to materialize grace or to think of grace as a power or energy implanted in a person. The Holy Spirit works by personally engaging us as responsible, moral, historical persons. Union with Christ is a personal relationship with Christ through the power of the Holy Spirit. It finds its closest analogy in deeply human relationships.

The Holy Spirit also elicits faith from our hearts. This, Calvin contends, is the principal work of the Holy Spirit, as will be noted in the next chapter. Faith is the human response to the gracious presence of God whereby we come to trust God.

Testimony is the third work of the Holy Spirit. We come to know scripture as the Word of God through testimony of the Holy Spirit.

> For as God alone is a fit witness of himself in his Word, so also the Word will not find acceptance in men's hearts before it is sealed by the inward testimony of the Spirit. The same Spirit, therefore, who has spoken through the mouths of the prophets must penetrate into our hearts to persuade us that they faithfully proclaimed what had been divinely commanded. . . . Let this point therefore stand: that those whom the Holy Spirit has inwardly taught truly rest upon Scripture, and that Scripture indeed is self-authenticated; hence, it is not right to subject it to proof and reasoning. And the certainty it deserves with us, it attains by the testimony of the Spirit. For even if it wins reverence for itself by its own majesty, it seriously affects us only when it is sealed upon our hearts through the Spirit. Therefore, illumined by his power, we believe neither by our own nor by anyone else's judgment that Scripture is from God.[7]

The Holy Spirit also makes us alive to the presence of Jesus Christ in the sacrament of the Lord's Supper. The Holy Spirit provides the power by which the sacraments promote and confirm faith. The sacramental elements cannot establish and increase faith by any inherent power which they themselves possess.

> The sacraments properly fulfill their office only when the Spirit, that inward teacher, comes to them, by whose power alone hearts are penetrated and affections moved and our souls opened for the sacraments to enter in. If the Spirit be lacking, the sacraments can accomplish nothing more in our minds than the splendor of the sun shining upon blind eyes, or a voice sounding in deaf ears. Therefore I make such a division between Spirit and sacraments that the power to act rests with the former, and the ministry alone is left to the latter—a ministry empty and trifling, apart from the action of the Spirit, but charged with great effect when the Spirit works within and manifests his power.[8]

The Spirit moves in human hearts to keep them alive to the presence of God in the sacraments, as well as in the words of scripture. The power of the Holy Spirit to make believers alive to the presence of God in the sacraments also extends to the whole created order. The Holy Spirit transforms human words and relationships, the beauty and wonder of nature, historical events into the means of God's grace in human life.

Sanctification is the fourth work of the Holy Spirit. The Holy Spirit not only unites us with Christ, elicits faith from our hearts, makes us alive to the presence and to the voice of God, but also moves our hearts to fashion us in the image of Jesus Christ. To be "sanctified in Christ" (1 Corinthians 1:2) is a broad term including the whole of the Christian life and also the status of being set aside for God of places and institutions and persons. In Reformed theology, however, sanctification refers to the transformation of human life into the image of Christ. This work is always attributed both in the New Testament and in Reformed theology first of all to the Holy Spirit.[9]

The Holy Spirit is active not only in the order of salvation but also in nature and human history; the Spirit of God is the sole fountain of truth. Those who depreciate the arts and mathematical sciences "dishonor the Spirit of God."[10] Later Reformed theologians developed a doctrine of common grace that is active in all creation and human history, in addition to the special grace that is operative in the order of salvation. Reformed theology has classically emphasized that the Spirit works in all creation, that the Christian life is lived in the world and that "religious" exercises are never a meritorious work in themselves.

## How Does the Holy Spirit Work?

The Holy Spirit is the mystery of the divine presence that encounters us, calls us, transforms us, makes us alive to God. As such the Holy Spirit is beyond our comprehension. The Gospel of John declares that the Holy Spirit is like the wind. We "do not know where it comes from or where it goes" (John 3:8).

Yet we do know that the Holy Spirit is the Spirit of Christ; furthermore, we know that the Holy Spirit is free. We cannot coerce the Spirit or control the Spirit. We must wait for the Spirit. We also know that the Holy Spirit, as the personal presence of God, deals with human beings as persons, not as sticks or stones. The Holy Spirit elicits our willing response.

The Holy Spirit's presence is always mediated. No one has seen God. The Holy Spirit promises to work through worship, scripture, Christian fellowship, the sacraments, where two or three are gathered in the divine name. These are the means appointed in the New Testament, yet the Holy Spirit is not bound and cannot be limited to any means.

❖

## CHAPTER 11

# THE BEGINNINGS
# OF THE CHRISTIAN LIFE

It is Christ, the Word of God, brought to the hearing of man by the out-pouring of the Holy Spirit, who is man's possibility of being the recipient of divine revelation. Therefore this receiving, this revealedness of God for us is really a self-revelation. In no less sense than the incarnation of the Word in Christ, it is the divine act of lordship, the mystery and the miracle of the existence of God among us, the triumph of free grace.

Karl Barth, *Church Dogmatics* I/2, 249

But to all who received him, who believed in his name, he gave power to become children of God, who were born, not of blood or of the will of the flesh or of the will of man, but of God.

John 1:12–13

The transformation of human existence which is the beginning of the Christian life is a complex experience![1] In the New Testament this experience is described in terms of an adult who is moving from an old life into a new life, or who is being reborn into the kingdom, or who is entering upon a new order of existence. The New Testament does not focus on the problem that arises when we attempt to describe the origins of the Christian life in the person who has been born in the providence of God into the fellowship of a Christian home and the Christian church. In general the New Testament assumes a radical shift in one's personal existence rather than growth into Christian maturity, which became the accepted pattern of Christian life in established churches. The New Testament deals with a situation that differs from the established church but that, increasingly in a pluralistic, secular society, has its counterparts today. The problems concerning the origin of the Christian life for established churches are very similar to the controversies about infant versus adult believer's baptism.

The Gospels, which come out of the context of a Jewish community, do expect a reorientation of life. John the Baptist called for repentance that demanded a radical change (Luke 3:7–14). Jesus repeatedly called upon his hearers to make drastic reorientations of life (Luke 19:1–10; Matthew 19:16–22). The kingdom takes priority over personal relations in the family (Mark 3:31–35). The rich young man must sell his goods; the anxious must trust God, who cares for the lilies of the field (Luke 12:22–31). The consistent call for a new life is addressed to those within the church as well as those without.

The transformation of life that is rebirth into the kingdom or the new creation of which Paul speaks cannot be simply described, because it involves the total life of a person. Many factors enter into this transforming experience. We cannot speak of them all at the same time; yet to speak of them chronologically or logically is to distort what is a unified human experience.

The New Testament description of the transformation which is the origin of the Christian life is always dramatic and decisive. The Gospels begin with Jesus' calling people to repent and believe the gospel (Mark 1:15), and the New Testament concludes with very decisive sayings in the pastoral epistles encouraging growth in the Christian life (e.g., 1 Timothy 4–6).

The beginning of the Christian life as described in the New Testament startles established churches that have practiced infant baptism. In these churches it is assumed that a child is born into the Christian family and that the origin of the Christian life begins perhaps before birth.[2] In any case, the Christian life begins with birth and is continually nourished in the life of the community. The child has no memory of life outside the community of faith and outside the context of the means of God's grace. Yet the typical or characteristic description of the origin of the Christian life in the New Testament, especially as it moves from the community of Israel to the society of the Roman Empire presupposes a radical shift in one's style and manner of living. The Christian life begins with the call to acknowledge Jesus as the Messiah or the chosen one whom God had raised from the dead. "Repent, and be baptized every one of you in the name of Jesus Christ so that your sins may be forgiven; and you will receive the gift of the Holy Spirit" (Acts 2:38).

The origin of the Christian life is described as a new creation. "So if anyone is in Christ, there is a new creation: everything old has passed away; see, everything has become new!" (2 Corinthians 5:17). "For neither circumcision nor uncircumcision is anything; but a new creation is everything!" (Galatians 6:15).

The New Testament also describes the Christian life as the resurrection from the dead. "You he made alive, when you were dead through the trespasses and sins in which you once walked" (Ephesians 2:1–2, RSV). "Even when we were dead through our trespasses, [God] made us alive together with Christ — by grace you have been saved — and raised us up with him" (Ephesians 2:5–6). The writer to the Colossians declares, "When you were buried with him in baptism, you were also raised with him through faith in the power of God, who raised him from the dead. And when you were dead in trespasses and the uncircumcision of your flesh, God made you alive together with him, when he forgave us all our trespasses" (Colossians 2:12–13).

A third image of the new life is birth. "But to all who received him, who believed in his name, he gave power to become children of God, who were born, not of blood or of the will of the flesh or of the will of man, but of God" (John 1:12–13). The Gospel of John quotes Jesus saying to Nicodemus, "Very truly, I tell you, no one can see the kingdom of God without being born from above" (John 3:3).

The radical change of a new creation, of a resurrection from the dead, of a rebirth had been proclaimed by Jeremiah in the Old Testament, "I will put my law within them, and I will write it on their hearts; and I will be their God, and they shall be my people" (Jeremiah 31:33). This is the radical change or transformation that is anticipated in the conversation of Jesus with Nicodemus (John 3:1–8).

In all these passages, the new creation, the resurrection from the dead, the new birth, and the writing of law on the heart are attributed to the action of God. The Christian life begins with God's grace and action. Just as we can feel the wind but do not know whence it comes, so it is with the power and the presence of God that elicits this transformation. Yet in the New Testament this action of God is generally within the context of the means of grace. Hearing the word of God comes by preaching. Paul also asks how they can hear without a preacher (Romans 10:14). The new birth is called forth by the witness who bears testimony to what God has done. Jesus himself came calling people to repent and believe the gospel (Mark 3:15). Many of the most remarkable stories in the Gospels tell of the presence of Jesus at dinners attended by sinners in whose presence the power of God was mightily demonstrated in the transformation of human life (Matthew 9:10–13; Luke 5:27–32; 7:36–50; 15:1). In the presence of the witness, in the context of the Christian family and the fellowship of the Christian community, through preaching, teaching, sacraments, diaconal service, prayer, and the conversation of Christians, the Holy Spirit, the personal presence of God, transforms and shapes human life.

Karl Barth has described the beginnings of the Christian life as an awakening. The scriptural admonitions "So then let us not fall asleep as others do, but let us keep awake and be sober" (1 Thessalonians 5:6); "It is now the moment for you to wake from sleep" (Romans 13:11); "Sleeper, awake! Rise from the dead, and Christ will shine on you" (Ephesians 5:14) are not so much missionary preaching as a call primarily to the Christian community. The awakening is "the relentless downward movement consequent upon Christian sloth." Yet the sleep which we sleep is the sleep of death and what is needed is that we should be awakened and awakened from death. But this requires a new and direct act of God, if there is to be an awakening in which a person becomes a disciple, a Christian.[3]

Barth's analogy of awakening is very suggestive, and his emphasis that it is God who does the awakening is crucially important. The Christian life has its origin and its goal in God. It is something that God does; the awakening of the human being, a conversion, is first of all an act of God. In the church we count on the fact that God himself "gives and creates and actualizes it."

> The basis of Christian existence lies as deep as this. It is not the Christian who guarantees it. It is God Himself. God Himself takes responsibility for its reality. We are given the simple task. Do we believe in God? We do so only if we believe in the awakening of man to conversion. Conversely do we believe in the awakening of man to conversion? We do so only if we believe in God.[4]

In the classic Reformed theologics of the seventeenth century, the beginnings of the Christian life were designated regeneration and conversion.[5] Regeneration can mean the entire process of the transformation of human life to the image of Christ, or it can refer to the beginning of that life and in particular to the interior roots of the beginning of the Christian life in the depth of the human self.

Conversion traditionally referred to the outward manifestation of the regeneration that had taken place in the heart. Conversion likewise can refer to the whole lifetime of the Christian, but generally it was restricted to the dramatic experience at the beginning of the Christian life.

The nature of the church itself partly determines the usage of these terms. In a church that practices the baptism of infants, the words have different connotations than they do in those churches which place the emphasis on a historical conversion experience and on believers' baptism. Such churches can point to a time before which the believers were not in the church and after which they are in the church.

How shall we understand the concept of regeneration? What is it that happens in the human self when one becomes a Christian? As John's Gospel puts it, the work of the Holy Spirit in the human heart is a mystery (John

3:7). We cannot know how the Holy Spirit lays hold of the human self. Yet we can emphasize that no one has ever seen God and that God's presence to us is mediated through persons and through objects. In the church we speak of the means of grace. Ordinarily the Holy Spirit works in the human heart through means, through the Bible as the written word of God, through the Christian life of the family, through the fellowship of the church, through preaching, through prayer, through stewardship, through images, metaphors, and stories, and through the witness of Christians in the world. Regeneration, in the words of Emil Brunner, is "the creation of the person through God's historical self-communication." The Spirit of God creates life, "yet not in disregard of Word and Spirit, but through them both."[6]

Contemporary psychology has much to teach us about human behavior, but the human self remains a mystery to the psychologist.[7] The Holy Spirit cannot become an object for study. As Christians we can learn what wisdom psychology and sociology may give us about how human character is formed and how human life is shaped. Yet there is no possibility that a psychology and a sociology, which methodologically rule out the divine presence, can give a definitive description of what Christians believe happens in the transformation of human life.

How shall we understand conversion? What is the appropriate public behavior that corresponds to the regeneration of the human heart? In America revivalism called for a dramatic conversion, a radical decision, before which one was not a Christian and after which one is. The decision frequently involved "walking down the aisle" to meet the minister in response to the call to accept Jesus Christ as Lord and Savior, followed by baptism. For churches that practice infant baptism the usual pattern is for persons to grow up in the life of the church experiencing no radical change, with no point before which they were not Christians and after which they are. Yet in such situations the need to heed the injunctions of the New Testament to grow into the image of Christ may be all the greater. Increasingly in a highly pluralistic society many persons born in the church come under alien influences. The fall from the Christian life may be radical, and the church in some way must acknowledge this and provide help in "turning human life around." Churches that practice infant baptism do not always have, or do not always provide, adequate opportunities for the kind of dramatic change of direction and repentance that is required of those reared in the church who have fallen under the tyranny of drugs or alcohol or the various temptations of a secular society.

❖

## CHAPTER 12

# FAITH

If you confess with your lips that Jesus is Lord and believe in your heart that God raised him from the dead, you will be saved. For one believes with the heart and so is justified, and one confesses with the mouth and so is saved.

Romans 10:9–10

Now faith is the assurance of things hoped for, the conviction of things not seen. Indeed, by faith our ancestors received approval. By faith we understand that the worlds were prepared by the word of God, so that what is seen was made from things that are not visible.

Hebrews 11:1–3

Faith on the primitive level is a universal human act.[1] It is consciously or unconsciously the decision a human being makes to orient and to direct human life. As such it is on its highest level the most significant personal act. It is an action of the whole person, yet it is also the principal work of the Holy Spirit.[2]

In the *Institutes of the Christian Religion,* John Calvin provides two formal definitions of faith. "We hold faith to be a knowledge of God's will toward us, perceived from his Word."[3] Calvin then goes on to what he understands is the right definition of faith. Faith is "a firm and certain knowledge of God's benevolence toward us, founded upon the truth of the freely given promise in Christ, both revealed to our minds and sealed upon our hearts through the Holy Spirit."[4]

Karl Barth defines faith as

at once the most wonderful and the simplest of things. In it a man opens his eyes and sees and accepts everything as it—objectively, really and ontologically—is. Faith is the simple discovery of the child which finds itself in the father's house and on the mother's lap. But this simple thing is also the mystery of faith because only in Jesus Christ is it true and actual that things are as man discovers them, and because man's own discovery can itself be an event only in the fact that man is again awakened by Him to see and accept everything as it is: that the night has passed and the day dawned; that there is peace between God and sinful man, revealed truth, full and present salvation. This simple thing, and this mystery, constitute the being of the Christian, his being by the one in whom he believes.[5]

Barth also goes on to a more formal theological definition of faith. Faith

is an acknowledgment, a recognition and a confession. As all these terms indicate, it is a knowledge. And as the object and basis is the same in every case, so in every case it is an active knowledge. Why a knowledge? As we have seen, underlying it there is the presupposition of a creative event—the being and activity of Jesus Christ in the power of his Holy Spirit awakening man to faith. As the event of a human act on this basis, faith is a cognitive event, the simple taking cognisance of the preceding being and work of Jesus Christ. But we are not dealing with an automatic reflection, with a stone lit up by the sun, or wood kindled by a fire, or a leaf blown by the wind. We are dealing with man. It is, therefore, a spontaneous, a free, an active event. This active aspect is expressed in the three terms: acknowledgment, recognition and confession.[6]

How then can we understand faith?

# A Personal Act

Faith is first of all a personal act. Faith is an act and an attitude which touches the totality of our existence. It is "I" who believed, not just with my intellect, my will, or my emotions, but that "I" in its totality.

Faith as ultimate concern is an act of the total personality. It happens in the center of the personal life and includes all its elements. Faith is the most centered act of the human mind. It is not a movement of a special section or a special function of man's total being. They all are united in the act of faith. But faith is not the sum total of their impacts. It transcends every special impact as well as the totality of them and it has itself a decisive impact on each of them.

Since faith is an act of the personality as a whole, it participates in the dynamics of personal life.[7]

Faith can be distorted when it is made simply a matter of the intellect, affirming certain propositions as true. It can also be distorted when it is centered in the emotions, the affections. Faith is something more than assenting to propositions or feeling or desiring. Finally, faith can be distorted when it is simply made a matter of the will. The will to believe is important, but no person has ever believed on the basis of willing alone. Faith is as much beyond the power of the human will as are such human decisions as love, gratitude, and humility.

It is important to note that faith has a double meaning. It can refer in the primary sense to the act of the human person. It can also refer in a secondary sense to the faith which is believed. Generally in the New Testament, faith refers to the act of believing, but it can also refer to the content of faith (1 Timothy 3:9; 4:6; Jude 3, 20). The act of believing and faith as the content of the act of faith are not to be confused, and yet they cannot be separated. In their own spheres both the act of faith and the faith that is believed are crucially important.

## Faith as Knowledge

Faith is knowledge. John Calvin was emphatic on the cognitive character of faith. The medieval church had tolerated a notion of implicit faith, that is, a faith which is taken on someone else's authority.

> Faith rests not on ignorance, but on knowledge. And this is, indeed, knowledge not only of God but of the divine will. We do not obtain salvation either because we are prepared to embrace as true whatever the church has prescribed, or because we turn over to it the task of inquiring and knowing. But we do so when we know that God is our merciful Father because of reconciliation effected through Christ . . . , and that Christ has been given to us as righteousness, sanctification, and life.[8]

Yet having said this Calvin goes on to say, "When we call faith 'knowledge' we do not mean comprehension of the sort that is commonly concerned with those things which fall under human sense perception. For faith is so far above sense that man's mind has to go beyond and rise above itself in order to attain it."[9] Faith as knowledge is comparable to the knowledge we have of our friends, not to the knowledge we have of the contents of a scientific textbook. Faith "is more of the heart than of the brain, and more of the disposition than of the understanding."[10] Karl Barth likewise emphasizes faith as knowledge, but he too, seeks to avoid the notion of faith as assent or the knowledge that we may have of propositions or of objects. Barth prefers to speak of faith as acknowledgment and recognition.[11]

Barth rightly argues:

> Without an initial knowing there can be no initial faith, for faith takes place only in that sphere of Scripture and the community in which Jesus Christ has a form and is an object of knowledge and can be known, in which,

therefore, everyone in his own measure can know something concerning him. . . . We can even dare to say that every Christian — in however primitive and rudimentary a way — can and must be a theologian, and that no matter how primitive and rudimentary he can and must be a good theologian, having a true vision of the one in whom he believes, having true thoughts concerning Him and finding the right words to express these thoughts. Of course, if what he feels and wants is something without form, then he is not a theologian, but he is also not a Christian. For Jesus is not without form, but in the sphere in which he encounters Him He is both form and object — and . . . he can know Him.[12]

The Heidelberg Catechism (1563) answers the question, "What is true faith?" with these words: "It is not only a certain knowledge by which I accept as true all that God has revealed to us in his Word, but also a wholehearted trust which the Holy Spirit creates in me through the gospel, that, not only to others, but to me also God has given the forgiveness of sins, everlasting righteousness and salvation, out of sheer grace solely for the sake of Christ's saving work" (Question 21). This answer of the Heidelberg Catechism emphasizes that faith is knowledge as well as trust. It leaves open the possibility that a reader can distort it by reducing faith to believing that what the Bible says is true. No person has ever had faith in a friend without having knowledge that can be expressed in propositions about that friend. Yet friendship can never be reduced to assent to propositions concerning one's friend. For this reason Augustine once said that only those who have had friends can understand the meaning of faith.[13]

## Faith as Trust

Faith is trust. It is confidence and joy in God. It is the sense of God's presence and God's lordship. Faith as trust involves the affective life of the believer. Faith as emotion in the "oceanic" sense is a pervasive human experience. Faith is never less than trust, but it is never a diffused trust in which the personal, moral historical qualities of life are lost. Faith in its affective dimensions can never be separated from the cognitive ones. It is always a responsible personal act.

## Faith as an Act of the Will

Faith is an act of the will. William James spoke of the will to believe and emphasized the importance of willing to believe in the actual fruition of faith. Yet faith is beyond the power of the will, just as are such human emotions as gratitude, humility, and love. No one, however, has faith without willing to do so, just as no one is grateful or humble or loving without willing to be so.

It is impossible to analyze faith in any specific way in terms of the faculties of the soul. All of the "faculties" of the human self are involved. It is an act of the "I" or of the person.

## The Object of Faith

The object of faith for Christians is God, as God is made known in Jesus Christ.[14] Faith in the formal sense is a universal human experience. Every human being lives by faith. The content of faith is fixed by its object.

Christian faith is intimately related to scripture. While faith is not mental assent to the text of scripture, it cannot be separated from the language, the metaphors, the worldview of scripture. Indeed, it is the scriptures that bear witness to Jesus Christ, in whom God is the specific subject of Christian faith. Yet it must always be emphasized that Christian faith is faith in God who was incarnate in Jesus Christ and who continues to reveal himself through the words of scripture.

## Faith and Love

Martin Luther insisted that the person who has faith has everything.[15] Faith is not some quality of the soul that makes people Christian or, in the Christian sense, spiritual — that is, true personal beings in the image of God. Faith is not becoming like God, as in mystical theology;[16] not a soul purified by love; not an infused grace that conforms the soul to God or that properly relates the soul to God. Faith is trust, confidence that delivers the believer from fear, doubt, and uncertainty and that properly orients the Christian to God. Christian faith is not becoming like God so much as trusting God. Christian faith is not so much meditation on Christ as obedience and a life conformed to the kingdom of God. The human problem for the early Protestants was not primarily mortality and separation from God — and certainly not humanness — but guilt and lives lived in the rejection of God's purposes. Salvation is not found in escape from personal, historical existence through the loss of self and the loss of the sense of divine transcendence but in the recovery of the integrity of moral, personal, historical life. Human beings are formed by their thoughts and acts and above all by faith, the unconditional commitment of their lives.[17]

This understanding of the Christian life shaped Calvin's thought. Faith as a responsible personal act of trust, confidence, and commitment is therefore the foundation of everything else in the Christian life. The end of the Christian life is not the vision of God, or union with God, but a life conformed to the kingdom of God and embodying the purposes of God.

The Protestant understanding of faith repudiated medieval notions of an unformed faith and of faith that was formed by love.[18] Love thus became the dominant quality of the Christian life.

Luther and Calvin alike insisted that love is a consequence of faith. Luther writes:

> Behold, from faith thus flows forth love and joy in the Lord, and from love a joyful, willing, free mind that serves one's neighbor willingly and takes no account of gratitude or ingratitude, of praise or blame, of gain or loss. . . . Our faith in Christ does not free us from works but from false opinions concerning works. That is, from the foolish presumption that justification is acquired by works. Faith redeems, corrects and preserves our consciences, so that we know that righteousness does not consist in works. . . .[19]

Calvin also rejects "the teaching of the Schoolmen, that love is prior to faith and hope, . . . for it is faith alone that first engenders love in us."[20]

## Faith and Hope

Faith is related to hope. The hope we have for the future, our own future and the future of human history, is based on faith and is the expression of faith's convictions about the future.

> Without faith in God's providence the freedom of man is intolerable. Hope is subordinate to and yet identical with faith. It is faith with regard to the future. The future is the symbol of the unpredictable possibilities of eternity which may appear in time. Without faith and hope these possibilities represent an intolerable threat to man's little universe of meaning. They may in any moment introduce uncalculated and incalculable elements into the little system of meaning by which men live and by which they seek to maintain their sense of domestic security. History is not rational. At least it does not conform to the systems of rational coherence which men construct periodically to comprehend its meaning. These systems are inevitably anchored in some specific anchor of meaning, which is itself subject to the vicissitudes of history. History can be meaningful, therefore, only in terms of a faith which comprehends its seeming irrationalities and views them as the expression of a divine wisdom, which transcends human understanding. Faith in the wisdom of God is thus a prerequisite of love because it is the

condition without which man is anxious and is driven by his anxiety into vicious circles of self-sufficiency and pride. As we have previously noted, the admonition, "Be not anxious," has meaning only in conjunction with the faith expressed by Jesus: "Your heavenly father knoweth that ye have need of these things."[21]

Calvin likewise saw hope as a consequence of faith.

Hope is nothing else than the expectation of those things which faith has believed to have been truly promised by God. Thus, faith believes God to be true, hope awaits the time when his truth shall be manifested; faith believes that He is our Father, hope anticipates that he will ever show himself to be a Father toward us; faith believes that eternal life has been given to us, hope anticipates that it will sometimes be revealed; faith is the foundation upon which hope rests, hope nourishes and sustains faith.[22]

# Faith Is Not a Work

Faith, Martin Luther insisted, is not a work, but faith is always very busy doing many works of love and mercy. Faith is being in right relationship to God, and out of this relationship good works flow. Faith is the human awareness that one is grasped by God, that one is laid hold of by God. Faith is called forth by God's grace, in a manner analogous to the human responses that are elicited by human grace. Thus faith is not a work explained by the human will, but it is the source out of which all Christian works are done.

❖

## CHAPTER 13

# JUSTIFICATION BY FAITH

You have heard, dearly beloved, that true faith is the justification of the church or faithful of God; that is, I say, the forgiveness of all sins, a receiving into the grace of God, a taking by adoption into the number of the sons of God, and assured and blessed sanctification, and finally, the well-spring of all good works. Let us therefore in true faith pray to God the Father, in the name of our Lord Jesus Christ, that he will vouchsafe to fill our hearts with this true faith; that in this present world, being joined to him in faith, we may serve him as we ought; and, after our departure out of this life, we may forever live with him in whom we believe. To him be praise and glory forever. Amen.

Heinrich Bullinger, *Decades,* Sermon 6

For by grace you have been saved through faith, and this is not your own doing; it is the gift of God—not the result of works, so that no one may boast.

Ephesians 2:8–9

John Calvin declared that justification is "the main hinge on which religion turns. . . . For unless you first of all grasp what your relationship to God is, and the nature of his judgment concerning you, you have neither a foundation on which to establish your salvation nor one on which to build piety toward God."[1]

Christian salvation is a twofold experience. It is first of all the experience of God's grace as mercy that forgives our sins. It is, second, the experience of God's grace as power by which we are transformed. As Calvin put it, "By partaking of Him [Jesus Christ] we principally receive a double grace: namely, that being reconciled to God through Christ's blamelessness, we may have in heaven instead of a Judge a gracious Father; and secondly, that sanctified by Christ's spirit we may cultivate blamelessness and purity of life."[2] Calvin goes on to define justification, simply as the "acceptance with which God receives us into his favor as righteous men. And we say that it consists in the remission of sins and the imputation of Christ's righteousness."[3]

178

# Faith Righteousness versus Work Righteousness

Martin Luther, more than anyone in the history of the Christian church, understood the righteousness of God as the justification of the sinner. He knew better than anyone else that salvation cannot be earned, that heaven cannot be guaranteed by human effort, and that the attempt to earn salvation and guarantee heaven leads to arrogance and self-righteousness. He also more than any other knew that good people sin in their best deeds as well as their worst deeds and therefore cannot save themselves.

Luther's doctrine of justification was shaped by his own personal experiences, first of all in his personal life and second in his dealings with self-righteous church leaders. Luther was tormented by the question of how a sinful person can stand in the presence of a righteous God. On the one hand he had an unusually sensitive awareness of the holiness of God, and on the other he was acutely aware of his own sin.[4]

Luther sought to resolve the personal crisis of his life in the ways that medieval Catholicism provided. Luther became a monk, and by all reports he became a very good monk. He himself would say that if anyone ever got to heaven by monkery, he should have gotten there. Yet Luther always knew that he could be a better monk than he was; therefore, he could never be sure that he had earned God's favor by becoming a religious.

Medieval Catholicism also offered the way of the confessional. Luther confessed his sins. He confessed them so repeatedly and so persistently that his confessors suggested he should go out and commit some real sins rather than the peccadilloes that were troubling his conscience, if he were to continue to confess. Yet Luther knew long before Freud that we do not remember the most painful things in our own lives, and therefore he could never be sure that he had confessed all of his sins.[5]

Medieval Catholicism likewise offered the way of mysticism, whereby human beings lose themselves in the deity. Luther was influenced by the mystics, particularly Staupitz. Yet Luther was too aware of the transcendence of God and of the sinfulness of finite human beings to find the fulfillment of his life in the contemplation of God or in union with God.

The great, decisive experience in the life of Martin Luther was the new awareness that God's favor cannot be earned, cannot be bought, cannot be achieved by any human effort. God's favor is freely given. It is all grace. This awareness came to Luther as he studied the Psalms and Romans. This understanding of Christian faith and of justification by faith found its pre-eminent expression in Luther's great writings of 1520, particularly the *Treatise on Christian Freedom* and the *Sermon on Good Works*.[6]

The life and work of Martin Luther represent, Reinhold Niebuhr has observed, the point in the history of the church when Christians have been most aware of the sins of good people, that is, most aware that all people need forgiveness.[7] Salvation is not something that can be achieved or earned. The favor of God is like the love of a parent; it can only be received.

Luther was an Augustinian, and he was also acutely aware that human beings cannot complete their own lives. The human spirit transcends every human achievement. Every achievement opens up new possibilities of achievement and every act of love opens up new possibilities of love that finally elude us.[8] For this reason also salvation cannot be earned or bought. Salvation is given by the grace and mercy of God.

Modern people do not experience guilt before God in precisely the same way Martin Luther did. He lived in Christendom and in a very religious culture, but our culture is secular. Yet the experience of lostness, of damnation, of alienation is widespread. If modern people do not feel guilty before God, they do feel guilty that they have not been good parents, that they are not successful in social relationships, that they have not achieved their expectations in their careers. Persons everywhere have a sense of the disparity between what they know life was made to be and what life is. Furthermore, even in a secular society the greatest of human achievements likewise leaves human life unfulfilled, as the biographies of most successful persons clearly indicate.[9]

There are brief moments in life, especially when we are young, when we feel no need for God who forgives our sins and redeems our life from destruction. Our personal endowments enable us to exult in the freedom of the secular cities; our rationalizations easily convince us of our own righteousness. But these moments are brief. Health breaks down; hopes are unfulfilled; the limits of our willpower become painfully clear. Finally we become aware that the achievements in which we have invested so much of our lives were possibly not worth the cost, or that our involvement is not so free of self-interest as once we imagined. Sooner or later we discover that life is an uphill battle, which in the end every person loses. We know finally that no one ought to underestimate the vicissitudes of life or the precariousness of the human enterprise.

Human life, as Reinhold Niebuhr astutely pointed out, is pathetic, tragic, and ironic.[10] The pathetic and pitiable dimensions of life are seen most vividly in the case of a deformed child or the case of a person overwhelmed by forces beyond his or her control. Other aspects of life are tragic, as when we have to deny one loyalty for the sake of another loyalty, when we have to do evil for the sake of good, or when the only choices open to us are evil. Some aspects of life are ironic, as when human wisdom becomes our undoing because we did not know its limits, or when our strength becomes our downfall because we trusted it too much. The final human predicament is the irony that our finest achievements have human flaws for which we are responsible.

Once we reflect on the pathetic, the tragic, and the ironic aspects of human life as well as on sin itself, it becomes clear that we grossly over-simplify life when we make unqualified distinctions between good people and bad, between the successful and the failures. One of the great failures of "fundamentalism," in theology as well as in politics, is its inability to recognize the pitiable, the tragic, and the ironic dimensions of human existence. Fundamentalism in any of its various forms, whether on the left wing or the right wing of the ideological spectrum, makes too simple a distinction between people. Fundamentalism says that on the one hand there are good people who work hard and who have money, who obey the laws and who go to heaven, who are identified with the right causes and make the right pronouncements about society. On the other hand there are lazy people who do not work hard and who do not have money, who disobey God and who do not go to heaven, who have wrong ideas about the issues of our day. Those who make these distinctions always think of themselves as hardworking people who deserve money, as the good who are going to heaven. There is no gospel in this, only a self-righteousness that is self-deceiving. The gospel is hidden from those who in their self-righteousness cannot see the sorrow and the tragedy in the worst life. The gospel is hidden from those who do not understand that success is not even a possibility for those who have a poor biochemical inheritance or an impossible social environment. The gospel is hidden from those who in their self-righteousness are proud of their moral achievements, who know that they are righteous by their identification with the proper causes, who are vindictive toward those who fail, who have only one solution for failures—to discard them, to electrocute them, to destroy them.

There is no gospel for the "righteous." In the New Testament the basic cleavage between human beings is not between rich and poor, powerful and oppressed, male and female, free and enslaved, but between those who believed they were righteous and those who knew they were sinners. The gospel is for the poor in the biblical sense—that is, for those who know that they cannot save themselves, who know that their only defense is God. As Jesus, who ate with sinners, put it, "Those who are well have no need of a physician, but those who are sick. Go and learn what this means, 'I desire mercy, not sacrifice.' For I have come to call not the righteous but sinners" (Matthew 9:12–13). Two important truths about life are set forth in these words. First, Jesus could help only those who knew they were sinners. Second, only those who know that they are sinners, only those who have received mercy, can show mercy.

The Christian gospel is directed to the sinfulness, the incompleteness, the pathetic, the tragic, and the ironic dimensions of life. This gospel is the Christian community's witness to the question, Is there a grace that forgives our sins, that gives us courage before an unknown future, that enables us to live with poise and dignity in the presence of the pathetic, the tragic, and the ironic, and that enables us to accept the incompleteness of our lives with hope?

The Christian gospel is God's forgiveness. It is dependent neither on our goodness nor on our achievements. The gospel finds in the New Testament its foundational statement in the simple assertion of Jesus, "Son, your sins are forgiven" (Mark 2:5). This gospel of forgiveness is not the whole of Christian faith, but everything else presupposes it.

Justification by faith was important for Luther not only for his personal life but also for his life in the church. Luther had experienced the self-righteousness of church leaders, and for this reason he spoke of the pope as the Antichrist. Contemporary sensitivities have led Protestants to remove the assertion that the pope is the Antichrist from their creeds, but a much wiser course would have been to observe that all church leaders are in danger of becoming the Antichrist. Sin is the corruption of the good as well as defiance of the good.[11] Justification by faith rather than works is the Christian gospel for the minister, the priest, the bishop, and the pope or church bureaucrat as well as for the individual Christian.

## An Imputed Righteousness

The righteousness conferred by justification by faith is an imputed righteousness. The older dogmatics distinguished between the passive obedience of Jesus Christ and active obedience. On the one hand, forgiveness rests on the atonement for sins in the death of Jesus Christ. He bore the penalty and paid the price. On the other hand, the righteousness of faith is the imputation whereby we are accepted as righteous, not because of our own deeds but because of the righteousness of Jesus Christ.

Imputation has always had an abstract and legalistic connotation. Yet through the word "imputation," theologians were attempting to say something that is very important and very personal. As has been noted in the discussion on the work of Christ, forgiveness is not the simple dismissal of sin. It is the acceptance of the sinner because the price has been paid. Even in human experience forgiveness always requires suffering, the suffering of atonement on the part of the forgiver and of repentance on the part of the forgiven. Likewise we know in human experience how the righteousness of one person is accepted for the righteousness of another. Imputation has to do with a person's ultimate worth and destiny. Christian theology in this doctrine endeavors to say that Christians are accepted as righteous because in the death on the cross Jesus bore the penalty for our sins and in his righteous life he covers us with his righteousness.

## Received by Faith

The righteousness of Christ is received by faith. Faith is a human act, yet it is first of all the gift of grace. The Christian does not earn forgiveness by believing. Faith itself, Luther insisted, is not a work.

Faith is a human response that is elicited by God's grace, whereby we receive the divine forgiveness. Analogies can be found in human experience. We do not come to trust a person through our work or achievement but in response to the impact of a person's life on our ours. In even a deeper way we do not receive forgiveness from another human being by earning it. Our acceptance is elicited by the offer for forgiveness.[12] Some contemporary Lutheran theologians object to the phrase "justification by grace through faith," because it obscures the "complete interdependence between grace and faith" (grace is the gift of faith; faith alone lets grace be grace).[13]

> All legal and moral schemes are shattered. Such justification comes neither at the beginning nor at the end of a movement; rather, it establishes an entirely new situation. Since righteousness comes by imputation only, it is absolutely not a movement on our part, either with or without the aid of what was previously termed "grace." The judgment can be heard and grasped only by faith. Indeed, the judgment creates and calls forth the faith that hears and grasps it. One will mistake the Reformation point, if one does not see that justification by "faith" is in the first instance precisely a polemic against justification "by grace" according to the medieval scheme. Grace would have to be completely redefined before the word could be safely used in a Reformation sense.[14]

Justification by faith is the divine forgiveness that calls forth the response of faith. It is the end of all schemes of work righteousness whether they are religious or secular and declares that human salvation is given by God's grace. God accepts us as his people not on the basis of our achievement but on the basis of his mercy.

## A Completed Act of God

Justification does not have to be repeated. God's forgiveness is complete and covers the whole of life.

The Christian never outgrows the need for forgiveness. Forgiveness is not the first stage of the Christian life, but the presupposition and condition for the entire Christian life. Luther was profoundly aware that we sin in our best deeds as well as our worst, and at the highest level of sainthood we are still forgiven sinners. The Calvinists and Reformed in their emphasis on sanctification sometimes forgot that the saints too need to be forgiven. Yet Calvin insisted that even those who are most saintly need to confess their sins and thank God for his forgiveness.[15]

## Consequences of Justification

The early Reformed theologians emphasized two consequences of the doctrine of justification. First, they insisted that justification by faith gives all the glory to God. Human beings do not glory in their own achievements but in God's mercy, which forgives them. Generally the Reformed did not suffer the anguish of heart about their sins that Luther did. Hence the emphasis in Reformed theology has been primarily on the glory of God, not on deliverance from personal anguish and guilt. Calvin insisted that the salvation of the human soul is not the most important concern of the Christian.[16] Therein lies the Calvinist critique of certain forms of revivalism, and one must think that Calvin himself also had Luther in mind. The Christian's first concern is the glory of God, and only in the light of this concern is salvation possible.[17]

Calvin likewise insisted that justification provides a serenity, a tranquillity of life that is not possible when salvation is a human work. Calvin would later make the same claims for the doctrine of predestination.[18] It can be argued that justification by faith and predestination are attempting to say the same thing and to describe the same Christian experience. In each case, salvation is solely the work of God, which elicits a human response.

Martin Luther argued that the Christian had no need for the law, something that John Calvin in his most ecstatic moments would never have said.[19] The experience of being forgiven not only initiated and called forth the Christian life; out of the experience itself the Christian knew how to love God and neighbor. As Luther put it, no one has to tell a man how to love his wife. This knowledge comes out of the experience of love. So the experience of divine grace and forgiveness frees a person to live the Christian life.

Calvin would never have said that the Christian can get along without the law, but he knew also that the law in and of itself is insufficient. The rigor of the law undercuts the possibility of the Christian life. The experience of forgiveness provides the tranquillity and the peace of soul, the security and the confidence out of which Christians can live for the glory of God and for the welfare of other human beings.

## The Doctrine by Which the Church Stands or Falls

Protestants have always been confident that justification by faith is the heart of the Christian message for every time and place. It stands over against every human effort to complete life and declares that salvation is given by God, not earned by human achievements, whatever they are. In the sixteenth century, religious works were demonstrated to be inadequate to relieve the bruised spirits and wounded consciences of human beings. In the twentieth century it is increasingly clear that secular works in spheres of politics, economics, social planning, and human development likewise are unable to complete life and to give it any final meaning. The Christian gospel is that forgiveness, the meaning and significance of life, cannot be earned but can only be accepted as God's gracious gift. This is the presupposition of the Christian life. Yet Barth rightly argues that the doctrine by which the church stands or falls is not justification but its basis, the confession of Jesus Christ in whom are hid all the treasures of wisdom and knowledge.[20]

❖

## CHAPTER 14

# SANCTIFICATION

What is meant by sanctification (*sanctificatio*) might just as well be described by the less common biblical term regeneration (*regeneratio*) or renewal (*renovatio*), or by that of conversion (*conversio*), or by that of penitence (*poenitentia*) which plays so important a role in both the Old and the New Testaments, or comprehensively by that of discipleship which is so outstanding especially in the synoptic Gospels. The content of all these terms will have to be brought out under the title of sanctification. But there is good reason to keep the term sanctification itself in the foreground. It includes already, even verbally, the idea of the "saints," and therefore in contradistinction to the other descriptions of the same matter it shows us at once that we are dealing with the being and action of God, reminding us in a way which is normative for the understanding of the other terms as well as of the basic and decisive fact that God is the active Subject not only in reconciliation generally but also in the conversion of man to Himself. Like his turning to man, and man's justification, this is His work, His *facere.* But it is now seen and understood, not as his *iustificare,* but as his *sanctificare.*

Karl Barth, *Church Dogmatics* IV/2, p. 500

Be perfect, therefore, as your heavenly Father is perfect.

Matthew 5:48

Work out your own salvation with fear and trembling; for it is God who is at work in you, enabling you both to will and to work for his good pleasure.

Philippians 2:12–13

I appeal to you therefore, brothers and sisters, by the mercies of God, to present your bodies as a living sacrifice, holy and acceptable to God, which is your spiritual worship.

Romans 12:1

He chose us in Christ before the foundation of the world to be holy and blameless before him in love.

Ephesians 1:4

Justification and sanctification are indissolubly united in the one experience of salvation.[1] They are dimensions of the same experience and cannot be separated. God not only forgives our sins; God also calls us to be holy. The New Testament has as much to say about the transformation of life as it does about forgiveness. Christians are called to be disciples of Jesus Christ and to be perfect, as their Father in heaven is perfect.

## The Relation Between Forgiveness and Sanctification

The relation of justification and sanctification has been a perennial and difficult problem for theology in every age.[2] A tendency persists in life as well as in theology to subordinate justification and sanctification to each other or to confuse them. Forgiveness can become so significant to the Christian that sanctification is forgotten, and sanctification can become so important that the need for forgiveness is likewise forgotten.

Martin Luther protested against the subordination of justification to sanctification in the Middle Ages. From Luther's perspective Augustine understood well enough grace alone but failed to understand faith alone. Luther understood better than any other theologian the persistence of sin in the life of the redeemed.

John Calvin may have put together justification and sanctification more carefully than any other theologian.[3] He was of a different temperament from Luther, and there is no real evidence that he experienced guilt before God in the powerful way that Luther did. For him the question was more, Is there a word from God and does human life have any meaning? Furthermore, Calvin was aware of criticisms that were made against Luther's emphasis on forgiveness, an emphasis that was judged to be subversive of the moral life both of the individual and of society. When Calvin came to write about justification and sanctification, he spoke first of sanctification or, to use his language, repentance. Sanctification then became an emphasis of Calvin's ministry in Geneva and of the Reformed community ever since.[4]

Calvin himself declared that justification is the principal hinge on which Christian faith depends;[5] and he knew that however sanctified we become, we still need the forgiveness of God.[6] In the formulation of his theology Calvin put together sanctification and justification in a remarkably nuanced way. Justification and sanctification can neither be separated nor confused. "By partaking of him, we principally received a double grace: namely, that being reconciled to God through Christ's blamelessness, we may have in heaven instead of a Judge a gracious Father; and secondly, that sanctified by Christ's spirit we may cultivate blamelessness and purity of life."[7] Again Calvin writes:

> There is, therefore, a double washing. The first is that God does not ascribe our faults and corruption to us, but receives us as his children. It is necessary that we be pure, but this is an imputed purity inasmuch as we borrow it from Jesus Christ. There is also an actual purity, or, as it is said, the goodness which God works in us. This shows itself by its effects, for God renews us by his Holy Spirit and corrects our evil affection. In short he lives in us and rules in us.[8]

Calvin is adamant that justification and sanctification cannot be separated. There is no justification apart from sanctification, and likewise there is no sanctification apart from justification.

> The faithful are never reconciled to God without the gift of sanctification, yet, to this end we are justified, that afterwards we might worship God in holiness of life. For Christ does not otherwise wash us with his blood, and by his satisfaction reconcile God to us, unless he makes us partakers of his spirit, which renews us into a holy life.[9]

Calvin is equally emphatic that just as the gifts of justification and sanctification cannot be separated, neither can they be confused. This was his polemic against medieval Catholicism and also against the Catholicism of Trent.

> The Fathers of Trent pretend that it [justification] is twofold as if we were justified partly by forgiveness of sins and partly by spiritual regeneration; or, to express their view in other words, as if our righteousness were composed partly of imputation, partly of quality. I maintain that it is one, and simple, and is wholly included in the gratuitous acceptance of God. I . . . hold that it is without us because we are righteous in Christ only.[10]

Calvin was convinced that the Catholicism of Trent and of the medieval church alike had overturned the whole doctrine of salvation by mangling and confounding the pardon of sins and repentance. When justification is made to depend partly on repentance, there can never be peace of conscience. Salvation, as the forgiveness of sins, is wholly God's gift. Confusion of sanctification with forgiveness undercuts the basis for the Christian life, which is God's mercy that forgives our sins.

The relation between justification and sanctification must not be construed in an abstract and barren manner. The relation between the two gifts of the gospel is always dynamic and vital. Justification by grace through faith provides the living context out of which the Christian life lives and grows. Calvin regarded the confidence that comes from the experience of justification by faith alone as the only possible basis for real sanctification. As long as human beings are engaged in a frantic search for salvation and standing before God, the moral life is impossible. Until consciences have been brought into a state of peace with God, they cannot be at peace with other human beings.[11] Furthermore, we cannot worship God in a proper manner without composure of mind. Alarm and dread make real worship impossible.[12] Furthermore, God does not accept forced service. His service must be from a pure and free affection. In this sense the Christian life is spontaneous. It is ecstatic; it grows out of the experience of being forgiven. The dominant motive that Calvin ascribes to the Christian life is gratitude. The widespread notion that Calvin conceived of the Christian life legalistically is refuted by his very pervasive insistence that confidence in God's mercy is the absolute precondition for the Christian life, the confidence that is based on the doctrine of justification and also on the doctrine of predestination.

The relation of justification and sanctification has received expression with classic precision and clarity in the Westminster Larger Catechism in answer to the question, "Wherein do justification and sanctification differ?" (Question 77).

> Although sanctification is inseparably joined to justification, yet they differ, in that God in justification imputes the righteousness of Christ; in sanctification his spirit infuses grace, enables to the exercise thereof; in the former sin is pardoned; in the latter it is subdued: the one frees all believers equally from the revenge and wrath of God, and that perfectly in this life, so that they never fall in to condemnation; the other is neither in all nor in this life perfect in any but grows into perfection.

Karl Barth reaffirms the classic Reformed tradition in his discussion of justification and sanctification, but he also carries it forward with an open inquiry into the ways in which justification may be superior to sanctification and sanctification superior to justification. Justification, Barth concludes, has priority over sanctification in that it is the presupposition and condition of the Christian life. It is in virtue of the forgiveness of sins that a person is "called and given a readiness and willingness for discipleship, for conversion, for the doing of good works, for the bearing of his cross. It is in virtue of the fact that he is justified in the presence of God by God that he is sanctified by Him."[13] Yet one must also say that teleologically sanctification is superior to justification and not the reverse. The goal of the Christian life is not to be forgiven but to be transformed into the image of Christ.

> In the *simul* of the one divine will and action justification is first as basis and second as presupposition, sanctification first as aim and second as consequence; and therefore both are superior and both subordinate. Embracing the distinctness and unity of the two moments and aspects, the one grace of the one Jesus Christ is at work, and it is both justifying and sanctifying grace, and both to the glory of God and the salvation of man.[14]

Barth is aware that Calvin handled the problem of justification and sanctification with profound precision and clarity. Yet Barth concludes:

> There can be no doubt that in practice [Calvin's] decisive interest is primarily in the problem of sanctification. Those who come to him from Luther will be almost estranged when right at the beginning of the third book (1,1), although not without justification in the linguistic usage of the Bible, he lays all the emphasis on the sanctifying power of the Holy Spirit, and it is not for a long time (only in chapter 11) that he comes to speak of justification at all.[15]

Calvin, therefore, must be called the theologian of sanctification. We have to learn from Calvin to give a twofold answer to the question of priority in the relation of justification and sanctification.

> Calvin was quite in earnest when he gave sanctification a strategic precedence over justification. He was also quite in earnest when he gave the latter a tactical precedence. Why could he be so free, and yet so bound, in relation to the two? Because he started at the place which is superior to both because it embraces both, so that in the light of it we can and must give the primacy, now to the one and now to the other, according to the different standpoints from which we look. The basic act in which they are a whole, in which they are united and yet different, and in which—without any contradiction—they have different functions according to which they must each be given the primacy, is as Calvin sees it (and as he describes it in the first chapter of the third book) the [participation in Christ] given to man by the Holy Spirit.[16]

## The Doctrine of Sanctification

Calvin's treatment of justification and sanctification set the course for Reformed theology in the future and gave it its distinctive character over against Lutheran theology with its emphasis on justification by faith. Calvin, as a theologian of sanctification, also contributed significantly to the prevailing ethos of Reformed theology, which in the English-speaking world was shaped mightily by Puritanism. Puritanism was not simply a Reformed movement but had sources in the much broader Christian tradition. As it developed in England and in America, Puritanism is inconceivable in a Lutheran context and it included in its theology the work of Heinrich Bullinger and John Calvin.[17]

The traditional Reformed emphasis on sanctification contributed not simply to well-known Reformed virtues but also to well-known problems. Reinhold Niebuhr observed that this emphasis on sanctification easily turned into legalism whereby the Christian life was understood in terms of laws and regulations, into an obscurantism whereby the Christian life and the kingdom of God were prematurely identified with established patterns of life in society. The result was often self-righteousness. As Niebuhr put it, God commands us to be perfect as our Father in heaven is perfect. Yet we must remember that our best deeds are always corrupted by our own self-interests. We have to pray for forgiveness not simply when we are at our worst but also when we are at our best.[18]

The carefully developed Reformed theology of the seventeenth century made distinctions between justification and sanctification that clarify these two moments of the one experience of salvation. Justification is an *act* of God that is complete and final. Nothing has to be added to our justification. God's forgiveness is complete and permanent. Sanctification is a *work* of the Holy Spirit in and through human life. It is a continual process, and it is never complete, at least in human history.

Forgiveness is equal in all people; sanctification is unequal. Sanctification does not add anything to forgiveness, but sanctification is the end for which we are forgiven. In justification God turns toward human beings; in sanctification God turns human beings toward himself. Sanctification is not completed in one act but is a process that continues throughout human life, and it involves the whole human person.

In sanctification character is formed, and the good and virtuous person comes to be. The Christian life is expressed in actions, but it is first of all the freedom, the disposition, the intentions, and the commitments of the self. Augustine declared that the immutably good God had created human beings mutably good. If they had decided for goodness they would have been confirmed in goodness. Adam did not choose goodness, and now salvation has as its goal the transformation and confirmation of sinners into the maturity in which they can no longer sin. Under the power of the Holy Spirit and in the community of faith, the human self is formed by its actions, its dispositions, its intentions, and its commitments of faith. The Reformed had a vision of perfection, but they also knew that it is never realized in history, only in glory. Character, the consistency and direction of the self, is established — or, in traditional theological language, the person is sanctified. "What is willed becomes part of the soul." Character and sanctification are the mystery of the self, but they are partially revealed in public actions and dispositions.

Calvin's theology also set the direction of future Reformed theology in emphasizing that progress must be made in the Christian life.[19] The Christian is involved in a race and in a warfare. The most pervasive metaphors that Calvin used for the Christian life come from the military. The Christian needs the discipline and commitment that are appropriate to military life; moreover, the Christian is confronted by principalities and powers that must be taken captive for Christ. Contemporary sensitivities may be repelled by Calvin's military images, but it needs to be recognized that a characteristic of Reformed theology is its emphasis on growth in grace and growth in the Christian life and on the conquest of evil.

Early Reformed theology was characterized by an optimism of grace that has frequently been obscured both by the observable facts that Christian lives fall so short of the Christian goal and by a theological awareness that even our best deeds are corrupted by our self-interests. As Niebuhr put it, the ultimate judgment that we all fall short of the glory of God and that we all have to ask divine forgiveness sometimes obscures the proximate or penultimate judgment that among us sinners there are very significant differences. On the human level, for example, when one is employing people to be responsible for money, these human differences are very significant.[20] Reformed theology generally, however, has emphasized that progress is possible in the Christian life and that Christians themselves should be making daily progress.

Progress in the Christian life is very difficult to quantify or to measure. Furthermore, human judgments are limited by time and space, by ideology, and by sin. Yet it is possible to note ways in which progress in the Christian life does take place.[21] It is obviously difficult to measure growth in poise and dignity that trust in God gives to human life, growth in gratitude and humility, growth in love for neighbor, and growth in capacity to give up things. Yet these qualities are detectable by human judgment, though any final judgment belongs to God alone.

Growth in Christian imagination is likewise possible and is enhanced by biblical and theological reflection. A. D. Lindsay once said that the saints are distinguished from ordinary Christians in that they do what ordinary Christians never think of doing.[22]

Growth in the means of grace is more easily detectable. From the beginning of human history human life has begun very much in the same way at birth. A newborn child cannot inherit the parents' character. In the moral and spiritual realm human beings begin now very much as they began ten thousand years ago. Yet there can be a growth in the means of grace, that is, in those practices, rituals, and traditions that impact human life. In the Christian church these would be preeminently scripture, the sacraments, and the fellowship of the church. It would also include the tradition of the Christian family and the inherited wisdom of the human race concerning how human life should be lived. Arnold Toynbee has suggested that it is precisely in the means of grace that progress can be observed in human history, which often seems to be bereft of any really great progression in human goodness.[23]

The Calvinists at their best have always been aware that on every new level of goodness a new form of evil appears. Yet the Calvinists find in the relative achievements of history a confirmation of the theological conviction that growth in grace is possible. Hence no Reformed theologian can set predetermined limits to the possibilities for sanctification either in an individual life or in the life of society.

The Reformed emphasis on growth in grace, on sanctification, also is supported by psychologists such as Gordon Allport, who emphasize that the most important fact you can know about any human being is that human being's intention for the future.[24] At its best Reformed theology has given to Christian people the goal of a human life conformed to the will of God and of a society under the rule of God. Calvin intended in Geneva not simply that Christians should express their faith in their lives but that Geneva itself should be a Christian community. The Reformed carried with them this vision, as, for example, in England, where they sought to build the new Jerusalem in England's green and pleasant land, or in Massachusetts, where they sought to demonstrate to a decaying society in Europe the possibilities of a Christian society in a new land.

## The Content of Sanctification

What does it mean to be sanctified? John Calvin's treatment of sanctification is developed in the third book of the *Institutes* under the rubric of repentance. Repentance for Calvin included mortification, the dying of the old person to sin, and vivification, the making alive of the person to the grace and the glory of God.

Calvin then goes on to develop the Christian life under the themes of self-denial, cross bearing, and meditation on the future life and the right use of this world's goods. By self-denial Calvin meant the economical use of life's energies for the purposes for which God gave them. Calvin was no ascetic; his own particular manner of life can be described as moderation. The world is good and one ought to rejoice in it, but one's use of the world must be disciplined by gratitude for God's gift and by the purposes for which God made the world. Cross bearing was the acceptance of the life of service. Cross bearing for Calvin was not something a Christian uses or something a Christian chooses or seeks out. Calvin was convinced that God lays on both the good and bad the burden of the cross. The patience of the saints, therefore, consists in bearing willingly the cross that has been laid on them.[25] By meditation on the future life Calvin meant something very close to faith itself, yet it is faith that is very much aware of human destiny. Peter Brunner has written, "Faith and trust are not thinkable without eschatology. . . . Expectation of eternal life is very closely connected with faith. It is in this being anxious of something future, eternal, other worldly, which encloses this expectation in itself, that the eschatological element in the faith is most clearly recognized."[26]

The Christian life is finally the proper use of human life, of history, and of this world's goods. Calvin was profoundly convinced of the goodness of God's creation and of the goodness of human life. His asceticism therefore is not a denial of creation but an economical use of the gift of life and of the created world in thanksgiving to God and in accordance with God's purposes for his creation. Finally the Christian life is vocation, the conviction that God has called one, not only to be but to do, that God has called his people to embody in their lives individually and in their lives together the divine purposes of the creator. Calvin concludes his section on the Christian life by saying that this conviction that God calls us to embody his purposes in our lives transforms even the humblest task into something that is very precious in the sight of God.[27]

Calvin had provided a detailed exposition of the Ten Commandments in book 2 of the *Institutes*. It is very significant that Calvin does not include the Ten Commandments in his discussion of the Christian life. At the beginning of the discussion of the Christian life he notes that the law of God contains in itself that newness by which the image can be restored in us, but then he proceeds to say that it would be "profitable to assemble from various passages of scripture a pattern for the conduct of life in order that those who heartily repent may not err in their zeal."[28] Finally, Calvin declares that in addition to scripture we also have "Christ, through whom we return into favor with God, [who] has been set before us as an example, whose pattern we ought to express in our life. What more effective thing can you require than this one thing?"[29] In order to understand the Christian life and to be guided about how we should live as Christians, we should know the stories of the Bible and assimilate the scriptures into our own person. Above all we should know the New Testament account of Jesus Christ, what he said and what he did, and what the early church found that God had done in and through Christ for our salvation. This is the true guide to the Christian life.

Later Reformed theology, however, would emphasize the Ten Commandments. Traditionally catechisms had expositions of the commandments as a guide to Christian living. One of the finest descriptions of a Reformed ethic in the seventeenth century is the Westminster Larger Catechism's exposition of the commandments. In this the catechism followed the tradition of Calvin's exposition in *Institutes,* book 2. Yet those who give priority to the commandments must somehow justify themselves over against Calvin's emphasis on the study of the scriptures generally and on the example of Jesus Christ, as guides to Christian living.

A Reformed Christian must ask what is the place of the Sermon on the Mount in an exposition of the Christian life. Gordon Rupp, a Methodist theologian, has insisted that one of the great contributions of John Wesley is that he replaced the Protestant emphasis on the Ten Commandments as the guide to Christian living with an emphasis on the Sermon on the Mount.

Karl Barth's discussion of sanctification represents a recent break with the exposition of the Ten Commandments as the primary basis for the sanctified life. The sanctified life involves the call to discipleship, the awakening to conversion, the praise of good works, and the dignity of the cross, which Barth interprets in very much the same sense as Calvin.[30] Barth's discussion of sanctification is followed immediately by his treatment of the work of the Holy Spirit in building up the Christian community. He thus ties the individual Christian life very closely to life in the community. The sanctified life is lived in the fellowship of the people of God. The sanctified life is lived by the Christian who has experienced God's grace as forgiveness by the power of the Holy Spirit in the context of the Christian community. It is informed by the scriptures, in which God has made himself known and in which he calls human beings to be his people. It is in particular informed by the life, death, and resurrection of Jesus Christ. The Christian life cannot be learned in terms of precepts or regulation or laws. It grows out of the experience of a community's life that is informed by scripture, by Jesus Christ, and by the presence of the Holy Spirit.

Can we say anything more specific about the pattern of the Christian life? What does it mean to live as a Christian? In the simplest definition, a Christian is one for whom God, the ground and source of our being, the mystery that encompasses us, is defined by Jesus Christ. To be a Christian is to know God's grace as mercy in Christ bearing our sins on the cross and as power in the resurrection of Jesus Christ from the dead and the giving of the Holy Spirit. Can we say anything further about the specific forms of human behavior that are shaped by these convictions about God and God's revelation of himself in human history?

Certainly no one description of the Christian life can ever be complete and final. The Christian life in part is determined by the historical situation in which it is lived and every perception of the Christian life is limited by the experience, intelligence, and saintliness of the perceiver. Nevertheless, Christians must in some sense attempt to conceive what it is to live as Christians in a particular time and place. A fair description of the Christian life would at least include the following qualities.

A Christian is one who trusts God and who lives with the serenity, dignity, and poise that faith in the living God wrests from the raw stuff of life. The Christian knows that God is the Father in heaven and the world is our Father's creation. Part of the Christian life is expressed in Francis of Assisi's "Canticle of the Sun," which we sing as a hymn, "All Creatures of Our God and King," or in the great hymn of the American frontier "How Firm a Foundation, Ye Saints of the Lord."

A Christian is one who lives with gratitude and with humility. Gratitude and humility belong together. The grateful person is humble, and the humble person is grateful. Christian piety is expressed in sheer wonder in the presence of the mystery of life and thanksgiving for the gift of life, of time, and of space. The wonder and the goodness of human life lead not simply to gratitude but to humility.

The Christian also lives with an openness to the neighbor, with a readiness to forgive, with compassion and humaneness.

The Christian life is characterized by a capacity to detach oneself from things. The Christian rejoices in the sheer wonder of being alive and in the goodness of creation. There is a proper Christian exultation in the vitalities and energies of life. Yet the Christian also knows that human life does not consist in the abundance of what one possesses. A Christian lives *with* things as one who can live *without* things. The apostle Paul in his letter to the Corinthians wrote:

I mean, brothers and sisters, the appointed time has grown short; from now on, let even those who have wives be as though they had none, and those who mourn as though they were not mourning, and those who rejoice as though they were not rejoicing, and those who buy as though they had no possessions, and those who deal with the world as though they had no dealings with it. For the present form of this world is passing away. (1 Corinthians 7:29–31)

The art of the Christian life is to use the things of this world as God's gracious gifts with gratitude but with the capacity to live without them.

This particular virtue of being able to detach oneself from things comes to a climax in that great event in the life of a Christian when the Christian community gathers at death to commit the human person to the care of God, who raised Jesus Christ from the dead, and to commit the body to the ground, dust to dust and ashes to ashes. This committal of life to God which comes to its climax at death is a characteristic of the Christian life.

The Christian life is characterized by a deep sense of responsibility, of answerability, of obligation. The Christian knows that he or she did not just happen but is by the will and the intention of God. Out of that deep conviction there comes the further conviction that the Christian is answerable to God and responsible for the use of life's good gifts, including time and space.

The Christian life is lived with a sense of embodying the purposes of God. This has been an especially strong emphasis in the Reformed tradition. The conviction that God calls us not only into our existence but to our daily work fills the most humble task with a sense of meaning. Life is lived not simply to maintain human existence but to fulfill the purposes of the creator.

The Christian life is characterized by simplicity. This was a pervasive virtue in early Reformed theological writings. Calvin in particular emphasized the simple life; he did not want to use two words when one word would do. He emphasized moderation in dress and in food, and in particular in human behavior. From the beginning the Reformed and the Calvinists in particular were opposed to the pretentious, the pompous, the ostentatious, the baroque, the contrived, and even the artificial. In contrast, they emphasized directness, openness, and authenticity. For Calvin simplicity was close to sincerity. The ostentatious, the pompous, the pretentious—whether it is expressed in automobiles, clothing, housing, or literary style—obscures reality. The simple opens up life to what is real. Sainthood is characterized by the kind of simplicity that is transparent to the reality of human life as God created it. It is a simplicity in which there is a transparent consistency between word and deed.

Finally, the Christian life is characterized by a sense of freedom in Christ.

This was the primary emphasis of Martin Luther. The Christian is a person who has been made free by God in Jesus Christ, and out of this freedom the Christian spontaneously knows how to live. The Reformed were never comfortable with Luther's emphasis on the spontaneity of the Christian life, and yet this also belonged to Reformed theology at its best. The Christian is a person who has been made free in Christ and therefore does not take too seriously his or her own sanctification. He knows that his salvation is ultimately in God's grace and not in human achievements. It is this awareness that makes the Christian free, so that there is a joy in seeking the kingdom and at the same time knowing that one has never fully found the kingdom.

The Christian life is lived in the world. For Calvin the gathering of the Christians for worship and the hearing of the sermon is the indispensable and decisive moment of the Christian life. Calvin also provided prayers for Christians for special times in each day: on arising from bed, on eating, or going to work or to school, on going to bed. He encouraged reading of the Bible and catechetical instruction. But Calvin resisted the establishment of exercises. Neither he nor his successors encouraged religious practices. Apart from the exercises specified in the New Testament (worship, the Bible, prayer, stewardship of possessions) the Christian calling is in the world, in human history. It is lived out in housework, in rearing children, in participation in political processes of the civil community, in work, and in the arts. The Christian life and sanctification are embodying the purposes of God in our daily lives in the world. Reformed piety is simply life lived in the time and place God puts us. It is never a "religious" withdrawal from the world.

## Good Works

Good works, which Christian faith encourages, must be carefully distinguished from work righteousness, which Christian faith condemns. Jesus spoke harshly of those who prayed on the street corners (Matthew 6:5), who sounded trumpets when they gave alms (Matthew 6:2), and who tithed "mint" and "every herb" but who neglected justice and the love of God (Luke 11:42, RSV). Jesus praised those who gave bread and water to the hungry and thirsty but were unaware they had done so (Matthew 25:31–46). When a woman poured a costly ointment on his head (Matthew 26:6–13), some protested that she should have given the money to the poor. But Jesus said, "She has done a beautiful thing" (v. 10, RSV).

The works that the Christian praises[31] are distinguished from work righteousness, which enhances the ego or seeks to earn glory in heaven.

1. Good works are those that God commands. "Good works are only such as God hath commanded in his holy Word, and not such as, without the warrant thereof, are devised by men out of blind zeal, or upon any pretense of good intention" (Westminster Confession 16.1). Protestantism was a rebellion against "good works" that had been imposed by medieval Catholicism. This definition of good works as works that God commands is a protestation against churches, movements, causes, and ideologies that seek to impose on people their own agenda while claiming the authority of God. Good works are those commanded by God in scripture.

2. Good works are the expression of thanksgiving and gratitude for God's goodness and mercy. They are done out of the joy of doing them and out of a personal awareness that they are right and appropriate. Good works are not a means to an end. They are the expression of faith and affection. Martin Luther declared that good works do not make a good man. A good man does good works.

3. Good works are covered by God's mercy; their flaws are forgiven. T. S. Eliot in "Little Gidding" declared that one of the gifts reserved for age was the awareness that the deeds we once thought were pure were in fact corrupted by self-interest. Good works are accepted by God even though they are flawed.

4. Good works are not distinguished by their own nature. Christians do the same works as non-Christians. Good works in the Christian definition are distinguished by the faith, the disposition, and the commitment with which they are done. There are no distinctively Christian works apart from the faith that motivates them and shapes them.

5. Good works are used by God to enhance human life and to accomplish his purposes. They have an importance that must not be minimized. They relieve human suffering, build up human community, and accomplish God's purposes in human history. The verdict of Jesus, "She has done a beautiful thing," can be applied to many human deeds.

## The Vision of the Holy Commonwealth

Reformed theologians from the beginning cherished the vision of the holy commonwealth.[32] Neither Zwingli nor Bullinger in Zurich nor Calvin in Geneva repudiated Christendom or a society whose official commitments were Christian. Calvin and Zwingli were concerned that Zurich and Geneva should be Christian cities. They differed only in the respective roles they assigned to the church and the magistrate. None of the early Reformers could have imagined a secular society, much less a pluralistic society. Calvin, unlike Zwingli and Bullinger, fought for a church independent of the state, but all agreed on the significance of the Christian magistrate.

John Calvin was concerned that Geneva should be a Christian community. Wherever the Calvinists went they carried with them this vision of the Christian community, of a holy commonwealth. Sanctification has to do with public as well as private life. The doctrine of vocation means that daily work, political life, or social activities are not activities Christians do in addition to being Christian or in spite of being Christian. They are the activities in which Christians embody and express their convictions.

The sanctification of the Christian includes life in the family and in the economic, social, and political spheres. The justification (forgiveness) of the Christian likewise covers public and social life as well as private and personal life. Hence the Christian can participate vigorously in political or social life without being a fanatic or self-righteous.

The sanctification of the Christian in public life begins with justification, the awareness that we are sinners in political, economic, and social life and that in these orders as well as in personal life we live by the mercy of God, who forgives our sins. As Reinhold Niebuhr said in so many different ways, our causes are not as righteous as we think they are and our participation in them is never as devoid of self-interests as we claim.[33] The Christian brings to public life a sense of contrition.

Perfectionism in public life is as disastrous as perfectionism in private life. It has always led to self-righteousness, fanaticism, and brutality. Protestants have historically been hesitant to speak of a Christian culture or a Christian society or a Christian state.[34] From the perspective of Protestant understanding of Christian faith there is no such thing as a Christian economic, political, or social order. There is, however, the reality of Christians who live out their faith in political, economic, and social life.

Alongside the awareness that no society is Christian there has always existed among Reformed Christians a profound conviction that they were elected by God to fulfill his purposes in human history. This was especially true of the English Puritans. For them the New World offered opportunities for the glorification of God, freedom to establish Christian communities that would be models for the decaying society of Europe and would bring salvation to the natives. There were other motives, of course, but the significant role of religious and theological motives cannot be gainsaid. Richard Hakluyt, a Puritan preacher and advocate of colonization, wrote in *Discourse on the Western Planting* that English sovereigns "are not onely chardged to mayneteyne and patronize the faithe of Christe, but also to inlarge and advance the same. Neither oughte this to be their laste worke but rather the principall and chefe of all others."[35] Louis B. Wright, distinguished authority on English and early American history, comments that Hakluyt's *Principal Navigations, Voyages, and Discoveries* "quickly found a place beside Fox's *Book of the Martyrs* and the King James version of the Bible as reading deemed necessary to all good Englishmen."[36] Wright also concludes:

> To the 20th century the motives and purposes of the religious groups who so powerfully affected the expansion of English-speaking peoples may seem narrow and hypocritical. But that interpretation ignores the spirit of the times which produced the movements which we have been discussing. Self-interest there certainly was. But to doubt the sincerity of these people is to misunder-stand the age in which they lived. Once more let me emphasize that they were conscious of being a part of a great undertaking, of being the instru-ments of God's will, and if profits accrued to them it was a clear indication of the favor of the Almighty. The Hebraic, Old Testament faith of the men and women of the 17th century and of their spiritual descendants in later periods was often harsh and conducive to bigotry. But it had sinews and strength.[37]

Any notion of manifest destiny or of a Christian nation or society has been subjected to criticism by a secular and pluralistic culture. The Christian community must be grateful for this criticism, for the organized church is as susceptible to the corruptions of power as is the political order. Faith can also become ideology. Protestant Christianity in the beginning empha-sized the principle of self-criticism, which was implicit in the doctrine of justification by faith. A Protestant when true to the faith is critically self-critical not only in personal life but of loyalties and commitments in public life.[38]

The criticism of the Christian mission is full of anomalies. Within the church, critics of those who have identified the church with political causes and social orders in the past have no hesitancy in identifying the church with their own social and political agendas today. Critics from outside the church, as in secular humanism, are as self-righteous and as without principles of self-criticism as the church has ever been at the height of its power.

The Protestant principle that God's judgment rests on good and evil, conservative and liberal, bond and free, black and white people alike is the beginning of sanctification for the church in public as well as in private life. The great contribution that Christians of every social agenda and of every racial, social, and ethnic origin can bring to political, social, and economic life is an awareness of the need for contrition on their *own* part.

The sanctification of the Christian—that is, the disposition, the attitudes, and the directions of political and social activities—is determined by Christian faith. In the earlier days of the ecumenical movement those involved in the study of life and work proclaimed a slogan that doctrine divides but work unites. This is true on a limited basis as people with a fair consensus of belief unite, for example, to relieve human suffering. Today, however, it is increasingly evident that work—economic, political, and social activities—divides people as bitterly and as clearly as Christian doctrines ever did. The reason for this is evident. Work is determined by doctrine, and sooner or later differences in work reflect differences in doctrine.

The sanctification of the Christian in public life is a working out of Christian faith in political, economic, and social decisions. Hence the presupposition of sanctification on the human level is Christian faith and life, especially in the worshiping, believing community.

In personal and public morality, courses in ethics are not as significant as participation in believing, worshiping communities that shape character. It is also significant that the translators of the Bible into English intended for the Bible to be the basis for life in the commonwealth as well as for life in the church. The Bible, incomparably more than any other book shaped the ethos, the institutions, and the commitments of the people who constitute the United States at least up until the middle of the twentieth century. The loss of the Bible as part of the memory of the people will very likely have serious consequences in the political and social life of the nation.[39]

The form of Christian life in the public sphere is significantly determined, limited, or enhanced by history. Christians have lived in a great variety of economic, political, and social orders—for example, the Roman Empire, medieval Europe, and the modern nation-state. They have lived in rural and urban societies, in feudal, communist, and capitalist economic orders, in developed countries and third-world countries. The possibilities for the sanctification of the Christian to express itself in public life differs significantly from one society to another. The possibilities of sanctification in a free society are radically different from those in a totalitarian society. Hence there is no one pattern of Christian sanctification. Every Christian is called to affirm the faith in the light of the possibilities that are open in the time and place in which in the providence of God he or she lives.

Pietism that defines the Christian life as the relation of the person to God with little reference to public responsibilities may in some historical situations be the only possibility open to the Christian. Yet Reformed Christianity can never be satisfied with sanctification defined simply in personal categories. God calls the Christian to sanctification in public as well as private life, to live out the commitments of Christian faith in the decisions and activities that constitute society in general as well as in the church.

## CHAPTER 15

# CHRISTIAN FREEDOM

A Christian man is a perfectly free lord of all, subject to none.

A Christian man is a perfectly dutiful servant of all, subject to all. . . .

For his works do not make man a believer, so also they do not make him righteous. But as faith makes a man a believer, and righteous, so faith also does good works. Since, then, works justify no one then a man must be righteous before he does the good work, it is very evident that it is faith alone which, because of the pure mercy of God through Christ and in His Word, worthily and sufficiently justifies and saves the person, and a Christian man has no need of any work or of any law in order to be saved, since through faith he is free from every law and does all that he does out of pure liberty and freely, seeking neither benefit nor salvation, since he already abounds in all things and is saved through the grace of God because of his faith, and now seeks only to please God.

Martin Luther, *The Freedom of a Christian*

God alone is Lord of the conscience, and hath left it free from the doctrines and commandments of men which are in anything contrary to his Word, or beside it in matters of faith or worship. So that to believe such doctrines, or to obey such commandments out of conscience, is to betray true liberty of conscience. . . .

Westminster Confession of Faith, 20.2

For freedom Christ has set us free. Stand firm, therefore, and do not submit again to a yoke of slavery.

Galatians 5:1

Christian freedom was the subject of Martin Luther's best-known writing, the deeply moving treatise on the freedom of a Christian, written in 1520. It was also the subject of a very moving chapter in Calvin's *Institutes of the Christian Religion;* it appeared in the first edition of 1536 and remained with few changes through the final edition of 1559.

He who proposes to summarize gospel teaching ought by no means to omit an explanation of this topic. For it is a thing of prime necessity, and apart from a knowledge of it consciences dare undertake almost nothing without doubting; they hesitate and recoil from many things; they constantly waver and are afraid. But freedom is especially an appendage of justification and is of no little avail in understanding its power.[1]

Calvin, like Luther, was very much aware of the oppressive character of medieval Catholicism, imposing on the consciences of human beings countless religious practices and human laws.

Jesus Christ makes human beings free from all human bondages. As Luther exclaimed,

One thing and one only is necessary for Christian life, righteousness, and liberty. That one thing is the most holy word of God, the gospel of Jesus Christ. . . . Let us then consider it certain and conclusively established that the soul can do without all things except the Word of God, and that where this is not there is no help for the soul in anything else. But if it has the word it is rich and lacks nothing, since this word is the word of life, of truth, of light. . . .[2]

# God Alone Is Lord of the Conscience

Christian freedom means first of all that the human conscience cannot be bound by human laws. No one has ever emphasized this freedom of the Christian conscience more than John Calvin. God alone has authority over the consciences of human beings.[3]

Laws that bind the conscience must be distinguished from civil and ecclesiastical regulations, which order life in church and society. These laws are to be obeyed on the authority of the state or the church, but they do not bind the conscience before God and neither can they in and of themselves establish the goodness or evil of any person. Calvin's purpose in protesting against laws that bind the conscience was to eliminate constitutions and regulations that are made "to bind souls inwardly before God and to lay scruples on them, as if in joining things necessary to salvation." God alone has ordained what is necessary for salvation and, if one wishes a more secular statement, what is necessary for human well-being.[4]

Freedom of conscience has reference not simply to the constitutions of ecclesiastical bodies but also to the unofficial "laws of society," or what is called political correctness. Christian conscience is bound to God and not to the ideologies of a society.

The Westminster Confession of Faith has remarkable paragraphs on freedom of conscience. The authors, writing amid the Puritan revolution, were very much aware that God alone is the Lord of the conscience and that the human conscience has been left free from the commandments of human beings whether these commandments are issued by the state or by the church or by the reigning political ideologies. God alone determines what is necessary for human salvation and human excellence.[5]

## Freedom from the Rigor of the Law

Christian freedom means, second, that Jesus Christ has delivered us from the rigor of the law.[6] The rigor of the law was the doctrine that perfect obedience to the law is necessary for salvation. Christian freedom is the gospel that human salvation does not rest on our works or our achievements or on our keeping the law. Salvation is God's free gift. God has borne our sins and freed us from the penalty. In short, God has forgiven us. This is Christian freedom. The Christian is no longer under the tyranny of the law. The Christian has been made free by the grace of God to live joyously in God's presence.

## Willing Obedience

Christian freedom means, third, that the Christian, having been freed from the necessity of obeying the law, now willingly obeys God's will.[7] Calvin put it thus:

> Those bound by the yoke of the law are like servants assigned certain tasks for each day by their masters. These servants think they have accomplished nothing, and dare not appear before their masters unless they have fulfilled the exact measure of their task. But sons, who are more generously and candidly treated by their fathers, do not hesitate to offer them incomplete and half-done and even defective works, trusting that their obedience and readiness of mind will be accepted by their fathers, even though they have not quite achieved what their fathers intended. Such children ought we to be, firmly trusting that our service will be approved by a merciful Father, however small, rude, and imperfect these may be.[8]

Martin Luther thought of the Christian life as a life made free by Christ. The Christian joyously loves and serves God. In ecstatic moments Luther would say that the Christian has no need for the law. He knows how to serve God out of the experience of being forgiven. As Luther put it, no one has to tell a man how to love his wife; he knows how to love his wife out of the very experience of love. The Christian is made free by Christ for this kind of love and service.[9]

Calvin, even in his most ecstatic moments, would never say that the Christian has no need for the law, but he too emphasizes the joy of Christian freedom whereby one can obey the law without the cringing fear that one's salvation is dependent on perfect obedience. Freedom relieves the Christian of anxiety and morbid introspection about one's own goodness.

## Things Indifferent

The fourth part of Christian freedom has to do with things indifferent, particularly in regard to "outward things."[10] The New Testament teaching about outward things, in and of themselves indifferent, centered on the question of eating meat offered to idols (Romans 14; 1 Corinthians 8). The Christian knew that the idols had no reality and that the meat was good. Therefore the eating of the meat was open to Christian freedom. Yet many people within the Christian community were offended if meat that had been offered to idols was eaten by Christians. Regulations by the church prohibiting eating meat offered to idols would deny the freedom of Christians to eat meat that was perfectly good in and of itself. Nevertheless the question of one's obligation to the neighbor remained. Paul therefore concluded, "Do not let what you eat cause the ruin of one for whom Christ died" (Romans 14:15).

John Calvin was insistent that the church must not lay prohibitions upon Christian consciences concerning matters that are in and of themselves indifferent.

> These matters are more important than is commonly believed. For when consciences once ensnare themselves, they enter a long and inextricable maze, not easy to get out of. If a man begins to doubt whether he may use linen for sheets, shirts, handkerchiefs, and napkins, he will afterward be uncertain also about hemp; finally doubt will even arise over tow. For he will turn over in his mind whether he can sup without napkins, or go without a handkerchief. If a man should consider daintier food unlawful, in the end he will not be at peace before God, when he eats either black bread or common victuals, while it occurs to him that he could sustain his body on even coarser foods. If he boggles at sweet wine, he will not with clear conscience drink even flat wine, and finally he will not dare touch water if sweeter and cleaner than other water. To sum up, he will come to the point of considering it wrong to step upon a straw across his path, as the saying goes.[11]

Calvin summed up his teaching in these words:

> We see whither this freedom tends: namely, that we should use God's gifts
> for the purpose for which he gave them to us, with no scruple of conscience,
> no trouble of mind. With such confidence our minds will be at peace with
> him, and will recognize his liberality toward us. For here are included all
> ceremonies whose observance is optional, that our consciences may not be
> constrained by any necessity to observe them but may remember that by God's
> beneficence their use is for edification made subject to him.[12]

Calvin goes on to say that Christian freedom is a spiritual thing and
its whole force lies in quieting frightened consciences before God. Thus
it must not be used as an excuse to abuse God's gifts—for example, by
gluttony or by "delight in lavish and ostentatious banquets, bodily apparel,
and domestic architecture." Christian freedom has to do with things
indifferent, "provided they are used indifferently. But when they are coveted
too greedily, when they are proudly boasted of, when they are lavishly
squandered, things that were of themselves otherwise lawful are certainly
defiled by these vices."[13]

The second qualification of Christian freedom is found in responsibility
for one's neighbor. The apostle Paul had insisted that he would give up
meat if eating meat caused his neighbor to stumble. In a similar manner,
Calvin argues that many practices that are in themselves indifferent and
that belong to Christian freedom may be and in some circumstances should
be given up by Christians in concern for their neighbor. An illustration
of this particular problem in our time is the use of alcoholic beverages.
There is no divine prohibition against drinking alcoholic beverages. The
drinking of alcoholic beverages is part of Christian freedom. Yet this
freedom has to be assessed in the light of the fact that the consumption
of alcohol constitutes the most serious drug problem in American society
and that alcoholics need support for total abstinence. How and under what
circumstances can a Christian in exercise of Christian freedom make use
of alcoholic beverages?

Calvin was greatly concerned that the Christian in the exercise of his
or her freedom should not give offense to those who are weak. Yet Christians must not allow those who enjoy taking offense to control their
behavior. Calvin very significantly makes a distinction between an offense
given and an offense taken.[14]

Christians should be careful not to give offense, but at the same time
they must be concerned not to take offense. Just as it is possible to give
offense unnecessarily so it is also possible to be too easily offended and

to be looking for an opportunity to take offense against one's neighbor. The Christian life calls for a disposition that is not easily offended as well as a disposition that seeks not to offend.

Calvin likewise insisted that just as freedom must be subordinate to love, so in turn love itself must abide under the purity of faith.[15] The weak must be fed with milk, as Paul declared (1 Corinthians 3:2). But feeding with milk does not mean feeding with poisons or falsehoods. Christian freedom is not a cover for falsehood or for heresy; Christians must accept the scandal that truth causes.

Finally, Calvin insisted that freedom of conscience does not relieve one from obeying civil laws and the regulations of society, which are necessary for the ordering of human life. Christian freedom has nothing to do with laws governing speed on the highway or with regulations such as worship at eleven o'clock.

Conscience for Calvin was an "awareness of divine judgment."[16] Conscience has reference to God, and a good conscience is nothing but inward integrity of heart. A law or regulation or religious rite is said to bind the conscience when it has to do with a person's status in the presence of God. Luther and Calvin alike were insistent that God has left the consciences of human beings free from all human rules in church and in society. Consciences can be bound by God alone.

❖

## CHAPTER 16

# THE LAW
# AND MORAL DECISIONS

The will of God is made known to us in His revelation in Jesus Christ as a single will which always and everywhere wills the same. As the One who imparts Himself unconditionally, as love, he wills to be known and recognized by us in this self-communication He wills to make Himself known and to rule as "the One He is." . . .

Hence the Divine Command is *one* and one alone, namely to acknowledge this God as the God who is, to know that he is our God; it is the "first commandment": "I am the Lord thy God, thou shalt have none other Gods before Me." That is: to believe in God as the only Center, as the Origin and End of our life, upon whose love and grace alone our life is based, and in which it is made complete, to fear Him and to love Him.

Emil Brunner, *The Divine Imperative*, 132–133

Do not think that I have come to abolish the law or the prophets; I have come not to abolish but to fulfill. For truly I tell you, until heaven and earth pass away, not one letter, not one stroke of a letter, will pass from the law until all is accomplished.

Matthew 5:17–18

The law is God's gracious intention for the world and for human life.[1] It is not some order arbitrarily imposed on either the world or human existence. Law is rightly understood as the gracious and loving will of the creator for his creation. Because the law is God's gracious will, it is good. Jesus Christ delivers us not from the law but from the "rigor" of the law, from the misunderstanding of the law. Jesus Christ delivers us from the law as it operates among sinful human beings.

The law as God's gracious will for his creation will endure as long as creation itself. Its purpose will always be God's intention for his creation. The gracious promise of the law for human life has been graciously fulfilled by Jesus Christ.

The law is the enemy or an evil only from the standpoint of sin.[2] It is a burden for sinful human beings who can no longer fulfill the law. It is an evil when the fulfillment of the law becomes the means of earning God's favor and of fulfilling the meaning of one's own existence through one's own efforts. Jesus Christ came not to destroy the law but to fulfill it. He abrogates not the law but the rigor of the law for sinful human beings. He saves us from the sinful use of the law as a means of earning what can only be given as God's gracious gift.

The law as God's gracious will for his creation is one. By reason of their finiteness, which is now complicated by sin, human beings have to receive the law in fragmentary ways. Hence, Christians know the law of God, which is one, in a variety of ways.

## Natural Law

The law of God has been written into the very structure of created existence and into human existence itself. For this reason Paul in the letter to the Romans could write:

> For what can be known about God is plain to them, because God has shown it to them. Ever since the creation of the world his eternal power and divine nature, invisible though they are, have been understood and seen through the things he has made. So they are without excuse; for though they knew God, they did not honor him as God or give thanks to him, but they became futile in their thinking, and their senseless minds were darkened. (Romans 1:19–21)

The Christian community came into existence in a world in which the Stoics already had a doctrine of natural law.[3] They believed that the purposes of creation and human existence were present in the world and accessible to human reason. The early theologians, Justin, Irenaeus, and Tertullian, appropriated the concept of the natural law. They believed that the law as we have it in the Ten Commandments and even in the law of Christ was revealed in the creation and that this revelation was sufficiently opened to all human beings as to leave them without excuse.

John Calvin also accepted the tradition of natural law.[4] He believed that we know God in the immediacy of human experience. The sense of divinity has been imprinted in the depths of human experiences. We know God not only in human nature but also in the general revelation in creation. This revelation is sufficient to convict human beings and to leave them without excuse. For Calvin the Ten Commandments make clearer what has already been revealed in the creation. Calvin understands natural law in a relative, broken sense. Sin has blinded the eyes of human beings, and they cannot clearly decipher God's will by studying the creation. Hence the emphasis of Reformed theology has always been on scripture, not on the natural law tradition.

Yet the affirmation of natural law is crucially important. On the basis of natural law Christians say to the world that the law they affirm is the same law that God has written into the very structure of things. Even Enlightenment Christians such as Thomas Jefferson appealed to natural law beyond human laws. Human beings have rights that are not in the first place granted by a government but have been given to them as an original endowment by God and as such are inalienable. Natural law in the moral and political sense is not to be confused with natural law in the natural sciences. Yet it must be observed that a creative Reformed theologian, Thomas F. Torrance, has been arguing in recent years that God's will for the universe is one, and that natural law in the sense of the natural sciences has its foundation in moral law. Moral law is not less certain than natural law and is indeed the basis of natural law, Torrance argues.[5]

## The Ten Commandments

The law has been expressed in the Decalogue, or the Ten Commandments. Calvin, who treats the Ten Commandments primarily in the second book of the *Institutes* under the general theme of Christ our redeemer, understood that the inward law, which is "written, even engraved, upon the hearts of all, in a sense asserts the very same things that are to be learned from the two Tables."[6]

Brevard Childs in his study of Exodus emphasizes the covenantal and personal context of the Ten Commandments.[7] This context provides exegetical controls for the interpretation of the Ten Commandments in every new situation.

(1) The commandments are given by God as an expression of his will for his covenant people. They are not to be seen as simply moral directives apart from the living authority of God himself, who has made himself known.

(2) The commandments are given by God to his people in the context of a covenant. Whatever broader implication the Commandments may have, their primary function is directed toward shaping the life of his chosen community.

(3) The commandments are addressed to the church both as a gracious gift pointing to the way of life and joy, and as a warning against sin which leads to death and judgment.

(4) The intent of the commandments is to engender love of God and love of neighbor. The two sides cannot be fused into one command, nor can either be used at the expense of the other. . . .

(5) The church tries to be obedient to the will of God through the gift of the Spirit of Christ, which continues to open up new and fresh avenues of freedom. . . .[8]

Calvin also lays down three principles for the interpretation of the commandments. First, the commandments have to do not only with "outward honesty but [with] inward and spiritual righteousness."[9] Second, the commandments and prohibitions always contain more than is expressed in words. For example, every negative commandment involves a positive obligation.[10] Third, "we ought to ponder what the division of the divine law into two Tables meant."[11] The beginning and the foundation of righteousness is the worship of God. Calvin concludes his exposition of the commandments by insisting that they have to be understood in the light of the teachings of Christ and the summary of the law as love for God and for neighbor.

It is significant that Calvin treats the Ten Commandments under the topic of the knowledge of God the redeemer. He does not discuss the commandments under God the creator,[12] nor does he treat them in any specific way when he talks about the Christian life. Finally, he does not use the Ten Commandments except as background in his discussion of the order of the church and of the state.

Calvin adopted the doctrine of the threefold use of the law.[13] The law is useful to convict us of our sins; it restrains public unrighteousness; and it serves as a guide for Christian living. The distinctiveness for Calvin's theology lies in his insistence that the third use of the law, as a guide for the Christian, is its primary use. Calvin understands the law in terms of the gracious purposes of the creator, not in the light of human sin, which made the righteousness of the law an impossibility for human beings, or in the light of the sinful use of the law as a means for self-righteousness.

The Ten Commandments continued to play an extensive role in traditional Reformed theologies. The exposition of the Ten Commandments in the Westminster Larger Catechism is a splendid summary of the ethical thinking of the Puritan Christians.

The Ten Commandments have played a less conspicuous role in recent Reformed theology. Reinhold Niebuhr pointed out three weaknesses in any summary of the law such as the Ten Commandments as a guide for human behavior.[14] First, no law can anticipate all the possibilities that are open to human freedom in a particular situation. Therefore, in many situations the law is an inadequate guide. Second, the law as such cannot transform and move the heart. Third, the law not infrequently elicits a negative response. In older, stable societies it was easier to summarize the Christian life simply in terms of the Ten Commandments. Without minimizing the role of the commandments in history and their continuous significance as one statement of the law of God, the question may legitimately be raised whether the almost exclusive emphasis of Reformed Christians on the Ten Commandments at various times ever offered an adequate guide for Christian life and society. Gordon Rupp has contended that Methodism went beyond the third use of the law in Protestant orthodoxy by defining the law as the "commands of Christ briefly comprised in the Sermon on the Mount."[15] This insistence, Rupp believes, safeguards justification against perfectionism and also prevents Methodism from relapsing into rigid moralism. Reformed theology also needs this safeguard against legalism.

## The Law of Christ

Paul called upon his converts "to fulfill the law of Christ" (Galatians 6:2) and also referred to the Lord's commands (1 Corinthians 14:37–38). The New Testament does not contain any simple summary of morality comparable to the Ten Commandments. It does, however, contain the Sermon on the Mount, as well as many precepts, sayings, and summaries of moral advice. Matthew especially emphasizes the work of Jesus as the teacher and lawgiver. The disciples of Jesus hear and obey his words. In contrast to the Ten Commandments, the teaching of Jesus is more specifically directed to the quality and the disposition of life. The teachings of Jesus also assume that one can truly obey specific rules without knowing the meaning of mercy, justice, and love.

The Christian church has always had difficulty understanding how the law of Christ is to be obeyed. At times the church has suggested that those who wish to follow the law of Christ should become religious and enter a monastery. In contrast, the Mennonites and the left wing of the Protestant Reformation, as well as the perfectionist movements of the eighteenth and nineteenth centuries such as the Nazarenes, have sought to be guided by the Sermon on the Mount in social and civic responsibilities as well as personal life.

Reinhold Niebuhr argued that the simple teachings of Jesus were an inadequate guide for life in contemporary society and further that history would not sustain a life lived simply on the basis of love.[16] Human existence cannot be maintained by those who turn the other cheek and give to everyone who asks of them. Hence Niebuhr continued to argue that the simple teachings of Jesus needed to be supplemented by a prudential ethic that takes seriously the sinful context in which human life must be lived. Finally, Niebuhr argued that the teachings of Jesus always stand in judgment on the prudential ethics. Those who modify the teachings of Jesus to meet their responsibilities in a sinful society seldom do all they can. The teachings of Jesus also serve not simply as judgment but as encouragement and as a stimulant to Christian living in a sinful world.

C. H. Dodd has cogently argued that the teachings of Jesus in the Sermon on the Mount and throughout the Gospels should become part of the Christian's life and thought and give a *quality* and a *direction* of action which reflect the standards set by the divine agape (love). "The quality may be present in its degree at a quite lowly level of achievement. The right direction may be clearly discernable in the act even though the goal may be still far off but the demand that our action in concrete situations shall have this direction and this quality is categorical."[17]

Jesus was aware that one may keep many rules and yet be a stranger to love and mercy. Hence in his teachings the emphasis is not so much on the external act as on the inner disposition and quality of life. In addition, there is a naturalness about the teachings of Jesus which says that this is the way God made human beings to live. Jesus reinforced his teachings by pointing to the creation. The Sermon on the Mount and the occasional teachings of Jesus are not arbitrarily imposed on life but are descriptions of the way human life is meant to be lived.

## The Bible and the Example of Jesus

It is important to observe that when Calvin came to write specifically about the Christian life he did not rely on the exposition of the Ten Commandments but referred to scripture and to the example of Jesus.[18] This seems to mean that the material of scripture—the narratives, the wisdom literature, the biographies, or, as some would say today, the stories—is the material from which we learn how to live as Christians in a new time and place.

The same is true of the example of Jesus. The words of the old hymn, "Tell me the old, old story . . . of Jesus and his love," have not only theological significance but also significance for ethical reflection and moral action. If one wishes to know how Christians live in the world, let this person assimilate the stories of the patriarchs, of the kings of Israel, of the prophets, of Jesus and his disciples, of Paul.

## Gospel and Law

John Calvin distinguished between law and gospel, but he did not separate them.[19] Behind both the law and the gospel is the gracious will of God. The law contains the gospel. The original law was the gospel for the human beings as they were created. Calvin argued that God's benevolence has been set forth for us in the law, if we could merit it by works, but that it never comes to us by this merit.[20] The promise of the law, because of human sin, is fulfilled only in Christ. The gospel of Christ, however, contains the law. As has been noted, forgiveness is the presupposition of the Christian life, but the end of the Christian life is sanctification, the transformation of human existence into the image of Christ. Law and gospel are different and cannot be confused, yet each contains the other. They can be distinguished but not separated.

## Moral Inquiry

The Ten Commandments and even the Sermon on the Mount can be studied in such a way that the Christian life appears to be obedience to clear and simple rules. In many situations in life simple rules are adequate, but when we begin to reflect on the Ten Commandments and the Sermon on the Mount, on our human situation, and on the convictions we have about God, we see that Christian life is deeper and more complex than simple conformity to rules. Moral inquiry and reflection are a Christian necessity and duty. We have to think about the way we must live as Christians.

The attempt to define the moral life simply in terms of external rules leads to *legalism*. The Christian life cannot be defined by rules alone. Rules may be superficial, dealing only with surface behavior, and they can never fully anticipate the possibilities that are open to human freedom. Rules can never adequately deal with all the factors that are involved in many human situations. Those who live simply by rules, the legalists, frequently become self-righteous and brutal toward those who fail by their rules; moreover, they sometimes become excessively concerned with their own purity. Finally, rules do not move the hearts of human beings. They are not able in themselves to sustain human relations. They are most effective in coercive situations, as when supported by the power of the state with its police force or its tax-collecting machinery.

The attempt to define the Christian life in terms of rules also leads to *moralism,* which is closely related to legalism. Moralism is defined in different ways, but here it means the insistence on a particular rule, value, or principle at the expense of other rules or values and with no regard for the complex facts in the human situation. Moralism always has a simple answer to a very complex problem. Thus the attempt to define the moral life in terms of rules or laws leads to irrelevance, a loss of contact with what is actually happening. A pattern of life or law is sooner or later rejected as arbitrary and out of touch with the real world when it is imposed on people without an understanding of their situation.

Living morally requires the use of the mind as well as the support of a good heart. We have to think about how we shall live as Christians. We are not given ready-made answers to how we should live from Bible reading alone, from prayer alone, or from good intentions alone. In many situations we do not have the choice between the simple good and the simple evil. The most notable instance of such a situation historically has been war. No Christian could ever believe that war is a simple good, but Christians have participated in war. In some situations the choice of one value or good means the denial of another value or good. In certain instances the refusal to take a life means the loss of life, or the feeding of hungry children means taking food from hungry older people. Furthermore, rules or values are most helpful not when they are arbitrarily imposed but when they are internalized, assimilated into one's own personal existence. This happens when a rule or value is meaningfully related to a person's actual situation and to other rules and values. Hence, moral inquiry, the task of thinking responsibly about conduct, is a basic Christian obligation.

How do we determine how we shall live as Christians? We have at least six guides or aids to help us to decide how we shall live.

1. Rules that prescribe conduct as well as values and principles, which give more general guidance for conduct than rules, are very significant indications of how Christians should live. The fact that rules and principles when taken alone are inadequate guides does not mean that they are unimportant. They are the embodiment in propositions of the wisdom of experience. In Christian theology they are rooted in what is believed to be the revelation of God. They are an indispensable element in understanding Christian conduct. For Christians, laws—the Ten Commandments, in particular—are more than inherited wisdom. They are the revelation of God expressed in rules.

2. Theology is also important in determining moral behavior, especially

the doctrine of God and the understanding of God's purposes in the world. Theological convictions about who God is, about who a human being is, and about the meaning of history influence—indeed, determine—in no small measure how we act in the world. It can be argued that communism, for example, collapsed in part because of a defective doctrine of the human being.

3. Our analysis and interpretation of the actual human situation and our interpretation of the moral significance of particular circumstances are also important factors in moral inquiry. We need to know what is actually happening, what is possible, and how our different values such as respect for human life and truth-telling relate to the situation and to each other in that situation.

4. A fourth factor that helps us to determine how we live as Christians is our basic understanding of the nature of the Christian life. Thomas à Kempis conceived of the Christian life as the imitation of Christ; Martin Luther as the life a person made free by Christ; John Calvin as obedience or the fulfillment of the divine purposes; H. Richard Niebuhr as the answering, responsible life. Each of these visions of the Christian life has its own strengths and weaknesses, and each gives a particular style to the Christian life.

5. A fifth factor in moral decisions is the assimilation of the content of the Bible, especially its narratives and biographies, the life of Jesus and his teaching, into one's own personal life. The knowledge of how Christians have lived in various times and places is also of great significance. Christians make moral decisions in the context of this participation in the life of faith.

6. The sixth factor in moral decisions is participation in the fellowship of a believing, worshiping congregation. The community in which we live guides our decision-making far more than the reading of a book, especially when the center of the community's life is worship and fellowship in a great tradition. The worship and ethos of the community provide not only support but perspective and sensitivity in moral inquiry. Life in the community of worship determines in considerable measure who we are and what we do.

All six factors are important in our thinking as Christians about the moral life. When any of the six is neglected, our ability to think constructively about how we should live is weakened.

The moral life for Christians presupposes trust in God and a good heart. It also requires the use of the mind to discover how the purposes of God can be fulfilled in our lives, in our community, and in the world. Hence, as we grow in trust and devotion to God, we need also to grow in our ability to think responsibly about how we should live as Christians.

Finally, just as it is possible to overemphasize the simplicity of the Christian life and to restrict it to rules, so it is possible to overemphasize its complexity. In most situations it is enough to know that we as Christians must tell the truth and respect other human beings as children of God.

CHAPTER 17

❖

# THE PREVENIENCE OF GRACE

The predominating sense of Grace in the New Testament is that which the word bears in the writings of Saint Paul, who thinks of the Divine salvation primarily as a "boon" flowing from the generous, unmerited graciousness of God to sinful, lost humanity, as expressed supremely on the cross of Christ. For Saint Paul the free outgoing and self-imparting of the redeeming love of God to man in Christ is constitutive of the whole of salvation. God deals with men in Christ purely on the basis of infinite, undeserved mercy.

William Manson, "Grace in the New Testament,"
in *The Doctrine of Grace,* ed. William T. Whitley, 59

For you know the generous act of our Lord Jesus Christ, that though he was rich, yet for your sakes he became poor, so that by his poverty you might become rich.

2 Corinthians 8:9

We know that in everything God works for good with those who love him, who are called according to his purpose. For those whom he foreknew he also predestined to be conformed to the image of his Son, in order that he might be the first-born among many brethren. And those whom he predestined he also called; and those whom he called he also justified; and those whom he justified he also glorified.

Romans 8:28–30 (RSV)

Grace means the loving-kindness of God, but in the scripture it has a more specific meaning. It refers in particular to God's spiritual initiative in choosing a people, in forgiving sins, in transforming human hearts. It is the active favor and goodness of God directed especially to his people. "Saint Paul, keeping steadfastly to the original sense of the word, thinks of the grace of God as becoming effectual in various ways, now as giving men a new status, now as conferring various special gifts, now as inspiring to fresh tasks and responsibilities."[1]

## Grace as God's Favor

Calvin and Reformed theology after him have generally been content to speak of God's grace without analyzing it according to various functions.[2] The only distinction that became general was between God's common grace, which supports and enhances all of creation, and special grace, which calls the human creature to his or her true destiny. John Wesley, a Protestant more open to the Catholic tradition, specified accompanying, convincing, following, cooperating, justifying, regenerating, sanctifying, and glorifying grace. As Albert Outler notes, "All of these, and each in its own way, signify God's unstinted benevolence, his spontaneous love and mercy. In each case, grace is a gift of God unmerited in the most literal sense. Grace as 'given' is also a moral influence in the human heart and yet enlarging its freedom and making its dispositions graceful."[3] It is typical of Calvin's theology and that of most of his followers that detailed analyses of grace have been omitted. It was enough to affirm God's grace, which gives to human beings a new status and transforms their lives. All the Protestant Reformers were agreed on the prevenience of grace, that it goes before, that it is the first word, that everything flows from it. This was their primary emphasis.

A second emphasis of the Protestant Reformers and of Calvinist theology is the insistence that grace is the personal favor of God. Christian theology has always faced the temptation to materialize grace into a thing. Over against materialization of grace the first Protestants were adamant. Hence they refused to think of grace as some infused quality. Grace is God's personal engagement of human beings. God is related to human beings as free, moral, historical persons.

Leonard Hodgson in a very perceptive study of grace insists that we understand God's grace by the analogy of our experience in personal relationships.

> When we are thinking of it [grace] in Paul's secondary sense of the word, as "the Divine influences" which operate from within the Christian nature, it is only too easy to slip into thinking of grace as a sub-personal something given by God to work on its own, as a doctor may give a patient a bottle of medicine to be taken three times a day after a meal. This materialized conception of grace led to sacramental abuses and practices. Furthermore when we think of grace in materialistic terms we cannot understand how a human act can both be caused by God's grace and also be the expression of a man's own free will.
>
> It is not so in the realm of personal relationships. We may not be able

fully to understand it, but we find no difficulty in accepting as a reality in
our experience the fact that one man can help another to be and to do what
he himself wills to be and do. We know what it means for a man to say,
"I could never have been what I am were it not for so-and-so coming into
my life—speaking with heartfelt gratitude for the coming of so-and-so."[4]

Of course, the influence of one person on another may be for good or
evil, and there may be undue influence that disregards a person's freedom.
But there is a personal influence which approaches another person in a
fully personal manner, "willing him to action for which he is fully responsible." We cannot limit the divine action to that of which we are consciously
aware. The influence of divine grace may transform our lives without con-
frontation and perhaps without our noticing it, just as we are not always
aware of the personal influence of a friend on our lives.

The insistence of Luther and Calvin on God's grace as personal, according to the analogy of human relationships, enabled them to insist on the
prevenience of grace and at the same time hold together the divine initiative
and human responsibility. Theologians have also maintained a distinction between uncreated grace and created grace. By created grace they have
referred to those qualities in human life such as love, peace, and freedom
that are the consequence of divine grace. Paul spoke of the charismatic
qualities of the Christian life. Reformed theologians, however, have not
generally used this distinction. They were opposed to the notion of "infused
grace," that is, a divine energy that was infused into the human person.
For this reason they were skeptical of talking about created grace and preferred to speak of human graces that are the consequence of divine grace.
John Calvin was reluctant to use technical theological vocabulary and was
certainly reluctant to invent theological vocabulary. He sought to express
theology in the language of ordinary human discourse. For this reason
one does not find in Reformed theology elaborate analyses of grace or the
detailed discussions of the distinction between divine grace and created
grace.

The chief point that runs through all Reformed theology is its insistence
on the prevenience of grace, the fact that God's grace is prior to all things,
that God's grace is personal and influences human beings as free, responsible, moral, historical persons.

Barth has defined the very being of God in the language of grace. God
seeks and creates fellowship in himself and in his creation. "He is Father,
Son and Holy Spirit and therefore alive in his unique being with and for
and in another."[5] What God is in himself he is also in relation to his creation. "Therefore what He seeks and creates between Himself and us is in

fact nothing else but what he wills and completes and therefore is in Himself. . . . That He is God—the Godhead of God—consists in the fact that He loves, and it is the expression of His loving that He seeks and creates fellowship with us."[6] Barth's favorite definition of God is one who loves in freedom.

## Grace in Creation

The prevenience of grace in the creation of the world has been a notable theme in the theology of Karl Barth.

> Creation is the freely willed and executed positing of a reality distinct from God. The question thus arises: What was and is the will of God in doing this? We may reply that He does not will to be alone in His glory; that He desires something else beside Him. But this answer cannot mean that God either willed or did it for no purpose, or that He did it so as to satisfy need. Nor does it mean that He did not will to be and remain alone because He could not do so. And the idea of something beside Him which would be what it is independently of Him is quite inconsistent with His freedom. In constituting this reality He cannot have set a limit to his glory, will and power. As the divine Creator He cannot have created a remote and alien sphere abandoned to itself or to its own teleology. If, then, this positing is not an accident, if it corresponds to no divine necessity and does not in any sense signify limitation of its own glory, there remains only the recollection that God is the One who is free in His love. In this case we can understand the positing of this reality—which otherwise is incomprehensible—only as the work of His love. He wills and posits the creature neither out of caprice nor necessity, but because He has loved it from eternity, because He wills to demonstrate His love for it, and because He wills, not to limit His glory by its existence and being, but to reveal and manifest it in His own co-existence with it. . . . That is why even the very existence and nature of the creature are the work of the grace of God.[7]

The origin of the universe is in the grace of God.

Barth's discussion of the Reformed controversy concerning infralapsarianism and supralapsarianism underscores the same point. Infralapsarianism as it developed in the last part of the sixteenth and the first part of the seventeenth century modified the seeming arbitrariness of supralapsarianism, but it also undercut some of the virtues of the supralapsarian position. In its initial impulse, Barth contends, supralapsarianism made some advance over the substance of Calvinistic dogma. It emphasized the priority of grace. It attempted to reverse the relationship between predestination and providence, that is, to understand providence in the light of predestination and not vice versa. While Barth is quite clear that supralapsarianism was not a viable theological position, he insists that it did attempt to say something important by saying that God's grace is prior to everything else. Infralapsarianism may have been more comfortable for the human sense of justice, but it did not resolve the problem. And it did not add anything, Barth contends, to what Calvin and other theologians of the sixteenth century had said.[8]

This emphasis on the priority of grace comes to special focus in the existence of the human person. It means that human life is rooted in the transcendent love of God. As Paul wrote in Ephesians, [God] "chose us in Christ before the foundation of the world to be holy and blameless before him in love. He destined us for adoption as his children through Jesus Christ, according to the good pleasure of his will, to the praise of his glorious grace that he freely bestowed on us in the Beloved" (Ephesians 1:4–6). This truth about life is celebrated in the sacrament of baptism when the child's name is called. God gives the child the name; God knows the child by name; God wills the child to be. This child did not just happen; behind every life is the purpose of God. God, not human beings, guarantees the identity of the child and gives to the child a dignity that no one should dare to abuse. When the Bible pronounces a final judgment on human beings, it declares that God will blot out the name, destroy the identity, take from the person the dignity of a life that has been undergirded by the power and love of God (Exodus 32:33; Revelation 3:5). On the other hand, there is no greater declaration that can be made about any person than the confidence that God chose this person before the foundation of the world and elected this person to be his son or daughter. The significance of this doctrine becomes clear when you put over against it the alternatives — that human beings are accidents, that they are the product of forces with no provision of their end, that in a casual way a man and a woman come together and a child results. Behind and beyond all these forces of biology, nature, and history, the Bible declares that the ultimate origin of human life is in the will and the intention of God. Nikolai Berdyaev, the Russian philosopher who died in exile, found profound meaning in this faith: "Where there is no God, there is no man."[9] When God is left out of the assessment of human worth, a human being has value only by belonging to the right nation, the right party, or the right race or by being the beneficiary of some political fiat. Over against the casualness of human life apart from God, Christian faith affirms that human life is established in the purposes of God.

# Predestination

Reformed theology has always been identified with the doctrine of predestination. While all Christian theologies have some doctrine of predestination, no other major theology has emphasized it so much. Predestination more obviously than any other doctrine is based on pre-venient grace. Election means that God chose human beings before the foundation of the world, and it also means that those whom he chose had to be rescued from the sinful condition in which they had fallen.

Predestination stands over against all forms of work righteousness, over every effort to achieve heaven by our own willpower, to earn our salva-tion. Predestination means that salvation is a gift and that in electing us God does for us what we could not do for ourselves.

Many of life's highest achievements, even apart from sin, are beyond the power of our wills. On every level of human life we are saved by "com-mon grace," which elicits from us what we ourselves could not have done. This common grace may be the kind word of a friend, the discipline of a teacher, or a crisis which somehow lays hold of our persons and elicits what we could not have done. When a plane crashed into the 14th Street Bridge across the Potomac to Washington, an ordinary man leaped out of his car and rescued a number of persons before he himself was over-come with fatigue and died in the icy waters. It is reasonable to conjec-ture that this great act of heroism and sacrifice was in some measure due to a "grace" in the situation. It was not something that he could have deliberately planned and accomplished. The situation called out of him that which he himself was not able to do. In some such way human life is continually blessed by an anonymous, or a common, grace, as Calvinists would say, that is pervasive in the whole created order.[10]

The most significant qualities of human greatness are beyond the power of the human will—namely, gratitude, humility, and love. No one can feel grateful by trying hard even though one may write thank-you notes according to the dictates of Emily Post. No one can feel humble by trying hard. If a person could be humble by his or her own efforts, then he or she would be proud of that humility. Literature reveals the comic and the tragic in such persons. Gratitude and humility are always the consequences of something that has happened to us. They are qualities that have been in some measure elicited by the situation in which we live. We often say that we ought to love, but no one loves out of obligation. "Oughtness" and love are in contradiction. We love only when we cannot help loving. We love only when it is spontaneous and uncalculated. Love is something that is elicited from us by the person whom we love.

For this reason the experience of falling in love is the closest analogy that we have in human experience, according to William Temple, to what Christian theology means by predestination.[11]

In Christopher Fry's play *The Dark Is Light Enough,* the Countess explains why she never fell in love:

> I mean, simply,
> It never came about.
> There we have no free-will.
> At the one place of experience
> Where we are most at mercy, and where
> The decision will alter us to the end of our days,
> Our destination is fixed;
> We're elected into love.[12]

Whenever a person falls in love, there is always something about the person who loves that reaches out and elicits love. Yet the act of love is very much one's own. Perhaps one is never so free and never so truly oneself as in the act of love. Yet every act of love must be explained first of all not in terms of human effort but in terms of a grace that reached out and called it forth.

The human predicament, according to Christian faith, is that we are self-centered when we ought to be God-centered. The human tragedy is that there is no way a self-centered person can become unself-centered by his or her own efforts. The ranges of our self-centeredness can be broadened from self to family or even to community or to the world. The self-centered person may overcome the selfishness on lower levels only to fall victim to it on the highest level — in the words of T. S. Eliot's great play *Murder in the Cathedral,* wanting to be last on earth in order to be first in heaven. Thomas à Becket's plight is an apt description of the predicament of every person. Can sinful pride be cast out only by more sinful pride? "The last temptation is the greatest treason: To do the right deed for the wrong reason."

Predestination embodies the Christian conviction that God lays hold of us and does for us what we could not do for ourselves. The prevenient grace of God comes perhaps in our birth and nurture in a Christian home and fellowship, perhaps in the gradual maturation of youth, perhaps in some great crisis. There is an analogy between what the church talks about in relation to predestination and the principles of Alcoholics Anonymous.

The alcoholic's only hope is to admit that he or she cannot save himself or herself. Salvation in a real sense comes from without. In a deeper and a broader sense this is what predestination is saying about the whole of human life. A sinful person can only wait for salvation. Some mediating Calvinists have sought to modify the more stringent forms of the doctrine, contending that while we cannot save ourselves, there are some things we can do, and that if we do them it is more likely that the salvation which is beyond our willpower will be ours. For example, a person may not be able to believe in God, but it is more likely that this person will come to believe in God if he or she associates with believing people, if he or she participates in the worship of God, and if he or she seeks to do God's will. Yet even those who have sought to modify the doctrine in these ways have always recognized that salvation sometimes comes when we least expect it and least hope for it.[13]

Predestination undercuts the structures of the church and even the sacraments. It means, as medieval churchmen well understood both in the Gottschalk and in the John Wyclif controversies, that salvation is God's gift and is not dispensed by the church or by its structures. Predestination has significance not simply for personal life but also for the nature of the ecclesial community.

Predestination is not to self-centered privilege but to service and responsibility. God's elect are not God's favorites so much as God's servants. John Calvin did not relegate God's sovereignty to the ultimate destinies of heaven and hell. He believed that God's election gives a human being something to do here and now in time and space. God's purposes are being worked out in history, and to be elect is to become an instrument of the divine purpose. The Calvinist is a person who is convinced that God is using his or her life to accomplish his divine purposes in human history.

It is clear enough that what has been said does not solve the mystery of those who reject God. Many Calvinists eliminated the mystery by saying quite frankly that God passed over the reprobates and left them to their just fate. The mystery of election is resolved in a very rational decision, however arbitrary it may appear to us, that God simply chose some for heaven and condemned others to hell for their sins. Generally the Calvinist always insisted that election and reprobation were not equal decrees. In the one case God chooses out of "a mass of perdition" some for salvation. In other cases God in his justice condemns them to their rightful fate, to their just destiny, and passes over them to show forth his justice.

Some of the Reformed, including Zwingli and Bullinger, preferred to emphasize simply the positive aspect of election and to leave in mystery the damnation that is so clearly a part of human experience and human history.[14] We do not know how or why it is that the love of God can be rejected. We do know that when we reject God the causes are with us, and that when we turn to God we do so because he first laid hold of us.

It is interesting to note that Calvin located the doctrine of predestination at the conclusion of the third book after he had discussed the Christian life and just before his discussion of the resurrection of the dead. In earlier editions of the *Institutes* he treated it as a part of providence. The final location, at the conclusion of the doctrine of salvation and just before the discussion of the resurrection, apparently pleased Calvin. This location of the doctrine suggests that predestination can best be understood not at the beginning of the Christian life but at the end, when the Christian looks back over Christian experience and explains, "This is what God has done in and through my life!"[15] This seems to be the testimony of the great saints. They regarded their own lives, insofar as they were good, not as their own achievements but as the work of God's grace. Calvin himself declared that the knowledge of predestination is nothing more than the testimony that we are sons of God, that is, of the grace and mercy of God.[16] The location of the discussion of the doctrine of predestination at the conclusion of the Christian life is not without its problems. It obscures the important theological conviction that predestination is prior to providence and that providence is subordinate to election. In other words, it obscures the prevenience of God's grace, which is the source of all things that are.

No one has stated more clearly than William Temple the way in which predestination functions as a testimony that one renders about one's own life in retrospect.

> All is of God; the only thing of my own which I can contribute to my own redemption is the sin from which I need to be redeemed. My capacity for fellowship with God is God's gift in creation; my partial deliverance from self-centeredness, my response to truth, beauty and goodness is God's gift through the natural world which he sustains in being and the history of man which he controls. One thing is my own—the self-centeredness which leads me to find my apparent good in what is other and less than the true good. This true good is the divine love and what flows from it appreciated as its expression. In response to that good, man finds his only true freedom, for only then does the self act as what it truly is and thus achieves true self-expression. . . . As the experience of grace becomes deeper, the conviction of its all sufficiency becomes more inevitable and more wholesome, until at last a man knows, and is finally "saved" by knowing, that all good is of God alone. We are clay in the hands of the potter and our welfare is to know it.[17]

# Perseverance of the Saints

The Reformed emphasis on the prevenience of grace also comes to expression in the doctrine of the perseverance of the saints.[18] On a very popular level this doctrine was formulated in the question whether a person who was once saved was always saved. Calvinists and Arminians disputed about the possibility of falling from grace with an intensity that is, in the light of contemporary human experience, unintelligible.

The remoteness of these questions underscores a twofold problem. On the one hand there is the disparity between human experience in the twentieth century and what we have known as Christian faith. Is faith in God after all a possibility? On the other hand our problem is the meaning of faith itself. What does the faith mean for those who stand within the circle of faith? Moreover and in particular, what does faith mean for those who once stood within the circle of faith but no longer do so?

The name of the doctrine was established in controversy and is unfortunate. The perseverance of the saints seems to suggest that the doctrine is about saints and their perseverance. Saints ought to persevere, but the doctrine is about the perseverance of God. The whole matter is stated in the words of Paul to the Philippians: "Work out your own salvation with fear and trembling; for it is God who is at work in you, enabling you both to will and to work for his good pleasure" (Philippians 2:12–13).

This doctrine has significance especially for those who know the dark night of the soul either in their personal lives or in society. The doctrine gives expression to the Christian hope that God will complete the work that he has begun in an individual life and in society. This doctrine is not so much a boast or an argument as it is a confession, a prayer, a hope that once we have known God's grace we shall never finally lose it.

The gospel has particular significance for an increasing number of people in the Western world who were once Christian but are no longer Christian. Here the issue is much more personal and pragmatic than the theoretical debates that once concerned Calvinists and Arminians.

The doctrine has some relation to the fact of experience that once a person has stood in the circle of faith he or she is always a person who has stood in the circle. The experience is indelible. No matter what one does, one always is the person who has known at one point God's presence and God's grace. No one can argue in an abstract way that this experience is a simple, easy guarantee of the particular outcome of a person's life. Nevertheless, the significance of the indelibility of this experience cannot be overestimated. José Ortega y Gasset, a social critic, has testified to this indelibility: "When I was a child, I was a Christian; now I am no longer. Does this mean strictly speaking, that I do not go on being a Christian? The Christian I was—is he dead, annihilated? Of course not; of course I am still a Christian but in the form of having been a Christian."[19] In Dostoevsky's *The Brothers Karamazov,* Alyosha exclaims, "Some good, sacred memory, preserved from childhood, is perhaps the best education."[20]

Ortega y Gasset's comment is confirmed in Christian experience. Baptism and Christian nurture are indelible. No matter how violently a teenager or a young adult may rebel against them and seek to deny the facts, he or she is always the person who has known life in the Christian community. Human beings are significantly determined by that against which they rebel.

The doctrine of the perseverance of the saints has reference not simply to the dark night of the soul and to tragic experiences of history, not simply to the indelibility of having been once a Christian; it also has application to world history. What, after all, are the significance and fate of this human history of which we are a part? Is human existence in the history of the universe simply an accident? Shall human beings someday disappear from this planet leaving no memory that they ever were? This is one possible fate, but it is the fate that is too frightful to contemplate and that does violence to our experience of the meaningfulness of life. The doctrine of the perseverance of the saints gives expression to the conviction that God, having begun a work, will see it through to completion.

## Assurance of Salvation

The assurance of salvation is the third doctrine that has reference to the prevenience of grace. Martin Luther himself had experienced terrible anguish over the question, Am I among the elect?[21] How can a person know his or her own salvation without concrete, tangible evidence? The emphasis in Reformed theology on election made this an increasingly serious question so that assurance of salvation became an article in the Westminster Confession of Faith, written during the high-water mark of Puritan theology in England.[22] The development of Covenant theology encouraged, according to Perry Miller, a new form of work righteousness whereby the believer had to demonstrate his or her election.[23] No one ever insisted more than Calvin that election was to vocation, to the Christian life. Yet Calvin himself never made works the mark of election.

The assurance of election must come, Calvin insisted, within the experience of faith itself.[24] Furthermore, the early Calvinists all insisted that the attention of the believer must be on the promises of God, not on the achievements and failures of his or her own heart. Luther in the dark night of the soul remembered that he had been baptized. Assurance is possible in this life. Indeed, "it is the duty of everyone to make his calling and election sure" (Westminster Confession 18.1). Yet it does not belong to the essence of faith. Calvin could not "imagine any certainty that is not tinged with doubt" (*Institutes* 3.2.17).

The grounds of assurance are the promises of God, justification by faith, predestination, the Holy Spirit, and, secondarily, vocation and sanctification. Salvation is God's gift and is not at the mercy of human frustration. The assurance of this gift is not in any human work but in the experience of faith itself and in particular of the promises of God. The assurance of salvation is not in human works but in the promises of God.

## Reprobation and Damnation

Any discussion of prevenient grace must take note of reprobation and of the evidences of damnation in the world. William Temple has pointed out that a doctrine of election is inevitable and by inference so is the doctrine of reprobation.

> The real difficulty of the position concerns the relation of God to those selves whom divine grace has not called, and apparently is not so far calling out of their self-centeredness. If grace can call the Buddha or Saint Francis to the great renunciation which inaugurates their career of sacrifice and service, why does it leave so many unstirred? We cannot say that it is because these responded while others do not respond to the activity of grace everywhere equally active, for it is only by grace that they could respond. Is it that God elects some to salvation and others to perdition? We all know the history of that doctrine and in our recoil from it have often failed to make due allowance for the strength of the argument leading to it. But it will not stand. Neither justice nor love could be intelligibly predicated of a God who could act so; and if these be denied, deity is denied. Yet we cannot escape the doctrine of election in some form; it is not so much an inference as the only possible reading of the facts when Theism is accepted. What the ultimate issue is to be lies beyond the bounds of terrestrial experience and must be considered in connection with eternal life.[25]

Evidences of damnation abound in the world. They range from the wastefulness of evolution to the frightful perversions of the human heart. Some human beings are born into situations in which they are blessed by a remarkably good genetic inheritance and are born into the nurture of a Christian family, a worshiping church, and a well-ordered community.

By contrast, many persons are born with a genetic inheritance that makes normal human life impossible, or into highly disordered and irregular families, or into chaotic communities — outside the limits of the ordinary means of grace. Furthermore, the accidents of human history seem destructive of good beyond any point that these evils can be justified theologically. Why is there so much evidence of damnation, so great a distinction between the Jacobs and the Esaus of the world?

Calvin and those who followed him in the Reformed tradition were right in refusing to evade the problem. As Calvin well understood, the question of salvation is simply part of a larger question, for example, of why one mother can nurse her baby and another cannot. Why is there such a radical difference in the situation into which human beings are born?[26] Calvin no doubt erred in too simply identifying damnation with the will of God. Yet in some sense damnation must be God's will. It is, as Temple indicated, an inevitable conclusion of any theistic view. Calvin also knew that damnation must be treated with respect and a certain awe, which is perhaps the real meaning of his words about the horrible decree. For those who believe in the God and Father of our Lord Jesus Christ, evil, damnation, and reprobation must be faced as facts but also as awesome facts and therefore as mysteries. In some sense they are the will of God, but because we know God in the face of Jesus Christ, we trust him.

## Grace and Freedom

The Reformed emphasis on the prevenience of grace led to extreme statements that called forth a reaction, particularly the Remonstrance in the Low Countries.[27] In the medieval church Augustine's doctrine of prevenient grace had been modified by a semi-Pelagianism. Some theologians insisted that grace alone provided the initial turning toward God but that the recipient of this grace then had to carry it further. This response of the human will was rewarded by further grace. Other theologians modified Augustine's doctrine by postulating an initial turning to God on the part of the sinner which was then confirmed and advanced by grace. Over against these modifications of Augustine's doctrine of grace alone, Luther and the Reformers generally insisted that salvation is by grace alone and by faith alone. It is a gift of God.

The doctrine of salvation by grace alone and the doctrine of irresistible grace were sometimes formulated in extreme and theoretical ways that denied the integrity of human action. Augustine, Luther, and Calvin knew quite well that, if from one perspective salvation is 100 percent the work of God, from another perspective it is truly a human act; yet it is a human act that is elicited by divine grace. Apart from the affirmation of the integrity of a human act, the doctrine of prevenient grace, of grace alone, of irresistible grace, became destructive of the human person.

At Saumur,[28] and also in the Low Countries, Reformed theologians themselves protested against the extreme statements of the doctrine. James Arminius defined Calvinism in such a way as to create a controversy between his followers and the hyper-predestinarians in the Low Countries that resulted in the Synod of Dort (1619). Out of this synod came the so-called five points of Calvinism: (1) total depravity, (2) unconditional election, (3) limited atonement, (4) irresistible grace, (5) the perseverance of the saints. These so-called five points of Calvinism were defined in controversy, and the titles are not an accurate indication of their meaning. Total depravity did not mean that human beings are totally evil; it meant that human beings are corrupt in every dimension of their existence and that at the one critical point of existence — namely, turning to God — they were totally unable to do so. Irresistible grace did not mean that grace could not be resisted, for grace is frequently, if not always, resisted. It did mean that God's grace cannot be thwarted. Limited atonement did not mean for the majority of Calvinists that Christ died only for a select few people; the atonement is adequate for all people. It did mean that it was efficacious only for the elect or for believers. Unconditional election did not mean that salvation is by an arbitrary decree; it meant that God redeems us not because we deserve to be redeemed or because of anything we do but only out of his free love. The perseverance of the saints meant not so much that the saints persevere, as that God's grace perseveres and brings the work of salvation to its completion.

The theological controversies of the medieval church as well as subsequent theological efforts have demonstrated that the problems of God's grace and human freedom cannot be resolved by dividing up the work. Salvation is not partly the work of God and partly the work of human beings. It is not that God begins what human beings may complete, or completes what human beings may have already begun. The best solution seems to be to affirm that salvation from one perspective is completely the work of God. From another perspective — that is, the historical and psychological — it is completely the work of human beings.

CHAPTER 18

❖

# THE CHURCH
# AND THE MEANS OF GRACE

I shall start, then, with the church, into whose bosom God is pleased to gather his sons, not only that they may be nourished by her health and ministry as long as they are infants and children, but also that they may be guided by her motherly care until they mature and at last reach the goal of faith. "For what God has joined together, it is not lawful to put asunder" [Mark 10:9], so that for those to whom he is Father the church may also be Mother. . . .

Although the melancholy desolation which confronts us on every side may cry that no remnant of the church is left, let us know that Christ's death is fruitful, and that God miraculously keeps his church as in hiding places.

John Calvin, *Institutes of the Christian Religion* 4.1.1–2

To the church of God that is in Corinth, to those who are sanctified in Christ Jesus, called to be saints, together with all those who in every place call on the name of our Lord Jesus Christ, both their Lord and ours.

1 Corinthians 1:2

To be a Christian and to be the church are one and the same existence. Yet it is not simple to conceptualize the relation of the individual to the community or the Christian to the church. Without individuals there would be no community, and without a community there would be no individuals. The individual and the community cannot be separated, but neither should they be confused.[1]

The Christian is not first a Christian and then the church. Neither does the church exist first and then the individual Christian. They exist together. Calvin's theology, for example, has been criticized for first discussing the individual Christian, as has been the case in this particular study, and then finally arriving at the community. This is the human problem of not being able to say everything at once. For reasons of clarity and comprehension it is simpler and safer to begin with the individual Christian and then move

234

to the church. But this can be done only if one knows that one will speak about the church and is aware that the individual Christian exists only within the church.

Calvin's theology has also been criticized for making the church instrumental to the Christian life, an aid to maintaining the Christian life that gives it direction as well as support. We need outward helps, Calvin said, because we have not yet reached the ranks. Therefore God "in his wonderful providence accommodating himself to our capacity, has prescribed a way for us, though still far off, to draw near to him."[2] Basic truth resides in these words of Calvin. The community in which one lives is one of the most important factors in the shaping of any human life in general as well as in the shaping of faith. Faith cannot easily, if at all, be sustained apart from a supporting community. Yet the church cannot be described simply as an aid or support. In a very basic way, life in the church is the life of the individual Christian. God, who calls us to be Christian, also calls us to be his people, that is, his church.

# Creation of God

The church is God's creation; it has its origin in God's love and in God's call. God chooses a people and covenants that he will be their God and they will be his people.

The church has its origin in the life, death, and resurrection of Jesus Christ and in particular in his calling disciples to be associated with him in a life of faith and love. He taught these disciples as well as nurtured them in his way, and he sent them forth into the world to bear witness to what they had experienced.

The origin of the church is found also in the outpouring of the Holy Spirit (Acts 1–2). After the departure of Jesus Christ his work was carried on by his Spirit. In John's Gospel we are told that the risen Christ breathed on his disciples and said to them, "Receive the Holy Spirit" (John 20:22). In the Acts of the Apostles, Jesus said to his disciples, "You will receive power when the Holy Spirit has come upon you; and you will be my witnesses in Jerusalem, in all Judea and Samaria, and to the ends of the earth" (Acts 1:8). The church has its foundation in the action and call of God, and it lives in obedience to the risen Lord.

Nowhere in the New Testament is there the slightest indication that the church is a human organization that came into being according to human plans. Everywhere in the New Testament the actions of the Christian community indicate that the believers suddenly found themselves to be a community without ever planning to be. Therefore they were always improvising for the needs of the community that they had not anticipated. However the origin of the church may be described, there is always the emphasis on the prior activity of God. The first Christians were those who had experienced the impact of the life, death, and resurrection of Jesus Christ and who had received the Holy Spirit. The life of Jesus, his resurrection from the dead, and the gift of the Spirit had created the New Testament church. In this way the church differs from every human organization.

The church as a creation of God is also rooted in the doctrine of election. The church is a community that is called out of the world by the power of God. Christians are persons whom God thought about before they were, and whom he called into being and elected to be his church, his holy people. The church as a creation of God is proclaimed in the baptism of infants. Children are baptized because in the providence of God they were born into the membership of the church.

The church as a creation of God received powerful emphasis in the theology of John Calvin. "And certainly the source and origin of the church is the free love of God; and whatever benefits he bestows on his church, they all proceed from the same source. The reason, therefore, why we are gathered into the church and are nourished and defended by the hand of God is only to be sought in God."[3] In his tract *On the Necessity of Reforming the Church* Calvin points to the same fact. "The restoration of the church is the work of God, and no more depends upon the hopes and opinions of men than the resurrection of the dead or any other miracle of that description."[4]

This Reformed emphasis on the church as the creation of God means that churches do not come into being through committee meetings, presbytery actions, or human planning. We must first pray for and then wait for the reality of the church. The church always comes as God's gracious gift.

# The Church Lives
# by Hearing the Word of God

The church lives by hearing the word of God. The Protestant Reformation began with passionate conviction of Martin Luther.

To put aside all kinds of works, even contemplation, meditation, and all that the soul can do, does not help. One thing, and only one thing, is necessary for Christian life, righteousness, and freedom. That one thing is the most holy Word of God, the gospel of Christ. . . . Consider it certain and firmly established that the soul can do without anything except the Word of God and that where the Word of God is missing there is no help at all for the soul. If it has the Word of God it is rich and lacks nothing since it is the word of life, truth, light, peace, righteousness, salvation, joy, liberty, freedom, power, grace, glory and of every incalculable blessing. . . . On the other hand, there is no more terrible disaster with which the wrath of God can afflict men than a famine of the hearing of his Word. . . . The Word is the gospel of God concerning his son, who was made flesh, suffered, rose from the dead, and was glorified through the Spirit who sanctifies. To preach Christ means to feed the soul, make it righteous, set it free and save it, provided it believes the preaching. Faith alone is the saving and efficacious use of the Word of God.[5]

In answer to the question Where does the church exist? all the Reformers answered that wherever the Word of God is rightly preached and the sacraments rightly administered, there is the church.[6] Calvin writes:

From this the face of the church comes forth and becomes visible to our eyes. Wherever we see the Word of God purely preached and heard, and the sacraments administered according to Christ's institution, there, it is not to be doubted, a church of God exists. For his promise cannot fail: "Wherever two or three are gathered in my name, there I am in the midst of them."[7]

Emil Brunner has criticized this early Protestant formulation for leaving open the possible substitution of doctrine or a liturgy for the hearing of the word of God. The church appears to affirm the "right" preaching or the "right" administration of the sacraments or the actual hearing of the word of God.[8] In a fundamental sense Luther's statement goes to the heart of the matter. The one essential for the existence of the church is the word of God. Wherever the word of God is heard there is the church; and without the word of God there is no church, no matter what doctrine, sacraments, or structure the church may have.[9] In contemporary theology no one has emphasized more than Karl Barth that both the reality of the church and its unity consist in hearing the word of God.[10] Whenever people hear the word of God the church exists, and in hearing the word of God they are united one with another in the true catholicity of the church.

Reformed theology has always qualified the emphasis on the word alone by insisting that there is no power in the word of preaching or in the sacraments or even in the word of scripture apart from the action of the Holy Spirit. "The Christian community, the true church arises and is only as the Holy Spirit works—the quickening power of the living Lord Jesus Christ and it continues and is only as he sanctifies men and their human work, building them up and their work into the true church."[11] Yet the Reformed always emphasized, in distinction from the Lutheran concern for the word alone, that the church exists not by the word alone but by the word enlivened by the power of the Holy Spirit.

## Congregation, the People of God

The problem that arises in distinguishing and holding together the individual and the community likewise arises in distinguishing between the community and its structures, offices, and institutions while at the same time acknowledging the importance of the latter. In the New Testament we see the church primarily as a community held together by shared experience and enriched by the mutuality of gifts. The necessity of offices, structures, and institutional forms is also present from the beginning, but there can be little doubt about the priority of a community created by a common experience in the life of the Spirit and in a common remembrance of Jesus Christ.

The tragedy of church history, as theologians such as Emil Brunner observe, is the perennial temptation to turn the congregation or the community into the church conceived as an institution with a hierarchy, with offices, and with structures.[12] Martin Luther at the time of the Reformation had wanted to substitute "I believe in a holy Christian people" for "holy catholic church" in the Apostles' Creed. He thought that the church had acquired such an institutional connotation that it could never again mean the congregation. The church in its basic form is the congregation of people, but it is not an aggregation of individuals — or a pile of sand, to use Barth's words.[13] It is a community that lives a shared life, a common life in the Spirit, and that shares faith, hope, and commitment, as well as the various graces with which individuals have been endowed and by which they mutually enrich each other.

The congregation is both local and universal in the New Testament.[14] The most frequent reference is to the Christian community, congregation, or assembly in a particular place, but it is always assumed that the congregation in this particular place is also the universal community. All those who acknowledge Jesus Christ as Lord are the church in whatever place they may be.

The communion of saints, which can refer to saints in a particular sense or to holy things, may also be understood, with Calvin, as the life of the Christian community. This phrase, Calvin writes, expresses what the church is. It is as if one said that the saints are gathered into the society of Christ on the principle that whatever benefits God confers upon them, they should in turn share with one another. This does not, however, rule out diversity of graces, inasmuch as we know the gifts of the Spirit are variously distributed. Nor is civil order disturbed which allows each individual to own his private possessions, since it is necessary to keep peace among men that the ownership of property should be distinct and personal among them. But a community is affirmed, such as Luke describes, in which the heart and soul of the multitude of believers are one; and such as Paul has in mind when he urges the Ephesians to be "one body and one Spirit, just as" they "were called in one hope." If truly convinced that God is the common Father of all and Christ the common Head, being united in brotherly love, they cannot but share their benefits with one another.[15]

This basic understanding of the church as a community of people, a congregation, is endangered on the one hand by individuals who wish to go to a church service to have their spiritual needs replenished and on the other hand by the inclination for the church to be identified with certain structures and individuals. Nothing is more clearly illustrated in the history of the church than a deeply ingrained tendency for individuals to identify the church with themselves and with their place in the structure, whether that place is the office of the bishop of Rome, the pope, or the minister or priest or seminary professor or "governing body" executive or the bureaucracies of Protestant churches. The church always needs a Luther to cry out that the church is not the curia (bureaucracy) but the people.[16]

The church is a community that acknowledges Jesus Christ as Lord. The first creed of the church was "Jesus is Lord." "If you confess with your lips that Jesus is Lord and believe in your heart that God raised him from the dead, you shall be saved" (Romans 10:9). This emphasis on the lordship of the risen Christ in the church was expressed in the old Presbyterian slogan "the crown rights of the Redeemer." In this way, too, the church differs from human organizations, which in a real sense belong to the organizers who set the rules. In the church Jesus Christ is Lord, and to him the community owes its unqualified allegiance.

The theme of the lordship of Jesus Christ is also expressed in Paul's writings about Jesus as the head of the church and about the church as his body. The concept of body when applied to the church easily leads to misunderstandings.

Applied to the Church, it does not primarily denote the sociological structure but its existence in the person of Christ, whose reality it expresses in the same way as the body translates the impulses of the soul. It is simply an epithet attached to this name, a form of his existence, a part of his own essence. . . . In its humanity it is the expression of his life, work and presence.[17]

Protestantism and Reformed theology in particular have emphasized the human reality of the church and have a reluctance to speak of the church as the body of Christ except in the sense of a community that expresses the will, purpose, and intentions of Jesus Christ in his full humanity. For this reason Reformed theologians have not spoken of the church as an extension of the incarnation. It is a consequence of the incarnation, but the church lives by the forgiveness of sins.

Karl Barth has put it this way.

> The community is not *sōma* because it is a social grouping which as such has something of the nature of an organism. . . . It is *sōma* because it actually derives from Jesus Christ, because of Him it exists as His body. . . . Even the *kerygma,* baptism, the Lord's Supper, the faith and love and hope of Christians, the work and word of the apostle, cannot have this function. It is the function of Jesus Christ alone. As the Head He is Himself and primarily the body, and He constitutes and organises and guarantees the community as His body. . . . Therefore the mystery of the community is not in the first instance its own. In the first instance it is His mystery: the mystery of His death in which He was this Victor; the mystery of His resurrection in which He was its Revealer. In His body He is elected, called and instituted from all eternity as this Victor and Revealer. It is His body which includes them all to their salvation and the salvation of the world. Because it includes them, it is their body and they are His body.[18]

# One, Holy, Catholic, Apostolic

The Niceno-Constantinopolitan Creed provides four predicates for the church. The church is *one, holy, catholic,* and *apostolic.* These four marks of the church in Reformed theology have always been subordinate to the preaching of the word of God and the right administration of the sacraments. The church is not constituted by its oneness, its holiness, its catholicity, or its apostolicity. Yet when subordinate to the affirmation that the real mark of the church's existence is the word of God, they have a useful role.

There is *one* church of Jesus Christ. Christians make this affirmation over against a geographical diversity. In the New Testament the word "church" is applied to the congregation in a particular place, but it is always assumed that the congregation in a particular place is likewise the whole body of believers. There is no hint in the entire New Testament that

Christian congregations were a separate community from other congregations. There is always the assumption that those who confess Jesus Christ as Lord are the church.

The unity of the church is easier to confess than to conceptualize. In what does the unity of the church consist? The classic Protestant and Reformed answer is that the unity consists in hearing the word of God or confessing Jesus Christ as Savior and Lord. Calvin is careful to insist that deviation on doctrines as important as justification by faith is not grounds for schism.

> For not all the articles of true doctrine are of the same sort. Some are so necessary to know that they should be certain and unquestioned by all men as the proper principles of religion. Such are: God is one; Christ is God and the Son of God; our salvation rests in God's mercy; and the like. Among the churches there are other articles of doctrine disputed which still do not break the unity of faith.[19]

For Calvin the unity of the church consists in trusting God, present in Jesus Christ, for salvation.

The real unity of the church can never be achieved on the basis of organization, sacraments, doctrinal orthodoxy, or ideological orthodoxy. Yet the church has always been tempted to define unity in these concrete terms. Attempts to achieve unity on any basis other than hearing the word of God in Jesus Christ have led to disunity and to schism.

In a very remarkable paragraph, Robert L. Calhoun astutely observed that some organizational divisions may contribute to unity, and by the same token some organizational mergers or unions may actually contribute to disunity.

> A first fundamental insight, shared by all of us, is that both our unity and diversity—even our division—arise out of God's working with men in history. To try to separate divine initiative and human response in the life of the Church is to obscure the real nature of our problem. To assign diversity and division, for example, solely to human obliquity gives a false impression of the depth and subtlety of the task of seeing the unity that is vital to the Church's being. It is necessary to recognize that the unity we seek cannot exist at all without diversity, in which are disclosed the bounty of God and the manifold gifts of his Spirit, not less truly than the weaknesses of men. Even our divisions and dissensions, which we are in duty bound to overcome, bear witness—sometimes in tortured ways—to God's demand for devotion to truth, as well as to man's frequent confusion as to what is true. It may well be that more vivid realization of other dimensions of our problem than those we are accustomed to see and to stress can bring us an important step closer to the unity we need.[20]

The unity of the church is a mark of its existence, but it is a unity that is first of all established in the hearing of the word of God in faith and in obedience and in love. This unity cannot be guaranteed by any structure, office, liturgy, or organization.

The church is *holy*.

> Holy means set apart, marked off, and therefore differentiated, singled out, taken (and set) on one side as a being which has its origin and nature and meaning and direction—and all this with a final definiteness, decisively, inviolably and unalterably because it is God who does it. . . . [The church] is not a society of necessity and compulsion like the state, nor is it a free society for a particular purpose like an order or a club or an economic or cultural union. It has its own basis and its own goal. It cannot, therefore, understand itself in the light of the basis of other societies or follow their goals.[21]

Yet in what sense is the church holy, and how is it set apart from the world? Some early churchmen answered this question by affirming that the church is holy because its members are holy. The church sought to restrict forgiveness to one sin after baptism and to be in actual fact a holy people.[22] When the holiness of the members became the condition for the existence of the church, impossible situations immediately arose. A church that cannot exist without the holiness of its members has a highly precarious basis. A second attempt at answering the question about the church's holiness insisted that, if the members cannot be holy, at least the priest shall be holy. This came to a head in the persecutions in the middle of the third century.[23] What happens to the person who was baptized by a priest who became a *traditor*, that is one who burned incense to the emperor or handed over the sacred writings? The imperial persecutions sought to destroy the church by destroying its ministry and its sacred books. The insistence that at least the ministers should be holy led to several of the major schisms of the early church, including that of the Donatists in northern Africa.[24]

The answer that Augustine gave to this question proved more adequate. The church is holy because within the church the Holy Spirit works through the appointed means of grace to transform human lives.[25] The church therefore is holy not primarily because its members are holy, not primarily because its priests or ministers are holy, but because within the church the Holy Spirit is at work through the appointed means of grace.

The church is a community of forgiven sinners. "The Lord is daily at work in smoothing out wrinkles and cleansing spots. From this it follows that the church's holiness is not yet complete. The church is holy, then, in the sense that it is daily advancing and is not yet perfect: it makes progress from day to day but has not yet reached its goal of holiness."[26]

The church is *catholic*. In the early church, catholic came to mean the orthodox church, but it had a prior meaning as a confession of the universality of the church. No one has ever expressed the true catholicity of the church more forcefully than Cyril of Jerusalem in his catechetical lectures.

> The Church, then, is called Catholic because it is spread through the whole world, from one end of the earth to the other, and because it never stops teaching in all its fulness every doctrine that men ought to be brought to know: and that regarding things visible and invisible, in heaven and on earth. It is called Catholic also because it brings into religious obedience every sort of men, rulers and ruled, learned and simple, and because it is a universal treatment and cure for every kind of sin whether perpetrated by soul or body, and possesses within it every form of virtue that is named, whether it expresses itself in deeds or words or in spiritual graces of every description.[27]

Finally, the church is *apostolic*. This expresses the concern of Christians to remain in continuity with the church of the New Testament, with the ministry of Jesus and his disciples. How can we be sure that the church today is in living communion with the church of the apostles? The church attempted to maintain its apostolicity by the consecration of bishops in unbroken succession back to the first apostles. Jesus consecrated the apostles and they in turn have consecrated their successors on through human history.[28] The apostolicity of the church is guaranteed by apostolic succession.

The notion of apostolic succession was radically rejected by Protestants in general but in particular by Reformed Christians. Calvin insisted that, even if apostolic succession were a historical reality, it could not guarantee that one was in communion with the first apostles.[29] True apostolicity is maintained by obedience to the living Lord of the church. Those who obey Jesus Christ today are in communion with the first disciples, who in their time believed in him on earth and now praise him in heaven.

There is a succession of believing people that goes back to the first disciples. From every Christian person living today there is an unbroken succession of believing people going back to those who were gathered in the upper room, as reported in Acts 2, as well as to those who were the disciples of Jesus Christ. This is a compelling and moving fact. Moreover, this succession of believing people has left behind documents of faith in every generation. Finally, there is the Holy Scripture that was acknowledged by the church as an authoritative apostolic witness to the mighty acts of God that created the church through the life, death, and resurrection of

Jesus Christ and the giving of the Holy Spirit at Pentecost. The canon of the New Testament is not authoritative in itself, but it is an authoritative action of the church affirming the authority of the New Testament documents as authentic witnesses to what God did in Jesus Christ.

There is in the church an unbroken succession of believers and witnesses, a true apostolic succession.

> Thus the existence of His community is always its history in its encounter with this witness—the history in which it is faithful or unfaithful to it in its exposition and application. There is, therefore, a legitimate apostolic succession, the existence of a Church in the following of the apostles, only when it takes place in this history that the apostolic witness finds in a community discipleship, hearing, obedience, respect and observance. But it is in the fact that they serve that the apostles follow the Lord Himself and precede the community. It would, therefore, be very strange if the community for its part tried to follow them in any other authority, power and mission than that of their service, if, for example, it tried to follow them in an institutional possession of and control over the high mystery of the free Holy Spirit, in the power to overrule His work and gift, as though it were a matter of money or property or of the legal regulation of certain human demands and interests.[30]

## Visible, Invisible

The church is *visible* and *invisible.* This distinction goes back to Augustine. It does not mean that the church is not visible. Wherever the church exists, it is visible. The invisibility of the church refers to the inability of human beings to set the exact boundaries of the church. The visible church must always be a judgment of charity. Calvin insisted that those "who by confession of faith, by example of life and by partaking of the sacraments profess the same God and Christ with us" are to be regarded as members of the church. This is practical judgment. Calvin as well as Augustine knew that there are many sheep without and many wolves within the church.[31] Within the visible church that we define in a practical way as God's people, we believe that the church of God, the church known only to God, exists.

The church is "visible-invisible" in the sense that it is not demonstrably true that the church as the people of God exists. Hence the existence of the church becomes a confession of faith that in this mixed company there does in fact exist the church of God. The existence of the church can no more be proved than any other article of faith. Yet Paul could write with confidence that in Corinth the church of God existed, though a sociologist could explain that community solely in secular terms, including its divisions, greed, and sexual aberrations.[32]

## Militant, Triumphant

The church is the church *militant* and the church *triumphant*. The church is a community composed of the living and those who have gone from us, and in Jesus Christ, the head of the church, we still have communion one with another. The confessions of the church have all insisted that the membership of the church includes all those who have trusted God in ages past and also in expectation those who will trust him in the future. The dead as well as the living form the communion of saints. As Barth has put it, "It is not only the living who speak and act, but their predecessors, their words and works, their history, which does not end on their departure, but on their departure often only enters its decisive stage among their successors, standing in an indissoluble relationship with the history of the present."[33] The church which was, which is, and which will be is one church. Some of the old liturgies of the Lord's Supper publicly acknowledge that as we gather at the Lord's table we do so in communion with all the hosts of heaven.[34]

## The Church as Israel

The church is the eschatological people of God. Jesus was a Jew reared in all the traditions of the religion of Israel, and so were all of his disciples. Peter addressed his fellow Israelites declaring what God had done in Jesus Christ. The Christian congregation began among Israelites who were convinced that the promises of scripture were fulfilled in Jesus Christ. The first worship of the church as well as the sacrament of baptism bears the marks of the worship of Israel. The scriptures of Israel became the scriptures of the Christian community before it was possible to speak of a New Testament. The early Christians all accepted the scriptures as their sacred book. Indeed, it was the book in which they had been nurtured but which was now read in a new way. Paul, more than any other, provided the way for Christians to read the scripture as their own book.

> For all that, in his relationship to Scripture as a Christian Paul does undergo a profound change, and radically parts company with every variety of belief in Scripture to be found within Judaism. For Paul reads the Scripture from the standpoint of Christ, and therefore in a new spirit. This is not simply

to say that the Biblical statements are now interpreted with appropriate pains and skill, as referring to Christ and to Paul's own community; Qumran has already done as much. Rather does it mean that now the historical experience of Christians and the new life that flows from this are consciously understood and affirmed as a new and unique starting-point, an independent way into the ancient Scriptures. The Spirit which searches all things, even the depths of the Godhead, did not derive from the Scriptures but was given for the first time as something quite new, with belief in Christ. Paul turns to the one who "raised from the dead Jesus our Lord," and finds—as the Jew had found in the Torah—that now in Christ "are hid all the treasures of wisdom and knowledge." To this extent the Christian has become spiritually independent and in his relationship with God is so to speak a law to himself. . . . All the promises which God had made find their fulfillment and their goal only in Christ.[35]

At first the writings which became the New Testament simply supplemented the scriptures. The designation Old Testament and New Testament did not come into being until the first part of the third century. From the beginning of the third century onward no one anywhere knew a different arrangement: the sacred scripture of the orthodox church consisted of an Old and a New Testament.[36] The current designation of the Old Testament as the Hebrew Scriptures is without warrant in the Christian tradition. The Christian community always regarded the scriptures of Israel out of which the first Christians came as their own book and the New Testament to be the fulfillment and proper interpretation of those scriptures.

A few Christians from Marcion in the second century down to the German Christians in the Nazi era in the twentieth century have sought to eliminate the Old Testament from the Christian canon. The Christian community, however, has always regarded the Old Testament as truly the book that found its fulfillment in the coming of Jesus Christ. The church also rejected the notion that Greek philosophy could serve as an introduction to Jesus Christ and Christian existence.[37]

The early Christians came to think of themselves as the people of God and therefore the continuation of Israel (Acts 2:14–36; Galatians 5:12–16). The writer of the letter to the Hebrews regarded the Old Testament saints as the cloud of witnesses that surrounded the Christian community (12:1). The author of First Peter likewise spoke of the Christian community as the people of God.

> But you are a chosen race, a royal priesthood, a holy nation, God's own people, in order that you may proclaim the mighty acts of him who called you out of darkness into his marvelous light.
>     Once you were not a people,
>     but now you are God's people;

once you had not received mercy,
but now you have received mercy.

1 Peter 2:9–10

The good news in Jesus Christ, in whom the promises of God were fulfilled, was preached to Jews and to Gentiles. The first preaching was by
Jews to Jews. The only controversy in the New Testament is not whether
the gospel should be preached to the Jews but whether it should be preached
to the Gentiles. The New Testament church insisted that the Christian
gospel is God's word for human beings as human beings, and therefore
it is to be preached not only to the people of Israel but to all the world.

The continued existence of the Israel that had rejected Jesus Christ was
a puzzlement to the Christian community, as Paul clearly indicates in
Romans 9–11. It has always been a theological problem, and today the
problem is complicated by the responsibility of some Christians at various
times for injustices done to Jews. It is further complicated by the political
orthodoxies of a secular culture and by difficult political and cultural
problems. The response of Christian theology to this problem must be
determined out of faith itself, free from cultural and political pressures.

Paul addressed the theological issue in Romans 9–11. He affirms that
God is sovereign and elects whom he will. Yet God's judgment on Israel
is not arbitrary, for in fact the Jews' own disobedience led to their downfall.[38]
Yet in chapter 11 he insists that God's judgment is not the last word. The
rejection of Israel is part of a larger plan. "God's plan, says Paul, runs
from God choosing Israel, to his hardening Israel to save gentiles, and then
to his saving gentiles in order finally to save Israel."[39] Israel has not been
finally rejected. As Paul understood, this is a great mystery; and we must
be modest in deciphering the purposes of God in the existence of the Christian community, which believes that the promises of God are fulfilled in
Jesus Christ, and in the continuing existence of Israel.

Evangelism of the Jews must be modified by the Christians' own origin
in Israel and the claim that the scriptures of the Old Testament are a Christian book.

Paul Achtemeier has well written:

There is no indication here that Jews are to be ignored and not told of the
good news in Christ. But any evangelization of Jews must take a different
form from that of the evangelization of non-Jews. Evangelization of Jews
must take the form of recalling members of the family to their own home,
and it must be done in the humility of adopted children bringing pleas of
return to those who have prior claim on the family inheritance. Every Christian may not have the opportunity for such evangelization, but every Christian

can and must resist and reject every form of anti-Semitism in whatever form it occurs. Any other reaction is inappropriate to the history of God's grace.[40]

Karl Barth likewise insisted that the evangelization of the Jews must have a unique character.

First, in relation to the Synagogue there can be no question of the community proclaiming the true faith in place of a false, or opposing the true God to an idol. The God whose work and Word it has to attest to the world was the God of Israel before the community itself ever came forth from this people, and to this day He can only be the God of Israel. . . . Above all, it was of their flesh and blood that Jesus Himself was born, so that . . . He is first their Christ. They are the people of God loved by Him in free grace, elected and called to His service, and originally sent into the world as His witnesses. . . .

Secondly, however, there is the shattering fact that at the decisive moment the same Israel denied its election and calling, that when the hour struck it did not know the fulness and goal of its history, that when it eventuated it did not receive the promised consolation, that when it was fulfilled it did not believe the Word of God spoken to it by Moses and the prophets, that when its King appeared among it He was despised and rejected and delivered up to the Gentiles. . . . Necessarily, therefore, the Jew who is uniquely blessed offers the picture of an existence which, characterised by the rejection of its Messiah and therefore of its salvation and mission, is dreadfully empty of grace and blessing. . . . We certainly can and should hold talks with the Jews for the purpose of information. But how can the Gospel help as proclaimed from men when already it has been repudiated, not just accidentally or incidentally, but in principle, *a priori* and therefore with no prospect of revision from the human standpoint? . . .

Does this mean that the Christian community has no responsibility to discharge its ministry of witness to the Jews? Not at all! What it does mean is that there can be only one way to fulfil it. To use the expression of Paul in Rom. 11:11, 14, it must make the Synagogue jealous. . . . To this day Christianity has not succeeded in impressing itself upon Israel as the witness of its own most proper reality and truth, of the fulfilled Word of God in the Old Testament. . . . But for the most part it has not done for the Jews the only real thing which it can do, attesting the manifested King of Israel and Saviour of the world, the imminent kingdom, in the form of the convincing witness of its own existence. And thus it still owes everything to those to whom it is indebted for everything. This failure, which is often unconscious, or perhaps concealed by all kinds of justifiable or unjustifiable countercharges against the Jews, is one of the darkest chapters in the whole history of Christianity and one of the most serious of all wounds in the body of Christ. Even the modern ecumenical movement suffers more seriously from the absence of Israel than of Rome or Moscow. The Church must live with the Synagogue, not, as fools say in their hearts, as with another religion or confession, but as with the root from which it has itself sprung.[41]

The Christian church is unintelligible apart from the history of Israel, in which it originated. Jesus as the Christ is impossible apart from the history of Israel, which enabled the disciples to acknowledge Jesus as the Christ. The Old Testament was from the beginning the scripture of the church. There is no substitute for the Old Testament either in philosophical traditions or in religious traditions. John Calvin and the Reformed tradition in general have emphasized that the substance and reality of the covenant made with the patriarchs is the same as the covenant in the New Testament, differing only in mode of dispensation (*Institutes* 2.10.2). The disciples of Jesus in the New Testament believed that all things that happened in Jesus were according to the scriptures. The church cannot reject Israel. The New Testament must be read in the light of the Old and the Old Testament in the light of the New.

Israel as it continues today rejects Jesus as the Messiah of Israel. This rejection of Jesus as the Christ and the Christian relation and mission to Israel today are complicated by factors that are not strictly theological: (1) the history of injustices done to the Jews and the response of Jews to this history, (2) the contemporary state of Israel, and (3) the ideologies of a secular, humanist society, which penetrate both communities and distort theological judgments. The relation of the Christian community to Israel is unique and delicate. Yet in this grateful and sensitive relation the Christian lives by the conviction that God's action in Jesus Christ not only fulfilled the promises of God to Israel but also is the salvation of God for all people.

## Organization or Institution

The church as an *organization* or *institution*. The church is above all a community that lives the common life in the body of Christ, constituted by a common faith, a common hope, and a common love. Yet as Calvin well knew, human beings are not angels and therefore there is a need for structures. This need becomes more and more apparent as the enthusiasm of an initial faith or of a period of revival begins to wane. Hence Calvin in particular among the Reformers emphasized the great significance of the church's structures. The structures are an aid to faith, and as Calvin was aware, they may distort faith or even become a substitute for faith. For this reason he placed a great emphasis on structures that had biblical warrants and were congruent with the faith. While Calvin insisted on biblical authority for church offices and structures, he was well aware that there is no simple pattern in the New Testament that can be duplicated in any and every society.[42] Furthermore, he was well aware that many aspects of church life have to be governed by the particular time and place in which the church exists.

In contemporary theology Emil Brunner has emphasized the personal, communal character of the church, to the point of depreciating the structures.[43] Karl Barth rejected Brunner's position because structures are necessary and serve good and useful purposes. Yet for Barth structures must always be subordinate to the gospel. In this he is in accord with Reformed theology. No Reformed theology has ever identified a particular structure with the existence of the church. The church exists wherever there is the word of God.

> No church order is perfect, for none has fallen directly from heaven and none is identical with the basic law of the Christian community. Even the orders of the primitive New Testament community (whatever form they took) were not perfect, nor are those of the Western Papacy, the Eastern Patriarchate, the Synodal Presbyterianism which derives from Calvin's system, Anglican, Methodist, Neo-Lutheran and other forms of Episcopacy, or Congregationalism with its sovereignty of the individual community. Nor are the orders of all different systems which are derivative variations of these basic types. There is no reason to look down proudly and distastefully from one to the others. At one time they may all have been living law sought and in a certain exaggeration found in obedience, and therefore legitimate forms of the body of Jesus Christ. Indeed, they may be this still. Thus for all the problems to which they give rise they must be respected by the others.[44]

Reformed theology has generally been identified with Presbyterianism. John Calvin as well as later Presbyterians opted for representative church government on theological grounds. On the one hand the masses of people are neither wise enough nor good enough to be entrusted with the government of the church. On the other hand no individual or small group of individuals is good enough or wise enough to be entrusted with power. The will of God, according to Presbyterianism, is more likely to be done in councils composed of wise persons elected by the people.[45] Some very vital Reformed communities in the seventeenth, eighteenth, and nineteenth centuries were organized as congregations. Calvin's support has been claimed for episcopacy, but the most that can be said is that in certain situations Calvin tolerated bishops as administrative officers of the church. He always rejected their theological significance.

In Reformed theology the structures of the church are radically subordinate to the gospel. No particular structure is essential to the church's
existence.

## The Means of Grace

Reformed theology has always emphasized the freedom of the Holy
Spirit. Yet along with other Christian communities it has acknowledged
that the Spirit ordinarily uses means in transforming human life and bringing into being the communion of saints. Calvin himself seldom used the
phrase "means of grace," but its later use in Reformed theology is in accord
with his writing about the sermon, the sacraments, and prayer.[46] Generally
speaking, Reformed theology has emphasized preaching, prayer, and
sacraments as intentional means of grace. Hendrikus Berkhof adds to these
the church supper, the conversation, the church meeting, and the ministry
of compassion.[47] There is no definitive list of the means of grace, but any
intentional means of grace used in the life of the church must have its basis
in the New Testament. Furthermore, Reformed theology has always emphasized the freedom of the Holy Spirit in the use of means. This emphasis
comes to expression not only in the doctrine of the Holy Spirit but also
in the doctrine of election.

## Sacraments

Sacramental actions have been a universal means of human communication. Eating together and drinking together confirm friendships in a way
that supplements what words can communicate, and the same is true of
a handshake or the giving of a ring. In this sense sacraments are universal
and are important in human communication.

Sacramental actions have been universal in the life of the Christian church.
From the beginning, Christians practiced baptism and celebrated the Lord's
Supper. In addition there were other sacramental acts such as the church
supper, the washing of feet, the kiss of peace, and the anointing with oil.
Baptism and the Lord's Supper had preeminence not only in the New Testa-
ment but also in the early church.

Sacramental practice and doctrine grew rapidly in the Middle Ages.[48]
This development was influenced by the mission of the church to persons
who could neither read nor write and for whom sacramental actions were
increasingly important. Many practices acquired some sacramental status
in the medieval church. The sacramental doctrine and practice were

consolidated in the theology of Thomas Aquinas (c. 1225–1274) and in the action of the Ecumenical Council of Florence in 1439:

> There are seven sacraments of the New Law, viz. baptism, confirmation, Eucharist, penance, extreme unction, orders, and marriage. These are quite different from the sacraments of the Old Law which did not cause grace but foreshadowed the grace that was to be bestowed solely through the passion of Christ. Our sacraments, however, not only contain grace but also confer it on those who receive them worthily. . . .
>
> Three elements are involved in the full administration of all these sacraments, viz. things as the matter, words as the form and the person as the minister performing the sacrament with the intention of doing what the church does. If any one of these is lacking, the sacrament is not affected. There are three of the sacraments, baptism, confirmation and orders, which imprint on the soul an indelible character, i.e., the kind of spiritual seal distinct from the others. They are therefore not to be received more than once by the same individual. The rest, however, do not imprint a character and may be performed more than once.[49]

The dogma of transubstantiation had been affirmed at the Fourth Lateran Council in 1215.

> In this church the priest and the sacrifice is the same Jesus Christ Himself whose body and blood are truly contained in the sacrament of the altar under the figures of bread and wine, the bread having been transubstantiated into His body and the wine into His blood by divine power, so that, to accomplish the mystery of our union, we may receive from him what he has received of us. And none can effect the sacrament except the priest who has been rightly ordained in accordance with the keys of the church which Jesus Christ himself granted to the apostles and their successors.[50]

The dogma of transubstantiation not only affected the nature of the bread and the wine but also greatly increased the power of the priest, who was given a power and an authority that did not belong to anyone else to perform an action essential to the life of the church.

Luther's great tract *On the Babylonian Captivity of the Church* undercut the whole sacramental system of medieval catholicism and was regarded by his contemporaries as the radical break. Erasmus exclaimed, "The breach is irreparable!" Luther reduced the sacraments to two, though he had difficulty deciding about penance. A sacrament, he said, must be instituted by Jesus Christ. Luther also rejected the notion that the power of the sacrament cannot be invalidated by human weakness, either of the priest or of the recipient. He denied that sacraments confer grace from the performance of the act, *ex opere operato.* There is no sacrament, he insisted, apart from faith.[51] Essential to the sacrament is the word of promise that is heard and believed.

Luther objected in particular to the doctrine of the Mass as a sacrifice. As such it became another human work to obtain salvation. In addition he denied the doctrine of transubstantiation—that the bread and wine became in actual fact the body and blood of Christ. But in ways that were never clear to Zwingli or even to Calvin he insisted that the body and blood of Christ were present with the elements.

Calvin as well as Luther maintained the Augustinian doctrine of the sacrament as an outward and visible sign of an inward and spiritual grace. They alike affirmed that the sacraments confer grace by the power of the Holy Spirit. Calvin and Heinrich Bullinger, Zwingli's successor in Zurich, would in 1549 come to an agreement about the sacraments in the Helvetic Consensus.[52] The differences between Zwingli and Calvin were more in emphasis, in personal religious experience, and in personality than in substance. They were alike concerned to emphasize that Jesus Christ is truly present in a spiritual and personal, not in a physical way, that the bread and wine remain bread and wine. Zwingli had no problem in saying this clearly and emphatically. Calvin is so realistic in speaking of partaking of the body and blood of Christ that his conviction that the bread and wine remain bread and wine is sometimes obscured. Zwingli has been accused of turning the supper into a memorial, but for Zwingli it was surely more than that. Christ was present, but he was personally or spiritually present. Zwingli no less than Luther or Calvin or medieval Catholicism insisted on a real presence.

A real crisis for sacramental teaching in Protestant churches began in the 1930s, precipitated by the problems of infant baptism.[53] Emil Brunner and Karl Barth were both concerned about the sociological fact that everyone in Europe was baptized and it did not seem to make any difference. As Barth put it, the pope is baptized, Hitler is baptized, Stalin is baptized—what difference does it make?[54] At the same time, historians were calling into question the origins of infant baptism and some were insisting that the church did not really baptize infants until the third century. In 1943 Barth delivered a lecture to theological students in which he defined baptism as a portrayal of death and resurrection. As such the sacrament belonged to the proclamation of the church, but enough remains of the sacramental function for Barth to speak of the flat quality of Zwingli's teaching.[55] Later Barth would say that he did not object to being called a Zwinglian.[56]

In traditional Reformed theology the sacraments have three functions:

(1) to show forth the grace of God, (2) to confer the grace of God, and (3) to testify to the faith and commitment of the recipient. In 1943 Barth had rejected the sacraments as means of grace but maintained the cognitive and ethical functions of baptism. In his discussion of the sacraments in *Church Dogmatics* (IV/4), the sacrament of baptism is only an ethical action. The real sacrament, the outward and visible sign of the grace of God, is Jesus Christ, and the real sacramental action is the baptism of the Holy Spirit. The significance of water baptism is the ethical action whereby the baptized confirms in his or her own life that which has happened in Jesus Christ and through the baptism of the Holy Spirit. Barth himself makes clear the diminished role of the sacraments.

> In the Introduction to IV, 1, I had in mind that the doctrine of baptism and the Lord's Supper should be treated in the two first and constitutive parts of the doctrine of reconciliation (in each case in the sections on the Church). But on a nearer approach to the problems I have adopted a different course. And it will perhaps have been noted in Volumes II and III that I made less and less use — and finally none at all — of the general term "sacrament," which was so confidently bandied about in Volume I. I cannot now explain the reasons. . . . I can only indicate that here, if anywhere, I have learned to regard a cautious and respectful "demythologizing" as expedient and practicable. Baptism and the Lord's Supper are given only incidental mention in the present volume. But they are not forgotten, and will be given what seems to be their appropriate and worthy place as the basis and crown of the fourth and ethical section of the doctrine of reconciliation.[57]

Emil Brunner is not as bold in reducing the role of sacraments in the life of the church as Karl Barth, but it is quite clear in his writings that he finds it difficult to relate the traditional understanding of the sacraments to his understanding of faith and of the church.[58] Likewise, Hendrikus Berkhof in his *Christian Faith* notes that the sacraments play a much larger role in the life of churches than they do in the New Testament, and he elevates practices such as the church supper and Christian conversation to the level of the sacraments.[59]

## Baptism

"Baptism is a sign of the initiation by which we are received into the society of the church, in order that, engrafted in Christ, we may be reckoned among God's children."[60] Baptism serves our faith as a token and proof of our cleansing; it is a sealed document to confirm to us that all our sins are abolished, remitted, and effaced. As Christians we "ought to recall the memory of our baptism and fortify our mind with it, that we may always be sure and confident of the forgiveness of sins."[61] Baptism also "serves as our confession" before others; hence baptism is an ethical action.[62]

The major controversy that arose about baptism was over the baptism of infants. The radical Protestants from the beginning insisted on a believer's baptism and regarded the baptism of infants as one of the sources of the corruption of the church. The reaction of the Anabaptists in the sixteenth century was similar to the reaction of many church leaders to the indiscriminate practice of baptism in Europe in the 1930s.

Calvin maintained the baptism of infants on the grounds that infants are born into the membership of the church and therefore by right of birth are entitled to be baptized. The primary context for Calvin's doctrine of the baptism of infants is the doctrine of the covenant and the promise, "the covenant which the Lord once made with Abraham is no less in force today for Christians than it was of old for the Jewish people."[63] The covenant is for believers and for their seed. The children of Christian parents, even one Christian parent, are considered holy. The community of birth, of nature, and of history has significance for the community of faith. The church cannot ignore birth, nature, and history and spiritualize away their significance. "The children of believers are baptized not in order that they who were previously strangers to the church may then for the first time become children of God, but rather that, because by the blessing of the promise they already belonged to the body of Christ, they are received into the church with this solemn sign."[64]

In our highly personalistic, voluntaristic, and rationalistic culture such a strong emphasis on the community of birth, nature, and history immediately raises questions, as it did with Emil Brunner and Karl Barth. They were in part moved to their position by the disparity between the baptized and any reasonable understanding of their lives. They were impelled in the direction of asserting that the church is constituted on the human level by the free act of faith. Yet just as they found evidence to indicate that birth is not a simple, automatic entrance into the church, there is also evidence that the significance of birth, of the natural community of faith, cannot be minimized. Most of those who are in the church are there first of all because they were born into the church. It is a clear fact of life that human existence is shaped by the nature and history into which a person is born. Students of personality have in recent years emphasized the social context into which a person is born, but increasingly attention is now being given even to biochemical and genetic inheritance. The ambiguity created by the fact that the church can be neither identified with the natural community nor separated from it is the source of our ambiguity concerning baptism.

Churches that do not baptize infants have the problem of determining the relation of unbaptized young people to the church. This is reflected in Baptist churches, which are committed to adult baptism, in the practice of pushing baptism back to the ages of five, six, and seven in many instances.

Calvin also found that the baptism of infants has at least four consequences that are significant. First, baptism confirms the promise given to pious parents. The sacrament certifies, confirms, attests, and seals the promises of the action of God. Second, Calvin finds that children receive some benefit from their baptism. They are engrafted into the body of Christ and are therefore commended to the church, that is, to other church members. In baptism the congregation obligates itself to be the child's sponsor to the end that this child will grow up trusting God and seeking to do his will. Third, Calvin finds also that when the baptized grow up, "They are greatly spurred to an earnest zeal for worshiping God, by whom they were received as children through a solemn symbol of adoption before they were old enough to recognize him as Father."[65] Martin Luther, as is well known, appealed in moments of crisis to the fact that he had been baptized.[66]

Baptism celebrates a work that is complete in the work of Jesus Christ; it also celebrates a work that is never complete in human history, namely, our sanctification. Baptism looks to the future. As Donald Baillie put it, "Baptism is for all Christians, the beginning of the Christian life."[67] Or, as Barth says, "Baptism is the first step of the way of a Christian life which is shaped looking to Jesus Christ."[68] The Westminster Larger Catechism speaks of the task of improving our baptism.[69] In this sense baptism is ordination to the Christian ministry. It is consecration or ordination to take part in the mission which is committed to the whole church. As Barth put it, "All those baptized as Christians are by that very fact consecrated, ordained, and dedicated to the ministry of the church. They cannot be consecrated, ordained, and dedicated a second, third, or fourth time without devaluing their baptism."[70]

The fourth benefit that comes from baptism is the effective work of the Holy Spirit through the sacraments. "Infants are baptized into future repentance and faith, and even though these have not yet been formed in them, the seed of both lies hidden within them by the secret working of the Spirit."[71] Here the mystery of the sacrament is hid from our eyes.

## The Lord's Supper

The gathering of the people of God at the table of the Lord has been from the beginning of the church a crucial moment in the church's life. It is a thrilling fact to remember that for almost two thousand years not a Sunday has passed, perhaps not a day, that Christians somewhere on this planet have not gathered at the table of their Lord. The earliest account of the Lord's Supper is found in Paul's letter to the Christians at Corinth (A.D. 50–52), and in the accounts that are found in the *Didache* as well as in the *First Apology* of Justin Martyr. In these descriptions we find all the acts that are familiar to us in the celebration of the Lord's Supper today. The prayer of thanksgiving, the breaking of the bread, the taking of the cup, the anticipation of the coming of the Lord, the recollection of his life, and the words of institution—all of these acts call to mind the life and death of Jesus Christ.

The bread and wine are appropriate symbols. Bread and wine have always been symbols of the truth that human beings are dependent on something besides themselves. Common eating has been a clear symbol of our common need and the significance of human fellowship. In addition, the bread and the wine have been symbols of God's blessing and human toil. In the ancient celebrations of the Lord's Supper, the people brought the bread and the wine from their own homes. This was the origin of the offertory. Here, the offering of the people, the fruit of creation and of human toil, became a means of the gracious presence of Jesus Christ among his people. When we make our offering in money today, it is more difficult to imagine that the bread and wine are our gifts, yet this is what they are.

The elements are not simply bread and wine; they are broken bread and poured wine. The breaking of the bread and the pouring of the wine, symbols of the broken body and the shed blood, are as important as the elements themselves. The symbolism of the one loaf and one cup emphasized the unity of the church. We all eat from one loaf and drink from one cup because we are one body. Today the celebration of the Lord's Supper in large gatherings does not make it practical to use literally one loaf or one cup. Moreover, our knowledge of germs has made it seem advisable to many Christians to have individual cups for the celebration of the communion. An ancient prayer that goes back to the days of the New Testament declared, "As this piece [of bread] was scattered over the hills and then was brought together and made one, so let your Church be brought together from the ends of the earth into your Kingdom. For yours is the glory and the power through Jesus Christ forever."[72]

What are the meanings of the Lord's Supper? First of all the Lord's Supper means the *gospel*. It is the proclamation of the gospel as is baptism. It is the gospel acted out. It has no purpose apart from the purpose of the word, which is to preach Jesus Christ as Lord and Savior. "Therefore, let it be regarded as a settled principle that the sacraments have the same office as the Word of God: to offer and set forth Christ to us, and in him the treasures of heavenly grace. But they avail and profit nothing unless received in faith."[73]

The Lord's Supper means the *presence* of Jesus Christ. Christians have always believed that Jesus Christ is truly present in the celebration of the sacrament. The broken bread and the poured wine have been the occasions of his presence by the power of the Holy Spirit. Yet Christians have and do differ over how he is present. Reformed theology has always emphasized the real but spiritual or personal presence of Jesus Christ in the sacrament. Donald Baillie, who has written with great perception on the sacraments, has said:

> But what do you mean by real presence? Is it different in the sacraments from the kind of presence we have at any time when we draw near to God?
>
> It is important to note that even apart from the sacrament we are bound to distinguish several degrees or modes of the divine presence. To begin with the most general, we believe in the omnipresence of God. He is everywhere present and yet we also say that God is with those who trust and obey him in a way which he is not with others. We say, God is with them. And we say that God's presence is with us *more* at some times than at others. We speak of entering into his presence at worship, and we ask him to come and be with us and grant us His presence. We say that wherever two or three are gathered in His name, He is there in the midst of them. And then in apparently a still further sense we speak of the real presence in the sacrament. What does it all mean?
>
> Surely the first thing we have to remember is that God's presence is not strictly speaking a *local* or spatial *presence* at all but a spiritual, personal relationship which we have to symbolize by spatial metaphors. . . .
>
> There may be even two persons together in a room without their being in more than a minimal way *with* each other because they are not encountering each other in a genuine relationship so "we can . . . have a very strong feeling that someone is sitting in the same room as ourselves, sitting quite near us, someone whom we can look at and listen to and whom we can touch if we want to make a final test of his reality is nevertheless more distant from us than some loved one who is perhaps thousands of miles away, or perhaps, even, no longer among the living. We could say that the man sitting beside

us was in the same room as ourselves, but that he was not really *present* there, that his presence did not make itself felt."[74]

The Lord's Supper means *remembrance*. It is a memorial that refreshes our memory. It focuses our attention on the actual historical life, death, and resurrection of Jesus Christ. Zwingli's doctrine has sometimes been characterized as a mere memorial, but Zwingli always meant more than a mere recollection of facts. Remembrance for Zwingli meant realization, the actualization of the presence of Jesus Christ.[75]

The Lord's Supper is a *thanksgiving*. The Orthodox churches of the East called the Lord's Supper the Eucharist, that is, a thanksgiving. From the beginning, the celebration of the Lord's Supper has been a time for thanksgiving for creation, for the good things of this life, and above all for the love of God shown in the redemption of the world in Jesus Christ and for the means of grace and for the hope of glory.

The Lord's Supper is a *communion*. It is a communion with Jesus Christ and also a communion of Christians one with another in the body of Christ.

The Lord's Supper is a *supper*. We are fed at the Lord's Supper spiritually, by faith. Those who come to the supper with understanding, expectancy, commitment, and faith are nourished by all that Jesus said and did, by his resurrection from the dead, and by his intercession at the right hand of God.

The Lord's Supper is a *declaration of faith*. Those who partake in the Lord's Supper declare before human beings their highest allegiance. It is a pledge of allegiance.

The validity of the sacraments according to Reformed theology resides in the work of the Holy Spirit. Neither the work of the receiver nor the work of the person who administers the sacrament can cause grace. The sacraments can only be received by faith, which is a conscious and deliberate act, and apart from this act the sacraments cannot confirm the grace of God. Faith in the baptism of infants is the faith of the parents and the faith of the congregation.

Reformed theology has always denied that the grace of God is tied to the sacraments. They are not essential for salvation. Hence, Calvin rejected the baptism of infants by those who are not ministers, as though salvation depended on the administration of the sacrament.[76] Normally Reformed churches limited the exercise of sacraments to ordained ministers. The reason for this is that the ministers are those who are certified to teach in the church and the sacraments are to be celebrated in the order and discipline in the church's life. There is, however, no inherent power in the minister that qualifies him or her to administer the sacrament. In principle every member of the congregation could administer the sacrament. Yet the sacraments must be properly administered in the context of teaching and preaching and in the presence of the congregation.

## Preaching

Preaching in the actual practice of the Protestant churches replaced the central role of the sacraments in the medieval church. Gottfried W. Locher has written that the Protestant doctrine of faith and justification by faith overturned the public worship of God.

> The miracle and the power lay henceforth in the fact that, in the word of man, the divine word of grace comes through, just as in man, Jesus, the eternal son of God has appeared. The same function which belongs to the sacrament in the Roman divine service is performed henceforth by preaching: the real presence of the Lord. This as from old is named the Holy Ghost. Although Lutherans and Reformed describe the internal relation between the word and spirit differently, this need not detain us here; at this point we are confronted by their insoluble connection. From here on the sacrament will be "relativised."[77]

Relativizing does not mean devaluing. "The word can exist without the sacrament, the sacrament never without the word. It lives from the personal word of promise which, according to Luther appeared in encapsulated power in the words of the institution."[78] The same truth holds for Calvin. Calvin would like to have celebrated the Lord's Supper each Sunday in Geneva, but he compromised for a celebration much more infrequent. It is inconceivable that he would have ever settled for the celebration of the sacrament without the preaching of the word. This is the reason Karl Barth does not like the phrase "word and sacrament" and prefers "word *plus* sacrament."[79] Calvin speaks of sacraments as an appendix to the gospel.[80]

Preaching not only replaced the sacrament in practice in the life of the church, but preaching itself came to be understood in a sacramental way. The Holy Spirit uses the words of the preacher in the same manner that the Holy Spirit uses the water or the bread and wine as occasions for the very presence of God. In this sense the word of the preacher—indeed the word of a poor sermon—may become the very word of God. By the same token, the word of a brilliant sermon may simply be the word of a very clever preacher without being the word of God. The Westminster Shorter Catechism declared that the reading of the Bible, but *especially* the preaching of the word of God, is a means of God's grace.[81] The explication of scripture and the application of scripture to personal life and public affairs became the primary means of grace in most Protestant churches. Calvin understood preaching to be God's will for the church. No other practice or exercise can be substituted for it.

## Mutual Conversation and Consolation

Traditionally the means of grace have been defined as the word of God, the sacraments, and prayer.[82] Luther had included in the means of grace "mutual discussion and comforting of the brethren."[83] Mutual discussion or conversation has seldom appeared in the listing of the means of grace in the church, but in actual experience, the faith has been transmitted and the presence of God has been known in conversation and discussion. The practice has good warrant in the example of Jesus. It may well be that for some a conversation or words of consolation have been the occasional presence of God to a greater degree than the sacraments. The problem with elevating conversation to sacramental status is the danger of trivializing the faith in superficial conversations that are little more than human emotion and have little to do with the disciplined life of faith.

Many other church acts have New Testament precedent and in the actual experience of people have been the means of the divine presence, such as church suppers, the church's diaconal ministry of compassion, and the instructional program of the church. Yet there are good reasons why Reformed churches for four centuries have limited the official means of grace to the sermon, the two sacraments, and prayer. In any case, the intentional means of grace must find their institution in the ministry of Jesus Christ and their warrant in the New Testament.

## CHAPTER 19

# PRAYER

For some time I have employed a simple device in forming a judgment on the systematic writings of theologians, new and old. I read what they have to say about prayer. It provides a significant clue. There are three things I look for.

(1) I look to see how much space the theologian devotes to prayer. Not that the amount of space is important in itself, but it serves as an index of how seriously the theologian takes the subject. And if he takes prayer seriously, I take him seriously, even if I am not able to agree with him in everything. I am disappointed with the theologian who disposes of the subject briefly with a few commonplace observations or pious platitudes. I am impatient of those who omit the subject altogether (a group which contains some surprising names). And I am ambivalent toward those who show a serious concern to attach some real significance to prayer, but who reduce it to the practice of the presence of God or to some kind of sensitivity training.

(2) I look to see whether the theologian thinks of prayer as an act of the individual wrestling with his life in face of the mysterious workings of providence, or as an act of the community of Christ arising out of their faith in Christ. . . .

(3) I look to see what the theologian says about prayer as petition. For prayer is basically petition—asking, seeking, making requests. Of course, it is not all petition; there are other things—adoration, confession, thanksgiving, and so forth. But if these elements are so enlarged as to crowd out petition, prayer is denatured; for petition is the heart of prayer. This is the crucial point.

George Hendry, "The Lifeline of Theology"<br>
Princeton Seminary Bulletin, December 1972

Prayer means conversation with God, calling upon God. The theological problem is exclusively connected with the true character of prayer, that it aims at conversation with God, and that its true and decisive intention is that God should hear and that man should be heard. The person who has

grown up in the traditions of the Church takes this for granted. He is not conscious of the astonishing character, the boldness and the "irrationality" of
this act. To make him aware of this is the first theological task.
> Emil Brunner, *The Christian Doctrine of the Church,*
> *Faith, and the Consummation,* 325

That Christian obedience includes prayer means first that prayer is the most
intimate and effective form of Christian action.
> Karl Barth, *Church Dogmatics* III/3, 264

But whenever you pray, go into your room and shut the door and pray to
your Father who is in secret; and your Father who sees in secret will
reward you.
   When you are praying, do not heap up empty phrases as the Gentiles do;
for they think that they will be heard because of their many words. Do not
be like them, for your Father knows what you need before you ask him.
   Pray then in this way:
   Our Father in heaven . . .
> Matthew 6:6–9

Prayer is a universal human activity.[1] According to the common proverb,
there are no atheists in foxholes. John Calvin likewise found prayer to be
a natural activity, inevitable for human beings.[2] Human beings pray because
God made them so that they cannot help praying. To be truly human is
to pray.

## Prayer and Faith

Prayer, as a human act, is determined by the character and by the faith
of the one who prays.[3] Prayer can be confused, incoherent, selfish, and
corrupted by the prayer's own interests—therefore, evil. Prayer easily
becomes magic, the human effort to get control of God and to use God,
on the one hand, or mysticism, the effort to identify with God, on the
other. Again, the Reformed emphasis on human beings as moral, responsible, historical persons determines the character of prayer. Prayer is not
the loss of personhood but the intensification of responsible existence in
the presence of God.
   Prayer is also determined by the suppliant's understanding of God. Prayer
as petition presupposes the reality of God, who hears prayer and acts
personally in the created order. This presupposition is true of any serious
prayer of adoration, thanksgiving, confession, or intercession. Apart from
the presupposition of a God who is more, not less, than personal, prayer
becomes meditation or an exercise in self-development.

For these reasons theologians such as John Calvin in the sixteenth century and Karl Barth in the twentieth century have been concerned to understand prayer in the light of the Christian faith. Calvin devoted a chapter to prayer in the *Institutes* of 1536, and that chapter remained throughout all successive editions, becoming one of the great treatises in church history on prayer. Karl Barth treats prayer under the general heading of providence. He also discusses it in connection with ethics and in particular with the life of the Christian community and its ministry in the world.

John Calvin declared that prayer is a chief exercise of faith,[4] and Emil Brunner stated that it is at the center of the Christian life.[5] There are other crucial exercises of faith: the worship of the congregation, the activities of the congregation, Bible reading, deeds of compassion and mercy, stewardship of possessions, and Christian conversation with fellow Christians. Prayer is not necessarily any more important, especially in certain moments of life, than these other activities of faith; but without prayer the life of faith is greatly impoverished, if it is possible at all.

Prayer brings into focus our Christian beliefs on the one hand and our Christian commitments on the other. Theological commitments distinguish prayer from exercises in self-development, meditations, and psychological stimulants. Christians pray because they believe, at least when they think about it, that God hears prayer and is able to answer it in their lives and in the created order. Prayer also involves deep human commitments that acknowledge the reality of God in adoration and in thanksgiving, that move the believer to confess sins and to ask for forgiveness. Prayer acknowledges one's needs and asks for God's help for oneself and for other human beings. Prayer reveals our deepest commitments in faith and also makes known our deepest commitments in life.

Prayer is a human activity that can either enhance life or corrupt it and can either confirm the reality of God as God has been made known in Jesus Christ or become the instrument of some idolatry. For this reason the theology of prayer is crucially important, and theologians such as Calvin and Barth have always insisted that prayer must be discussed and practiced in the context of Christian faith commitments.

## The Rules of Prayer

John Calvin began his discussion of prayer by laying down four rules to govern prayer. These rules, to which he adds others in a less formal way, serve as a very good introduction to the Christian understanding of prayer. They, as well as everything Calvin wrote about prayer, presuppose what he said about God, about Jesus Christ, about the Holy Spirit, and about human beings as sinners who are redeemed by Christ.

The first rule of prayer is "that we be disposed in mind and heart as befits those who enter conversation with God. This we shall indeed attain with respect to the mind if it is freed from carnal cares and thoughts by which it can be called or led away from right and pure contemplation of God. . . ."[6] Calvin does not insist that the mind should be totally free from anxiety or vexations, but that in prayer *our human attentions should be concentrated.* "Whoever engages in prayer should apply to it his faculties and efforts, and not, as commonly happens, be distracted by wandering thoughts." And whoever engages in prayer should take care "not to ask any more than God allows."[7] For this reason Calvin recognizes that to pray rightly is a rare gift. Prayer is intimate conversation with God, and true prayer requires greater intensity and concentration of human energies than are required in intimate conversation with another human being.

The second rule is that we should be aware in prayer of our own insufficiency and earnestly ponder why we need all we seek.[8] This sense of need should be joined with a burning desire to attain that for which we pray. Prayer is no perfunctory discharge of a duty to God. It arises out of serious human need. Prayer requires an awareness of reality. It is not an exercise of whim or illusion. "Vain repetition" is a folly in practice, against which Calvin repeatedly protested.

The third rule of prayer is "that anyone who stands before God to pray, in his humility giving glory completely to God, abandon all thought of his own glory, cast off all notions of his own worth, in fine, put away all self-assurance."[9] We do not come to God as those who deserve that for which we ask. We plead our own insufficiency.

Calvin insisted that at the heart of prayer is the petition that God shall forgive our sins. The old practice of concluding every prayer with the petition for God to forgive our sins was more than rote piety. It gave expression to the conviction that in prayer, as in the Christian life, the forgiveness of sins is the presupposition of everything else.

The fourth rule of prayer is that "we should be nonetheless encouraged to pray by a sure hope that our prayers will be answered."[10]

The fifth rule is that prayer must be in the name of Jesus Christ.[11] It must be in the name of Jesus Christ because the risen Christ is our intercessor. We stand in confidence before God because God in Christ bore our sins and God raised Jesus Christ from the dead. Now Christ has risen to the right hand of God, where he is our intercessor.

Calvin's insistence that prayer be made in the name of Jesus Christ also stands over against any notion that prayer should be made in the name of a human being, even of the saints of heaven. All that God can give us has been given to us in Jesus Christ. Calvin held that Christian prayer can be made on account of what Christ has done for us and in the light of Christ's intercession for us, and this is the foundation for the practice of concluding every prayer in the name of Jesus Christ. Moreover, the revelation of God in Jesus Christ determines the character and quality of a Christian prayer. Christians pray for what is in accord with the life that Jesus Christ lived in our midst.

Calvin's sixth rule is that prayer must be according to the will of God. In prayer the deepest needs and desires of the heart are laid before God with authenticity, honesty, and supplication, especially in private prayer; but they are presented to God in the context of the deep conviction that God will answer our prayer according to his will, not according to our own.

Calvin's seventh rule opposed all prayer for the dead. He found no warrant for it in scripture, and he found the basis for the practice in human sorrow. "They were seeking comfort to relieve their sorrow, and it seemed inhuman to them not to show before God some evidence of their love toward the dead. All men know by experience how man's nature is inclined to this feeling."[12] Calvin was adamant on this point because he understood quite well how human sorrow and sympathy can become the context in which evil corruptions arise. Calvin's opposition to prayers for the dead grows out of his emphasis on the decisiveness of life here and now and on the "more perfect solace": "Blessed are the dead who . . . die in the Lord" (Revelation 14:13). For it is our belief that "we ought not to indulge our affection to the extent of setting up a perverse mode of prayer in the church."[13]

An eighth rule that is implicit in all that Calvin wrote and did is authenticity in prayer. Calvin himself prayed both extemporaneously and also with the use of written prayers that had grown out of the tradition of the church.[14] Later, Puritans, greatly influenced by Calvin's theology, would protest against read prayer, a protest that was alive in the Presbyterian church until after the Second World War. The Westminster Assembly prepared a directory of worship giving general instructions rather than a book of worship with established forms. Many of the Puritans settled for what they called studied prayers, that is, prayers that had been prepared but were rendered in worship extemporaneously. The point is that prayer must come from the heart.

Calvin's general rule of simplicity also applies to prayer. He was opposed to windy prayers designed to elicit applause from the hearers rather than from God. The tongue without the mind is displeasing to God.[15] Simplicity was for Calvin and the early Reformed tradition very close to sincerity. The pompous, the pretentious, the ostentatious, and the contrived cover up reality, especially in prayer. The Calvinist opted for plain-style preaching and also for plain-style prayers, though Calvin insisted that the plain style of prayer had to reflect the transcendence and majesty of God, using the kind of language, for example, that Isaiah used.[16]

A ninth rule is Calvin's insistence that prayer should be in the language of the people. No one now prays in Latin, but the admonition is still appropriate. Calvin regarded congregational singing as the prayers of the people. The admonition that prayers should be in the language of the people would surely hold for singing, even though Calvin himself never contemplated a choir, much less a special anthem or a solo in worship.[17] Bodily gestures such as kneeling, uncovering the head, or standing have value as means of expressing reverence. In prayer every act or form is justified only as it contributes to the personal and theological integrity of prayer.

Finally, prayer should be offered according to the model of the Lord's Prayer.

> We would not have it understood that we are so bound by this form of prayer that we are not allowed to change it in either word or syllable. For here and there in Scripture one reads many prayers, far different from it in words, yet composed by the same Spirit, the use of which is very profitable to us. Many prayers are repeatedly suggested to believers by the same Spirit, which bear little similarity in wording. In so teaching, we mean only this: that no man should ask for, expect, or demand, anything at all except what is included, by way of summary, in this prayer; and though the words may be utterly different, yet the sense ought not to vary. . . . Here nothing is left out that ought to be thought of in the praises of God, nothing that ought to come into man's mind for his own welfare.[18]

## The Forms of Prayer

Prayer takes many forms: adoration, thanksgiving, confession, intercession, and petition. All of these forms of prayer are essential to the nature of prayer itself. Comprehensive prayers should include all of these elements; however, in certain situations one form may be paramount.

In a contemporary, humanistic, and secular culture the form of prayer that is at greatest risk is petition. The tacit assumption of a secular culture is that even if God can hear prayer, God cannot answer prayer in a world of cause and effect. Christian theology has always insisted on the personal activity of God in the created order. This is surely true of the scriptures from beginning to end. It is precisely this conviction—that God works personally in the created order—that is most at risk in our society.

Karl Barth in his discussion of prayer raises the question of whether worship, penitence, and petition are not equally important; he answers that in practice they may well be so, but in substance they are not.

> In all languages the word prayer is itself against it. For it speaks only of petition as the constitutive element in what takes place in prayer. It shows us that while prayer is a matter of worship and penitence, it is not so in the first instance. In the first instance, it is an asking, a seeking and a knocking directed towards God; a wishing, a desiring and a requesting presented to God. And the actuality of prayer is decidedly against not merely a precedence of the other two elements but even their equality with petition. The man who really prays comes to God and approaches and speaks to Him because he seeks something of God, because he desires and expects something, because he hopes to receive something which he needs, something which he does not hope to receive from anyone else, but does definitely hope to receive from God.[19]

The psalms have always been models for Christian prayers. Calvin understood the singing of psalms in worship as the prayers of the people.

## Occasions for Prayer

The occasions for prayer are coextensive with life itself. Calvin distinguished between but did not separate public and private prayers. According to the example of Jesus, who prayed in public and in private, Christians should do likewise. Public and private prayer reinforce each other.

> We must consider that whoever refused to pray in the holy assembly of the godly knows not what it is to pray individually, or in a secret spot, or at home. Again, he who neglects to pray alone and in private, however unremittingly he may frequent public assemblies, there contrives only windy prayers, for he defers more to the opinion of men than to the secret judgment of God.[20]

Calvin's emphasis on the constancy of prayer was so great that he even prescribed a set practice for the discipline for prayer.

> It is fitting each one of us should set apart certain hours for this exercise. Those hours should not pass without prayer, and during them all the devotion of the heart should be completely engaged in it. These are: when we arise in the morning, before we begin daily work, when we sit down to a meal, when by God's blessing we have eaten, when we are getting ready to retire.[21]

Calvin composed prayers for these various times and also a prayer to be made as one went to school. These were published with his catechism.

Prayers may also be made — indeed, the most intense prayers frequently are made — in sudden and unexpected situations. God is not bound to particular circumstances or to times or places, and it is folly for human beings to attempt to bind God. We are free to pray in any situation, so long as we pray that everything be done according to God's will.

In summary, prayer is an exercise of faith in any particular situation in which Christians may find themselves. Prayer is faith in its self-expression and shares the spontaneity and freedom of faith. Fixed forms of prayer may be broken by the exigencies of the situation and the moment. Prayer, as intimate conversation with God, is a pervasive form of the Christian life and undoubtedly takes place more frequently than outward observation would suggest.

CHAPTER 20

❖

# THE BIBLE

From time immemorial the Church has always called the Scriptures of the Old and the New Testaments the "word of God." In so doing, the church expresses a fundamental truth of the Christian faith, namely, that in these books the historical self-manifestation of God is offered to faith in an incomparable, decisive, and unique manner; this means that no Christian faith can either arise or be preserved which ignores "Holy Scripture." . . .

The Christian Church stands and falls with the written New Testament, and the written Apostolic testimony to Christ is not only the foundation of all the later witness of the church to Christ; it is also its norm.

Emil Brunner, *Revelation and Reason,* 118, 127

The Holy Scriptures are both a means of grace and the norm of the church's life.[1] The Bible is the church's memory, inspired by the Holy Spirit, of those events that are the foundation of the Christian life in history. It is the church's witness to the gospel and the content of its preaching. In the church the Bible is read devotionally as a means of God's grace. In theological reflection, it is the warrant for Christian doctrine.

## The Word of God Written

The Bible is the original witness to and interpretation of God's revelation and work "for us men and for our salvation" in Jesus Christ. In this sense the Bible is the church's memory reduced to writing by the prophets and the apostles who were the original witnesses of and believers in God's revelation and work that constituted his people. More specifically, the Bible is the forward- and backward-looking testimony to Jesus Christ and as such sets the boundaries and is the unique authorization for Christian theology and life.

The Bible, however, is more than the original and authentic witness to God's revelation. It is, as the Westminster Confession of Faith declares, "the written word of God." This confession was adopted by the Westminster Assembly in 1646. The first paragraph was done with such care and precision that it can be affirmed today.

> Although the light of nature, and the works of creation and providence, do so far manifest the goodness, wisdom, and power of God, as to leave men inexcusable; yet are they not sufficient to give that knowledge of God, and of his will, which is necessary unto salvation; therefore it pleased the Lord, at sundry times, and in divers manners, to reveal himself and to declare that his will unto his Church; and afterwards for the better preserving and propagating of the truth, and for the more sure establishment and comfort of the Church against the corruption of the flesh, and the malice of Satan and of the world, to commit the same wholly unto writing; which maketh the Holy Scripture to be most necessary; those former ways of God's revealing his will unto his people being now ceased (1.1).

God reveals himself in great events in history, in eliciting images and ideas in the minds of the prophets, and supremely in Jesus Christ. Revelation in its diverse forms is so experienced as to cause the recipient to formulate its content in words, phrases, and sentences. Revelation by events always leads to revelation by words. Metaphors, images, and ideas elicited in the human mind have to be expressed in coherent sentences. If the facts or events or the metaphors of the mind were not translated into words they would remain ineffectual. Revelation in facts or events leads to revelation in words, and revelation in words is based on revelation in facts. Had facts or ideas and images not been translated into words, they would have remained powerless. Revelation as the word spoken or the word written stands midway between revelation in events and the experience of revelation today.[2] The Bible is therefore more than a witness to revelation. It is the word of God written. The Holy Scriptures are the word of God, but they are the word of God within the limitation of words and of the writers who composed it.

# The Authority of Scripture

The authority of scripture is that it is the word of God written, or, as John Calvin and the Westminster Confession declare, "God is its author."

> [The scriptures] attain full authority among believers only when men regard them as having sprung from heaven, as if there the living words of God were heard. . . . It is utterly vain, then, to pretend that the power of judging Scripture so lies with the church that its certainty depends upon churchly assent. Thus, while the church receives and gives its seal of approval to the

Scriptures, it does not thereby render authentic what is otherwise doubtful or controversial.[3]

## The Testimony of the Holy Spirit

The authority of scripture cannot be guaranteed by the church. The scriptures, under the power of the Holy Spirit, are self-authenticating. As Calvin put it, "Scripture exhibits fully as clear evidence of its own truth as white and black things do of their color, or sweet and bitter things do of their taste."[4] The credibility of doctrine "is not established until we are persuaded beyond doubt that God is its Author. Thus, the highest proof of Scripture derives in general from the fact that God in person speaks in it."[5] No human authority can guarantee the authority of scripture.

> We ought to seek our conviction in a higher place than human reason, judgments, or conjectures, that is, in the secret testimony of the Spirit. . . . Let this point therefore stand: that those whom the Holy Spirit has inwardly taught truly rest upon Scripture, and that Scripture indeed is self-authenticated; hence, it is not right to subject it to proof and reasoning. And the certainty it deserves with us, it attains by the testimony of the Spirit.[6]

Having asserted that the holy scriptures are self-authenticating as to their authority and that this self-authentication comes from the testimony of the Holy Spirit, Calvin turns to arguments to bolster the assertion that the Holy Scriptures are the word of God. These arguments are inconclusive, but they point to the truth that the testimony of the Holy Spirit is not in contradiction to human judgment. In other words, the Holy Spirit does not testify that something is true when we know that it is not true. The testimony of the Holy Spirit does not contradict human reason or require believers to sacrifice the integrity of the human mind. The conviction that the Bible is the word of God is reasonable and is validated in the lives of intelligent people as they read scripture.

Believers have become convinced that the scriptures are the word of God not so much by taking a course in the New Testament or the Old Testament but by reading the scriptures in the context of the worshiping, believing community. No scholar and no scientific study of the New Testament can ever convince anyone that it is the word of God. Yet highly intelligent critical persons reading it with affection in the context of the church's worship and faith become convinced that it is God's word written and the means of God's revelation to us today.

# The Canon of Scripture

The formation of the canon, that is, the certification that these books are authoritative in the life of the church, is an action of the church. Emil Brunner has well written:

> It is the Church, the community of believers, which decides what is "canonical" or "Apostolic," and hence what is the character of the primitive witness in itself. The formation of the canon is a judgment of faith, a decision of knowledge, a "dogma" of the Church. Therefore the question of the canon has never, in principle, been definitely answered, but it is continually being reopened. Just as the Church of the second, third, and fourth centuries had the right to decide, and felt obliged to decide, what was "Apostolic" and what was not, on their own responsibility as believers, so in the same way every Church, at every period in the history of the church, possesses the same right and the same duty. The dogma of the canon, like every other ecclesiastical decision of faith, is not final and infallible, but it is possible and right continually to re-examine it, test it, and revise it.[7]

The church renders its own verdict as to which books are authoritative, which books are authentic and original witnesses of the revelation of God. Yet in this decision the church is simply acknowledging the books that are authoritative in its own life. Hans von Campenhausen, an authority on the canon, has cogently observed:

> The content of this N.T. collection of writings and to a certain extent the writings themselves were something with which the church was presented as an already existing "Apostolic testimony." The church knew that she had been called into life by this testimony and had not herself created the Scriptures. She could merely accept, affirm, and confirm them. Hence one could also say, with equal or greater justification, that the canon (thought of in terms of its content) imposed itself, and was in any case not a product of the church on which it was binding.[8]

The decision concerning the authoritative books in the life of the church grew out of the life of the church itself, out of worship, out of preaching, out of teaching. For the most part, the acknowledgment of the authoritative books was clear and uncomplicated. "It is undisputed that both the Old and the New Testament had in essence already reached their final form and significance around the year 200. The minor variations which still persist, and are occasionally the subject of further discussions, coexist perfectly happy with the overriding conviction that Christians everywhere possess one and the same Bible."[9]

Von Campenhausen goes on to say:

> The Christian Bible—and this is the first and absolutely unshakeable fact that we know about it—comes into existence from the start as the book of Christ. The Scriptures of the Lord testify to the Lord—the Old Testament prophetically, the New Testament historically. Christ speaks in both Testaments and is their true content. This alone is what makes the Bible the Christian Bible, the book of the Christian church.[10]

# Inspiration

The Holy Spirit, who testifies that the scriptures are God's word, also inspired the writing of the Bible itself. Reinhold Seeberg defined inspiration as "certain effects worked by the spirit of God in the souls of the prophets and first witnesses of Christ through which they were enabled to understand revelation—its facts and words—and make it intelligible."[11] Inspiration refers not only to the reception of revelation but also to the proclamation of it in writing. Emil Brunner declares that just as this inspiration does not rule out

> human search, human weaknesses, and the possibility of mistakes in actions and in behavior, so it cannot be intended that the Scriptures are so completely under the control of the Spirit that this rules out all human activity of reflection and inquiry. Human research, such as Luke mentioned as the author of the gospel narrative, does not exclude inspiration, but it does exclude automatic dictation and verbal inspiration with its claim to an oracular divine infallibility.[12]

## Herman Ridderbos writes:

> Inspiration does not mean deification. We cannot say everything of Scripture that we say of the word of God nor can we identify the apostles and prophets during their writing with the Holy Spirit. The Word of God exists in eternity, is perfect. But Scripture is neither eternal nor perfect. Inspiration consists in this, that God makes the words of men the instrument of his word, that he uses human words for his divine purposes. As such the human words stand in the service of Christ and participate in the authority and in the infallibility of the Word of God, answer perfectly God's purpose, in short, function as the word of God and therefore can be so called. But this remains a human instrument in the hands of God. And it is not up to us, it is up to the free pleasure of God to decide what kind of effect divine inspiration should have in the mind, knowledge, memory, accuracy of those whom he has used in his service, in order that their words really can be accepted and trusted as the inspired word of God.[13]

The inspiration of scripture means that in God's providence and by the power of the Holy Spirit the scriptures are an infallible source for the church's life and authority for its doctrine and practice. When the scriptures are read as the Word of God, when the reader in the company of the faithful searches in them for God's Word addressed to him or her, the scriptures are an infallible declaration of God's salvation. The Holy Spirit speaking through scripture is the final norm on the church's existence.

Karl Rahner argued that scripture by inspiration became the work of God precisely in its role as the objectification of the faith of the primitive church that is the permanent norm of the faith of all later Christian ages. Yet he recognizes the contingent, historical nature of scripture.

> The human authors of the scriptures are not secretaries who, by their own intelligent understanding and free will, receive whatever is illuminated and presented by God. They are real originators and authors. We may even say that they are authors in no less a sense than men usually are in regard to their own writings. The divine authorship is neither a rival nor a diminution of human authorship, which is not to be limited or reduced to a secretarial function. The mental picture of the "instrumentality" of the human author, which is frequently stressed in the teaching statements of the Church, must not be misunderstood in that sense. It is precisely not a question of the instrumentality of a secretary in regard to the author, but of a human authorship which remains completely and absolutely unimpaired, which is permeated, embraced, but not diminished, by the divine authorship. Only in this sense is it an "instrument" of God. And it is an instrument in such a way that the instrumentality of the writer, linked with the divine authorship, does not only tolerate but also demands the human authorship, and that there would be no point in divine authorship if man were but a secretary.[14]

Karl Barth declared that the inspiration of scripture cannot be reduced to a proposition in which we believe. To believe in the inspiration of scripture is to believe in God whose witness it is. Verbal inspiration, according to Barth, does not mean the infallibility of the biblical word in its linguistic, historical, and theological character as a biblical word. It does mean that "the fallible and faulty human word is used by God and has to be received and heard in spite of its human fallibility."[15]

## The Bible and Tradition

The high place that Protestantism has always given to the Bible, as the norm and authority for the church's life, obscures the importance of the living tradition even for the Bible itself. Consequently, it is crucial to emphasize that the Bible was written within the living Christian community and tradition; and when it is properly understood, it is read and heard within the same living community and tradition. The importance of the living tradition can be illustrated if we imagine some disaster blotting out all traces of the Christian community so that no knowledge of it remained. Then let us further imagine someone walking among the ruins of a Western city and stumbling upon a sealed box containing the Bible. Let us now estimate the possibility of the Bible alone, without a living community, without a living interpreter, giving rise to a new community. The chances would be small or nonexistent.[16]

The Protestant Reformers, even though they placed great emphasis on returning to the sources, always read the sources in the context of the Christian community and in the light of much of the Christian community's reflection on those sources. Calvin interpreted the scriptures according to the analogy of faith, that is, within the context of the church's creeds. The relationship of scripture and tradition is dialectical. The scripture as the concretion in writing of the original and authentic witness in the church's tradition has authority over the tradition, as Luther insisted with great power. On the other hand, the Bible itself must be understood in the context of the living church and the church's understanding of the witness to which scripture attests.

## The Interpretation of Scripture

The first Reformed theologians, John Calvin in particular, insisted on the natural meaning of scripture.[17] By the natural meaning he meant that the interpretation must be under the authority of the text. He also meant that the text should be understood today in terms of the meaning that the writer intended to convey. All the early Reformers believed that scriptures are sufficiently clear that the ordinary Christian can read them with understanding. For this reason Protestants insisted that the Bible should be in the language that ordinary people understood. The translation of the Bible, in particular William Tyndale's translation into English, is one of the great, heroic stories in the life of the church, a story that continues today as the Bible is translated into the languages of the world. Portions of scripture have now been translated into 1,900 languages and dialects. No other book has been made available in so many languages.

The clearest early Reformed statement indicating the rubrics that should guide the interpretation of scripture is found in a sermon by Heinrich Bullinger. (1) Scripture, he said, should be interpreted by scripture, the more obscure passages by the clearer, (2) with attention to language, to historical setting, to the author's intention, (3) in the light of the church's understanding of scripture. (4) Any authentic interpretation of scripture will increase love for God and love for humanity, and finally (5) all true interpretations of scripture presuppose the heart of an interpreter who loves God and seeks to do his will.[18]

## The Bible and General Revelation

The Bible, as God's word written, does not minimize God's revelation in all of creation. This revelation is emphasized within scripture itself. John Calvin compared the scriptures to spectacles.[19] Without spectacles a person whose eyesight is failing sees things in vague, inchoate, and distorted ways. In a similar manner the eyes of human understanding have been distorted by human sin. The scripture provides the spectacles, the proper refraction of theological vision, that enable the believer to see and understand God's revelation in the created order, in history, and in the depths of human existence. The revelation of God in Jesus Christ attested in scripture clarifies, corrects, and completes our perception of God's revelation in all creation.

❖

## CHAPTER 21

# CHRISTIAN FAITH
# AND LIVING RELIGIONS

Jesus Christ is both the Fulfillment of all religion and the Judgment on all religion. As the Fulfiller, He is the Truth which these religions seek in vain. There is no phenomenon in the history of religion that does not point toward Him. . . .

He is also the Judgment on all religion. Viewed in His light, all religious systems appear untrue, unbelieving, and indeed godless.

Emil Brunner, *Revelation and Reason,* 270–271

For what can be known about God is plain to them, because God has shown it to them. Ever since the creation of the world his eternal power and divine nature, invisible though they are, have been understood and seen through the things he has made.

Romans 1:19–20

No one knows the Son except the Father, and no one knows the Father except the Son and anyone to whom the Son chooses to reveal him.

Matthew 11:27

There is salvation in no one else, for there is no other name under heaven given among men by which we must be saved.

Acts 4:12 (RSV)

The Christian church exists today in a pluralistic society. The basic dogmas of pluralism deny the foundation of Christian faith, namely, the conviction that Jesus Christ is the Word made flesh. The assumption of pluralism is that if there is a Word to become flesh then there cannot be just one word. The old dictum of the Enlightenment that many roads lead to God is broadened into the rubric that theology and philosophy consist of many conversations which may or may not lead to God. The influence of pluralism in our culture is greatly enhanced by its dominance in the mass media and the secular university.[1]

The contemporary situation is similar to the world into which Jesus came.

The Roman society tolerated many religions so long as they did not challenge the authority of the emperor or the claim of Rome to fulfill the meaning of life. So contemporary society tolerates all religions as long as none of the dogmas of a secular society are challenged.

Christians of the first three centuries were in continual struggle to maintain the integrity of their life and of their faith. In part the struggle was moral. In particular the Christian community insisted on a life controlled by the example of Jesus in a society where many found the meaning of life in the enhancement of its physical vitalities and energies. They insisted on the preciousness of life in a society in which human life was very cheap, as illustrated by the practice of exposure of babies and the brutalities of gladiatorial shows. They insisted on the life of love and devotion in a society in which greed and lust for power were rampant. This struggle for moral integrity is reflected in the New Testament, in the writings of the Apostolic Fathers and in the apologies of Justin Martyr and Tertullian.

The struggle for the integrity of faith was even more severe. The Mediterranean world would have welcomed Christian faith as one religion among many religions. Yet the early Christian could not accept tolerance on this basis. From the middle of the third century until Constantine's acceptance of Christianity in 313 it was clear to many observers that the claims of the Roman state and of Christian faith could not exist in the same society. This point was made decisively by the Council of Nicaea (A.D. 325) and in the Nicene Creed, which declared that Jesus was from the being of the Father, true God from true God, begotten not made, of the same substance (being, essence, reality) as the Father. Paul Tillich has noted that this declaration of the council meant that Jesus Christ is the mediator between God and humanity, not one of many mediators, and that Christian faith was not simply one of the religions of the Roman Empire.[2]

The question in the first four centuries as well as the question today is, How do we relate the Christian conviction that Jesus Christ is "of the same substance as the Father" to the fact of living religions? Any satisfactory answer to this question must confess the Christian conviction that Jesus Christ is the Word made flesh and that in his life, death, and resurrection God wrought the salvation of all human beings. In addition any satisfactory answer to this question must be faithful in representing the teaching of other religions and give some explication of their existence.

## The Universality of Religion

Religions, according to John Calvin, have their origin in the universal revelation of God in the created order. God has planted a sense or an awareness of deity in every human heart, and God's presence is mediated through all his creation.[3] Religion, according to Calvin, is the consequence of the human response to this universal revelation of God, a response that has been corrupted by human sin. Hence all religions reflect in some way God's universal revelation, and they also reflect the human response.

The Christian thesis concerning religions, writes Emil Brunner, is

> a twofold thesis: the religions, the religious life of the natural man, are the product of the original divine revelation and of human sin. Apart from real revelation the phenomenon of religion cannot be understood. . . . Therefore the Apostle, when he explains the nature of the pagan religion, speaks, first of all, of this universal self-manifestation of God to all men without exception through the works of creation and through the writing of the law upon their hearts. . . . The holy Scriptures teach us to understand all pagan religion from the standpoint of the revelation through the Creation. . . . [Religion] is the product of man's sinful blindness. In the same passage, and indeed in the same sentence, in which Paul speaks of the original revelation, he also speaks of the original sin of all men: "Because that, knowing God, they glorified him not as God . . . but became vain in their reasonings . . . and changed the glory of the incorruptible God for the likeness of an image of corruptible man, and of birds, and four-footed beasts, and creeping things." The God of the "other religions" is always an idol. . . .
>
> All empirical religion, to use mathematical terms, is a "product" of these two "factors" combined with others, which through this are brought into play. These two original elements, however, are so closely interwoven that in our efforts to explain we cannot always distinguish the one from the other. . . . In all religion, even in the most primitive form of idolatry, there is something of reverence and gratitude toward a power on which man knows himself to be dependent, which is different from his dependence on natural facts: but in all religion too, even in "higher religions," this reverence is mingled with fear of the absolutely Terrible, which only leads to a slavish submission to overwhelming Power, while gratitude is mingled with a selfish longing for happiness, for which the Deity is "used."[4]

Hendrik Kraemer, a Dutch Reformed theologian and missionary, spent his life studying the religions of the world and reflecting on the relationship of Christianity to them. He understood religion as the human response to God's universal revelation of himself.[5]

Every reader of the Old Testament knows that religion can be destructive and that religious practices can be a substitute for authentic trust in God (e.g., Amos 5:21–24). The Christian hope is not in religion or in religious communities or in religious practices. Religion and religious communities must be both appreciated and judged as human works in response to what is believed to be the revelation of God. Christians may gladly acknowledge every evidence of truth and goodness in every religion. On the other hand, Christian openness to the presence of God wherever he reveals himself does not mean that all religions are essentially the same or equally valid ways of salvation. As a matter of simple observation, some religions are very destructive of values Christians cherish. The evidence in history is overwhelming that religions are significant ingredients in shaping the character of political, economic, and cultural life as well as religious life.

Historians have commented on the historical fact that democratic societies and high economic productivity have been associated with Protestantism and especially with Reformed Protestantism. Other historians have noted the significance of the Judeo-Christian tradition for the development of modern science. Neither democracy nor high economic productivity nor scientific study is likely to thrive in cultures that are dominated by religions which deny or minimize the goodness of the created order, the significance of history, and the importance of vocation as a fulfillment of the purposes of God. Religions neither teach the same thing, nor do they contribute to the same type of economic, social, or political life and culture.

## The Uniqueness of Jesus Christ

The Christian claim is not that Christianity is a superior religion to the other religions of the world. Christian faith, like all other religions, is corrupted by human sinfulness. In saying this there is no intention to depreciate the notable achievements and constructive influences that Christian communities have had on society as well as the virtues of the communities themselves. The Christian claim, however, has to do with Jesus Christ. According to the Nicene faith, Jesus Christ is the Word made flesh. Jesus Christ is God insofar as God can be embodied in a human life. The revealing activity of God that we perceive in all creation comes to a sharp focus in Jesus Christ. In this sense Jesus Christ is the final revelation, not in a sense that God does not continue to reveal himself. Jesus Christ is the revelation in the light of which all other revelation is perceived.

Hendrik Kraemer has related this Christian affirmation to other religions in a sharp and decisive way.

> The Christian revelation, as a record of God's self-disclosing revelation in Jesus Christ, is absolutely *sui generis*. It is the story of God's sovereign acts having become decisively and finally manifest in Jesus Christ, the son of the living God in whom God became flesh and revealed his grace and truth. . . .

Religious experiences or ideas, of course, are not absent from the Bible, and they are by no means unimportant, but in no sense are they central. What is central and fundamental in the Bible is the registering, describing and witnessing to God's creative and redemptive dealings with man and the world.[6]

Emil Brunner writes of Jesus Christ as the fulfiller and the judge of all religions including Christianity. Brunner goes so far as to argue that there is no phenomenon in the history of religion that does not point toward Jesus Christ. For in the bloody sacrifice of expiation, the sacred meal, the ecstatic element, the seeking of the Holy Spirit, the magical element, the indication of the *dynamis* of God in the reality of his revelation, prayer, the divine father, and the divine judge all point to Jesus Christ. In Jesus, "the protest of the atheist has as much right as religion."[7] Brunner goes on to argue that Jesus Christ is not only the fulfillment but the judge of all religions. "Viewed in His light, all religious systems appear untrue, unbelieving, and indeed godless."[8]

Calvin, Brunner, and Kraemer all understand religions not simply in terms of the general revelation of God in all creation or of human sin but in particular in the light of the incarnation of the wisdom and the power of God in Jesus Christ.

The work of Jesus Christ as the Fulfiller of religion and the Judge of religion is found not only in God's general revelation in creation and history, and not only in the life, death, and resurrection of Jesus Christ, but also in the work of the crucified and risen Christ in human history today and in all religions. In addition, the judgment and the fulfillment is finally eschatological. Hence none of us can say except in a provisional and preliminary way how Jesus Christ judges and fulfills all religions including the Christian religion. In the meantime we must remember that the Christ who judges and fulfills is the incarnate Christ to whom the apostles witnessed, not an abstract reason or an unincarnate Christ.

## Inclusive and Exclusive

Christian faith speaks about revelation in strongly exclusive pronouncements.[9] This is true of the New Testament, and it is true of all subsequent theology. Yet it is also inclusive.

Both the universal and exclusive points of view expressed the peculiar genius of Christian faith. On the one hand it does not establish any limits around the divine revelation, but, on the other hand, it refuses to recognize any other god than him who reveals himself in Christ. In fact, every attempt to regulate and determine the boundaries within which the divine revelation might express itself appears to face an extreme presumption. . . . Rightly understood, the Christian faith has not the slightest interest in limiting and restricting the extent of the divine revelation. On the contrary it must be said that faith encounters with the divine revelation in Christ empower the eye of faith to discover what men in the ancient church called the broken rays of the divine Logos.[10]

Christian faith knows no other God than the God who is revealed in Jesus Christ and no other salvation than that which Jesus Christ has wrought.

While limiting salvation to Jesus Christ many Christians have argued that those who did not know the Christ according to the flesh were in some way saved by the unincarnate Christ. Justin Martyr in the second century declared that Socrates and other Greek philosophers were Christian on the grounds that the Logos whose presence was focused in Jesus Christ informs the whole of creation. All of those who live by "reason," Justin contended, are Christians.[11] Augustine knew that there were many wolves within the church and many sheep without the fold.

In Reformed theology the great theologians of Zurich took a generous position. Zwingli in a remarkable passage writes to the king of France about those whom he should expect to see in heaven.

> We believe, then, that as soon as they depart the body the faithful fly away to God, joining themselves to God and enjoying eternal felicity. Therefore, most religious king, if you discharge the office entrusted to you, as David, Hezekiah and Josiah did, you may look forward first to seeing God himself in his very essence and majesty and with all his attributes and powers. . . . After that you may expect to see the communion and fellowship of all the saints and sages and believers and the steadfast and the brave and the good who have ever lived since the world began. You will see the two Adams, the redeemed and the Redeemer, Abel, Enoch, Noah, Abraham, Isaac, Jacob, Judah, Moses, Joshua, Gideon, Samuel, Phinehas, Elijah, Elisha, Isaiah and the Virgin Mother of God of whom he prophesied, David, Hezekiah, Josiah, the Baptist, Peter, Paul; Hercules too and Theseus, Socrates, Aristides, Antigonus, Numa, Camillus, the Catos and Scipios; Louis the Pious. . . ![12]

Heinrich Bullinger likewise wanted to set no boundaries on who may be saved outside of the church: "It is certain, that there were an innumerable company of men dispersed throughout the whole world among the gentiles, who never did nor could, communicate with this visible company and congregation of God's people; and yet not withstanding they were holy members of this society in communion and the friends of almighty God."[13]

John Calvin probably had Zwingli in mind when he wrote that "vile is the stupidity of those persons who open heaven to all the impious and unbelieving without the grace of him whom scripture commonly teaches to be the only door whereby we enter into salvation."[14] It would be unwise to generalize too much from Calvin's remarks or from Zwingli's remarkable picture of heaven. These two statements do represent the poles between which Christian thinking must move. On the one hand there is the Christian conviction that Jesus Christ is the Word made flesh and that in his life, death, and resurrection God wrought the salvation of all people. Or, as Calvin put it, the only door is Jesus Christ. On the other hand, no Christian should want to limit the ways in which Jesus Christ may be known by those who do not call him by his right name. The Christian task is the proclamation of what God has done in Jesus Christ for the salvation of all people "in Jerusalem, in all Judea and Samaria, and to the ends of the earth" (Acts 1:8).

## Confessional

The Christian mission to the world is confessional.[15] The Christian confesses what God has done for all people in Jesus Christ and invites others to share this faith.

God alone knows what happens to people when they die. Willem Visser 't Hooft once wrote, "I do not know whether a Hindu is saved. I only know that salvation comes in Jesus Christ."[16] This "theology of neutrality" has been vigorously attacked for not declaring that those outside Christian faith are saved. Yet it is wise to leave the fate of all to the judgment of God.

Lesslie Newbigin argues that this is a poor question because only God can answer it. The fundamental question is, How can God be glorified and his grace made known?[17] Newbigin then proposes that Christians should welcome signs of God's grace in any life, that Christians will cooperate with people of all faiths in projects in line with Christian understanding, that in this association we shall discover where we must separate, and that the real contribution of Christians to the dialogue will be telling the story of Jesus and the Bible.[18]

The God who creates and sustains the world is the God incarnate in Jesus Christ. This is the inclusivism and exclusivism of Christian faith.

The awesomeness, wonder, and passion of this confession has been well expressed by John Baillie.

So when we ask ourselves why it should be ordained that there is only one Name whereby we all must be saved, our first answer is that, if we do not know why, we do not need to know and could hardly expect to know. And yet—this is my second point—I believe we can say a little more than that. We could not be wise before the event, but perhaps we can be a little wiser after it. Perhaps the event itself has enlightened us, so that we can now see something of the reason why things should stand thus. . . . If it had been so that each could find God in his own way, then each would be finding Him without at the same time finding his brother. If the love of God were revealed to each in a different place, then we could all love Him without meeting one another in love. If the various tribes of mankind could find salvation in different names, then the human race would forever be divided. . . .

Was it not then a gracious ordering of things on God's part that there should be salvation in one Name only; that we can meet with Him only by meeting with one another; by betaking ourselves all together to one place—to one "green hill far away, without the city wall"; by encountering there a single figure to whom we all together give our whole allegiance; by listening to the self-same story; by reading in the same Holy Book; by being baptized in the same Name into the same fellowship; by eating and drinking at the same Holy Table—"all made to drink [as St. Paul says] into one Spirit"; so that [as he also says] "there is no difference between the Jew and the Greek; for the same Lord over all is rich unto all them that call upon him"; and Jew and Greek, Barbarian, Scythian, bondman, and freeman are all one in Him? . . . We understand a little more of what St. Paul had in mind, and can enter more deeply into his burning zeal for the propagation of a gospel which should transcend all differences of race and tongue and tribe and nation—with "one body, and one Spirit . . . , one Lord, one faith, one baptism, one God and Father of all, who is above all, and through all, and in you all."[19]

❖

## CHAPTER 22

# THE CHRISTIAN HOPE

God summons the Church of Jesus Christ today to speak plainly about hope. Jesus Christ is our hope. In all humility and boldness we are bound to tell the good news of the hope given to us in him.

The hope of which we speak is something different from what men usually mean when they speak of hope. In common speech "hope" means a strong desire for something which may be possible but is not certain. What is spoken of here is something that we wait for expectantly yet patiently, because we know it can never disappoint us.

We have this confidence because our hope is based upon what we know of God, and because we know of him through what He has done. Our hope is not the projection of our desires upon an unknown future, but the product in us of God's acts in history and above all, of his act in raising Jesus Christ from the dead. That mighty event is faith's assurance that Christ has overcome the world and all the powers of evil, sin, and death; it is the beginning of a new life in the power of the Spirit; it is a guarantee of God's promise that in his good time his victory will be manifest to all, his Kingdom come in glory, and he himself be known everywhere as King. It therefore begets a living hope, an ardent longing for that glorious consummation, and an eager expectation of its coming.

"Christ: The Hope of the World," report
of the Advisory Commission on the main theme
of the Second Assembly of the World Council of Churches
(1954), in *The Christian Hope and the Task of the Church*

For God alone my soul waits in silence,
    for my hope is from him.
He alone is my rock and my salvation,
    my fortress; I shall not be shaken.

Psalm 62:5–6

. . . Christ in you, the hope of glory.

Colossians 1:27

Christian faith is very realistic about the human situation. It knows both the fragility of life and the limits of life. It is futile to vest one's final hopes in wealth (Proverbs 11:28; Psalm 49:6–12; 52:7; Job 31:24); in houses (Judges 18:7, 10, 27; Job 18:14; Isaiah 32:17, 18); in horses (Isaiah 30:16); in princes (Psalm 146:3); in empires and armies (Isaiah 31:1–3; 2 Kings 18:19–24); or even in the Temple of Zion (Jeremiah 7:1–7). Far stronger than all these is the hope from God that enables those who believe to wait silently for him.[1]

This modesty concerning the possibilities of human life stands in opposition to the optimism of modern culture.

> The modern world, for very good reasons, does not have a vernacular of fate. Cultures that live by the values of self-realization and self-masteries are not especially good at dying, at submitting to those experiences where freedom ends and biological fate begins. Why should they be? Their strong side is Promethean ambition: the defiance and transcendence of fate, material and social limits. Their weak side is submitting to the inevitable.[2]

The modern secular city seems to offer a solution to all human problems with its achievements in speed of transportation, in antibiotic medicines, in computers with vast stores of information, in political processes and programs, in human comforts such as indoor plumbing, heat, and air conditioning.[3] Yet no solution to any basic human problem has yet been found that enables human beings to overcome the limits either of life or of human sin.

When Pilgrim and Faithful arrived at Vanity Fair (Secular City) they had "to learn that the one and only true heaven" was not the secular city.[4] Nor is this the first time in human history that the limits of human achievements have had to be acknowledged. As a young man Augustine joined in the optimism of the age of Theodosius, singing that "the whole world has become a choir praising our Christ"; but as an old man witnessing the fall of Rome to the barbarians from the north and to corruption from within, he wrote one of the great books of human history, *The City of God,* to say that Rome was not eternal, that the only abiding security is God.

The Bible, over against the realism with which it accepts the consequences of human sin and the limitations of created existence, is always a book of hope. Within the Bible there are reasons for despair, if the life of Jeremiah, or the crucifixion of Jesus Christ, or the foibles of the New Testament church are isolated from the biblical context. Yet through the Bible from the assertion in Genesis that God looked at the world and found it to be very good to the great vision of the new heaven and the new earth with which scripture concludes there is this solid base of hope.

The Second Assembly of the World Council of Churches, meeting in Evanston, Illinois, in 1954 had as its theme "Christ—the Hope of the World." The basic document for the assembly was prepared by a remarkable committee of theologians including Emil Brunner, Karl Barth, John Baillie, Robert L. Calhoun, C. H. Dodd, T. S. Eliot, Hendrik Kraemer, Lesslie Newbigin, and Reinhold Niebuhr. It begins by making clear that the hope of which they spoke was "no mere existence or reaffirmation of our desires." Christian hope begins with the crucifixion of Jesus Christ and God's raising him from the dead.

> When we stand at that place where the Son of God died for our sins, all our human desires are judged by Him. We are stripped naked of all our claims and pretensions and clothed afresh with His mercy. We are dead and made alive again. In the words of the apostle, we are begotten again to a living hope. This act of God himself is the beginning of our hope that the Creator and Lord of all has come forth in wrath and loving kindness to shut up every false way, and to bring us face to face with himself, the living Lord. He, by his own act, has put us in the place where we must hope and can hope only in him.[5]

Neither is Christian hope an extension of human desires, nor is it based on human achievements. Christian hope is built on convictions about God's acts in creation and in redemption. The Christian hope is the conclusion of all that has gone before in this book. For what then can we hope?

## What Can We Hope for in History?

The hopes for individual human life have already been discussed in the chapter on sanctification. The possibilities of life are determined by our creation as human beings in the image of God. As created beings we are limited by time, space, energy, and intelligence; and finally life is cut off by death. There are no promises in the Bible that these limitations of life will ever be overcome or that they should be. The real achievements of human life are within these parameters of created beings, and here there is the promise that God's grace is sufficient in all things (2 Corinthians 12:9). The promise is that all who are in Christ are a new creation (2 Corinthians 5:17). Jesus commanded his disciples to be perfect as their Father in heaven is perfect (Matthew 5:48). The possibilities for human goodness, for increasing the breadth and depth of human life, for the serenity and poise of faith are indeterminate. Yet there is always a warning for those who believe they are already righteous and who feel no need to live by the mercy and forgiveness of God.

The possibilities of achievement in human history have been the concern of contemporary people. Those who have experienced remarkable achievements in human society, whether they are the ancient Romans or the contemporary Americans, find it difficult to acknowledge the limits of historical achievements. Yet the twentieth century has known catastrophic wars, economic disasters, and genocide or mass murder.

The theologians who prepared for the Second World Council Assembly were aware of the optimism and despair of human society in 1954 and addressed them both.

> Because God is the Lord of history, Christians must reject all doctrines of automatic progress or of fated decline. Man's hope is not in any process or achievement of history. It is in God. There can be no identification of any human act or institution with God and His righteousness. Yet we have been given the assurance that God's grace works in and through and all about us, that he grants us the gift of sharing in his Kingdom even now, and that continually repentant and continually forgiven, we can go forward in hope of the consummation of all things in Christ.[6]

The report goes on to warn against a double temptation: the temptation on the one hand to expect too much in terms of human achievement and the temptation on the other hand to expect too little.

> On the one hand [the believer] is tempted to despair of this world and to fix his whole attention on that which is to come. He may forget that God keeps him in this world precisely as a minister of its reconciliation to Himself. He may be so daunted by the apparently unconquered power of evil that he loses all faith in the possibility that God who created and sustains the world can also make his power known in it. In his longing for the heavenly city with all of its blessedness he may pass by his fellow-man, fallen among thieves, and leave him by the roadside.
>
> On the other hand the believer is tempted in the opposite way. Because he has been brought out of darkness into light and made a sharer here and now in Christ's risen power, he may forget that what is given here is still only a foretaste. He may so confine his attention to the possibilities of this present world as to forget that the whole world lies under judgment. He may confuse man's achievements with God's kingdom and so lose the only true standard of judgment upon human deeds. He may forget the true dimension of man's existence as a child of God created and redeemed for eternal life and by seeking the end of human life within earthly history make man the mere instrument of an earthly plan, and so dehumanize him.[7]

The German sociologist Max Weber observed that John Calvin rejected the vocation of the monk in the monastery and called upon every Christian to live as a monk in the world.[8] This understanding of the Christian life, Weber believed, gave to the Calvinists the energy to shape history and to determine mightily the future. The image that Weber evokes, which in many ways fits Calvin, goes back to the New Testament, where Jesus warned his disciples to build up treasures in heaven, where Paul reminded the Philippians that their true citizenship was in heaven, and where the writer of the first epistle of Peter urged his readers to live in the world as aliens. The theme of the Christian as resident alien continued in the *Letter to Diognetus* and in particular in the writings of Augustine. This particular vision of the Christian life was given classic expression in the great paragraphs on peace in Augustine's *City of God:*

> The families which do not live by faith seek their peace in the earthly advantages of this life; while the families which live by faith look for those eternal blessings which are promised, and use as pilgrims such advantages of time and of earth as do not fascinate and divert them from God, but rather aid them to endure with greater ease, and to keep down the number of those burdens of the corruptible body which weigh upon the soul. Thus the things necessary for this mortal life are used by both kinds of men and families alike, but each has its own peculiar and widely different aim in using them.
>
> The earthly city, which does not live by faith, seeks an earthly peace, and the end it proposes, in the well-ordered concord of civic obedience and rule, is the combination of men's wills to attain the things which are helpful to this life. The heavenly city, or rather the part of it which sojourns on earth and lives by faith, makes use of this peace only because it must, until this mortal condition which necessitates it shall pass away. Consequently, so long as it lives like a captive and a stranger in the earthly city, though it has already received the promise of redemption, and the gift of the Spirit as the earnest of it, it makes no scruple to obey the laws of the earthly city, whereby the things necessary for the maintenance of this mortal life are administered; and thus, as this life is common to both cities, so there is a harmony between them in regard to what belongs to it. . . .
>
> This heavenly city, then, while it sojourns on earth, calls citizens out of all nations, and gathers together a society of pilgrims of all languages, not scrupling about diversities in the manners, laws, and institutions whereby earthly peace is secured and maintained, but recognising that, however various these are, they all tend to one and the same end of earthly peace. It therefore is so far from rescinding and abolishing these diversities, that it even preserves and adopts them, so long only as no hindrance to the worship of the one supreme and true God is thus introduced.
>
> Even the heavenly city, therefore, while in its state of pilgrimage, avails itself of the peace of earth, and, so far as it can without injuring faith and godliness, desires and maintains a common agreement among men regarding

the acquisition of the necessaries of life, and makes this earthly peace bear upon the peace of heaven; for this alone can be truly called and esteemed the peace of the reasonable creatures, consisting as it does in the perfectly ordered and harmonious enjoyment of God and of one another in God. When we shall have reached that peace, this mortal life shall give place to one that is eternal, and our body shall be no more this animal body which by its corruption weighs down the soul, but a spiritual body feeling no want, and in all its members subjected to the will. In its pilgrim state the heavenly city possesses this peace by faith; and by this faith it lives righteously when it refers to the attainment of that peace every good action towards God and man; for the life of the city is a social life.[9]

The resident alien is a useful metaphor because on the one hand it does emphasize that the Christian is a resident in the world, and therefore responsible for the world, and on the other hand it insists that a human being's true destiny is not in this world and that the person's true citizenship is in heaven. In other words, this world is not the only world there is, nor is it the most important, as the secularists continually claim.[10]

The possibilities and limits of history were the specific theme of Reinhold Niebuhr's greatest work, *The Nature and Destiny of Man*. In this work Niebuhr emphasizes that human beings are created and therefore limited by time, space, intelligence and energy. They are also very unique creatures with a capacity for self-transcendence, which means that no human society ever fulfills all the possibilities of life and that human beings can always imagine something better. Therefore no society is final. The capacity for self-transcendence also involves freedom; and wherever there is freedom, there is sin. Niebuhr concluded that force will always be a factor in human relationships, both because human beings are creatures of impulse and instinct and therefore need to be restrained and because they have the capacity to transcend the self, a capacity that is corrupted by sin. There is no evidence that self-centeredness will be overcome. Hence the best that we can hope for in human affairs is a society in which centers of power are reduced and balanced against one another in such a way as to make a tolerable measure of justice possible. Although religion and human reason are resources for justice, they can also be corrupted by the power of the human spirit and made instruments of injustice.

The possibilities for good and for evil are alike indeterminate. Niebuhr refused to set any limits on the possibilities of good. God himself has set limits on the possibilities of evil, for evil is parasitic and has to live on the good. It cannot sustain itself; it is always in the end self-destructive. The purposes of human beings are also thwarted by God's providence as expressed in natural factors such as oceans, rivers, mountains, and the changing seasons, as well as human weaknesses and limitations. Yet new forms of evil appear on every new level of goodness.

Niebuhr's understanding of the possibilities of history has been called constructive realism, which proposes a middle course between skepticism as to truth and fanaticism, between despair and romantic utopianism, between the conviction that problems cannot be solved and the notion that if sufficient money, technical skill, and intelligence are brought to bear, then all problems are solvable.

Niebuhr's convictions about the possibilities of human history are based not simply on his understanding of the meaning of human existence but also on the way he puts together salvation as God's mercy toward us, justification by grace through faith, and salvation as God's power in us — sanctification. Indeterminate levels of sanctification are possible, but no human being, however sanctified, ever in human history is free from self-interest, which corrupts every level of sanctification.

Reinhold Niebuhr and John Calvin are at one with the writers of the report *Christ: The Hope of the World* in their insistence that the kingdom of God is transcendent and stands in judgment on every human enterprise and that no human achievement, whether in democracy, secular humanism, Marxism, or capitalism, is exempt from the judgment of God. This insistence on the transcendence of God is necessary not only in times of great evil but also in moments when good people are tempted to identify human achievements in society or in personal life with God's kingdom.

The answer to the question of what is possible in history on the basis of Reformed theology is, first, that the possibilities of good and evil cannot be fixed beforehand. They are in a real sense indeterminate, yet the possibilities of achievement in the future are of the same order as achievements in the past. As long as human beings are creatures of instinct and impulse with the power and the freedom of self-transcendence, and as long as God continues to deal with human beings as he has in the past, the possibilities of the future will include both good and evil. The possibilities for good are great and indeterminate, but there is no utopia.

# Eternal Life

The Christian hope must be affirmed over against the fact of death and in the light of the promise of eternal life. Death is the moment in every human life when human limitations are made most clear and when the finiteness of every human achievement is laid bare.

Death is part of the created order. All living things die. Death is so much a part of nature that some have described it in the idyllic language of natural occurrences.[11]

Death, as a part of the created order, belongs to the goodness of creation. The world God looked at and saw to be very good was a world in which death is a prevailing fact. Yet the New Testament describes death as the last enemy to be destroyed (1 Corinthians 15:26). Although death is a natural fact, Augustine well knew that it is never simply a natural fact for human beings.[12] Dying and having to die, Augustine noted, are two different experiences. Some have solved the problem by noting that death is a consequence of sin. Yet it is an obvious fact that death was in the world before there was sin. Once sin occurred, however, the human experience of death was forever changed. If death is not the consequence of sin, sin always issues in death and complicates the fact of dying. Moreover, death is the occasion of great sin, namely, the fear of death.

A Christian doctrine of death contains at least the following convictions: (1) Death is a part of the natural order and therefore is not in and of itself evil, though it may be the occasion of evil. (2) Death is a solemn reminder of our created existence and should be accepted in humility. As the final limit to earthly life, death is a declaration of the boundaries within which human existence is possible. (3) Death is never experienced by human beings as simply a natural fact. It can only be a natural fact for animals, who have no power of self-transcendence. (4) Death can be the occasion of great sin, as seen in the frantic efforts to overcome it or to fortify ourselves against it. (5) Death is the event in which, in the providence of God, persons of faith participate in bringing this episode of human existence to an end. In this sense Christian theology denies that death is simply a fate that has to be endured. Death is the critically important event, in which the person who dies brings his or her own existence to a conclusion. Karl Rahner has insisted that death is the occasion of the highest human freedom, when we make the final commitment of our lives.[13]

Death was perceived very differently by Augustine and by Calvin.[14] For Augustine death even for the Christian believer is a great anguish, for it involves the wrenching and the tearing when the soul separates from the body. Calvin, on the other hand, approached death, at least according to all the records, with the equanimity of one who was sure that death was no more than the passage from this particular existence to existence more immediately in the presence of God. Hence he carried on the affairs of his final days as though he was simply making preparation to go on a trip to France or to Germany.

Any faith or philosophy that deals adequately with human beings and that can command their enduring allegiance has to deal constructively with the fact of death. The Christian proclamation of the hope of eternal life came as a gospel to people in the Mediterranean world of the first several centuries.[15] In our own time communists have had public difficulty and embarrassment in dealing with the fact of death, as the embalmed bodies of their first leaders on public view in the Kremlin indicate. Ambassador Charles Bohlen, who represented our country in Russia in the 1930s, once commented that communism was doomed because it had no sufficient answer to the problem of death. Ambassador George Kennan also bears the same testimony:

> As an adequate and enduring personal philosophy, Marxism has many deficiencies; but the greatest of them is that it has, in contrast to Christianity, no answer to the phenomenon of death. This is why there is nothing more pathetic than a Marxist funeral; for to the Marxist, this formality celebrates nothing more than an inexplicable, unpreventable, and profoundly discouraging event in the human experience. Unable to give meaning to death, Marxism is unable to give meaning to life. This helplessness is the guarantee of its impermanence and ultimate failure of the personal philosophy and political ideology.[16]

The Christian hope has been faithfully proclaimed throughout the New Testament and in every age since over against the fact of death. This Christian hope is summarized in three sentences from Paul's letter to the Philippians. Paul declares: "Our citizenship is in heaven, and it is from there that we are expecting a Savior, the Lord Jesus Christ. He will transform the body of our humiliation that it may be conformed to the body of his glory, by the power that also enables him to make all things subject to himself" (Philippians 3:20–21). "For to me, living is Christ and dying is gain. If I am to live in the flesh, that means fruitful labor for me; and I do not know which I prefer. I am hard pressed between the two: my desire is to depart and be with Christ, for that is far better" (Philippians 1:21–23). The third statement that gives expression to the Christian hope in this letter is Paul's conviction "that at the name of Jesus every knee should bend, in heaven and on earth and under the earth, and every tongue should confess that Jesus Christ is Lord, to the glory of God the Father" (Philippians 2:10–11). In these statements Paul makes clear his conviction that at death we immediately depart to be with Christ, and yet there is something more: the coming of the Savior will change our lowly body to be like his glorious body, and finally the time will come when every tongue will confess that

Jesus Christ is Lord. These convictions run throughout the New Testament, though they are never put together in any single, coherent form.

The expression of the Christian hope today should begin with the recollection that eternal life has been an important part of the Christian witness from the very beginning. Eternal life, Walter Lowrie once wrote, is the core doctrine that brings all Christian doctrines into systematic coherence. "'This is the Christian faith, apart from which, without doubt, a man must perish everlastingly.' These words which sound astonishing and offensive when used as an introduction of the so-called Athanasian Creed do not seem unreasonable when applied to belief in eternal life."[17] Christianity simply does not make sense apart from the Christian hope. Only in recent years, when a secular society has undercut many of the general warrants for immortality, has the continuation of personal existence beyond death been doubted in the Christian church. Austin Farrer has astutely commented that apart from the doctrine of eternal life Christian faith does not make sense.[18]

The grounds for believing in human immortality are broader than Christian faith. Immortality has been argued on the basis of human desire and the impossibility of fulfilling the claims of human existence in this life, on the basis of the powers of the human spirit to overcome transitoriness somewhat in memory, in the power of self-transcendence, and on the basis empirical research especially related to death experiences. Belief in immortality is found in Greek philosophy and in the burial rites of Neanderthal human beings. In fact, the notion of immortality is one of the oldest and most general of human ideas. Within the Christian church the doctrine of eternal life is based on Christian belief about God, on the witness to the resurrection of Jesus Christ attested in scripture, and on the life of the Christian under the power of the Holy Spirit and under the lordship of the risen Christ.

The Christian hope has been expressed in the terminology of the resurrection of the body, eternal life and everlasting life. Theologians in recent years, particularly under the influence of Karl Barth, have avoided using the word "immortality" and have preferred to speak of the resurrection of the body. In a nontheistic context, immortality does have a meaning that is foreign to Christian faith, indicating a belief that there is a human soul that is self-sustaining and imperishable in and of itself. In the context of Christian faith, however, the distinction of immortality and the resurrection of the body is not so clearly drawn. The immortality about which Christian theologians have spoken is an immortality that comes as a gift from God and is sustained by the divine power. The resurrection is likewise the resurrection to eternal life. The resurrection of the body emphasizes the importance of the historical life that was expressed in and through the body and means that immortality is not a nullification of historical existence.

The resurrection of the body cannot be precisely defined; for here, as in all of these matters, we are speaking of that which is beyond our experience. The apostle Paul speaks about our dying a mortal body and being raised a spiritual body. By this he may mean that in human history the person has a physical body appropriate to the environment in which the life is lived. In the life beyond death there will be a body appropriate to that existence in and through which the human self can express itself.

An inconsistency seems to exist in the New Testament's insistence that at death we depart to be with Christ and that some do rest in their graves until final resurrection. Paul never gives a single coherent statement in which all of his affirmations about hope for the individual Christian come together. The Christian hope is that we do depart immediately to be with Christ. The Christian hope also contains the awareness that individual existence is never simply individual but can only be fulfilled in the total community. Furthermore, the significance of a human life is not exhausted by that life but is caught up in history. In this sense there has to be a final resurrection and a final fulfillment that includes not only the individual but the community of which the individual is a part and the consequences of an individual life.

Eternal life is never described in detail in the New Testament. Here the Christian theologian and believer have to speak by hope and by faith, not by sight. Yet on the basis of Christian faith, it is reasonable to make certain inferences about existence beyond death.

Eternal life is personal existence, an assumption throughout the New Testament and generally throughout the history of Christian theology until quite recent times. In more recent years some theologians have defined eternal life as living on in the memory of God or the significance of one's life being included in the kingdom of God.[19]

Eternal life on the basis of the New Testament hope fulfills human existence. Historical existence, human decisions, and the historical experiences that are embodied in the self are not annulled; neither are they simply judged. They are fulfilled by the power of God. Eternal life is obviously not life in the body. In heaven persons are not given in marriage, as Jesus put it (Mark 12:25). Yet the very meaningful events of human life that occur in the flesh, including the sexual life of human beings, can live on as they have been embodied in personal existence. Within human experience some insight may be found in the analogy of dreams. In the dream, events that have occurred in the body and in history are very real; yet a dream is in a real sense "outside" the body.[20]

God, who chose us before the foundation of the world, destined us to be his children. The Nicene Creed declares: "I look for the resurrection of the dead, and the life of the world to come." This is the Christian witness which the church has made in the New Testament and has continued to make in good times and bad up to the present day. William Temple put the dilemma for those who would deny this witness in this way:

> For man's moral and spiritual life is in this world a baffled and thwarted enterprise; and the scene of our endeavor is slowly becoming uninhabitable, so that even though men labor for a remote posterity, yet if this life only is permitted to them, it will one day make no difference whether we have striven or not for noble causes and lofty ideals. An earth as cold as the moon will revolve about a dying sun. Duty and love will have lost their meaning.[21]

Heaven has been the traditional description of the human destiny of the saints. In scripture heaven is part of God's creation along with the earth. It stands under his lordship. Heaven will pass away with the earth. Yet heaven is also God's dwelling place, and to have heaven as one's destiny is life with God. Heaven as a human destiny is not a reward that is external to life itself. In popular mythology heaven is conceived as reward that has no relationship to the life lived. In Christian theology heaven is the reward of a Christian that is appropriate to the Christian life, just as becoming a mathematician is the reward for studying mathematics.

Human destiny, especially in the mythology of Dante and John Milton, is imprinted upon the Christian imagination as a duel between heaven and hell. As heaven is not a reward, so hell ought not to be conceived simply as a punishment. Hell is the fulfillment of human decisions. Hell may be conceived as God's ratification of the decisions that a human being has persisted in making for himself or herself. Someone has said that the only valid argument for hell is that if one wishes to go to hell there ought to be a hell for one to go to.[22]

Yet the Christian hope is that God is like the person who forgives seventy times seven, whose love never ceases to seek the lost, to restore the broken, and to heal the afflicted. Wisdom means that human beings should be modest in talking about either heaven or hell—and certainly never as rewards that are external to the lives human beings live. Perhaps the best conclusion of this matter is to note that the New Testament is everywhere emphatic concerning the cruciality of human decisions and the significance of the lives which we live now. Our final destinies are in the hands of the God who experienced the pain of death in Jesus Christ and who raised Jesus Christ for our salvation. As Barth argued, we ought to be open to greater possibilities for all people than we now expect.

## The End of History

The Christian hope also has to do not simply with the death of an individual but with the end of history. Reinhold Niebuhr once observed that it makes all of the difference in the world whether the end of history is the finish of history or is its fulfillment.[23] Does all of human existence come to an end in the debris of a universe in ruins? Here again Christians have to be modest if we talk about that which is beyond our experience. In the New Testament Christian convictions about the end of history are summarized in three very important symbols: the judgment, the resurrection of the body, and the second coming of Christ.

Jesus' parable of the last judgment in Matthew 25 is one of the most dramatic passages in the New Testament.

> When the Son of Man comes in his glory, and all the angels with him, then he will sit on the throne of his glory. All the nations will be gathered before him, and he will separate people one from another as a shepherd separates the sheep from the goats, and he will put the sheep at his right hand and the goats at the left. Then the king will say to those at his right hand, "Come, you that are blessed by my Father, inherit the kingdom prepared for you from the foundation of the world; for I was hungry and you gave me food, I was thirsty and you gave me something to drink, I was a stranger and you welcomed me, I was naked and you gave me clothing, I was sick and you took care of me, I was in prison and you visited me." Then the righteous will answer him, "Lord, when was it that we saw you hungry and gave you food, or thirsty and gave you something to drink? . . ." And the king will answer them, "Truly I tell you, just as you did it to one of the least of these who are members of my family, you did it to me." Then he will say to those at his left hand, "You that are accursed, depart from me into the eternal fire prepared for the devil and his angels; for I was hungry and you gave me no food, I was thirsty and you gave me nothing to drink. . . ." Then they also will answer, "Lord, when was it that we saw you hungry or thirsty or a stranger or naked or sick or in prison, and did not take care of you?" Then he will answer them, "Truly I tell you, just as you did not do it to one of the least of these, you did not do it to me." And these will go away into eternal punishment, but the righteous into eternal life. (Matthew 25:31–46)

This passage creates a theological problem in the light of what has been said about justification by grace through faith and the forgiveness of sins. How can we be saved by the forgiveness of sins and also by giving a cup of cold water? The same problem is inherent in the teachings of Jesus, who on the one hand said, "Do not think that I have come to abolish the law or the prophets; I have come not to abolish but to fulfill. For truly I tell you, until heaven and earth pass away, not one letter, not one stroke of a letter, will pass from the law until all is accomplished" (Matthew 5:17–18). On the other hand, Jesus ate with publicans and sinners and brought them into the very presence of God. Indeed, he declared that he could not help the righteous. "Those who are well have no need of a physician, but those who are sick. . . . For I have come to call not the righteous but sinners" (Matthew 9:12–13). Reinhold Niebuhr points out that in the parable of the judgment the righteous did not know that they were righteous and the sinners did not know that they were sinners.

Niebuhr goes further to interpret this conflict between the parable of the last judgment and the doctrine of the forgiveness of sins in the light of God's ultimate judgment that we are all sinners and that in the presence of God we all have to be forgiven. The ultimate judgment does not nullify the significance of the proximate judgment that on the level of history the differences between sinners are very significant. The final judgment that we are all saved by grace does not wipe out the distinction between good and evil. In the final judgment we are all saved by grace for we all sin in our best deeds as well as our worst deeds. Yet this judgment does not nullify the differences between good people and bad and the significance in human history of the partial goods that can be achieved.

The final judgment, according to Niebuhr, highlights three important truths. The first is that history is judged by Jesus Christ. The Christ who is rejected in history is the final judge, and the love which was crucified on Calvary is the standard of the judgment. The second is that there is a relative distinction between good and evil in history. Even the best deeds are corrupted by self-centeredness, but there remains a need for a final judgment to distinguish between relative good and evil. The atonement did not efface the distinction between good and evil. "God cannot destroy evil except by taking it into and upon Himself."[24]

The third truth is to be found in "the locus at the 'end' of history."

> There is no achievement or partial realization in history, no fulfillment of meaning or achievement of virtue by which man can escape the final

judgment. The idea of a "last" judgment expresses Christianity's repudiation of all conceptions of history according to which history is its own redeemer and is able by its process of growth and development to emancipate a human being from the guilt and sin of his existence, and to free him from judgment.[25]

Moreover, judgment must come at the end of history because the full significance of events in history is never known at the time of their occurrence. Their significance is revealed in their consequences and therefore can be judged only at the conclusion of history.

The second symbol of the end is the resurrection of the body. This does not necessarily mean the transformation of an earthly body but may mean, as Paul says, the provision of a spiritual body (1 Corinthians 15:35–50). The resurrection of the body in Paul's writings also refers to a general resurrection at the end of history. There is no simple way to put these two ideas together: what happens at the moment of one's death and what happens at the general resurrection at the end of history. The great truth contained in the resurrection of the body is the affirmation of the significance of the life that is lived in history, the affirmation that this life expressed in and through the body is fulfilled and not annulled by death.

The third symbol is the second coming of Jesus Christ.

> To believe that the suffering Messiah will return at the end of history as a triumphant judge and redeemer is to express the faith that existence cannot ultimately defy its own norm. . . . The vindication of Christ and his triumphant return is therefore an expression of faith in the sufficiency of God's sovereignty over the world in history, and in the final supremacy of love over all the forces of self-love which defy, for the moment, the inclusive harmony of all things under the will of God.[26]

These symbols of the judgment and the resurrection, climaxing in the second coming of Christ, express the conviction that the Christian knows how history is going to end. A possible analogy would be sitting at a football game and knowing the final score—not how the game is going to be played or who is going to make the touchdown, but how the game will come out in the end. Francis Pickens Miller, a church leader and statesman in the political life of Virginia, was on General Dwight D. Eisenhower's staff at the conclusion of the Second World War. A young lieutenant under his command was talking with a Russian officer, who asked the American lieutenant, "Have you read Karl Marx?" The American lieutenant replied that he had. In response the Russian said, "Then you know how it is going to come out." As Francis Miller commented, it would have been wonderful indeed if the American had been able to say to the Russian, "Have you read the New Testament? Then you know how it is going to come out."

Paul Minear asks: Was the expectation of Christ's return central or peripheral to Christian faith? He answers:

> Provisionally we conclude that neither of these alternatives is entirely satisfactory as an appraisal of the views of the New Testament writers. This expectation was not by itself constitutive of Christian hope as a whole, but neither was it a marginal or accidental encumbrance on Christian life. The living Christ was himself constitutive of the hopes; expectation of his final, decisive victory was an important corollary of life in him. There were sufficient varieties of expectation to furnish freedom of thought and to invite grave abuses, but sufficient common ground and the knowledge of Christ to maintain "the unity of the spirit in the bond of peace."[27]

The coming of Christ at the end of history cannot be precisely defined. The New Testament is replete with vivid images, and the history of the church shows the damage that has been done when these images have been taken too literally as well as when they have been explained away. The images of Christ coming on the clouds of heaven with a trumpet to slay the dragon are impressive, but they cannot be taken literally. The New Testament, as a matter of fact, never refers to the second coming. Christ comes in many ways. The best that we can do is to affirm that human history will not come to a conclusion either with a whimper or with a bang, nor will it come to a conclusion simply by some human act of destruction. Human history will come to a conclusion by the will and the intention of God. The important theological truth is the conviction that at the end of history the Christ who is crucified in history stands as its triumphant Lord and judge.

## A New Heaven and a New Earth

The writer of Isaiah 65 pictures the end of human history and of the earth in the dramatic language of a new heaven and a new earth.

For I am about to create new heavens
    and a new earth;
the former things shall not be remembered
    or come to mind.
But be glad and rejoice forever
    in what I am creating;
for I am about to create Jerusalem as a joy,
    and its people as a delight. . . .

The wolf and the lamb shall feed together,
  the lion shall eat straw like the ox;
  but the serpent—its food shall be dust!
They shall not hurt or destroy
  on all my holy mountain,
      says the LORD.

Isaiah 65:17–18, 25

These prophecies anticipated a future in history, but it is a future that God brings about. The writer of this passage did not know how this good society would be achieved, but on the basis of what the prophet knew about God, he dared to envision a new heaven and a new earth. The same vision is carried over to the New Testament in Paul's confession of the time to come when every knee would bow and every tongue confess that Jesus Christ is Lord (Philippians 2:9–11).

The New Testament concludes with the triumphant vision of Revelation:

Then I saw a new heaven and a new earth; for the first heaven and the first earth had passed away, and the sea was no more. And I saw the holy city, the new Jerusalem, coming down out of heaven from God, prepared as a bride adorned for her husband. And I heard a loud voice from the throne saying,
  "See, the home of God is among mortals.
  He will dwell with them as their God;
  they will be his people,
  and God himself will be with them;
  he will wipe every tear from their eyes.
  Death will be no more;
  mourning and crying and pain will be no more,
  for the first things have passed away."

Revelation 21:1–4

These passages of scripture do not tell us how the world will end, but they tell us the theological significance of that end.     The Christian hope for the world has been expressed with admirable insight and soberness by the confession of faith (1967) of the Congregational Church in England and Wales.

(1) *Though God's purpose for a universe is mysterious* . . . God's purpose for the physical universe is for the most part hidden from us in mystery. We do not suppose that its only purpose is the support and discipline which it provides to the bodies and minds of human beings during their lifetime on earth. We are certain that God's purpose will be worthy of his own majesty and consistent with the dignity which already appears in the splendor of the universe. How the universe is related to God's final and everlasting kingdom lies beyond our present possibilities of understanding. . . .

(5) *Creation glorified.* We look forward to acts of God which bring final transformation to human life and admit human beings to share in his own eternal joy and felicity. The unimaginable glory of the everlasting God is the destiny for which we have been made. Cleansed from sin we shall see God in Christ Jesus in open splendor, and he will make us like himself. We do not know in what universal framework our lives will be set nor how in that framework God's other purposes for his created universe will be fulfilled. We only know that God is the source, the guide, and the goal of all that is. To him be glory forever.[28]

The Christian doctrine of the end is simply the affirmation that the God who created the world and the God who redeems his people will bring his creation and his people to fulfillment and to judgment.

God reigns. This is the Christian hope. It is the persistent theme of scripture, from the creation of the world (Genesis 1) to the new heaven and the new earth (Revelation 20:1–4). The psalmists and the prophets proclaimed the reign of God in creation and in history. Jesus Christ embodied the reign in his person and life (Mark 1:14–15).

The kingdom is present and future. It is present now to the eyes of faith, preeminently in Jesus Christ, in individuals who live in loyalty to God, and in human history. It is present in creation and in the structures of the created order, so that sin cannot survive on its own and always self-destructs.

The reign of God is also future. It is an order of existence that moves through human history and is not contained in it but is concluded beyond it in the new heaven and the new earth. God has exalted Jesus, that at his name "every knee should bow . . . to the glory of God the Father" (Philippians 2:10).

God's reign is the final security. "The world passes away, and the lust of it; but he who does the will of God abides for ever" (1 John 2:17). There is the assurance, "We are God's children now; it does not yet appear what we shall be, but we know that when he appears we shall be like him, for we shall see him as he is" (1 John 3:2–3).

The God who created the world became incarnate in Jesus Christ. The heavenly king and the heavenly father are one. This God raised Jesus Christ from the dead. Believing this, the writer of the letter to the Ephesians concluded, "Now to him who by the power at work within us is able to do far more abundantly than all that we ask or think, to him be glory in the church and in Christ Jesus to all generations, for ever and ever. Amen" (Ephesians 3:20–21).

# EPILOGUE

Reformed theology, especially in its Calvinist origins, was simple, direct, and without pretension. It was realistic in its rejection of sophistry and in its abhorrence of illusion. Reformed theology in its original form may be rejected, but it is not easily misunderstood. In addition, it faces the hard realities of life, even if it has no easy solution, as in the case of "damnation."

Almost fifty years ago Robert L. Calhoun defined the summons of Christian faith in "two great moral principles that appear again and again in Jesus' teaching and practice," namely, intelligence and integrity on the one hand and a life of faith, hope, and love toward God on the other.

> The first is a demand for intelligence and integrity: not simply shrewdness nor technical competence nor rule-of-thumb honesty (though all these have their places) but a fundamental readiness in all situations to see and acknowledge what is so. The temptation stories, the Sermon on the Mount, the sayings that deal with cup and platter, unwhitened graves, ceremonial cleanliness, the Sabbath day, all reflect, in one way or another, Jesus' insistence on truthfulness and realism in the presence of an objective order that men disregard at their peril. It should not be necessary at this late day to insist that the moral and religious teaching of Jesus is not that of a light-hearted visionary but that of one who insists at every step that realities shall be squarely faced. Intellectual and moral integrity, clear eyes and candid minds, are required of all who seek to follow his lead. In a time like ours, it seems not too much to say, these things are prime necessities not merely for would-be Christians but for all men who have to share in the job of cleaning up wreckage and rebuilding a badly damaged world. One cannot work hopefully at that task without recognition of inexorable order—natural and moral order—maintained by the power of God.
>
> An equally essential factor in this moral summons is the demand that men live by faith, hope, and love toward God and their fellows. More concretely,

this is a call for unstinting generosity in thought and action, for readiness to give more than one expects to get, for refusal to see either God or man solely within the bounds of legal stringency. This is not a contradiction of either the realistic temper or the recognition of moral order. As regards every fellow man it is a well-warranted insistence that the complexity and incompleteness of his behavior at any particular moment be given full weight in our dealings with him. As regards oneself it is a reminder that callous or cruel action reacts promptly upon one's own character, and that generosity and forgiveness do likewise, so that in very truth life is measured to us with the measures we ourselves use. As regards God the demand exacts from us recognition that if he is inexorably just, his very justice is creative and gracious. He who is sovereign is Father, in whose utmost rigor there can be promise of new gifts.

Our gospel, then, begins and ends with imperatives that are grounded in the nature of man and the presence of God. It centers in the revelation of God in human history, especially in Jesus Christ crucified and the community of grace that widens around him. The God who has given himself and his Son thus freely has not yet failed those who trust him. He will not fail us in the hard years ahead![1]

These words are alike a summary and a description of Reformed theology. E. L. Mascall once described certain modern theologies as both sophisticated and naïve—sophisticated in that only a highly trained intellect could devise them, but naïve in that no "ordinary person . . . could think Christianity was worth practicing if he thought this position to be true."[2]

Reformed theology at its best has been neither sophisticated nor naïve but realistic about the world, about human existence, about what it is convinced is God's salvation of his people, the Christian gospel.

"If you confess with your lips that Jesus is Lord and believe in your heart that God raised him from the dead, you will be saved. . . . For there is no distinction between Jew and Greek; the same Lord is Lord of all and is generous to all who call on him" (Romans 10:9, 12).

---
❖
---

# NOTES

## Preface

1. Barth's theology was an energizing factor in responding to the crisis of "German Christianity" and to the development of the ecumenical movement during the period 1930–1960. The sales of his books, especially in English, indicate an enduring influence today in a secular culture. Charles Hodge's *Systematic Theology*, which modified seventeenth-century theology with the warmth of the revivals, was very influential with preachers and shaped the life of congregations probably on a greater scale than any other theology that has been written in America. See Mark Noll, ed., *Charles Hodge: The Way of Life* (Mahwah, N.J.: Paulist Press, 1987). Hugh Ross Mackintosh (1870–1936) is another example of a Reformed theologian who wrote out of the life of the church and who influenced the church on the congregational level. Dutch Reformed theologians also served the church well. Reinhold Niebuhr may have been read and heard by more persons outside the church than any other theologian since the Reformation.

2. Andrew Greeley, *Religious Change in America* (Cambridge, Mass.: Harvard University Press, 1989); Richard Neuhaus, ed., *Unsecular America* (Grand Rapids: Wm. B. Eerdmans Publishing Co., 1986).

3. Jeffrey Stout, *Ethics After Babel* (Boston: Beacon Press, 1988), p. 168.

4. It is instructive to note that John Wesley "converted" more eighteenth- and nineteenth-century people to Christian faith than Schleiermacher, who was preeminently concerned to express the faith in relevant terms. The same is also true of Wesley's influence on social problems such as slavery, mental sickness, prisons, education, in addition to the modern missionary movement.

5. Jaroslav Pelikan, *The Growth of Medieval Theology (600–1300)* (Chicago: University of Chicago Press, 1978), p. 7.

6. John Calvin, *Reply to Sadolet*, in *Calvin: Theological Treatises*, ed. J. K. S. Reid, Library of Christian Classics (hereafter LCC), vol. XXII (Philadelphia: Westminster Press, 1954), p. 233. See also Calvin's preface to the commentary on Romans for his judgment on literary style. See also his commentary on

307

1 Corinthians 1:26ff. Note: Quotations from Calvin's *Institutes* in this book are from *Calvin: Institutes of the Christian Religion,* ed. John T. McNeill, trans. Ford Lewis Battles, LCC, vols. XX–XXI (Philadelphia: Westminster Press, 1960).

7. Karl Barth, *Church Dogmatics,* ed. G. W. Bromiley and T. F. Torrance (Edinburgh: T. & T. Clark, 1936–62), vol. I/1, pp. 248ff.

8. Reinhold Niebuhr, *Faith and History: A Comparison of Christian and Modern Views of History* (New York: Charles Scribner's Sons, 1949), chap. 10.

9. James Turner, *Without God, Without Creed* (Baltimore, Md.: Johns Hopkins University Press, 1985), pp. 266–269.

10. Discussions with Stacy Johnson have been very helpful on this point. See also H. Richard Niebuhr, *The Meaning of Revelation* (New York: Macmillan Co., 1941), chap. 1; Thomas Kuhn, *The Structure of Scientific Revolutions,* 2nd ed. (Chicago: University of Chicago Press, 1970); Richard Bernstein, *Beyond Objectivism and Relativism: Science, Hermeneutics, and Praxis* (Philadelphia: University of Pennsylvania Press, 1983).

11. See chapter 1 for a definition of the Enlightenment.

## Chapter 1
## Christian Theology in Reformed Perspective

1. Anselm of Canterbury, for example, wrote his *Proslogion* as a prayer. See Anselm, *Basic Writings,* trans. S. N. Deane, with an introduction by Charles Hartshorne; 2nd ed. (La Salle, Ill.: Open Court Publishing Co., 1962), pp. 47–80.

2. Bruce Metzger, *The Canon of the New Testament: Its Origin, Development, and Significance* (New York: Oxford University Press, 1987), pp. 282–288. See also Brevard Childs, *Biblical Theology in Crisis* (Philadelphia: Westminster Press, 1970), p. 105.

3. See John H. Leith, ed., *Creeds of the Churches: A Reader in Christian Doctrine from the Bible to the Present,* 3rd ed. (Atlanta: John Knox Press, 1982), pp. 230–281.

4. Karl Barth was aware of this necessity to write theology from one's own situation: "Let us admit at once that when we speak of the Evangelical Church and therefore of the Church generally in this presentation of dogmatics we mean the Evangelical Reformed Church, in conformity with our own Church position, and the fathers and the dogma to which we owe loyalty in obedience to the Word of God until we are led by that same Word to something better. . . . We cannot practise indifferently Anglican, Lutheran or Reformed dogmatics, but only Reformed dogmatics. For us, therefore, Church dogmatics is necessarily Reformed dogmatics." *Church Dogmatics,* I/2, pp. 830–831.

5. James C. Livingstone, *Modern Christian Thought from the Enlightenment to Vatican II* (New York: Macmillan Co., 1971), chaps. 1–3.

6. See John E. Smith, *The Spirit of American Philosophy* (New York: Oxford University Press, 1963).

7. For ambiguity in Augustine's theology, see Reinhold Seeberg, *Textbook of the History of Doctrines* (Philadelphia: Lutheran Publication Society, 1905), vol. 1, pp. 367–368.

8. Calvin, *Institutes* 1.7.3. Calvin's dependence on Augustine's way of doing theology is enormous and freely acknowledged by Calvin in many places. See the Introduction to the Battles translation of the *Institutes*, section X. Luchesius Smits, *Saint Augustin dans l'oeuvre de Jean Calvin*, 2 vols. (Assen: Van Gorcum, 1958).

9. Charles N. Cochrane, *Christianity and Classical Culture: A Study of Thought and Action from Augustus to Augustine* (London: Oxford University Press, 1957), p. 417. See also Augustine, *Confessions* 3.4; *City of God* 9.17.

10. Augustine, *On the Profit of Believing* 31, trans. C. L. Cornish, *Nicene and Post-Nicene Fathers*, series 1, ed. Philip Schaff (1887; repr. Grand Rapids: Wm. B. Eerdmans Publishing Co.), vol. 3, p. 362. Cf. H. Richard Niebuhr, *Faith on Earth: An Inquiry Into the Structure of Human Faith* (New Haven, Conn.: Yale University Press, 1989).

11. Barth, *Church Dogmatics* III/3, pp. 230ff.

12. Calvin, *Institutes* 2.8.16–17.

13. Augustine, *On the Profit of Believing* 23.

14. Augustine, *On the Trinity* 5.3.7.

15. Augustine, *On the Profit of Believing* 22.

16. I have been unable to locate this statement from William Temple. John E. Smith has cogently argued for the importance of will in belief in *The Spirit of American Philosophy* (New York: Oxford University Press, 1963), pp. 69–79.

17. Anselm, *Basic Writings*, trans. Deane, p. 48. See the excellent discussion of Anselm and Augustine in John E. Smith, *The Analogy of Experience* (New York: Harper & Row, 1973), pp. 10ff.

18. Reinhold Niebuhr, *Faith and History: A Comparison of Christian and Modern Views of History* (New York: Charles Scribner's Sons, 1949), pp. 123ff.

Chapter 2
Faith and Doctrine

1. Geoffrey Wainwright, *Doxology* (New York: Oxford University Press, 1980), pp. 218–283.

2. John Wesley, Letter to Samuel Walker, September 3, 1756. In John Telford, ed., *The Letters of the Rev. John Wesley M.A.* (London: Epworth Press, 1931), vol. 3, p. 192.

3. Kenneth Scott Latourette, *A History of the Expansion of Christianity* (New York: Harper & Brothers, 1937–45).

4. Quoted by Steven Ozment, *The Age of Reform, 1250–1550: An Intellectual*

*and Religious History of Late Medieval and Reformation Europe* (New Haven, Conn.: Yale University Press, 1980), pp. 315–316.

5. Augustine, *City of God* 14.7.28.

6. Donald G. Tewksbury, *The Founding of American Colleges and Universities Before the Civil War* (New York: Teachers College, Columbia University, 1932), p. 323.

7. Edward Schillebeeckx, *Revelation and Theology,* trans. N. D. Smith (New York: Sheed & Ward, 1967–68), vol. 1, p. 95.

8. Karl Rahner, *Theological Investigations* (Baltimore: Helicon Press, 1961), vol. 1, pp. 66ff.

9. *The Third World Conference on Faith and Order,* ed. Oliver S. Tomkins (London: SCM Press, 1953), pp. 27–31, 249–252.

10. Albert Outler, *The Christian Tradition and the Unity We Seek* (New York: Oxford University Press, 1957), pp. 110–111.

11. H. E. W. Turner, *Pattern of Christian Truth* (London: A. R. Mowbray & Co., 1954), Lecture 3.

## Chapter 3
### The Human Situation, Mystery, and Revelation

1. Calvin, *Institutes* 1.1.1.

2. Daniel Bell, "The Return of the Sacred? The Argument on the Future of Religion," *British Journal of Sociology* 28, no. 4 (December 1977): 442, 443–444.

3. Langdon Gilkey, *Naming the Whirlwind: The Renewal of God-Language* (Indianapolis: Bobbs-Merrill Co., 1969), part 2, chaps. 2–4.

4. Robert Jastrow, *Until the Sun Dies* (New York: W. W. Norton & Co., 1977), chap. 1; idem, "Have Astronomers Found God?" *New York Times Magazine,* June 15, 1978.

5. S. W. Hawking, *A Brief History of Time: From the Big Bang to Black Holes* (New York: Bantam Books, 1988). On pp. 140–141 Hawking argues that if the universe is self-contained, there is no need for God, but on p. 174 he opens up the question again by asking why the universe goes to all the bother of existing.

6. Richard E. Leakey and Roger Lewin, *Origins: What New Discoveries Reveal About the Emergence of Our Species and Its Possible Future* (New York: E. P. Dutton & Co., 1977), p. 84.

7. *New York Times,* April 20, 1975, and February 18, 1979.

8. Theodosius Dobzhansky, *The Biology of Ultimate Concern* (New York: New American Library, 1967), pp. 4–5.

9. Barth, *Church Dogmatics* III/3, p. 122.

10. Gabriel Marcel, *Being and Having* (New York: Harper & Row, 1965), pp. 117–118; Milton Munitz, *The Mystery of Existence* (New York: Appleton-Century-Crofts, 1965), p. 8; Reinhold Niebuhr, *Discerning the Signs of the Times:*

*Sermons for Today and Tomorrow* (New York: Charles Scribner's Sons, 1946), pp. 152–173; Karl Rahner, *Foundations of Christian Faith: An Introduction to the Idea of Christianity* (New York: Seabury Press, 1978), pp. 57ff.; Barth, *Church Dogmatics* III/2, pp. 71–132; Peter Berger, *A Rumor of Angels: Modern Society and the Rediscovery of the Supernatural* (Garden City, N.Y.: Doubleday & Co., 1969).

11. William Hamilton, "A Secular Theology for a World Come of Age," *Theology Today* 18, no. 4 (1962): 435–459.

12. Marcel, *Being and Having,* pp. 117–118; Munitz, *Mystery of Existence,* pp. 14–32.

13. Munitz, *Mystery of Existence,* pp. 11–12.

14. Marcel, *Being and Having,* pp. 117–118.

15. Ibid.

16. Munitz, *Mystery of Existence,* p. 31.

17. Ibid., p. 262.

18. Rahner, *Foundations of Christian Faith,* pp. 57ff.

19. Gilkey, *Naming the Whirlwind,* p. 330.

20. Berger, *Rumor of Angels,* pp. 54–55.

21. Richard Rorty, *Philosophy and the Mirror of Nature* (Princeton, N.J.: Princeton University Press, 1979), pp. 365ff.

22. Robert Wuthnow, *Experimentation in American Religion: The New Mysticisms and Their Implications for the Churches* (Berkeley, Calif.: University of California Press, 1978), chaps. 1–2. See also Edmond C. Gruss, *Cults and the Occult* (Phillipsburg, N.J.: Presbyterian and Reformed Publishing Co., 1980), chaps. 9–10; and Marc Galanter, *Cults, Faith, Healing, and Coercion* (New York: Oxford University Press, 1989), chap. 7.

23. Barth, *Church Dogmatics* III/2, pp. 71ff., 78ff.

24. Hendrik Kraemer, *The Christian Message in a Non-Christian World* (New York: International Missionary Council, 1947), p. 142.

25. Cf. Wilfred Cantwell Smith, "Transcendence," *Harvard Divinity School Bulletin,* Fall 1988, pp. 10–15; Gilkey, *Naming the Whirlwind,* part 2, chaps. 2–3.

26. Avery Dulles, *Models of Revelation* (Garden City, N.Y.: Doubleday & Co., 1983), pp. 30–35. Cf. Wolfhart Pannenberg, *Systematic Theology,* vol. 1 (Grand Rapids: Wm. B. Eerdmans Publishing Co., 1991), pp. 189–257.

27. Robert L. Calhoun, *God and the Common Life* (New York: Charles Scribner's Sons, 1935; repr. Hamden, Conn.: Shoe String Press, 1954), pp. 172ff.

28. Kraemer, *The Christian Message in a Non-Christian World,* p. 69.

29. Augustine, *The Spirit and the Letter* 54.

30. Augustine, *Enchiridion* 7.20.

31. Thomas Aquinas, *Summa Theologiae* 2a-2ae, q. 1–7.

32. Martin Luther, *The Freedom of a Christian,* in *Selected Writings of Martin Luther,* ed. Theodore G. Tappert (Philadelphia: Fortress Press, 1967), pp. 21ff.

33. A. A. Hodge and B. B. Warfield "Inspiration," in Rev. J. Allanson Picton,

*New Theories and the Old Faith* (London: Williams & Norgate, 1870), pp. 69–103.

34. John Baillie and Hugh Martin, eds., *Revelation* (London: Faber & Faber, 1937), p. 53.

35. H. Richard Niebuhr, *The Meaning of Revelation* (New York: Macmillan Co., 1941), p. 109.

36. Ibid., pp. 170ff.; William Temple, *Nature, Man and God* (London: Macmillan & Co., 1934), p. 315.

37. John E. Smith, *The Analogy of Experience* (New York: Harper & Row, 1973), pp. 93ff.

38. Ibid., pp. 96ff.

39. Ibid., p. 94.

40. John Baillie, *The Idea of Revelation in Recent Thought* (New York: Columbia University Press, 1956), pp. 62ff.

41. Temple, essay on "Revelation," in *Revelation,* ed. Baillie and Martin, p. 108. For a critique of Temple's position, see Alan Richardson, *Christian Apologetics* (New York: Harper & Brothers, 1947), pp. 146–147.

42. Austin Farrer, *The Glass of Vision* (London: Dacre Press, 1948), chaps. 3–4.

43. William Abraham, *Divine Revelation and the Limits of Historical Criticism* (New York: Oxford University Press, 1982), p. 45.

44. Ibid.

45. Emil Brunner, *Revelation and Reason: The Christian Doctrine of Faith and Knowledge* (Philadelphia: Westminster Press, 1946), chaps. 6–8; Reinhold Niebuhr, *The Nature and Destiny of Man* (New York: Charles Scribner's Sons, 1964), vol. 1, chap. 5.

46. Calvin, *Institutes* 1.6.1.

47. Temple, *Nature, Man and God,* p. 306.

48. H. H. Farmer, *The World and God* (London: Nisbet & Co., 1942), pp. 85, 87.

49. Reinhold Niebuhr, *Nature and Destiny of Man,* vol. 1, chap. 5; Temple, *Nature, Man and God,* p. 306.

50. Sergius Bulgakov, "Essay on Revelation," in *Revelation,* ed. Baillie and Martin, pp. 125–126.

51. Hendrikus Berkhof, *Christian Faith: An Introduction to the Study of the Faith* (Grand Rapids: Wm. B. Eerdmans Publishing Co., 1980), pp. 108ff.

52. Ibid.

53. Ibid., pp. 60–63.

54. F. G. Downing, *Has Christianity a Revelation?* (London: SCM Press, 1964), p. 275.

55. Gustaf Aulén, in *Revelation,* ed. Baillie and Martin, pp. 275–276.

56. James Barr, *Old and New in Interpretation: A Study of the Two Testaments* (New York: Harper & Row, 1966), p. 92.

57. Rorty, *Philosophy and the Mirror of Nature,* pp. 357ff.

58. Gordon Kaufman, *Systematic Theology: A Historicist Perspective* (New York: Charles Scribner's Sons, 1969), p. 26.

59. Calhoun, *God and the Common Life,* p. 172.

60. See Rorty, *Philosophy and the Mirror of Nature,* pp. 357ff.

Chapter 4
The Doctrine of God

1. Some significant works of this century on the doctrine of God include Karl Barth, *The Doctrine of God,* vol. II/1–2 of *Church Dogmatics;* Donald G. Bloesch, *The Battle for the Trinity: The Debate Over Inclusive God-Language* (Ann Arbor, Mich.: Servant Publications, Vine Books, 1985); Emil Brunner, *Dogmatics,* vol. 1: *The Christian Doctrine of God* (Philadelphia: Westminster Press, 1950); John Macquarrie, *In Search of Deity: An Essay in Dialectical Theism* (New York: Crossroad, 1987); Eberhard Jüngel, *God as the Mystery of the World: On the Foundation of the Theology of the Crucified One in the Dispute Between Theism and Atheism* (Grand Rapids: Wm. B. Eerdmans Publishing Co., 1983); Jürgen Moltmann, *God in Creation: A New Theology of Creation and the Spirit of God* (San Francisco: Harper & Row, 1985); Wolfhart Pannenberg, *Systematic Theology,* vol. 1 of a projected 3 vols. (Grand Rapids: Wm. B. Eerdmans Publishing Co., 1991).

2. Daniel Bell, "The Return of the Sacred? The Argument on the Future of Religion," *British Journal of Sociology* 28, no. 4 (December 1977): 422, 443–444.

3. Austin M. Farrer, *The Freedom of the Will,* 2nd ed. (London: A. & C. Black, 1963), pp. 82–116, 309–315. Cf. Owen Gingerich, "Kepler's Anguish and Hawking's Query: Reflections on Natural Theology," in James I. McCord Memorial Lectures, Fall 1990, in *Reports from the Center,* no. 4 (Princeton, N.J.: Center of Theological Inquiry, 1991), pp. 38–55.

4. Barth, *Church Dogmatics* II/1, pp. 205–206.

5. Blaise Pascal, *Pensées,* trans. Martin Turnell (New York: Harper & Brothers, 1962), pp. 115 (no. 17) and 183 (no. 280).

6. Barth, *Church Dogmatics* II/1, p. 284. See John E. Smith, *The Analogy of Experience* (New York: Harper & Row, 1973), pp. 95–97, for an excellent discussion of what it means to say that God is personal.

7. See also Paul Tillich, *Systematic Theology,* 3 vols. (Chicago: University of Chicago Press, 1951–63), vol. 1, p. 245.

8. See Paul Tillich, *A History of Christian Thought* (New York: Simon & Schuster, 1968), pp. 112–113.

9. Tillich, *Systematic Theology,* vol. 1, p. 235; Barth, *Church Dogmatics* II/1, pp. 269–270.

10. Helmut Gollwitzer, *The Existence of God as Confessed by Faith* (Philadelphia: Westminster Press, 1965), p. 152.

11. Ibid., pp. 152–153.

12. Ibid., p. 153.

13. Ibid., p. 214.

14. Augustine, *On the Trinity,* trans. A. W. Hadden and W. G. T. Shedd, *Nicene and Post-Nicene Fathers,* series 1, vol. 3.

15. "Joint Statement of the Official Dialogue Between the Orthodox Church and the World Alliance of Reformed Churches, Klappel, Switzerland, March 9–15, 1992" (mimeographed). Cf. Thomas F. Torrance, *Trinitarian Perspectives: Toward a Doctrinal Agreement* (Edinburgh: T. & T. Clark, forthcoming in 1993).

16. G. L. Prestige, *God in Patristic Thought,* 2nd ed. (London: SPCK, 1952), p. 162.

17. Ibid., p. 174.

18. Barth, *Church Dogmatics* I/1, pp. 344, 408–414.

19. Karl Rahner, *Foundations of Christian Faith: An Introduction to the Idea of Christianity* (New York: Seabury Press, 1978), pp. 136–137.

20. Tertullian, *Treatise Against Praxeas* 7–9.

21. Augustine, *On the Trinity* 10.

22. Arthur C. McGill, *Suffering: A Test of Theological Method* (Philadelphia: Geneva Press, 1968), pp. 59ff.

23. Barth, *Church Dogmatics* I/1, p. 403.

24. Prestige, *God in Patristic Thought,* pp. 300–301.

25. McGill, *Suffering,* p. 66.

26. Augustine, *On the Trinity* 6.7–9.

27. This was especially true for Calvin in his sermons. See Richard Stauffer, *Dieu, la Création et la Providence dans la prédication de Calvin* (Bern: P. Lang, 1978).

28. See, for example, Barth's discussion of the problem of ordering the attributes in *Church Dogmatics* II/1, pp. 348–350.

29. Ibid. II/1, secs. 30–31.

30. Ibid., pp. 276–281.

31. Gustaf Aulén, *The Faith of the Christian Church* (Philadelphia: Muhlenberg Press, 1961), pp. 102–106.

32. Rudolf Otto, *The Idea of the Holy: The Non-Rational Factor in the Idea of the Divine and Its Relation to the Rational* (London and New York: Oxford University Press, 1923).

33. Barth, *Church Dogmatics* II/1, pp. 276–280.

34. Origen, *Contra Celsum,* trans. with introduction and notes by Henry Chadwick (London and New York: Cambridge University Press, 1953), 3.70, p. 175.

35. Barth, *Church Dogmatics* II/1, p. 522.

36. Brunner, *Christian Doctrine of God,* pp. 248ff.

37. Ibid., p. 254.

38. Ibid., pp. 266ff.

39. Aulén, *Faith of the Christian Church*, p. 128.

40. Tillich, *Systematic Theology*, vol. 1, pp. 277–278. See also Karl Heim, "Faith in Absolute Time and Absolute Space and Its Disruption by the Theory of Relativity," chap. 3 in idem, *The Transformation of the Scientific World View* (New York: Harper & Brothers, 1953); Ian G. Barbour, *Issues in Science and Religion* (Englewood Cliffs, N.J.: Prentice-Hall, 1966), pp. 297–298, 316, 455.

41. Brunner, *Christian Doctrine of God*, p. 23.

42. Aulén, *Faith of the Christian Church*, p. 149.

43. Brunner, *Christian Doctrine of God*, p. 267.

44. See, e.g., Jürgen Moltmann, *The Crucified God: The Cross of Christ as the Foundation and Criticism of Christian Theology* (London: SCM Press, 1974), and the work of the process theologians, such as Charles Hartshorne and John B. Cobb, Jr.

45. Prestige, *God in Patristic Thought*, p. 7.

46. Ibid.

47. Barth, *Church Dogmatics* II/1, p. 495.

48. Ibid., pp. 412–413.

49. For the influence of covenant idea on church and on American society, see Charles S. McCoy and J. Wayne Baker, *Fountainhead of Federalism* (Louisville, Ky.: Westminster/John Knox Press, 1991).

50. Thomas Aquinas, *Summa Theologiae* 1a, q. 3, 4.

51. John Dillenberger, *Protestant Thought and Natural Science* (Garden City, N.Y.: Doubleday & Co., 1960), pp. 115, 121.

52. Rudolf Bultmann, *Jesus Christ and Mythology* (New York: Charles Scribner's Sons, 1958), p. 68.

53. William Temple, *Nature, Man and God* (London: Macmillan & Co., 1934), pp. 283–284.

54. Barbour, *Issues*, pp. 446–447.

55. Wilder Penfield, *The Mystery of the Mind: A Critical Study of Consciousness and the Human Brain* (Princeton, N.J.: Princeton University Press, 1975), p. 77.

56. Barth, *Church Dogmatics* II/1, p. 200.

57. Ibid., IV/3.2, pp. 554ff.

58. Charles N. Cochrane, *Christianity and Classical Culture: A Study of Thought and Action from Augustus to Augustine* (London: Oxford University Press, 1957), p. 407.

59. Calvin, *Institutes* 1.1–6. See also Alvin Plantinga, "The Reformed Objection to Natural Theology," *Christian Scholar's Review* 11, no. 3 (1982), 187–198; a revised edition of that essay may be found in *Faith and Rationality: Reason and Belief in God*, ed. Alvin Plantinga and Nicholas Wolterstorff (Notre Dame, Ind.: University of Notre Dame Press, 1984), pp. 63–73. The nature of this immediacy is debated in theology. It seems to me that this knowledge is in some sense mediated. We could not know God without words, metaphors, and what the church calls

the means of grace, which qualify the immediacy of our knowledge. See Barth, *Church Dogmatics* III/2, sec. 46; see also Wayne Proudfoot, *Religious Experience* (Berkeley, Calif.: University of California Press, 1985), pp. 1–40.

60. Calvin, *Institutes* 1.3.

61. Anselm, *Proslogion,* in *A Scholastic Miscellany: Anselm to Ockham,* ed. and trans. Eugene R. Fairweather, LCC, vol. X (Philadelphia: Westminster Press, 1956), p. 75 (chap. 4).

62. Robert L. Calhoun, "Lectures on the History of Christian Doctrine," vol. 2, p. 278 (unpublished ms., 1948; private circulation).

63. See Karl Barth, who argues that Anselm is trying to show that faith in God has its own intelligibility and is inviting nonbelievers to come and stand where the believers stand.

64. Thomas Aquinas, *Summa Theologiae* 1a, q. 2.1–2, q. 3; *Summa Contra Gentiles* 42–44.

65. Thomas Aquinas, *Summa Theologiae* 1a, q. 2.3.

66. Calhoun, "Lectures," vol. 2, p. 306. See also idem, *God and the Common Life* (New York: Charles Scribner's Sons, 1935; repr. Hamden, Conn.: Shoe String Press, 1954), pp. 145ff.

67. Owen Gingerich, "Kepler's Anguish and Hawking's Query: Reflections on Natural Theology," James I. McCord Memorial Lectures, Fall 1990, in *Reports from the Center,* no. 4 (Princeton, N.J.: Center of Theological Inquiry, 1991), pp. 35–57.

68. Temple, *Nature, Man and God,* pp. 129–134.

69. Ibid., p. 262.

70. Gingerich, "Kepler's Anguish," p. 54. Remarkable is Gingerich's quote of Pierre Lecomte du Noüy: "Events which, even when we admit very numerous experiments, reactions, or shakings per second, need an infinitely longer time than the estimated duration of the earth in order to have one chance, on the average, to manifest themselves can, it would seem, be considered as impossible in the human sense. . . . To study the most interesting phenomena, namely Life and eventually Man, we are, therefore, forced to call on anti chance, as Eddington called it, a 'cheater' who systematically violates the laws of large numbers, the statistical laws which deny any individuality to the particles considered" (p. 41). Cited from Lecomte du Noüy, *Human Destiny* (New York: Longmans, Green & Co., 1947), pp. 35, 38. Cf. Fred Hoyle, "The Universe: Past and Present Reflections," *Engineering and Science* (November 1981).

71. A. E. Taylor, *The Faith of a Moralist,* Series II: Natural Theology and the Positive Religions (London: Macmillan & Co., 1930), vol. 2, p. 1; Bell, "The Return of the Sacred?" pp. 422, 443–444.

72. Arthur James Balfour, *Theism and Humanism* (New York: Hodder & Stoughton, 1915), p. 90.

73. Bell, "The Return of the Sacred?"

74. Immanuel Kant, *Critique of Pure Reason,* trans. Norman Kemp Smith (New York: St. Martin's Press, 1965), 2.2, pp. 384–484.

75. Richard Kroner, *How Do We Know God? An Introduction to the Philosophy of Religion* (New York: Harper & Brothers, 1943), lecture 5.

Chapter 5
Creation

1. Significant recent books on the doctrine of creation are Bernhard W. Anderson, *Creation Versus Chaos* (Philadelphia: Fortress Press, 1987); Georges Florovsky, *Creation and Redemption* (Belmont, Mass.: Nordland Publishing Co., 1976); Langdon Gilkey, *Maker of Heaven and Earth: A Study of the Christian Doctrine of Creation* (Garden City, N.Y.: Doubleday & Co., 1959); Karl Heim, *The World: Its Creation and Consummation* (Philadelphia: Muhlenburg Press, 1962); George Hendry, *Theology of Nature* (Philadelphia: Westminster Press, 1980); Stanley Jaki, *Cosmos and Creator* (Edinburgh: Scottish Academic Press, 1980); Jürgen Moltmann, *God in Creation* (San Francisco: Harper & Row, 1985); Roland M. Frye, ed., *Is God a Creationist?* (New York: Charles Scribner's Sons, 1983).

2. Barth, *Church Dogmatics* III/1, pp. 42, 81ff., 253.

3. C. J. Webb, *God and Personality* (London: George Allen & Unwin, 1918), p. 168.

4. Barth, *Church Dogmatics* III/1, pp. 3, 12.

5. Ibid., p. 28.

6. Calvin, *Institutes* 1.5.2, 1.5.6, 1.14.20; *Commentary on the Book of Psalms,* trans. James Anderson (Edinburgh: Calvin Translation Society, 1845), vol. 1, pp. 308f.; *Treatises Against the Anabaptists and Against the Libertines,* ed. and trans. Benjamin Wirt Farley (Grand Rapids: Baker Book House, 1982), pp. 242–245.

7. Fred Hoyle, "The Universe: Past and Present Reflections," *Engineering and Science* (November 1981), 8–12. Quoted by Owen Gingerich in "Kepler's Anguish and Hawking's Query: Reflections on Natural Theology," James I. McCord Memorial Lectures, Fall 1990, in *Reports from the Center,* no. 4 (Princeton, N.J.: Center of Theological Inquiry, 1991), p. 39.

8. Hendrikus Berkhof, *Christian Faith: An Introduction to the Study of the Faith* (Grand Rapids: Wm. B. Eerdmans Publishing Co., 1980), p. 152.

9. Leonard Hodgson, *For Faith and Freedom,* 2 vols. (Oxford: Basil Blackwell, 1956), vol. 1, p. 148.

10. Barth, *Church Dogmatics* III/1, pp. 30, 44.

11. Ibid., p. 321.

12. Justin, *The First Apology of Justin, the Martyr,* in *Early Christian Fathers,*

ed. Cyril C. Richardson, LCC, vol. I (Philadelphia: Westminster Press, 1953), pp. 242–289.

13. Theophilus of Antioch, *Ad Autolycum,* trans. Robert M. Grant (Oxford: Oxford University Press, 1970), 2.10, pp. 38–41.

14. Athanasius, *Defense of the Nicene Definition* 3.11.

15. Augustine, *Confessions* 1.1.

16. Hodgson, *For Faith and Freedom,* vol. 2, p. 159.

17. Ibid., vol. 2, pp. 155–156.

18. Stephen Jay Gould, *Hen's Teeth and Horse's Toes* (New York: W. W. Norton & Co., 1983), pp. 32–35.

19. Augustine, *City of God* 11.22, 12.9.

20. The debates about sexuality seem to reveal a hatred of sex by secular culture, which is uninhibited in its practice of sex. There are signs, I think, that a secular humanist culture may collapse for the same reason secular communist societies collapsed, an inability to give plausible answers to the deepest questions of life.

21. Barth, *Church Dogmatics* III/3, pp. 289ff.

22. Berkhof, *Christian Faith,* p. 170.

23. Augustine, *City of God* 11.22.

24. Ibid. 11.23.

25. Marcus Aurelius, *The Meditations of Marcus Aurelius,* trans. George Long, in *Great Books of the Western World,* ed. Robert M. Hutchins and M. Adler (Chicago: Encyclopaedia Britannica, 1952), vol. 12.

26. Augustine, *Confessions* 2.20.

27. Barth, *Church Dogmatics* III/1, p. 67.

28. Ibid., pp. 409–410.

29. Ibid., p. 19.

30. James M. Gustafson, *Ethics from a Theocentric Perspective,* vol. I: *Theology and Ethics* (Chicago: University of Chicago Press, 1981), pp. 90–91, 97–98, 108–111, 112–113.

31. Ibid., pp. 97ff.

32. Theodosius Dobzhansky, *The Biology of Ultimate Concern* (New York: New American Library, 1967), pp. 4–5.

33. Calvin, *Institutes* 1.1–5.

34. Paul Ramsey, *Fabricated Man: The Ethics of Genetic Control* (New Haven, Conn.: Yale University Press, 1970), pp. 121–160.

35. Andrew Greeley, "When Religions Cast Off Wonder, Hollywood Seized It," *New York Times,* Nov. 27, 1977, sec. 2, p. 1.

36. Otto Piper, *God in History* (New York: Macmillan Co., 1939), pp. 12–13.

37. Calvin, *Institutes* 1.14.21.

38. Ibid.

39. Ibid. 1.14.22.

40. Ibid. 3.10.

Chapter 6
Providence

1. Significant recent works on providence include Albert C. Outler, *Who Trusts in God* (New York: Oxford University Press, 1967); Benjamin Wirt Farley, *The Providence of God* (Grand Rapids: Baker Book House, 1988); Herbert Henry Farmer, *The World and God: A Study of Prayer, Providence and Miracle in Christian Experience* (London: Nisbet & Co., 1936); Austin Farrer, *Love Almighty and Ills Unlimited: An Essay on Providence and Evil* (London: William Collins Sons & Co., 1962); John Hick, *Evil and the God of Love,* 2nd ed. (San Francisco: Harper & Row, 1977); William Grosvenor Pollard, *Chance and Providence: God's Action in a World Governed by Scientific Law* (New York: Charles Scribner's Sons, 1958); Gordon Kaufman, *God the Problem* (Cambridge, Mass.: Harvard University Press, 1972).

2. Emil Brunner, *Dogmatics,* vol. 2: *The Christian Doctrine of Creation and Redemption* (Philadelphia: Westminster Press, 1952), p. 155.

3. Outler, *Who Trusts in God,* pp. 81–82.

4. Charles N. Cochrane, *Christianity and Classical Culture: A Study of Thought and Action from Augustus to Augustine* (London: Oxford University Press, 1957), pp. 456–516.

5. Ibid., p. 478; Augustine, *Exposition of Genesis According to the Letter* 2.17.35; *City of God* 5.1.

6. Herbert Butterfield, *Writings on Christianity and History,* ed. C. T. McIntire (New York: Oxford University Press, 1979), p. 8.

7. Bertolt Brecht, "Grande Chorale of Thanksgiving." Jacques Monod, a Nobel laureate in biology, has put the Christian in sharp perspective, "Man must at last wake out of his millenary dreams and discover his total solitude, his fundamental isolation" (*Chance and Necessity* [New York: Alfred A. Knopf, 1971], p. 160).

8. Barth, *Church Dogmatics* III/3, p. 15.

9. Ibid., p. 18.

10. See Brunner, *The Christian Doctrine of Creation,* p. 149; Otto Weber, *Foundations of Dogmatics* (Grand Rapids: Wm. B. Eerdmans Publishing Co., 1955), vol. 1, p. 505:

Creation and conservation, or creation and providence cannot be identified as one, although certainly the Creator is the Conserver and Ruler. The most illuminating reason for this is the simple fact that God's conserving and ruling activity, his providence, by no means takes place "out of nothingness," but conserves created existence as something already extant and active and thus presupposes it. Both Scholasticism and Orthodoxy were acutely aware of this. They attempted to respect it by distinguishing between God as the "first cause" and the "second causes" within created reality. Regardless of the way one proceeds terminologically, the distinction between creation and providence should be quite clearly obvious. Christian theology in general has never fallen prey to the temptation of assuming the Creator's omni-causality so that the reality of the creature's activity was severely restricted. Conversely, it has never assigned such importance to the creature's own causality that the effectiveness and reality of the Creator were made into nothing more than the initiative past. It has avoided both Pantheism and Deism. In doing so, however, it has confronted in the creature's own capacity to work effectively in the world one of the two great problems of the doc-trine of providence. The other great problem is raised by the fact of evil. How is God, in his preserving, accompanying, and ruling the creature (to use K. Barth's expression), to be seen in relationship to the evil which is also the evil in the creature? God's providence must cope not with something neutral, nor with something created good, but with the creature who is resisting God's will. The fact of sin makes our thinking about God's provi-dence fraught with profound tension. If faith states that God's will happens, then it cannot avoid the riddle that God's will does not in fact take place in our lives, and so it can then only speak of God's providence in the peti-tion which is confident of its own fulfillment, "Thy will be done."

11. See John H. Leith, *John Calvin's Doctrine of the Christian Life* (Louisville, Ky.: Westminster/John Knox Press, 1989), pp. 108–120.

12. Barth, *Church Dogmatics* III/3, p. 4.

13. Ibid., p. 28.

14. W. P. Stephens, *The Theology of Huldrych Zwingli* (Oxford: Clarendon Press, 1986), p. 96.

15. Ibid.

16. John Calvin, *Commentary on the Psalms,* Preface.

17. Calvin, *Institutes* 1.16.5, 7.

18. Ibid. 3.23.8; 1.17.9.

19. R. A. Markus, *Saeculum: History and Society in the Theology of St. Augustine* (London: Cambridge University Press, 1970), p. 87.

20. Calvin, *Institutes* 2.5.5–14.

21. Ibid. 1.17.6, 7.

22. See Richard Muller, *Post Reformation Reformed Dogmatics* (Grand Rapids: Baker Book House, 1987), vol. 1.

23. Barth, *Church Dogmatics* III/3, sec. 49, parts 1–3 (pp. 58–238).

24. Ibid. III/3, pp. 192ff.

25. Ibid., p. 201.

26. Ibid., pp. 204–226.

27. Ibid., p. 226.

28. Ibid., p. 227.

29. Ibid., pp. 230–231.

30. John Calvin, *Concerning the Eternal Predestination of God,* trans. J. K. S. Reid (London: James Clarke & Co., 1961), pp. 177–178.

31. Ibid., p. 176.

32. Calvin, *Institutes* 1.18.3.

33. Augustine, *City of God* 1.9–36.

34. This will be discussed further in chapter 14, "Sanctification."

35. Friedrich Schleiermacher, *On Religion: Speeches to Its Cultured Despisers,* trans. John Oman (New York: Harper & Brothers, 1958), p. 88.

36. Nathaniel Micklem, *Ultimate Questions* (Nashville: Abingdon Press, 1955), p. 57.

37. Nathan Söderblom, *The Living God: Basal Forms of Personal Religion* (Oxford: Oxford University Press, 1933).

38. Daniel Day Williams, *God's Grace and Man's Hope* (New York: Harper & Brothers, 1949), p. 53.

39. Barth, *Church Dogmatics* III/3, sec. 49, part 4 (pp. 239–288).

40. As found in Sherwood E. Wirt and Kersten Beckstrom, eds., *Living Quotations for Christians* (New York: Harper & Row, 1974), p. 92.

41. George A. Buttrick, *Prayer* (Nashville: Abingdon-Cokesbury Press, 1942), p. 93.

42. Calvin, *Institutes* 1.17.6.

## Chapter 7
## The Human Creature

1. Recent works in Christian anthropology include Emil Brunner, *Man in Revolt* (New York: Charles Scribner's Sons, 1939); Reinhold Niebuhr, *The Nature and Destiny of Man,* 2 vols. (New York: Charles Scribner's Sons, 1941–43); Wolfhart Pannenberg, *Anthropology in Theological Perspective* (Philadelphia: Westminster Press, 1985); Jürgen Moltmann, *Man: Christian Anthropology in the Conflicts of the Present* (Philadelphia: Fortress Press, 1974); Nikolai Berdyaev, *The Destiny of Man* (New York: Charles Scribner's Sons, 1937); John Macquarrie, *In Search of Humanity: A Theological and Philosophical Approach* (New York: Crossroad, 1983).

2. See page 293.

3. Claus Westermann, *Genesis 1–11: A Commentary,* trans. John J. Scullion (Minneapolis: Augsburg Publishing House, 1984), pp. 157, 158.

4. William Temple, *Nature, Man and God* (London: Macmillan & Co., 1934), pp. 219–221.

5. Augustine, *Confessions* (New York: Airmont Publishing Co., 1969), book 11.

6. See Temple, *Nature, Man and God,* chap. 9; Søren Kierkegaard, *The Concept of Dread,* trans. Walter Lowrie (Princeton, N.J.: Princeton University Press,

1944); idem, *Fear and Trembling,* trans. Walter Lowrie (Princeton, N.J.: Princeton University Press, 1941); Karl Jaspers, *Man in the Modern Age* (New York: AMS Press, 1978).

7. Augustine, *Confessions* 1.1; cf. Reinhold Niebuhr, *The Self and the Dramas of History* (New York: Charles Scribner's Sons, 1955).

8. Karl Barth, *Church Dogmatics* III/2, p. 176.

9. Reinhold Niebuhr, *Nature and Destiny of Man,* vol. 1, chap. 1.

10. Ibid., p. 270.

11. Ibid., pp. 288–289.

12. Lynn White, "The Historical Roots of Our Ecologic Crisis," *Science* 155 (March 10, 1967): 1203–1207.

13. Martin Luther, *Commentary on Genesis,* trans. Theodore Mueller (Grand Rapids: Zondervan Publishing House, 1958), commentary on Genesis 2; John Milton, *Paradise Lost: A Poem in 12 Books,* 7th ed. (London: Printed for J. Beecroft, 1770), book 9.

14. Gordon Kaufman, *Systematic Theology: A Historical Perspective* (New York: Charles Scribner's Sons, 1969), pp. 357–359.

15. Augustine, *City of God* (New York: Penguin Books, 1972), 14.28.

16. Peter Brown, *The Body and Society: Men, Women, and Sexual Renunciation in Early Christianity* (New York: Columbia University Press, 1988), esp. chap. 19.

17. Lewis Sherrill, *The Struggle of the Soul* (New York: Macmillan Co., 1952), chap. 2, pp. 23–47.

18. Arthur F. Smethurst, *Modern Science and Christian Beliefs* (London: James Nisbet & Co., 1955), pp. 146ff.

19. David Baltimore, "Can Genetic Science Backfire?" in *U.S. News and World Report,* March 28, 1983, pp. 52–53.

20. N. P. Williams, *The Ideas of the Fall and of Original Sin* (London: Longmans, Green & Co., 1927), pp. 513ff.

21. Reinhold Niebuhr at the end of his life raised questions about his use of the concept "original sin," as the secular human culture could not comprehend it; see *Man's Nature and His Communities* (New York: Charles Scribner's Sons, 1965), pp. 23–24.

22. T. S. Eliot, *Murder in the Cathedral* (New York: Harcourt, Brace & World, 1964), pp. 39–40.

23. Augustine, *City of God:* "If you try and find the efficient cause of this evil choice, there is none to be found. For nothing causes an evil will, since it is the evil will itself which causes the evil act" (p. 477). "The truth is that one should not try to find an efficient cause for a wrong choice. It is not a matter of efficiency but of deficiency; the evil will itself is not effective but defective" (12.7).

24. Kierkegaard, *Concept of Dread,* pp. 23–41.

25. Brunner, *Man in Revolt,* pp. 129–133.

26. John Hick, *Evil and the God of Love,* rev. ed. (San Francisco: Harper & Row, 1977), chap. 13.

27. Calvin, *Institutes* 2.1.4; Reinhold Niebuhr, *Nature and Destiny of Man,* vol. 1, chap. 7; Augustine, *City of God,* chap. 14.

28. Calvin, *Institutes* 2.1.2; Reinhold Niebuhr, *Nature and Destiny of Man,* vol. 1, pp. 186–187.

29. Niebuhr, *Nature and Destiny of Man,* vol. 1, pp. 186–203.

30. See Carlos Eire, *War Against the Idols* (Cambridge: Cambridge University Press, 1986); Edmond La Beaume Cherbonnier, *Hardness of Heart* (Garden City, N.Y.: Doubleday & Co., 1955).

31. Harvey Cox, *On Not Leaving It to the Snake* (New York: Macmillan Co., 1964), pp. xiii–xvii.

32. Barth, *Church Dogmatics* IV/2, p. 405.

33. Ibid. III/3.

34. Augustine, *City of God* 12.1–10.

35. Reinhold Niebuhr, *Nature and Destiny of Man,* vol. 2, chap. 9.

36. Augustine, *City of God:* "Therefore good may exist on its own, but evil cannot" (12.3).

37. Reinhold Niebuhr, *Nature and Destiny of Man,* chap. 8.

38. Søren Kierkegaard, *The Sickness Unto Death,* trans. Walter Lowrie (Princeton, N.J.: Princeton University Press, 1941), pp. 98, 107, 185.

39. Barth, *Church Dogmatics* IV/1, pp. 358ff.

40. Charles Hodge, *Systematic Theology,* 3 vols. (1872–73; repr. Grand Rapids: Wm. B. Eerdmans Publishing Co., 1960), vol. 2, p. 48.

41. Barth, *Church Dogmatics* III/4, p. 386.

42. Reinhold Niebuhr, *The Self and the Dramas of History,* chaps. 1–2.

43. Oscar Cullmann, *The Early Church: Studies in Early Christian History and Theology,* ed. and trans. A. J. B. Higgins (Philadelphia: Westminster Press, 1956), pp. 165ff. Cf. John A. T. Robinson, *The Body: A Study in Pauline Theology* (London: SCM Press, 1952).

44. Karl R. Popper and John C. Eccles, *The Self and Its Brain* (New York: Springer-Verlag, 1977), p. vii; see also Roger Penrose, *The Emperor's New Mind: Concerning Computers, Minds, and the Laws of Physics* (New York: Viking Penguin, 1991).

45. Wilder Penfield, *The Mystery of the Mind: A Critical Study of Consciousness and the Human Brain* (Princeton, N.J.: Princeton University Press, 1975), pp. 75–100.

46. Ibid.

47. Popper and Eccles, *The Self and Its Brain,* pp. 522–523.

48. John C. Eccles, *The Human Mystery* (New York: Springer-Verlag, 1979), pp. 235–236. See also Penrose, *The Emperor's New Mind.*

49. Eccles, *The Human Mystery,* p. 144.

50. J. N. D. Kelly, *Early Christian Doctrines,* rev. ed. (San Francisco: Harper & Row, 1978), pp. 345–346.

51. Westermann, *Genesis 1–11,* p. 220.

52. Ibid., p. 222.

53. John Calvin, *Corpus Reformatorum: Ioannis Calvini Opera Quae Supersunt Omnia* (Brunswick: C. A. Schwetschke et Filium, 1863–97), vol. 26, p. 297. *Sermons on Deuteronomy,* chap. 5.

54. Ibid., vol. 52, p. 164: *Commentary on I Thessalonians* 5:11; see also John H. Leith, *John Calvin's Doctrine of the Christian Life* (Louisville, Ky.: Westminster/John Knox Press, 1989), pp. 192–194.

55. Barth, *Church Dogmatics* IV/2, 285ff.

56. Westermann, *Genesis 1–11,* p. 157.

57. Barth, *Church Dogmatics* III/4, pp. 144–145.

58. Westermann, *Genesis 1–11,* p. 59.

59. Ibid.

60. Brown, *The Body and Society,* p. 424.

61. Ibid., pp. 432ff.

62. Reinhold Niebuhr, "Sex and Religion in The Kinsey Report," in *Union Seminary Quarterly Review* 9, no. 2, pp. 3–9.

63. John Milton expounded the position "that marriage is primarily companionship in a common endeavor. . . . The center of interest for the Puritan was, of course, religion" (Roland E. Bainton, *The Travail of Religious Liberty* [Philadelphia: Westminster Press, 1951], p. 192). See Roland Bainton, *What Christianity Says About Sex, Love, and Marriage* (New York: Association Press, 1957), pp. 91ff.; David G. Hunter, *Marriage in the Early Church* (Minneapolis: Fortress Press, 1992); and Rowan Greer, *Broken Lights and Mended Lives: Theology and Common Life in the Early Church* (University Park, Pa.: Pennsylvania State University Press, 1986).

64. Otto Piper, *The Christian Interpretation of Sex* (New York: Charles Scribner's Sons, 1941).

65. Richard B. Hays, "Relations Natural and Unnatural: A Response to John Boswell's Exegesis of Romans 1," in *Journal of Religious Ethics,* vol. 14, no. 1 (Spring 1986): 184–214. See also Karl Barth, *Church Dogmatics* IV/4, p. 166; and Helmut Thielicke, *The Ethics of Sex* (New York: Harper & Row, 1964), chap. 4, sec. D.

66. The Reformed–Roman Catholic Consultation (1976–1979) addressed the question of abortion. The following paragraphs are from the Roman Catholic response to "The Statement on Abortion," in *Ethics and the Search for Christian Unity* (Washington: United States Catholic Conference, 1981), p. 20:

The Catholic tradition would consider these mitigating circumstances but not sufficient to justify abortion. Among the more common assessments as to when the fetus possesses personhood might be included the following:

1) fertilization—the moment of the joining of the sperm and ovum to create a unique zygote with its own genetic code; 2) implantation—5–8 days after fertilization when the fetus implants itself in the uterine wall; 3) neo-cortex—at approximately 5 weeks when the neo-cortex, indispensable for human activity, begins to appear and develop; 4) formation—after about 7 weeks when the fetus is formed and looks like a human being; 5) quickening—the first detectable movement of the fetus in the womb; 14–20 weeks; 6) viability—somewhere between 20 and 28 weeks when the infant can survive outside the womb; 7) birth—when the child begins its natural life outside the womb.

Roman Catholics today, with some exceptions, appear to agree that human life begins at conception. In the past, however, and for several centuries, there was general agreement that human life began at the time of formation. It was only with the discovery of the ovum and sperm, and the gradual identification of conception with fertilization, that immediate hominization began to be generally accepted. But the condemnation of abortion was never dependent on theories of hominization. As already pointed out, the fetus was considered sacred and inviolable right from the time of conception because it had a human destiny. When it actually became a human being was of secondary importance. Today, those who want to justify abortion give primary significance to the time of hominization and base their position on theories of delayed hominization. Actually, there are stronger arguments to show that the fetus is a human being right from the moment of conception than there are for later hominization, at least prior to the actual appearance of human function. But there are still many who relate hominization to some intermediate biological change. It is not certain where members of the Presbyterian/Reformed churches would draw the line, but it does not seem that they would want to admit immediate hominization. It is clear that they want to allow abortion, at least prior to hominization, but it is not clear within what limits.

The Presbyterian Church (U.S.A.) at its General Assembly, Milwaukee, Wisconsin, June 2–10, 1992, adopted a report containing the following statement:

Presbyterians hold varying points of view about when human life begins. The five most common viewpoints are:

    1. at conception, when a woman's unfertilized egg is fertilized by a male's sperm, producing a zygote.

    2. when the following criteria, developed by the Harvard Medical School, are met: (a) response to external stimuli, (b) presence of deep reflex action, (c) presence of spontaneous movement and respiratory effort, and (d) presence of brain activity as ascertained by the electroencephalogram.

    These criteria would be met by the end of the third month in almost all cases.

3. at "quickening," when movements can be subjectively perceived by the woman, usually around 4–5 months.

4. at "viability," when the unborn child is potentially capable of living outside the woman's womb with artificial help (life support system). Today, our medical technology makes this possible at around 20 weeks.

5. at birth, when the baby is physically separated from the woman and begins to breathe on its own.

Those holding these varying points of view agree, however, that after human life has begun, it is to be cherished and protected as a precious gift of God. While Presbyterians do not have substantial agreement on when human life begins, we do have agreement that taking human life is sin.

A minority report that argued cogently that life begins at conception was rejected.

67. John Connery, *Abortion, the Development of the Roman Catholic Perspective* (Chicago: Loyola University Press, 1977), pp. 293ff.; Daniel Callahan, *Abortion: Law, Choice and Morality* (London: Macmillan & Co., 1970), pp. 349–401. John Calvin, so far as I know, typically did not comment on the beginning of human life. He did declare emphatically in his commentary on Exodus 21:22 that the "unborn, though enclosed in the womb of his mother, is already a human being."

68. For a discussion of this position, see Paul Ramsey, *Ethics at the Edges of Life: Medical and Legal Intersections* (New Haven, Conn.: Yale University Press, 1978), p. 46.

69. Augustine, *Enchiridion* 23; Thomas Aquinas, *Summa Theologiae* 1a, q. 92, a. 1, ad 1; 2a–2ae, q. 64, a. 8.

70. See the statement in n. 65.

71. See Paul Ramsey's conservative discussion of the beginning of human life in *Ethics at the Edges of Life*, pp. 43ff.

72. Eccles, *The Human Mystery*, p. 144.

73. Barth, *Church Dogmatics* III/4, p. 423.

74. Ibid.

75. Ramsey, *Ethics at the Edges of Life*, p. 187.

## Chapter 8
## Jesus Christ

1. Recent works on the doctrine of Jesus Christ include Aloys Grillmeier, *Christ in Christian Tradition*, vol. 1, 2nd rev. ed., and vol. 2, part 1 (Atlanta: John Knox Press, 1975, 1987); Jürgen Moltmann, *The Crucified God: The Cross of Christ as the Foundation and Criticism of Christian Theology* (London: SCM Press, 1974); Wolfhart Pannenberg, *Jesus — God and Man* (Philadelphia: Westminster Press, 1968); Eduard Schweizer, *Jesus* (Richmond: John Knox Press, 1971);

George S. Hendry, *The Gospel of the Incarnation* (Philadelphia: Westminster Press, 1958).

2. Emil Brunner, *Dogmatics,* vol. 2: *The Christian Doctrine of Creation and Redemption* (Philadelphia: Westminster Press, 1952), chaps. 10–12.

3. Gotthold Ephraim Lessing, *On the Proof of the Spirit and Power,* in *Lessing's Theological Writings: Selections in Translation,* trans. Henry Chadwick (London: A. & C. Black, 1956), pp. 53–55.

4. Paul Tillich, *A History of Christian Thought,* 2nd rev. ed. (New York: Harper & Row, 1968), pp. 80ff.; R. V. Sellers, *The Council of Chalcedon: A Historical and Doctrinal Survey* (London: SPCK, 1953), pp. 132ff.

5. Martin Hengel, *Acts and the History of Earliest Christianity* (Philadelphia: Fortress Press, 1980), pp. 50–58.

6. Ursula M. Niebuhr, ed., *Remembering Reinhold Niebuhr* (San Francisco: Harper, 1991), p. 389.

7. Paul Althaus, *Fact and Faith in the Kerygma of Today* (Philadelphia: Muhlenberg Press, 1960), pp. 67ff.

8. John Knox, *Criticism and Faith* (London: Hodder & Stoughton, 1953), chaps. 1–2. For a critique of Knox's approach see Robert E. Cushman, "Christology or Ecclesiology?" *Religion in Life* 27, no. 4 (1958): 515–526.

9. Herbert Butterfield, *The Origins of History* (Andover, Hampshire: Methuen, 1981), pp. 164–165.

10. Ibid.

11. Nils Alstrup Dahl, *Jesus the Christ: The Historical Origins of Christological Doctrine* (Minneapolis: Fortress Press, 1991), p. 92.

12. James H. Charlesworth, "The Foreground of Christian Origins and the Commencement of Jesus Research," in idem, ed., *Jesus' Jewishness: Exploring the Place of Jesus in Early Judaism* (New York: Crossroad, 1991).

13. James Kugel and Rowan Greer, *Early Biblical Interpretation* (Philadelphia: Westminster Press, 1986), p. 242.

14. Charlesworth, ed., *Jesus' Jewishness,* p. 80. David Flusser of Hebrew University has written, "It is possible to write the story of Jesus' life. . . . The early Christian accounts about Jesus are not as untrustworthy as people today often think" (ibid., pp. 153–154).

15. B. J. F. Lonergan, *The Way to Nicea: The Dialectical Development of Trinitarian Theology* (London: Darton, Longman & Todd, 1976); Robert C. Gregg, *Arianism: Historical and Theological Reassessments* (Philadelphia: Philadelphia Patristic Foundation, 1985); Emilianos Timiadis, *The Nicene Creed* (Philadelphia: Fortress Press, 1983).

16. William G. Rusch, ed., *The Trinitarian Controversy* (Philadelphia: Fortress Press, 1980), pp. 29–32, 161–162.

17. G. L. Prestige, *God in Patristic Thought,* 2nd ed. (London: SPCK, 1952), pp. 219ff.

18. J. N. D. Kelly, *Early Christian Creeds,* 3rd ed. (New York: Longman, 1981), pp. 247–263.

19. Athanasius, *Athanasius, Select Works and Letters,* vol. 14 of Philip Schaff and Henry Wace, *A Select Library of Nicene and Post-Nicene Fathers of the Christian Church,* 2nd series (New York: Christian Literature Co., 1892), *Discourse Against the Arians* 1.6.

20. Donald Baillie, *God Was in Christ: An Essay on Incarnation and Atonement* (London: Faber & Faber, 1948), pp. 60–71.

21. Tillich, *History of Christian Thought,* pp. 71–72. The framers of the Nicene Creed used nonbiblical concepts to maintain what they believed was New Testament faith.

A contemporary effort to state the doctrine of Nicaea is found in the remarkable statement by a committee reporting to the Federal Council of Churches, "The Relation of the Church to the War in Light of the Christian Faith" (1943):

> Revelation of God in Jesus Christ takes place whenever and wherever human persons find themselves effectively confronted, through the Gospel record or some spoken word, through personal contact or social heritage, inside or outside the institutional Church, by the person of Jesus of Nazareth as an embodiment of unqualified moral judgment and of regenerating power, "God's power and God's wisdom." Effectively confronted: that is to say, compelled to acknowledge him as a stubborn reality, as summons to repentance, and as source of drastic spiritual renewal. The person Jesus of Nazareth: the actual subject of that unique actual human life and death and triumph over death from which the Christian Church and the so-called Christian era of history, a new age and a new mode of life for mankind, have their beginnings. An embodiment of God's power and God's wisdom: one in whom, for Christian faith, the initiative of God for man's redemption uniquely assumed individual human form, so that uniquely and definitively "God was in Christ reconciling the world to himself" (see John H. Leith, ed., *Creeds of the Churches,* 3rd ed. [Atlanta: John Knox Press, 1982], p. 524).

Jean Daniélou argues that Jewish Christians expressed the same truth in a language out of the Jewish tradition (*The Theology of Jewish Christianity* [London: Darton, Longman & Todd, 1964], pp. 205–231, 407–408). Rowan Williams summarizes the significance of the Nicene Creed:

> The Nicene faith as interpreted by its greatest defender thus alters the nature of our reflection on apophatic theology. The unknowability of God ceases to be simply the inaccessibility of a kind of divine "hinterland," the mysteriousness of an indefinite source of divinity. The language of "source" or "cause" applied to the Father certainly continues to be used, but not in such a way as to suggest an actually prior reality about which nothing can be said except that it determines itself as Father of a Son or Utterer or a Word.

There is no overplus of "unengaged" and inexpressible reality, nothing that is not realized in and as relationship, in God. Thus post-Nicene Catholic theology turns away from the assumptions that so shaped Arius' thought. Arius' passionate concern to secure God against the claims of created understanding to mastery and possession had very naturally expressed itself as a theological transcription of the hierarchical and mathematically-influenced cosmology of Neoplatonism: God is pure singularity, and the purely single can only be known as the negation of duality; what it is apart from this negation is strictly beyond conceiving, yet it would be a mistake to reduce the One to being no more than a negative ideal limit. There is thus "more" to unity than duality can show. Post-Nicene theology, on the other hand, opposes not first and second principles but creator and creation: the divine simplicity is seen as belonging to the divine life, rather than to a primal monad. To say that in God there is absolute identity of nature, will and action is indeed to say something that challenges the claims of understanding and impels us towards the apophatic moment in our theology: it means that the divine nature cannot be abstracted from God's active relationship with the world. And since that relationship, in which the theologian as believer is caught up, is not susceptible of being distanced and exhaustively defined, neither is God's nature. His everlasting act is as little capable of being a determinate object to our minds as the wind in our faces and lungs can be held still and distant in front of our eyes. (*Arius, Heresy and Tradition* [London: Darton, Longman & Todd, 1987], p. 242).

22. James Orr, *Progress of Dogma* (1901; repr. Grand Rapids: Wm. B. Eerdmans Publishing Co., 1963). This is an old but very clear summary of the early councils. See also Sellers, *The Council of Chalcedon;* J. N. D. Kelly, *Early Christian Doctrines,* rev. ed. (San Francisco: Harper & Row, 1978).

23. Grillmeier, *Christ in Christian Tradition,* vol. 1, pp. 132, 166, 288. Theologians speak of a Christology from below and a Christology from above. Freeman Dyson, in *From Eros to Gaia* (New York: Pantheon Books, 1992), reports that physics also can be done from the bottom up and from the top down.

24. Ibid., pp. 452, 510, 524, 533, 543.

25. Ibid., pp. 331, 523–534, 543, 548, 553.

26. Leith, ed., *Creeds of the Churches,* pp. 35–36. Translation by Albert Outler.

27. Albert Outler in an unpublished lecture summarized the teaching of Nicaea and Chalcedon:

The episcopal committee that drafted this definition were not great theologians, but at least they knew what they were trying to do. They took the term *ousia,* that goes back to Origen, as referring to God's mysterious reality; then they took the *hypostasis* as the word for the mystery as self-revealed, which is mystery having a name in the eyes of faith in response to the light of revelation; they then took the *prosōpon* from the Antiochene vocabulary as a somewhat awkward synonym for *hypostasis,* but distinguished from *hypostasis* by its stress upon the personification of the self-presentation to the Triune God. The real apple of discord was the term *physis.* To change or to mix the metaphor, this was the bone in the Alexandrine throat. But the Chalcedonian bishops took it, as the Antiochenes had before them and as Maximus the Confessor would two centuries later, to mean "energy" rather than "entity," "process" rather than "produce," "agency" rather than "agent." As well as any modern existentialist they wanted to avoid the claim of objectivizing knowledge, and so they chose the verb *gnōrizomenon* to make this plain. Finally they were determined to spike the batteries on the extreme flanks of the battle lines, and this they did with the four famous adverbs.

The resulting definition said, in effect, the best or the best balanced explanation of the mystery of Christ begins with the recognition that the *hypostasis* of this mystery shares the *ousia* of man, that this *hypostasis* is a personification of God, that the energy systems of the proclaimer and the proclaimee exist in an integral agent and must not be confused or disjoined. The plain implication of such an explanation as this is that any further explanation is legitimate and orthodox if it strays out into barren wastes of heresy. And here you have the shaping of the dogma which is not a settlement of the question, but a definition of the playing field in which Christological reflection can go on. (From a tape recording of lectures given at Emory University, 1963. Used by permission.)

David Jenkins has also attempted to put in personal language the meaning of Chalcedon:

But the Chalcedonian Definition is a symbol of the discovery and assertion that in the purposes of the transcendent and independent God, and by the power of this God, a union has been achieved between that evolutionary product of cosmic dust which is a human being and that transcendent and wholly other purposeful personalness who is God. Transcendent and independent personalness is at one with derived, dependent, and evolved personality whose whole basis can be reduced to that impersonal materiality out of which it has developed and on which it depends. And the result is the personal union of God and man who is himself the person, Jesus Christ. In this there is discovered the personal fulfilment both of God and of man. We have the fulfilment of the personalness of God because God has achieved the expression of his purpose of love. This is the expression in conditions of materiality and history of an always perfect love so it is not a development of divine personalness. But to this we shall return in the last lecture. On the other hand we have the fulfilment of the personalness of man in the coming into existence of a perfection of relationship with God which is a personal and permanent union. But this we must consider in the seventh lecture. Meanwhile, we must be careful to note the shape of what is involved here. It is that God provides the fulfilment of his personal purposes for materiality and history by involving himself to the point where there is a personal union between transcendent personalness and derived personalness. This derived personalness is acknowledged as being wholly continuous with the impersonal stuff of the universe at large, but it is none the less asserted that such derived personalness can be lifted out of dependence on impersonal stuff, into a personal union with underived and transcendent personalness. Thus there is no denial of the immense difference between God and everything else nor of the fact that man's existence is rooted in the realm of "everything else." Man is clearly part of what we would call "the universe known to science," and this is *not* God nor continuous with God. But God unites the personal possibilities of this universe to himself in a personal union which does not destroy the distinction but achieves the personal purpose. Transcendent personalness and derived personalness are united by the immanence of the transcendent. Such is the pattern which the Chalcedonian Definition proclaims and defends. There is a union of two-foldness, of God and man, through the activity and presence of God. We do not have to choose between unique personalness and general impersonalness because God is concerned to produce and unite persons for himself out of the processes of materiality and history. (David Jenkins, *The Glory of Man* [New York: Charles Scribner's Sons, 1967], pp. 55–56.)

Robert L. Calhoun summarized the Second Council of Constantinople in class lectures:

i. When we say that Jesus Christ is a person, a crucial question arises: shall we say there is one will in Christ or two wills? Is there divine will and also a human will? Or a fusion? The Church has stated traditionally that there are two wills. Tertullian said that we are not to think of Jesus Christ as a kind of amalgam, like an alloy; that would make him something of which we know not. Toward the end of the 5th century the Monophysite controversy raised the question as to whether we should ask if there are two centers of thought and action in Christ. The Monothelites said that there were two natures and one will in Christ. The Church said no to this; that there were two wills, but in such complete harmony as to enable Christ to act in accord with God. This seems to be the right answer to this problem, though it is difficult to spell this out in terms. Certainly the alternatives to this position appear to be inadequate. Moreover, what is involved is a right understanding of the relation of a finite person to God. If we say that there is one will which is divine, or on the other hand one human will, we fall back to a one-sided Christology. The clue lies in seeing how two wills can be interrelated so that though there are two sources of impulse in Jesus, the net effect is unitary action. That this can happen is seen to some extent among men; the morale of a fighting unit is an example, in which there is individual will but also a group spirit. If this can happen among humans, then it seems to be possible for Jesus to have human and divine will. Our own wills are never so attuned to the will of God that we will do His will perfectly; in Jesus Christ we see one who does God's will perfectly.

ii. If Jesus Christ is an individual, how can he be a "universal man"? It is helpful to make use of a philosophic term here "concrete universal." This kind of universal is not an abstract character, but a concrete one which somehow embodies the character of an entire group. This term can be seen meaningfully when we consider Shakespeare, whose characters have endured more than the medieval Everyman plays in which the characters were stylized, because of his delineation of concrete persons who show a remarkable universality. The analogy of Jesus Christ is somewhat like this. He was an individual, but his life was significant for all men at all times. The universal problems of our lives are in direct focus in him.

iii. If we speak of Jesus Christ as "einmalig"— as "once for all," are we to say that there is at the same time eternal reality in the event? This is a paradox: the universal event and the eternal truth. In Jesus Christ we see the historical disclosure of God in an eternal way. The Incarnation is in some sense continuous with creation. The Incarnation did not make God into a God of love, but revealed what God had eternally been. Here God lets himself be seen most decisively. Because God always has these characteristics, then what we see in Christ is truly a revelation of God. ("Lectures on Systematic Theology," given at Yale Divinity School, 1954; compiled and mimeographed by Robert H. Smith.)

28. Leith, ed., *Creeds of the Churches,* pp. 51–52.

29. Albert C. Outler, "Jesus Christ as Divine-Human Savior," *Christian Century,* May 3, 1961, p. 555.

30. Barth, *Church Dogmatics* IV/1, pp. 351–352.

31. Ibid., p. 341.

32. Ibid., pp. 335–336.

33. Rodion Shchedrin, *Lenin in the People's Heart* (Moscow, 1972), pp. 25–32.

34. Paul Tillich, "Existentialist Aspects of Modern Art," in *Christianity and the Existentialists,* ed. Carl Michaelson (New York: Charles Scribner's Sons, 1956), p. 143.

35. Barth, *Church Dogmatics* IV/2, pp. 100ff.

36. A. M. Ramsey, "Ascension," in Alan Richardson, ed., *Theological Word Book of the Bible* (New York: Macmillan Co., 1951).

37. Oliver O'Donovan, *Resurrection and Moral Order* (Grand Rapids: Wm. B. Eerdmans Publishing Co., 1986), pp. 56–58.

38. Henry Chadwick, *The Early Church* (Baltimore: Penguin Books, 1967), pp. 84–85.

39. Hans Lietzmann, *History of the Early Church,* vol. 2: *The Founding of the Church Universal* (New York: Charles Scribner's Sons, 1938), pp. 173ff.

40. Ibid., p. 197; also vol. 3: *From Constantine to Julian,* pp. 288ff.

41. Oscar Cullmann, *The Early Church: Studies in Early Christian History and Theology,* ed. and trans. A. J. B. Higgins (Philadelphia: Westminster Press, 1956), pp. 23–28.

42. Ibid.

43. Ibid., p. 25.

44. William Haller, *The Rise of Puritanism* (New York: Harper & Brothers, 1938), p. 151.

45. For an exhaustive study of birth narratives, see Raymond E. Brown, *The Birth of the Messiah* (New York: Doubleday & Co., 1977).

46. Edwin H. Rian, *The Presbyterian Conflict* (Grand Rapids: Wm. B. Eerdmans Publishing Co., 1940).

47. Leonhard Goppelt, *Theology of the New Testament,* vols. 1–2 (Grand Rapids: Wm. B. Eerdmans Publishing Co., 1981–83), vol. 1, pp. 22–23. For a careful and able defense of the virgin birth, see J. Gresham Machen, *The Virgin Birth of Christ* (London: Marshall, Morgan & Scott, 1930); cf. Thomas Boslooper, *The Virgin Birth* (Philadelphia: Westminster Press, 1962). Also see Raymond E. Brown, *The Virginal Conception and Bodily Resurrection of Jesus* (Paramus, N.J.: Paulist/Newman Press, 1973); R. H. Fuller, "The Virgin Birth: Historical Fact or Kerygmatic Truth?" *Biblical Research* 1 (1956), 1–8; Otto Piper, "The Virgin Birth: The Meaning of the Gospel Accounts," *Interpretation* 18 (1964), 131–148; Vincent Taylor, *The Historical Evidence for the Virgin Birth* (Oxford: Clarendon Press, 1920).

48. Brown, *The Birth of the Messiah,* pp. 527–528.

49. Emil Brunner, *The Christian Doctrine of Creation,* p. 354.

50. Ibid., p. 355.

51. Karl Barth, *Church Dogmatics* IV/1, p. 207. Cf. Barth, *Dogmatics in Outline,* trans. G. T. Thomson (London: SCM Press, 1949), p. 97; and *Credo* (London: Hodder & Stoughton, 1936), pp. 62–72.

## Chapter 9
## The Work of Christ

1. Donald Baillie, *God Was in Christ: An Essay on Incarnation* (London: Faber & Faber, 1948); Sydney Cave, *The Doctrine of the Person of Christ* (London: Duckworth & Co., 1956); F. W. Dillistone, *The Christian Understanding of Atonement* (Philadelphia: Westminster Press, 1968); idem, *How Can the Life and Death of Christ Save Us?* (London: SPCK, 1964); idem, *Jesus Christ and His Cross: Studies on the Saving Work of Christ* (Philadelphia: Westminster Press, 1953); R. S. Franks, *The Work of Christ,* 2nd ed. (London: Thomas Nelson & Sons, 1962); George Smeaton, *The Doctrine of the Atonement* (Grand Rapids: Zondervan Publishing House, 1953); H. E. W. Turner, *The Patristic Doctrine of Redemption* (London: A. R. Mowbray & Co., 1952).

2. *Melanchthon: on Christian Doctrine: Loci Communes, 1555,* trans. and ed. Clyde L. Manschreck (New York: Oxford University Press, 1965); Albrecht Ritschl, *The Christian Doctrine of Justification and Reconciliation* (New York: Charles Scribner's Sons, 1900); idem, *A Critical History of the Christian Doctrine of Justification and Reconciliation* (Edinburgh: Edmonston & Douglas, 1872).

3. Augustine, *Tractates on the Gospel of John* 13.1–2. In *The Fathers of the Church,* trans. John W. Rettig (Washington, D.C.: Catholic University of America Press, 1988), vol. 79, 9.4; cf. vol. 80, *Tractate* 51.12.

4. Ibid.

5. Calvin, *Institutes* 3.6.3.

6. Leander E. Keck, *A Future for the Historical Jesus: The Place of Jesus in Preaching and Theology* (Nashville: Abingdon Press, 1971), pp. 36–40.

7. Thomas à Kempis, *The Imitation of Christ,* ed. Thomas S. Kepler (Cleveland: World Publishing Co., 1952); Charles Sheldon, *In His Steps* (New York: Grosset & Dunlap, 1935).

8. Baillie, *God Was in Christ,* pp. 157ff.

9. Turner, *The Patristic Doctrine of Redemption,* pp. 102ff.

10. Gustaf Aulén, *Christus Victor,* trans. A. G. Hebert (New York: Macmillan Co., 1931), pp. 47ff.

11. E. R. Hardy, ed. and trans., "Selections from the Work Against Heresies by Irenaeus, Bishop of Lyons," in *Early Christian Fathers,* ed. Cyril C. Richardson, LCC, vol. I (Philadelphia: Westminster Press, 1953), pp. 343–358.

12. Turner, *The Patristic Doctrine of Redemption,* p. 95. See also Gerald Bonner, "Augustine's Conception of Deification," *Journal of Theological Studies* 37, no. 2 (October 1986).

13. Anselm, *Why God Became Man,* in *A Scholastic Miscellany: Anselm to Ockham,* ed. and trans. Eugene R. Fairweather, LCC, vol. X (Philadelphia: Westminster Press, 1956), pp. 118–122, 134–144. For a very perceptive summary of Anselm's doctrine, see Paul Tillich, *A History of Christian Thought,* 2nd rev. ed. (New York: Harper & Row, 1968), pp. 165–167.

14. Robert L. Calhoun, "Lectures on the History of Christian Doctrine" (unpublished ms., private circulation).

15. H. R. Mackintosh, *The Christian Experience of Forgiveness* (New York: Harper & Brothers, 1927), pp. 181, 234.

16. Baillie, *God Was in Christ,* pp. 171ff.

17. G. L. Prestige, *God in Patristic Thought,* 2nd ed. (London: SPCK, 1952), pp. 6–7.

18. Peter Abailard, *Exposition of the Epistle to the Romans,* trans. Gerald E. Moffatt, in *A Scholastic Miscellany: Anselm to Ockham,* ed. and trans. Eugene R. Fairweather, LCC, vol. X, pp. 283–284.

Chapter 10
The Holy Spirit

1. Westminster Shorter Catechism, Question 29.

2. Calvin, *Institutes* 3.1.1.

3. John V. Taylor, *The Go-Between God: The Holy Spirit and the Christian Mission* (Philadelphia: Fortress Press, 1973), pp. 7ff.

4. Barth, *Church Dogmatics* IV/1, p. 648.

5. Claude Welch, *In This Name: The Doctrine of the Trinity in Contemporary Theology* (New York: Charles Scribner's Sons, 1952), p. 285.

6. Calvin, *Institutes* 1.9.3.

7. Ibid. 1.7.4, 5.

8. Ibid. 4.14.9.

9. See chapter 14, "Sanctification."

10. Calvin, *Institutes* 2.2.16.


Chapter 11
The Beginnings of the Christian Life

1. For treatments of the beginning Christian life, see Emil Brunner, *Dogmatics,* vol. 3: *The Christian Doctrine of the Church, Faith, and the Consummation* (Philadelphia: Westminster Press, 1962); H. R. Mackintosh, *The Christian Experience of Forgiveness* (New York: Harper & Brothers, 1927); Reinhold Niebuhr, *The Nature and Destiny of Man,* vol. 2 (New York: Charles Scribner's Sons, 1943), chaps. 4–5; Gordon Allport, *The Individual and His Religion* (New York: Macmillan Co., 1950).

2. Lewis Sherrill, *The Struggle of the Soul* (New York: Macmillan Co., 1952), chap. 2.

3. Barth, *Church Dogmatics* IV/2, pp. 554–556.

4. Ibid. IV/2, p. 558.

5. Charles Hodge, *Systematic Theology,* 3 vols. (1872–73; repr. Grand Rapids: Wm. B. Eerdmans Publishing Co., 1960); Heinrich Heppe, *Reformed Dogmatics* (1861; Eng. trans., New York: Macmillan Co., 1950).

6. Brunner, *The Christian Doctrine of the Church,* pp. 269–270.

7. Allport, *The Individual and His Religion,* esp. chap. 1; Wayne Oates, *The Psychology of Religion* (Waco, Tex.: Word Books, 1973); William James, *The Varieties of Religious Experience* (New York: Penguin Books, 1982).


Chapter 12
Faith

1. H. Richard Niebuhr, "Faith in Gods and in God," in idem, *Radical Monotheism and Western Culture* (New York: Harper & Brothers, 1960), pp. 114–126; Wilfred Cantwell Smith, *Faith and Belief* (Princeton, N.J.: Princeton University Press, 1979), pp. 129ff.

2. Calvin, *Institutes* 3.1.2.

3. Ibid. 1.2.6.

4. Ibid. 1.2.7.

5. Barth, *Church Dogmatics* IV/1, pp. 748–749.

6. Ibid., p. 758.

7. Paul Tillich, *The Dynamics of Faith* (New York: Harper & Brothers, 1957), p. 4. Cf. Emil Brunner, *Dogmatics,* vol. 3, *The Christian Doctrine of the Church, Faith, and the Consummation* (Philadelphia: Westminster Press, 1962), pp. 140ff.

8. Calvin, *Institutes* 3.2.2.

9. Ibid. 3.2.14.

10. Ibid. 3.2.8.

11. Barth, *Church Dogmatics* IV/1, pp. 751–758.

12. Ibid., pp. 764–765.

13. Augustine, *The Utility of Believing,* 23.

14. Calvin, *Institutes* 3.2.7.

15. Martin Luther, *The Freedom of a Christian,* in *Selected Writings of Martin Luther,* ed. Theodore G. Tappert (Philadelphia: Fortress Press, 1967): "True faith in Christ is a treasure beyond comparison which brings with it complete salvation and saves man from every evil" (p. 23).

16. As in mystical theology. Cf. Paul Tillich, *A History of Christian Thought* (New York: Simon & Schuster, 1972), pp. 201–203.

17. See Emil Brunner, *The Christian Doctrine of the Church, Faith, and the Consummation,* pp. 168ff., 270.

18. Calvin, *Institutes* 3.2.8–10, 41.

19. Luther, *The Freedom of a Christian,* in *Selected Writings,* ed. Tappert, pp. 43, 48–49.

20. Calvin, *Institutes* 3.2.41.

21. Reinhold Niebuhr, *The Nature and Destiny of Man,* vol. 1 (New York: Charles Scribner's Sons, 1941), p. 289.

22. Calvin, *Institutes* 3.2.42.


Chapter 13
Justification by Faith


1. Calvin, *Institutes* 3.11.1.

2. Ibid.

3. Ibid.

4. Compare Calvin, *Institutes* 3.4.16–18.

5. Compare Calvin, *Institutes,* ibid.

6. Roland Bainton, *Here I Stand: A Life of Martin Luther* (Nashville: Abingdon-Cokesbury Press, 1950), esp. chap. 3; Kurt Aland, *Four Reformers* (Minneapolis: Augsburg Publishing House, 1979), chap. 1.

7. Reinhold Niebuhr, *The Nature and Destiny of Man,* 2 vols. (New York: Charles Scribner's Sons, 1941–43), vol. 2, chap. 7.

8. Ibid., vol. 1, chaps. 6–7.

9. Donald M. Baillie, *God Was in Christ: An Essay on Incarnation and Atonement* (London: Faber & Faber, 1948), esp. chaps. 7 and 8.

10. Reinhold Niebuhr, *The Irony of American History* (New York: Charles Scribner's Sons, 1952).

11. Reinhold Niebuhr, *The Nature and Destiny of Man,* vol. 2, chap. 9.

12. William Temple, *Nature, Man and God* (London: Macmillan & Co., 1934), chap. 9.

13. Robert Jenson and Carl Braaten, eds., *Christian Dogmatics* (Philadelphia: Fortress Press, 1984), vol. 1, p. 422.

14. Ibid., p. 407.

15. Calvin, *Institutes* 3.3.11–14.

16. Calvin, *Reply to Sadolet,* in *Calvin: Theological Treatises,* ed. J. K. S. Reid, LCC, vol. XXII (Philadelphia: Westminster Press, 1954), p. 228.

17. Calvin, *Institutes* 3.16.3.

18. Ibid. 3.21.1.

19. Martin Luther, *The Freedom of a Christian,* in *Selected Writings of Martin Luther,* ed. Theodore G. Tappert (Philadelphia: Fortress Press, 1967), pp. 21–22.

20. Barth, *Church Dogmatics* IV/1, p. 527.

Chapter 14
Sanctification

1. Significant works on sanctification include R. Newton Flew, *The Idea of Perfection in Christian Theology* (New York: Humanities Press, 1968); Reinhold Niebuhr, *The Nature and Destiny of Man,* 2 vols. (New York: Charles Scribner's Sons, 1941–43); Daniel Day Williams, *God's Grace and Man's Hope* (New York: Harper & Brothers, 1949); Gordon Rupp, *Methodism in Relation to Protestant Tradition* (London: Epworth Press, 1954).

2. See esp. Reinhold Niebuhr, *Nature and Destiny of Man,* vol. 2.

3. Calvin, *Institutes,* esp. 3.3.19 and 3.11.1.

4. Steven Ozment, *The Age of Reform, 1250–1550: An Intellectual and Religious History of Late Medieval and Reformation Europe* (New Haven, Conn.: Yale University Press, 1980), pp. 372ff.

5. Calvin, *Institutes* 3.11.1.

6. Ibid. 3.17.15, 3.3.10–14.

7. Ibid. 3.11.1.

8. John Calvin, *Commentary on Romans,* in *Calvin's New Testament Commentaries,* ed. D. W. Torrance and T. F. Torrance (Grand Rapids: Wm. B. Eerdmans Publishing Co., 1960); *Corpus Reformatorum: Ioannis Calvini Opera Quae*

*Supersunt Omnia* (Brunswick: C. A. Schwetschke et Filium, 1863–97), vol. 46, pp. 359–360: *Sermon on Matthew 2:1–11 and Luke 2:21–24.*

9. *Corpus Reformatorum,* vol. 7, p. 448: *Antidote to the Acts of the Synod of Trent.*

10. Ibid., vol. 37, pp. 350–351: *Commentary on Isaiah,* chap. 59.

11. Ibid., vol. 36, p. 66: *Commentary on Isaiah,* chap. 2.

12. Ibid., vol. 45, p. 49: *Commentary on Luke,* chap. 1.

13. Barth, *Church Dogmatics* IV/2, pp. 507–508.

14. Ibid., pp. 508–509.

15. Ibid., p. 509.

16. Ibid., pp. 510–511.

17. William Haller, *The Rise of Puritanism* (New York: Harper & Brothers, 1938), chaps. 1–4.

18. Reinhold Niebuhr, *The Nature and Destiny of Man,* vol. 2, chap. 6.

19. John H. Leith, *John Calvin's Doctrine of the Christian Life* (Louisville, Ky.: Westminster/John Knox Press, 1989), pp. 82–86.

20. Reinhold Niebuhr, *The Nature and Destiny of Man,* vol. 2, chaps. 5–6.

21. Williams, *God's Grace and Man's Hope,* pp. 107–135.

22. A. D. Lindsay, *The Two Moralities: Our Duty to God and to Society* (London: Eyre & Spottiswoode, 1940), p. 49.

23. Arnold Toynbee in a Sherwood Eddy Seminar at Toynbee Hall (July 1951 in London) in answer to a question about progress (according to the memory of the writer).

24. Gordon Allport, *Becoming: Basic Considerations for a Psychology of Personality* (New Haven, Conn.: Yale University Press, 1955), pp. 89–90.

25. Calvin, *Institutes* 3.8.10–11.

26. Peter Brunner, *Vom Glauben bei Calvin* (Tübingen: J. C. B. Mohr [Paul Siebeck], 1925), p. 147.

27. Calvin, *Institutes* 3.10.6.

28. Ibid. 3.6.1.

29. Ibid. 3.6.3.

30. Barth, *Church Dogmatics* IV/1, pp. 533–613.

31. Ibid. IV/2, pp. 584ff.

32. Christopher Dawson, *The Judgment of the Nations* (New York: Sheed & Ward, 1942), pp. 44–46.

33. Reinhold Niebuhr, *The Nature and Destiny of Man,* vol. 2. Niebuhr discusses at length the limits and possibilities of history. Compare Glenn Tinder, *The Political Meaning of Christianity: The Prophetic Stance* (San Francisco: Harper, 1991). Tinder has an excellent discussion of the dangers of perfectionism in public life.

34. John Baillie, *What Is Christian Civilization?* (New York: Charles Scribner's Sons, 1945), chap. 1.

35. Louis B. Wright, *Religion and Empire: The Alliance Between Piety and Commerce in English Expansion, 1558–1625* (Chapel Hill, N.C.: University of North Carolina Press, 1943), pp. 45, 43.

36. Ibid.

37. Ibid.

38. Reinhold Niebuhr, "Christian Faith and Social Action," in *Christian Faith and Social Action,* ed. John Hutchison (New York: Charles Scribner's Sons, 1953), pp. 225–242.

39. For early Protestant hopes for a society informed by scripture, see Ozment, *The Age of Reform,* pp. 201–203.

## Chapter 15
## Christian Freedom

1. Calvin, *Institutes* 3.19.1.

2. Martin Luther, *The Freedom of a Christian,* in *Selected Writings of Martin Luther,* ed. Theodore G. Tappert (Philadelphia: Fortress Press, 1967), vol. 2, p. 21.

3. Calvin, *Institutes* 4.10.28–32.

4. Ibid. 4.10.1–4.

5. Westminster Confession of Faith 20.2.

6. Calvin, *Institutes* 3.19.6.

7. Ibid. 3.19.5.

8. Ibid.

9. Luther, *The Freedom of a Christian,* pp. 32–34, 37–43.

10. Calvin, *Institutes* 3.19.7.

11. Ibid.

12. Ibid. 3.19.8.

13. Ibid. 3.19.9.

14. Ibid. 3.19.11.

15. Ibid. 3.19.13.

16. Ibid. 4.10.3–4.

## Chapter 16
## The Law and Moral Decisions

1. C. H. Dodd, *Gospel and Law: The Relation of Faith and Ethics in Early Christianity* (New York: Columbia University Press, 1951); Emil Brunner, *The Divine Imperative* (New York: Macmillan Co., 1937); Karl Barth "Gospel and Law," in *Community, State, and Church,* ed. Will Herberg (Garden City, N.Y.: Doubleday & Co., 1960), pp. 71–100; Robert Jenson and Carl Braaten, eds., *Christian Dogmatics* (Philadelphia: Fortress Press, 1984); James Gustafson, *Can Ethics*

*Be Christian?* (Chicago: University of Chicago Press, 1975); idem, *Christ and the Moral Life* (New York: Harper & Row, 1968); Alasdair MacIntyre, *Three Rival Versions of Moral Enquiry* (Notre Dame, Ind.: University of Notre Dame Press, 1990); Oliver O'Donovan, *Resurrection and Moral Order: An Outline for an Evangelical Ethics* (Grand Rapids: Wm. B. Eerdmans Publishing Co., 1986).

2. Edward A. Dowey, *The Knowledge of God in Calvin's Theology* (New York: Columbia University Press, 1952), pp. 224–232.

3. Emil Brunner, *The Divine Imperative*, p. 269.

4. John T. McNeill, "Natural Law in the Teaching of the Reformers," *Journal of Religion* 26 (1946): 168–182. ("The moral law is nothing else than a testimony of natural law and of that conscience which God has engraved upon the minds of men." Calvin, *Institutes* 4.20.16.)

5. Thomas F. Torrance, *Reality and Scientific Theology* (Edinburgh: Scottish Academic Press, 1985); idem, *Juridical Law and Physical Law: Toward a Realistic Foundation for Human Law* (Edinburgh: Scottish Academic Press, 1982), pp. 22ff.

6. Calvin, *Institutes* 2.8.1.

7. Brevard Childs, *The Book of Exodus; A Critical, Theological Commentary* (Philadelphia: Westminster Press, 1974).

8. Ibid., pp. 438–439.

9. Calvin, *Institutes* 2.8.6.

10. Ibid. 2.8.8.

11. Ibid. 2.6.11.

12. A discussion of the Second Commandment is found in *Institutes* 1.11–12.

13. Calvin, *Institutes* 2.7.6–15.

14. Reinhold Niebuhr, *The Nature and Destiny of Man*, 2 vols. (New York: Charles Scribner's Sons, 1941–43), vol. 2, pp. 38–41.

15. E. Gordon Rupp, *Methodism in Relation to Protestant Tradition* (London: Epworth Press, 1954), pp. 21–22.

16. Reinhold Niebuhr, *An Interpretation of Christian Ethics* (New York: Harper & Brothers, 1935), pp. 37–161.

17. Dodd, *Gospel and Law*, chap. 4.

18. Calvin, *Institutes* 3.6.3.

19. Ibid. 2.7.1–2.

20. Ibid. 2.7.2.

Chapter 17
The Prevenience of Grace

1. William Manson, "Grace in the New Testament," in *The Doctrine of Grace*, ed. William T. Whitley (New York: Macmillan Co., 1932), p. 49.

2. Recent books on grace include Oscar Hardman, *The Christian Doctrine of Grace* (New York: Macmillan Co., 1947); Peter Brown, *Augustine of Hippo*

(Berkeley, Calif.: University of California Press, 1967); Albert Outler, *The Rule of Grace* (Melbourne: Uniting Church Press, 1982); Gerald Bonner, *Augustine and Modern Research on Pelagianism* (Villanova, Pa.: Augustinian Institute, 1970).

3. Outler, *Rule of Grace,* p. 16.

4. Leonard Hodgson, *For Faith and Freedom,* 2 vols. (Oxford: Basil Blackwell, 1956), vol. 2, p. 149.

5. Barth, *Church Dogmatics* II/1, p. 275.

6. Ibid.

7. Ibid. III/1, p. 95.

8. Ibid. II/2, pp. 129ff. Infralapsarianism and supralapsarianism refer to the order of the decrees of God in the mind of God. Supralapsarianism: Election, Creation, Fall, Redemption. Infralapsarianism: Creation, Fall, Election, Redemption.

9. Nikolai Berdyaev, *The End of Our Time* (New York: Sheed & Ward, 1933), p. 54.

10. Reinhold Niebuhr, *The Nature and Destiny of Man,* 2 vols. (New York: Charles Scribner's Sons, 1941–43), vol. 2, p. 123.

11. William Temple, *Nature, Man and God* (London: Macmillan & Co., 1934), chap. 9.

12. Christopher Fry, *The Dark Is Light Enough* (London: Oxford University Press, 1959), p. 99.

13. William Temple, *Christian Faith and Life* (London: SCM Press, 1950), chap. 6; John L. Girardeau, *The Will in Its Theological Relations* (Columbia, S.C.: W. J. Duffie, 1891), pp. 404–405.

14. Gottfried Locher, *Zwingli's Thought: New Perspectives* (Leiden: E. J. Brill, 1981), pp. 130–131; see also the Second Helvetic Confession, chap. 10.

15. John H. Leith, *John Calvin's Doctrine of the Christian Life* (Louisville, Ky.: Westminster/John Knox Press, 1989), pp. 134ff.

16. Ibid., p. 134.

17. Temple, *Nature, Man and God,* pp. 401–402.

18. Jürgen Moltmann, *Prädestination und Perseveranz: Geschichte und Bedeutung der reformierten Lehre "de perseverantia sanctorum"* (Neukirchen-Vluyn: Neukirchener Verlag, 1961).

19. José Ortega y Gasset, *History as a System, and Other Essays Toward a Philosophy of History* (New York: W. W. Norton & Co., 1941), p. 208.

20. Fyodor Dostoevsky, *The Brothers Karamazov* (New York: Modern Library, 1950), p. 938.

21. Roland Bainton, *Here I Stand: A Life of Martin Luther* (Nashville: Abingdon-Cokesbury Press, 1950), pp. 62, 356, 361.

22. Westminster Confession, Article 18. See Joel R. Beeke, *Assurance of Faith, Calvin, English Puritanism and the Dutch Second Reformation* (New York: Peter Lang, 1991).

23. Perry G. E. Miller, "The Marrow of Puritan Divinity," in idem, *Errand Into the Wilderness* (Cambridge, Mass.: Harvard University Press, 1956), pp. 48–98.

24. Calvin, *Institutes* 3.2.4. Cf. Barth's discussion of assurance in *Church Dogmatics* II/2, p. 235.

25. Temple, *Nature, Man and God,* p. 403.

26. Calvin, *Institutes* 3.21.1ff.

27. See Carl Bangs, *Arminius: A Study in the Dutch Reformation* (Nashville: Abingdon Press, 1971).

28. See Brian Armstrong, *Calvinism and the Amyraut Heresy: Protestant Scholasticism and Humanism in Seventeenth-Century France* (Madison, Wis.: University of Wisconsin Press, 1969).

Chapter 18
The Church and the Means of Grace

1. For studies of the church see D. Douglas Bannerman, *The Scripture Doctrine of the Church, Historically and Exegetically Considered* (Edinburgh: T. & T. Clark, 1887); Jürgen Moltmann, *The Church in the Power of the Spirit* (San Francisco: Harper, 1990); Paul D. Avis, *The Church in the Theology of the Reformers* (Atlanta: John Knox Press, 1981); T. W. Manson, *Ministry and Priesthood* (Atlanta: John Knox Press, 1959).

2. Calvin, *Institutes* 4.1.1.

3. *Corpus Reformatorum: Ioannis Calvini Opera Quae Supersunt Omnia* (Brunswick: C. A. Schwetschke et Filium, 1863–97), vol. 31, p. 439: *Commentary on Psalms,* Ps. 44.

4. Ibid., vol. 6, p. 510: *On the Necessity of Reforming the Church.*

5. Martin Luther, *The Freedom of a Christian,* in *Selected Writings of Martin Luther,* ed. Theodore G. Tappert (Philadelphia: Fortress Press, 1967), pp. 21–22.

6. Discipline is added in the Scots Confession of 1560 and in the Belgic Confession of 1561. Yet discipline can be conceived as a means to hearing the Word.

7. Calvin, *Institutes* 4.1.9.

8. Emil Brunner, *Dogmatics,* vol. 3: *The Christian Doctrine of the Church, Faith, and the Consummation* (Philadelphia: Westminster Press, 1962), chaps. 7–9.

9. Luther, *The Freedom of a Christian,* pp. 21–22.

10. Barth, *Church Dogmatics* I/2, pp. 542–546.

11. Ibid. IV/2, p. 617.

12. Emil Brunner, *The Christian Doctrine of the Church,* chaps. 5–6.

13. Barth, *Church Dogmatics* IV/1, p. 149.

14. "To the church of God that is in Corinth . . ." (1 Corinthians 1:1); "All the churches of Christ greet you" (Romans 16:16). See Newton Flew, *Jesus and His Church* (London: Epworth Press, 1951), chap. 1.

15. Calvin, *Institutes* 4.1.3.

16. Theodore G. Tappert, ed. and trans., *The Book of Concord* (Philadelphia: Muhlenberg Press, 1959), pp. 416–417.

17. Johan Christiaan Beker, *Paul the Apostle: The Triumph of God in Life and Thought* (Edinburgh: T. & T. Clark, 1984), pp. 307–315.

18. Barth, *Church Dogmatics* IV/1, pp. 663–664.

19. Calvin, *Institutes* 4.1.12.

20. Robert L. Calhoun, "Christ and the Church," in *The Nature of the Unity We Seek,* ed. Paul Minear (St. Louis: Bethany Press, 1958), p. 52.

21. Barth, *Church Dogmatics* IV/1, p. 685.

22. See *Shepherd of Hermas* and *Epistle of Barnabas,* in *Early Christian Fathers,* ed. and trans. Cyril Richardson, LCC, vol. I (Philadelphia: Westminster Press, 1953).

23. J. N. D. Kelly, *Early Christian Doctrines,* rev. ed. (San Francisco: Harper & Row, 1978), pp. 200–207.

24. Peter Brown, *Religion and Society in the Age of Saint Augustine* (New York: Harper & Row, 1972), part 3.

25. Ibid. Robert Markus has a remarkable essay on Augustine's defense of Christian mediocrity. He writes:

> The Church cannot be an elite in the world; it is necessarily holy and worldly at the same time, to be purified only at the end. The ecclesiology Augustine deployed against Donatism had been an attack on one brand of perfectionism. Pelagian perfectionism raised new problems and demanded new theological labours; but the direction of Augustine's answer to Pelagius was already settled. It had to be a vindication of Christian mediocrity.
>
> One thing that "being a Christian" was necessarily understood to involve in Augustine's age was some reference to baptism. A "Christian" could not simply be equated with being a baptised person, for the label could be given to others known to have committed themselves to Christ, for instance, to those intending to receive baptism; but baptism was the universal point of reference. To this extent Augustine and Pelagius agreed that baptism is what marks out a Christian among other men. Baptism establishes one as a new man, re-born in the Pauline sense, through Christ's death and resurrection into the circle of His grace and His new law. Where Augustine and Pelagius differed was in their views on what baptism achieved in renewing man. From the moment that Augustine perceived the affinity between Pelagianism and Donatism in their tendency to anticipate an eschatological purification, he also perceived that the nature of baptism lay at the roots of the problem. "Which of us would deny that in baptism all sins are forgiven, that all the faithful emerge from the water of regeneration without spot or wrinkle? What Catholic Christian will reject, what the Lord himself approves and what is to be realised in the future, a Church enduring without spot or wrinkle?"— all could agree on that; what Pelagius took no account of—as Augustine, perhaps somewhat unfairly, complained—was "the interim, the interval between the remission of sins which takes place in baptism, and the permanently established sinless state in the kingdom that is to come, this middle

time [*tempus hoc medium*] of prayer, while [we] must pray 'Forgive us our sins.'"

In Augustine's view baptism launched a Christian on a lifelong process of convalescence, rather than curing him at once and enabling him to make a clean break with his past. He had long ago learnt to appreciate the insidious force of habit. (*The End of Ancient Christianity* [Cambridge: Cambridge University Press, 1991], pp. 53–54.)

26. Calvin, *Institutes* 4.1.17. See also Markus, *The End of Ancient Christianity,* chaps. 4–5.

27. Cyril of Jerusalem, *Catechetical Lectures,* in *Cyril of Jerusalem and Nemesius of Emesa,* ed. and trans. W. Telfer, LCC, vol. IV (Philadelphia: Westminster Press, 1956), p. 186.

28. *First Letter of Clement,* in *Early Christian Fathers,* ed. Richardson, sec. 42, pp. 63–64.

29. Calvin, *Institutes* 4.10.18.

30. Barth, *Church Dogmatics* IV/1, p. 719.

31. Calvin, *Institutes* 4.1.8.

32. Ibid. 4.1.2–8; Barth, *Church Dogmatics* IV/1, p. 657.

33. Barth, *Church Dogmatics* IV/1, p. 669.

34. See Holy Communion prayer in *The Book of Common Worship* (Philadelphia: Presbyterian Church in the U.S.A., 1946), p. 161.

35. Hans von Campenhausen, *The Formation of the Christian Bible* (Philadelphia: Fortress Press, 1972), p. 27.

36. Ibid., pp. 102–209.

37. Kelly, *Early Christian Doctrines,* chap. 1.

38. Beker, *Paul the Apostle,* p. 336.

39. Paul Achtemeier, *Romans* (Atlanta: John Knox Press, 1986), p. 188.

40. Ibid.

41. Barth, *Church Dogmatics* IV/3.2, pp. 877–878.

42. Calvin, *Institutes* 4.10.27–31.

43. Emil Brunner, *The Christian Doctrine of the Church,* chaps. 4–5.

44. Barth, *Church Dogmatics* IV/2, p. 718.

45. James Henley Thornwell, "Commentary on Acts 15:2 and 15:6," in *Collected Writings of James Henley Thornwell* (Richmond: Presbyterian Committee of Publication, 1873), vol. 4, p. 10.

46. Calvin, *Institutes* 4.1.1.

47. Hendrikus Berkhof, *Christian Faith: An Introduction to the Study of the Faith* (Grand Rapids: Wm. B. Eerdmans Publishing Co., 1980), pp. 362–385.

48. Helmut T. Lehmann, ed., *Meaning and Practice of the Lord's Supper* (Philadelphia: Muhlenberg Press, 1961), chap. 3.

49. John H. Leith, ed., *Creeds of the Churches,* 3rd ed. (Atlanta: John Knox Press, 1982), pp. 60–61.

50. Ibid.

51. Roland Bainton, *Here I Stand: A Life of Martin Luther* (Nashville: Abingdon-Cokesbury Press, 1950), pp. 136–140.

52. Timothy George, "John Calvin and the Agreement of Zurich (1549)," in *John Calvin and the Church: A Prism of Reform* (Louisville, Ky.: Westminster/John Knox Press, 1990), pp. 42–58.

53. Kurt Aland, *Did the Early Church Baptize Infants?* (Philadelphia: Westminster Press, 1963); Oscar Cullmann, *Baptism in the New Testament* (London: SCM Press, 1958); Joachim Jeremias, *Infant Baptism in the First Four Centuries* (Philadelphia: Westminster Press, 1961).

54. Karl Barth, *The Teaching of the Church Regarding Baptism* (London: SCM Press, 1965), p. 60.

55. Ibid.

56. Barth, *Church Dogmatics* IV/4, p. 130.

57. Ibid. IV/2, pp. xi–xii.

58. Emil Brunner, *The Christian Doctrine of the Church*, pp. 60–69.

59. Berkhof, *Christian Faith*, p. 352.

60. Calvin, *Institutes* 4.15.1.

61. Ibid. 4.15.3.

62. Ibid. 4.15.1.

63. Ibid. 4.16.6.

64. Ibid. 4.15.22.

65. Ibid. 4.16.9.

66. Bainton, *Here I Stand*, pp. 140–142.

67. Donald M. Baillie, *The Theology of the Sacraments* (New York: Charles Scribner's Sons, 1957), chap. 3.

68. Barth, *Church Dogmatics* IV/4, pp. 149, 202.

69. Westminster Larger Catechism, Question 71.

70. Barth, *Church Dogmatics* IV/4, pp. 188–189.

71. Calvin, *Institutes* 4.16.20.

72. *Didache*, in *Early Christian Fathers*, ed. Richardson, p. 175.

73. Calvin, *Institutes* 4.14.17.

74. Baillie, *The Theology of the Sacraments*, pp. 98–99.

75. Gottfried Locher, *Zwingli's Thought: New Perspectives* (Leiden: E. J. Brill, 1981), pp. 220–223.

76. Calvin, *Institutes* 4.15.27.

77. Locher, *Zwingli's Thought*, pp. 307–308.

78. Ibid., p. 308.

79. Barth, *Church Dogmatics* IV/4, pp. 103–107.

80. Calvin, *Institutes* 4.14.3.

81. Westminster Shorter Catechism, Question 89.

82. Ibid.

83. Smalcald Articles 3.4, in Formula of Concord. See Wilbert Rosin, *A Contemporary Look at the Formula of Concord* (St. Louis: Concordia Publishing House, 1978).

## Chapter 19
## · Prayer

1. George A. Buttrick, *Prayer* (Nashville: Abingdon-Cokesbury Press, 1942); Barth, *Church Dogmatics* III/3, pp. 264ff.; H. H. Farmer, *The World and God: A Study of Prayer, Providence, and Miracle in Christian Experience* (London: Nisbet & Co., 1936); Peter Forsyth, *The Soul of Prayer* (London: Independent Press, 1916); Harry Emerson Fosdick, *The Meaning of Prayer* (New York: Association Press, 1915); Ford Lewis Battles, trans. and ed., *The Piety of John Calvin: An Anthology Illustrative of the Spirituality of the Reformer* (Grand Rapids: Baker Book House, 1978).

2. Calvin, *Institutes* 3.20.15.

3. Friedrich Heiler, *Prayer: A Study in the History and Psychology of Religion* (New York: Oxford University Press, 1958), pp. 356–357.

4. Calvin, *Institutes* 3.20.1.

5. Emil Brunner, *Dogmatics,* vol. 3: *The Christian Doctrine of the Church, Faith, and the Consummation* (Philadelphia: Westminster Press, 1962), pp. 324–325.

6. Calvin, *Institutes* 3.20.4.

7. Ibid. 3.20.5.

8. Ibid. 3.20.6.

9. Ibid. 3.20.8.

10. Ibid. 3.20.11.

11. Ibid. 4.20.17. Calvin lists the first four rules seriatim; without including them in a numerical order, he lists additional rules.

12. Calvin, *Institutes* 3.5.10.

13. Ibid.

14. Battles, ed., *The Piety of John Calvin,* chap. 4.

15. Calvin, *Institutes* 3.20.29–33.

16. Ibid. 3.20.29; see also Preface to the commentary on Romans.

17. Calvin, *Institutes* 3.20.33.

18. Ibid. 3.20.49.

19. Barth, *Church Dogmatics* III/3, pp. 267–268.

20. Calvin, *Institutes* 3.20.29.

21. Ibid. 3.20.50.

## Chapter 20
## The Bible

1. See C. H. Dodd, *The Bible Today* (Cambridge: Cambridge University Press, 1946); Emil Brunner, *Revelation and Reason: The Christian Doctrine of Faith and Knowledge* (Philadelphia: Westminster Press, 1946); Hans von Campenhausen,

*The Formation of the Christian Bible* (Philadelphia: Fortress Press, 1972); Herman Ridderbos, *Studies in Scripture and Its Authority* (Grand Rapids: Wm. B. Eerdmans Publishing Co., 1978), chap. 2; Karl Rahner, *Inquiries: Inspiration in the Bible . . .* (New York: Herder & Herder, 1964); Bruce Metzger, *The Canon of the New Testament: Its Origin, Development, and Significance* (New York: Oxford University Press, 1987).

2. Reinhold Seeberg, *Revelation and Inspiration* (London: Harper & Brothers, 1908), pp. 62ff.

3. Calvin, *Institutes* 1.7.1, 3.

4. Ibid. 1.7.2.

5. Ibid. 1.7.4.

6. Ibid. 1.7.4, 5.

7. Brunner, *Revelation and Reason*, p. 131.

8. Von Campenhausen, *The Formation of the Christian Bible*, p. 331; see also Metzger, *The Canon of the New Testament*.

9. Von Campenhausen, *The Formation of the Christian Bible*, p. 327.

10. Ibid., p. 328.

11. Seeberg, *Revelation and Inspiration*, p. 69. Inspiration can refer primarily to the work of the Holy Spirit in the hearts of the prophets and disciples as God revealed himself to them. It may also be used with primary reference to the writing of the scriptures.

12. Brunner, *Revelation and Reason*, p. 128.

13. Ridderbos, *Studies in Scripture and Its Authority*, pp. 25–26.

14. Karl Rahner, *Inspiration in the Bible* (Edinburgh and London: Herder, 1961), pp. 13–14.

15. Barth, *Church Dogmatics* I/2, pp. 527ff.

16. W. Norman Pittenger, *The Word Incarnate: A Study of the Doctrine of the Person of Christ* (New York: Harper & Brothers, 1959), pp. 57–58.

17. John H. Leith, "John Calvin: Theologian of the Bible," *Interpretation* 25 (July 1971): 329–344; idem, "The Bible and Theology" *Interpretation* 30 (July 1976): 227–241.

18. Heinrich Bullinger, *Decades,* Parker Society edition (Cambridge: Cambridge University Press, 1852), Third Sermon of the First Decade.

19. Calvin, *Institutes* 1.6.1.


Chapter 21
Christian Faith and Living Religions


1. For a position very different from that of this chapter, see Wilfred Cantwell Smith, *Towards a World Theology* (Philadelphia: Westminster Press, 1981); Leonard Swidler, ed., *Toward a Universal Theology of Religion* (Maryknoll, N.Y.: Orbis Books, 1987); John Hick and Paul F. Knitter, eds., *The Myth of Christian Uniqueness: Toward a Pluralistic Theology of Religions* (Maryknoll, N.Y.: Orbis

Books, 1987). For studies in line with the position taken here, see Lesslie Newbigin, *The Gospel in a Pluralist Society* (Grand Rapids: Wm. B. Eerdmans Publishing Co., 1990); Hendrik Kraemer, *Religion and the Christian Faith* (Philadelphia: Westminster Press, 1957); Karl Barth, *Church Dogmatics* I/2, pp. 280–361; Carl E. Braaten, *No Other Gospel! Christianity and World Religions* (Minneapolis: Fortress Press, 1992).

2. Paul Tillich, *A History of Christian Thought,* 2nd rev. ed. (New York: Harper & Row, 1968), pp. 71–72.

3. Calvin, *Institutes* 1.1–5.

4. Emil Brunner, *Revelation and Reason* (Philadelphia: Westminster Press, 1946), pp. 262, 264–265.

5. Hendrik Kraemer, *The Christian Message in a Non-Christian World* (Philadelphia: Westminster Press, 1961), pp. 101ff.

6. Hendrik Kraemer, "Continuity or Discontinuity," in *The Authority of Faith,* Madras Series (New York: International Missionary Council, 1939), p. 1.

7. Brunner, *Revelation and Reason,* p. 272.

8. Ibid.

9. Gustaf Aulén, *The Faith of the Christian Church* (Philadelphia: Muhlenberg Press, 1961), p. 34.

10. Ibid., pp. 35–36.

11. Justin, *The First Apology of Justin the Martyr,* in *Early Christian Fathers,* ed. Cyril Richardson, LCC, vol. I (Philadelphia: Westminster Press, 1953), p. 272.

12. Ulrich Zwingli, *An Exposition of the Faith,* in *Zwingli and Bullinger,* ed. G. W. Bromiley, LCC, vol. XXIV (Philadelphia: Westminster Press, 1953), p. 275.

13. *The Decades of Henry Bullinger* (Cambridge: Cambridge University Press, 1852), The Fifth Decade, Sermon 1, p. 20.

14. Calvin, *Institutes* 2.6.1.

15. H. Richard Niebuhr, *The Meaning of Revelation* (New York: Macmillan Co., 1941), pp. 38–42.

16. Quoted by Lesslie Newbigin, *The Gospel in a Pluralist Society,* p. 177. See my discussion of this problem in *From Generation to Generation* (Louisville, Ky.: Westminster/John Knox Press, 1990), pp. 109–114.

17. Newbigin, *The Gospel in a Pluralist Society,* pp. 177–179.

18. Ibid., pp. 180–183.

19. John Baillie, *A Reasoned Faith: Collected Addresses* (London: Oxford University Press, 1963), pp. 164–166.

Chapter 22
The Christian Hope

1. On Christian hope see John Macquarrie, *Christian Hope* (New York: Seabury Press, 1978); Daniel Day Williams, *God's Grace and Man's Hope* (New York:

Harper & Brothers, 1949); Jürgen Moltmann, *Theology of Hope: A Contemporary Christian Eschatology* (San Francisco: Harper, 1990).

2. Michael Ignatieff, "Modern Dying," *New Republic,* Dec. 26, 1988, p. 32.

3. For an optimistic perspective, see Harvey Cox, *The Secular City* (New York: Macmillan Co., 1965). For a sober assessment of the problems of the city, see Edward Banfield, *The Unheavenly City* (Boston: Little, Brown, 1970). For an indication of rapid changes in the city itself, see Tay K. Soon, *Megacities in the Tropics* (Ashgate Publishing Co., 1989).

4. John Bunyan, *Pilgrim's Progress* (London: Penguin Books, 1987), pp. 136ff.

5. *The Christian Hope and the Task of the Church* (New York: Harper & Brothers, 1954).

6. Ibid., pp. 27–28.

7. Ibid., p. 8.

8. Max Weber, *The Protestant Ethic and the Spirit of Capitalism* (Eng. trans. 1930; New York: Charles Scribner's Sons, 1958). See also Ernst Troeltsch, *The Social Teaching of the Christian Churches* (New York: Macmillan Co., 1931), vol. 2, pp. 583–589.

9. Augustine, *City of God* 19.17, in *The Works of Aurelius Augustine,* ed. Marcus Dods (Edinburgh: T. & T. Clark, 1872), vol. 2, pp. 326–329.

10. See *Letter to Diognetus,* in *Early Christian Fathers,* ed. and trans. Cyril Richardson, LCC, vol. I (Philadelphia: Westminster Press, 1953), pp. 104–105.

11. Marcus Aurelius Antonius, *To Himself* 2.12.36, Loeb Classical Library, ed. T. E. Page, E. Capps, and W. H. D. Rouse (New York: G. P. Putnam's Sons, 1930).

12. Cf. Paul Lehmann, "The Anti-Pelagian Writings," in Roy Battenhouse, ed., *A Companion to the Study of Augustine* (New York: Oxford University Press, 1955), p. 213.

13. Karl Rahner, "Ideas for a Theology of Death," in idem, *Theological Investigations,* vol. XIII, pp. 169ff. (New York: Crossroad, 1974).

14. See Margaret R. Miles, "Theology, Anthropology, and the Human Body in Calvin's *Institutes of the Christian Religion,*" *Harvard Theological Review* 74 (1981): 303–323.

15. Walter Lowrie, "Easter Only Once a Year," *Theology Today* 9, no. 1 (1952): 102.

16. From a letter to the author dated February 6, 1986.

17. Lowrie, "Easter Only Once a Year," pp. 97–106.

18. Austin Farrer, *A Celebration of Faith* (London: Hodder & Stoughton, 1970), p. 165.

19. Schubert M. Ogden, *The Reality of God, and Other Essays* (New York: Harper & Row, 1966), pp. 206–230.

20. John Hick, *Death and Eternal Life* (New York: Harper & Row, 1977), pp. 266ff.

21. William Temple, *Nature, Man and God* (London: Macmillan & Co., 1934), p. 452.

22. Nikolai Berdyaev, *The Destiny of Man* (New York: Charles Scribner's Sons, 1937), pp. 338ff.

23. Reinhold Niebuhr, *The Nature and Destiny of Man* (New York: Charles Scribner's Sons, 1941–43), vol. 2, p. 287.

24. Ibid., p. 292.

25. Ibid., p. 293.

26. Ibid., p. 290.

27. Paul Minear, *Christian Hope and The Second Coming* (Philadelphia: Westminster Press, 1954), p. 97.

28. Lukas Vischer, ed., *Reformed Witness Today: A Collection of Confessions and Statements of Faith Issued by Reformed Churches* (Evangelische Arbeitsstelle Oekumene Schweiz, 1982), pp. 147–149. See John R. Albright, "The End of the World: A Scientific View of Christian Eschatology," *Dialog: A Journal of Theology* 30 (Autumn 1991): 279–283, for a brief summary of various possibilities envisioned by modern science.

## Epilogue

1. Robert L. Calhoun, "The Gospel for This World," in *Making the Gospel Effective,* ed. William K. Anderson (Nashville: Commission on Ministerial Training, The Methodist Church, 1944), pp. 33–34.

2. E. L. Mascall, *Jesus, Who He Is and How We Know Him* (London: Darton, Longman & Todd, 1985), p. 19.